PERSONAL
RECORD
1920–1972

Gerald Brenan

PERSONAL RECORD

1920-1972

Alfred A. Knopf   New York
1975

THIS IS A BORZOI BOOK
PUBLISHED BY ALFRED A. KNOPF, INC.

Library of Congress Cataloging in Publication Data

Brenan, Gerald. Personal record, 1920–1972.
Includes index.
1. Brenan, Gerald—Biography.   I. Title.
PR6003.R3513Z525 1975   828'.9'1209 [B]   74–21286
ISBN 0–394–49582–9

Manufactured in the United States of America
First American Edition

Contents

12-75

Illustrations

Illustrations

The author and publishers wish to thank Mrs Frances Partridge for permission to reproduce nos. 2, 4–10, 13, 15, 16, 23, 25, 26, 29 and 30, Mr Noel Carrington for no. 3 and the Strachey Trust for no. 11.

'Moments si doux de la folâtre-jeunesse,
qu'il y a de temps que vous êtes partis.'

Jean-Jacques Rousseau
Les Confessions (Livre Cinquième)

Preface

I wrote this account of my life mainly between 1966 and 1969. I wrote it solely for my own satisfaction and without any idea of publishing it. If my literary executors wished to bring it out thirty years after my death they would be free to do so. But circumstances have changed, so that I have decided with some reluctance to agree to its being published now. This reluctance is natural, for the account it gives of my life is often very intimate.

It may be asked why I devoted several years to writing an autobiography which I did not intend to publish. One motive, which I can call the initial one, goes back to a feeling I first had when I was twenty-seven that the real tragedy of life is that we forget. Happy moments come and go, our friends die, everything is in the end destroyed, but this could be endured if only a purer and sharper reflection were kept. Forgetfulness is the real death, for if there is anything that we save and hoard up it is our memories. All the substance of our life is in them, so that to cease to recall and be affected by our past experiences is to suffer a diminishment of our personality.

So I wrote as a young man fifty-two years ago. Civilization, I thought, grew out of memory – both the collective memory that we call history and the individual memory which, since we change all the time, is the ground of our claim to be distinct persons. For this reason records must be kept. Yet I must admit today that I have lost much of the sharpness of feeling I used to have about the past and indeed rarely think of it. I live in the present and with the passage of time most of the experiences I have been through have grown unreal and faint. Yet the urge to recall them in writing has persisted. I think that the reason for this is that I have never been able to believe that anything had really and thoroughly happened to me until I had written it down, which usually meant communicating it in a letter to someone else. For writing a thing down means ordering it and arranging it. The letter writer or autobiographer takes the chaotic material he finds in his

11

memory and organizes it, eliminating what is trivial and thus allowing what is significant to stand out. Bringing order into my past experiences has thus been the principal motive I have had in writing this book.

Yet in doing so I am well aware that many of the things that have counted for me most and which have worked themselves in small fragments into my mind have had to be omitted. Every autobiography must take the form of a sequence of events and situations with interruptions to draw the portraits of friends. But the moments that come back to us most readily from the past are more impalpable and suggest rather the disconnected shots of a film by Fellini. The tone of a voice, a girl's smile, the chant of an Andalusian street vendor, the smell of crushed thyme after a flock of goats has passed, the shame left by a social gaffe or by a failure of response, my father's dry, positive cough, my mother's bouncing walk and kind, crumpled face . . . None of these moments of spontaneous recollection is easily fitted into a narrative such as this, though for a long time now they have made up the finer siftings of the rubble of my life. It is only in poems and novels that they can be given verbal expression since they are the bricks with which the imagination builds. Here in this work I have had to confine myself to lower and more prosaic levels.

Perhaps as a good historian I should give the written sources from which I have drawn this autobiography. For the first twelve years I have had at my disposal very ample material. This comprises a typescript of my letters to Carrington, totalling some 400,000 words, as well as all her letters to me and a copy of my *Journal*, which ran from August 1925 to March 1932. The originals of all of them are now in Texas University Library.

For the period after 1932 I have much less material – chiefly small pocket diaries recording social engagements, notes made at the time of Bertrand Russell's conversation, and a diary of my experiences during the first two months of the Spanish Civil War and the period just before it.

I was well on in my book when Michael Holroyd's admirable biography of Lytton Strachey appeared. The picture he gives of Carrington is fuller and more balanced than mine and some of the information he provided was new to me. However, I have not made any changes in my narrative since reading this book except that I have corrected two or three small points of fact and cut certain passages which repeated what he had said.

March 1974   G.B.

I

Yegen

I moved into my house in Yegen on Jan. 13th, 1920. From this day a new life began for me. I was almost twenty-six, but except for a few months in my early youth, when I had run away from home, I had never been free to live as I wished. School, crammers, the war and the circumscribed routine of my parents' house had left me with little time to call my own.

In *South from Granada* I have described at some length my house and village and the customs of that remote region of the province of Granada which is known as the Alpujarra, so I will here only give a brief sketch of the place for the benefit of those who have not read that book. The house to begin with. It was an irregularly shaped, ramshackle affair with eight or nine rooms on the first floor and above these an *azotea* or attic which was open in front and gave on to a flat roof. The ground floor was taken up with stables and store rooms. For this I paid in English money £6 a year and with the house went a garden, laid out in two terraces and containing a bitter orange tree, a persimmon tree and several apple trees as well as a large sweet bay, and a few rose bushes and chrysanthemums.

The village, or pueblo, as it is more properly called, for in constitution it was a little township with a mayor, a *juez* or magistrate and civic officers, presented at first sight an uncouth or barbaric appearance. From a distance it looked like something made out of the soil by insects. Silvery grey in colour, a jumbled conglomeration of cubes of different sizes, it ran down the hill slope in a stepped succession of planes, while the houses in each of its blocks communicated with one another by their flat roofs of stamped clay. It was in fact a Berber village, such as one finds in the more arid regions of North Africa, and down to the year 1575 it had been occupied, like all the other two hundred or so *lugares* or inhabited places of the Alpujarra, by Berbers from the Rif. Then these people, who had risen in revolt against the Crown, were turned out and new settlers brought in from Galicia and Asturias.

Yegen might be a poor sort of place to look at, but it was splendidly situated. To begin with, it stood at a height of nearly 4,000 feet above the sea. The Sierra Nevada rose in gradual slopes and spurs behind it, while in front it looked out over a great expanse of air to the coastal range – on the one hand to the vast, flat-topped Sierra de Gádor, treeless and waterless, and on the other to the snaky line of the Sierra la Contraviesa, with, dividing them, a gap cut by the river through which one caught a distant glimpse of the sea. Down below, in the trough that in early Quaternary times had been a lake, lay a tangle of red and yellow hills, bare and shrubless with precipitous edges, which dropped into narrow valleys where wheat and broad beans grew under the spreading olives and thick-set orange trees, and poplars and tamarisks and oleanders lined the stony or sandy bottomed streams. Poised on the edge of a steep descent, the houses of the lower quarter of the pueblo seemed about to slip down a thousand feet into the red ravine beneath, where the hawks and bee-eaters flew and the wild cats and foxes and badgers had their secret lairs.

This immense panorama gave its character to the humble village that looked out on to it. It could never be escaped from and it dwarfed everything else. In summer when the sun was high it became a pulsating jangle of reds and yellows and magentas in which nothing that was hard could be distinguished; then in the evening the shapes reaffirmed themselves while mauve and lilac tones gave a look almost of transparency to the mountains of the coastal range. In storms the scene became dramatic with mists swirling by and great rainclouds piled overhead, while at night, when I looked out from the flat roof of my house, the stars glittered as fiercely as they do in deserts. I would take out my star atlas and lantern and plot their constellations.

Yegen was a place of light and air and it was also a place of water. Streams ran down its slopes from the mountain above and were diverted into irrigation channels which in early summer, when the snow on the high summits was melting, filled the air with a continual burbling. The soil too, whenever it got enough water, was fertile. Nowhere have I seen wheat grow thicker or taller than on its *bancales* or terraces, nowhere were the figs and apricots and persimmons and melons and trellis-grown grapes better to the taste. A little higher up the slope, above the chestnut level, there grow cherry trees whose dark red succulent fruit no one bothered to pick, while from the next village came walnuts and pears and apples. This meant that in summer, if one liked fruit and vegetables, one lived well. The whole village blossomed out, the air was full of the songs of the men riding their mules to work and at night guitars twanged in the streets as the young men serenaded their *novias*. But at other seasons one fared more spartanly. The staple diet for eight months of the year was rice cooked with chick-peas and salt cod. The fresh fish, brought up at night on muleback from the sea, was of poor quality and there was no meat to be had unless someone happened to kill a kid. There were of course the *serrano* hams, but these, though delicious, were expensive because they fetched a high price in the towns and it was often hard to come by an egg because the hens laid so sporadically. Worst of all was the olive oil, in which all our dishes had to be cooked and fried. Crushed out in the village presses, crude and unrefined, it acted on the intestines like castor oil. The wine too, though held in much esteem, was undrinkable because it was never allowed to complete its fermentation, and there was no butter. To make up for these shortcomings however, the bread, while dense in texture, had a good taste; the honey, which I bought in large *orsas* or amphorae, fifty pounds at a time, was rich and aromatic and the Columbian coffee sold by the shop was excellent. I imported tea and, when I could afford it, tins of Dutch butter by carrier from Granada and I taught my servant Maria to make cherry, apricot and fig jam.

My village was a very isolated one. By starting at dawn and catching the coach (later the motor bus) at Ugíjar I could reach Almeria by the afternoon of the same day, but it took a thirty-five-mile walk followed next morning by a three hours' bus ride to reach Granada. I had never wished to live in such a remote spot. My first choice had been a village within half an hour's ride of Granada, where I hoped, as soon as I was more proficient in Spanish, to make friends in University circles, but no house there was available. Since I had an exaggerated idea of the summer heat, liked mountains yet did not wish to be penned up in a narrow valley, I was driven to moving further out into the wilds than I wished to go. But though I settled in Yegen reluctantly, I never regretted it. Its relative poverty, its lack of a gentry class, made it sympathetic to me. Living there I got a taste and feeling for Spain I could not easily have obtained anywhere else. No doubt its isolation had some drawbacks, but I came to love this village and the country round it more than I have loved any other place and to feel in time that I belonged to it.

My chief object in settling in Spain was to educate myself. Four years on the modern side of a public school followed by four years spent in the war had left me very ignorant about many things that I wished to know. I had therefore shipped off to Almeria a number of wooden cases packed with books that I had selected with care. In all there were more than two thousand titles, which included such bulky sets as the *Encyclopaedia Britannica,* the full edition of Frazer's *Golden Bough* and – an old but now very dated favourite – Reclus's *Geography of the World* in forty large tomes. Rather more than half the total collection was made up of the English and French poets and prose writers with a sprinkling of Germans and Italians and a small batch of Latin and Greek authors in the *Loeb Classics*. Besides these there was a bulky contingent on philosophy, books on psychology, anthropology and popular science, books on Christianity and Oriental religions, a couple of shelves of history and finally a fairly complete set of travel books on Central Asia and Arabia. As soon as they arrived I settled down, like a mouse that has got into a warehouse full of cheese, to work my way through them.

My usual programme of studies was to read steadily from breakfast to lunch, then take a walk during which I went over in my mind what I had read and after tea to read again, with a break for conversation in the kitchen, till midnight or later. But in the summer I often sat up reading till dawn and then went out to see the sun rise and hear the birds singing in the poplar trees before going to bed, after which I slept till lunch time. I am not a good student for I have a poor faculty of attention and a bad memory, but I was excited by what I read and anxious to absorb as much as possible before my money ran out.

One of the first things I had set myself had been to learn Greek and Latin, which I had not touched since leaving my prep school, sufficiently well to read Homer and Virgil in the original. I ended by mastering enough Latin to read the *Aeneid* with the help of a crib and by dint of much repetition to obtain a certain nebulous feeling for its poetry, but I never succeeded in getting my teeth into Greek and that is a thing that still rankles. The only grudge I bear today against my father is that he made me drop the Classics when I went to my public school and take up maths and science instead. Since I had no aptitude for these the time I spent on them was wasted.

What I most enjoyed reading was poetry; I had only a scattered acquaintance with the English poets before Wordsworth, so now I started in on Milton, Spenser and Marlowe. Before long all the poetry I had read before, including even that of my favourites Blake and Donne, was buried under the tidal wave of Milton's verse. Yet it was not so much those tremendous passages in *Paradise Lost* about Hell and Satan that moved me as those others, cited by Hopkins as examples of what he called 'counterpoint', in which a lyrical tone emerges in conflict with, or rather flowing back against, the general rhythm of the verse.

All this time I was of course learning Spanish. Every day I spent an hour or two in the kitchen talking to my servant Maria and her young daughter Angela and to any other people who happened to come in. As my fluency in the language increased I began to make friends among the villagers and in *South from Granada* I have described some of them. I also made expeditions to the sea and to the mountains. I was a good walker and got a pleasure from my strength and agility – the speed with which I came half leaping down rocky slopes and the ease and lightness with which I climbed. Although far from being an athlete, since I had no strength in my arms, I could outrun any shepherd boy on the mountain side and keep walking for more than twelve hours at a stretch without overtiring myself. I got a special exhilaration too from long solitary excursions into the mountains when the melting snow made them a little hazardous or from crossing the high passes at night. The feeling of my limbs moving easily under me elated me because it seemed a confirmation of my freedom and independence.

But the greatest pleasure to be had from these expeditions came from the contacts with Nature. It was when I was battling with it in some way, fording a river, clambering up a slope, shirt stuck to back with sweat, that it beat its way into my system. Most of all when I was tired or hurrying to get in before dark. Then the gleam of water in a pool, the cliffs of a gorge towering above me, the rose whorls of an oleander in a dry ravine, the waving of a tuft of esparto grass would hit me suddenly and leave an indescribable impression. Sometimes on arriving at dusk at a small town I would feel that I had been transported into another world. The crowds of people strolling aimlessly about, the swallows flying faster and faster overhead, the church bell clanging, the sense of being unknown to everyone and perhaps invisible would make me walk as if I was treading on air. Then came the nights in *posadas*, devoured by bugs or with a toothache no amount of aspirin would cure. Unable to sleep, I would lie listening to the cocks crowing from near or far off, watch the sky growing slowly pale and smell the strong stench of urine coming in from the jakes outside the door. When an hour later I stood drinking a glass of coffee at the muleteers' bar I would feel light-headed and as if my body did not belong to me.

Since travel of this sort is in large part a masochistic activity, offering flashes of vision as a reward for fatigues and privations, everyone who has tried it will know what I got from these experiences and how wonderful it was to be twenty-six, free and alone in a south Mediterranean country.

The only thing that troubled me was the smallness of my bank account. I had saved hard on my pay all through the war and handed over my savings to my friend John Hope-Johnstone, or Hope as he was always called, to invest for me. When I asked him for them again he told me that he had put them into Italian War Loan and that when the lira sank to nothing they had all been lost. At the time I believed him, but today I don't. He was a man who when he got hold of money spent it; and when he couldn't he would run up debts with the result that he was always being dunned by tradesmen. Obviously he had blown what I had given him and had to find an excuse to cover his extravagance. However I still had my captain's gratuity which, if I remember right, amounted to £250. As I had spent almost half of this on buying books I was left with only £160 in my bank when I moved into my house. Since the Spanish exchange was unfavourable and furniture had still to be bought, I did not see how, in spite of the basic cheapness of life in Yegen, I could manage on this sum for much more than a year.

However, before I had been in Spain for very long a piece of luck came my way. My grandmother had died that winter and though she did not leave me anything because she disapproved of my not taking up a career, her death led to a bitter quarrel between her elder sister, a strong-minded old lady of eighty-three, and my father. I forget how the quarrel began, but both of them were famous for the rude letters they could write and before long unforgivable things had been said on both sides. This led to my great-aunt taking up my cause. Since the opening of the war had found her a German subject, the widow of a Prussian colonel whom she had married around 1900 and the aunt of the commander of one of the battalions of the Prussian Guard, she had felt obliged, in disassociating herself from her enemy connections, to adopt an ultra-patriotic attitude. This made her indignant that my father had not treated his soldier son better. With a little prompting from Hope, whom I had introduced to her before leaving for Spain and whose sleek, bird-like elegance she found appealing, she suddenly announced that she would give me an allowance of £50 a year and besides that make me her heir. Not a very large sum was involved in this last transaction because she had some time before put most of her capital into an annuity, but, since I did not anticipate the decline in the value of money and had modest requirements, I imagined that it would be enough to allow me to do anything I wanted during the rest of my life. Meanwhile I should be able to get along for some years with the help of that £50.

I must now try to give some account of what I was like at this time, all the more as I was soon to change into a rather different sort of person. Since I had found at Yegen the Arcadian mode of life I was looking for, I felt very much at home there and for the first time since childhood completely sure of myself. Accustomed as I was to living without companions, I was immune to loneliness and so long as I had books to read, mountains to climb and Spanish country people to talk to, I was – for a year or two at least – immune to boredom also. But this charmed existence hung by a thread – the thread of money. All my self-assurance melted at that word. I have never felt any confidence in my ability to earn my living and now I resolved that, when forced to do so, I would not attempt to find an educated man's job in England but would take the boat to, say, Mexico, and try my luck there. But then, as I have explained, my great-aunt came to my rescue and the problem that had worried me for the past year was solved.

Set up and reassured in this way I became a very self-sufficient and secretly rather conceited person. Since I lived so much out of the world and never compared myself with other people, I had no conception of the inadequacies of my mind or of how dull and stupid I might appear in literary company. But even if I had realized this I would not have been greatly perturbed because I believed that I was a person with a vocation. A vocation for what? I did not define it, but what I could have said was for leading a full, intense and inwardly rewarding life with a certain amount of adventure in it. That and not talking or writing was to my mind the important thing and I looked just a little down on those who did not have the same aptitudes that I had, such as pride in physical toughness, a love of Nature and of foreign countries and a deep enjoyment of poetry. Literary people, I thought, read poetry chiefly in order to talk or write about it, whereas I lived with it, submitting myself to it in a passive and uncritical way for the pure delight of its language or for the new modes of feeling it led me into, and distinguishing only between the better and less good passages.

For I must make it clear that when I first settled in Yegen I had no thought of becoming a writer. My plans for the future were all of travel – to cross the Sahara, to live among the Tuareg or the Bakhtiari of Persia, to explore Guatemala and Ecuador. These were the things I had been dreaming of all through the war and I had the example of my hero Rimbaud to encourage me, though even if I had never read him I do not think that I should have felt any differently because, since the age of sixteen, the longing to travel and take my chance in the more remote and inhospitable regions of the world had been in my bones. It was only gradually that I began to lose interest in these projects and to wonder whether, since I was so fond of literature, I might not have it in me to become a writer and to earn my living like that.

There was however one question that I had not solved – that of women. In my village there was none that attracted me, but when I went down to the towns I became only too aware of their existence. Those proud, high-stepping girls with their long, finely-combed hair and their dark floating eyes who paced slowly up and down the street in the soft evening light leaving a trail of scent behind them made me deeply ashamed of my poverty. In my badly fitting corduroy suit, cut by a local tailor, and my rope-soled *alpargatas*, I did not draw even a glance from them. But some day, I said to myself, this would change. When I came into my great-aunt's money I would find myself one of these dark-haired, olive-skinned, amorous girls and make her my mistress.

19

2

Carrington

In the spring of 1920, Lytton Strachey, my war-time friend Ralph Partridge and Dora Carrington, the girl he was living with and was soon to marry, made the long journey on mule-back from Granada to see me. During the next seven or eight years she was to be the principal person in my life, the cause both of great happiness and great unhappiness, so I will say something of her past history.*

Carrington – she was never known by her first name – was the daughter of a retired Anglo-Indian railway engineer who at the age of fifty-six had married a young woman who was the governess to his sister's children. Born on March 29, 1893, which made her just a year older than I was, she showed such a talent for drawing that she was sent to the Slade School of Fine Art in 1909 or 1910. Here she got to know a fellow student called Mark Gertler, who fell violently in love with her.

She left the Slade in 1913 and after that lived chiefly in London where, as Gertler's friend, she belonged to the set that revolved round D. H. Lawrence and Middleton Murry and had affiliations with Aldous Huxley and Lady Ottoline Morrell. But her relations with Gertler were not happy ones. Although unwilling to give him up, she refused to sleep with him, then did so but declined to repeat it, so that she ended by reducing him to complete desperation.

Then in the autumn of 1915 she met the man who was to be the ruling passion in her life. This was Lytton Strachey, a homosexual aged thirty-five who had never been known to look at any woman. It seemed as if she had no chance, but she hung on to him, following him to London and from there to Cambridge where, half bored, half flattered, he displayed her to his friends as a new and strange acquisition. He was often maddened by her – this clumsy, uneducated girl of twenty-two, who could neither cook nor

*I have described this visit in *South from Granada*. Carrington's previous life is also described in great detail in Michael Holroyd's biography of Lytton Strachey and in *Carrington: Letters and extracts from her diaries*, edited by David Garnett.

spell – but he also recognized that she had talent and originality and that with her corn-coloured hair which she wore bobbed like a medieval page-boy's, and bright blue, restless eyes she was very striking. And then, though ignorant and unread, she was not stupid – merely a person so choked by her intense feelings about the world and so torn between her conflicting moods that she often could not express herself coherently.

So Lytton, though continuing to lead his own life, kept her in tow. Indeed it would have been hard for him to shake her off. Her slave-like devotion amazed everyone who knew her because in the past she had been so fanatically set on her independence. But now in her eyes he was God. He too must have felt drawn to her, both for the evident delight she took in visual impressions and for her boy's wiry figure, because the following summer saw them spending their holidays in Wales and sleeping in the same bed, though ineffectively.

However this happy, though for Lytton unnatural, state of affairs could not last. Before long she and Gertler resumed their interrupted affair and from time to time spent the night together. It is possible that Lytton encouraged her to return to him to see if their old relation, which had in many ways been so suitable, could be made to work. But within a year things had taken another turn. In February 1918 Lytton rented Tidmarsh Mill House near Pangbourne and invited Carrington to come and live with him and be his housekeeper. She accepted instantly while Gertler, as his letters show, was overwhelmed. From this time on a new life began for her. On Wednesdays she and Lytton would usually go up to London for the night and from Fridays to Mondays his Cambridge friends would come down, but during the rest of the week they were alone. It was a period of great strain and anxiety for her since only too often she had the feeling she bored him. He began to educate her, reading Gibbon's *Decline and Fall* aloud every evening, but even this did not always go off well. Once as he was finishing the chapters on the rise of Christianity, she interrupted him to ask what the word 'ecclesiastic' meant and he shut the book with a bang. There was a horrible instability about this life. She lived in continual dread that at any moment he would get tired of her and leave.

I now come to the time when Ralph Partridge appears on the scene. In the first volume of my autobiography* and also in *South from Granada* I have described this handsome, exuberant young man who had been a fellow officer of mine during the war and whose gay, carefree disposition and military prowess I so much admired. He had been at Oxford with Carrington's brother Noel before the war and one day in the summer of 1918 Noel introduced him to his sister and they had an argument. Ralph as a soldier had been full of belligerent feelings, while she was a pacifist with (at that

A Life of One's Own is to be reissued shortly by Jonathan Cape.

time) communist sympathies. But Ralph, feeling attracted to her, had given way. Then, not long after this, Carrington invited her new friend over to Tidmarsh. Though his first meeting with Lytton was not a success, Carrington became increasingly drawn to this dashing young soldier who sang her Italian songs and after he returned to Oxford early in the following year they began an affair, confirmed by a holiday in the South of Spain with Noel and Ralph's sister. Ralph fell deeply in love with Carrington and moved into the Mill House, coming down every week-end and spending his vacations there. Yet Carrington, though attracted to him, was not in love with him. The principal reason for her having invited him to join her was that Lytton liked him so much – was indeed for a short time in love with him – and had let it be known that he could not promise to stay on at Tidmarsh unless there was a capable and personable man about the place. It made him feel nervous, he said, to live alone with a woman. So since there was nothing in the world that Carrington would not do to hold on to Lytton and since she was becoming fonder every day of Ralph, she was only too glad to have him share the house.

Yet it was in every other way an unsuitable union. Since Ralph was strongly sexed and Carrington was not, quarrels were continually being hatched in the bedroom. Then with his fine war record and his lack of interest in the arts he was felt to be an intruder from another and coarser-skinned world, a man of Mars in a nest of artists and pacifists. People called him 'Carrington's Major' as if, to quote her brother, he was a boar or cheetah she led about on a chain. Gertler, unable to work, almost at the end of his tether, spoke of him as the 'policeman'. This was the way in which Bloomsbury resisted all new arrivals who did not bear their special trademark of literary culture and Ralph, like all soldiers just back from the war, had to go through a period of re-education and adjustment before he could be assimilated.

Besides, he dared to be jealous. Carrington could not pay a day's visit to London without being cross-questioned minutely as to whom she had seen. In this world of the Cambridge Apostles, governed by the moral philosophy of G. E. Moore, jealousy was regarded as a vice that infringed on the liberty of another person and which must therefore be suppressed. No doubt he felt insecure because he did not mentally or spiritually possess her and because so few of her friends at this time approved of him. Had their relations been of a more reciprocal kind he would almost certainly have behaved differently. But jealousy has a way of bringing about the opposite results to those it seeks, so that the only effect Ralph's suspiciousness had on Carrington was to increase the secretiveness which her mother's attempts at control had given her as a child and to make her almost automatically lie to him. When he found this out he was furious because, like the ancient

Persians, he put truth and frankness above everything and thought lying the act of a slave. The consequence was that their life, though delightfully gay and happy at times, was full of tensions. They quarrelled almost daily. If it had not been for Lytton's tact and wisdom and for his great influence over both of them, it is unlikely that they would have remained long together.

It was in the spring of 1919 that I saw Carrington for the first time. We met casually in London, after which Ralph brought her over for a two day walking tour in the Cotswolds and I joined them. Then in July I went down to Tidmarsh for the night. It was, as I remember, one of those dark, overcast summer days. The trees and the grass had turned to a uniform tint of green and the air was heavy and stagnant. I came down a straight road shaded by elms and then saw a low brick and plaster building, in size a small farmhouse, standing by an open meadow which must once have been the marsh. This was the Mill House.

Carrington came to the door and with one of her sweet, honeyed smiles welcomed me in. She was wearing a long cotton dress with a gathered skirt and her straight yellow hair, now beginning to turn brown, hung in a mop round her head. But the most striking thing about her was her eyes, which were of an intense shade of blue and very long-sighted, so that they took in everything they looked at in an instant. Passing a door through which I saw bicycles, we came into a sitting room, very simply furnished, in which a tall, thin, bearded man was stretched out in a wicker armchair with his long legs twisted together. Carrington introduced me to Lytton who, mumbling something I did not catch, held out a limp hand, and then led me through a glass door into an apple orchard where I saw Ralph, dressed in nothing but a pair of dirty white shorts, carrying a bucket. He came forward to meet me with his big blue eyes rolling with fun and gaiety and carried me off to see the ducks and grey-streaked Chinese geese that he had recently bought. He had discovered the pleasure of growing vegetables and keeping domestic poultry – anything that provided food appealed to him – and got a sensuous enjoyment from watching the processes of their generation and from handling their smooth, finely grained eggs. He led me through to the paddock where the geese stretched out their necks and hissed at us and then to the mill pond to watch the ducks swimming and copulating. After this I was introduced to the tortoiseshell cat, which to his delight was rolling on its back in the grass in the frenzies of heat, and taken on to the kitchen where a buxom, fair-haired village girl of twenty, whom he addressed in a very flirtatious manner, was busy among the pots and pans.

Tea was served in the dining room – a wonderful spread with farm butter, honey in the comb, home-made cakes and currant loaf, served in a pink lustre tea service. Carrington was a devotee of Cobbett and her housekeeping and furnishing expressed not only the comfort but the poetry of English cottage and farmhouse life. Her very English sensibility, in love with the country and with all country things, was already giving everything she touched a special and peculiar stamp. And her cooking had become excellent. But my memory of this particular meal has become confused with many later ones. I seem to see Lytton, elegant in his dark suit, with his squeaky voice that faded out at the end of the sentence and his strongly stressed pronunciation of certain words, seated remote and fantastic at the head of the table. Then I see Ralph with his look of a Varsity rowing man and his stylized way of speaking, which contrasted with his general air of gaiety and high spirits. And lastly Carrington with her coaxing voice and smile and gaily teasing manner and the extraordinary deference and attention she paid to her god. They all seemed very happy together and it was evident that she liked me for she suggested our meeting in London. We did, and spent the better part of two days together and when she left she asked me to write to her from Spain and promised to write back.

She did indeed write. Before I had settled into my house at Yegen I had received a long and decidedly oncoming letter from her. She said that she felt I was very like her in character, but that she did not believe I was as bored with *la Egyptienne* (the girl from Cairo I had been having a brief affair with on the Cotswolds) as I made out. Then came another letter in which she said that she would like to confide in me about a lot of things, but felt it would be wiser not to. She had lately become much fonder of Ralph as he had given up his slightly moral character which used to tire her.

> I will certainly never love him, but I am extremely fond of him. I believe that if one wasn't reserved and hadn't a sense of what is possible one could be *very* fond of certainly two or three people at a time. To know a human being intimately, to feel their affection, to have their confidences is so absorbing that it is clearly absurd to think one can only have the inclination for one variety ... But the days are too short and one has work to do.

Other letters followed in the new year. Ralph was now taking English Literature at Oxford and coming over at weekends. He was great friends with Lytton who delighted in teaching anyone literature. She was making him wear nice clothes, leather jerkins and knee breeches so that he looked like an Elizabethan serving man. 'I hate drabness,' she wrote.

Then she showed concern over my poverty: 'I think that the lack of money is more sordidly grim than anything. I've known it in London – walking from Waterloo to Hampstead because I hadn't a penny. Eating

24

twopenny soup packets meal after meal in a smelly studio in Brompton Road.'

From this she went on to speak of the comfort of Ralph's love, though even at the most intimate moments she was never submerged by it but 'Always outside, waiting'.

'For since I deserted all my friends except Alix for Lytton and there were moments when he didn't want me, when I recognized the isolation of it all, I turned in despair for a relation with a mortal to assure me that I was not entirely cut off.'

Then in April 1920 she, Ralph and Lytton made the long journey to Yegen. It was not a smooth nor an easy visit. She and Ralph were in a state of acute tension all the time and Lytton was upset by the food and exhausted by the journey. I had no conversation alone with her and Ralph was in one of his difficult moods. But as soon as she had got back to England she wrote me a letter which explained why the visit had not gone off better. Ralph wanted to marry her and had threatened to leave Tidmarsh and take a job on a sheep farm in Bolivia if she would not agree. But she had always hated the idea of marriage. She thought of it as a kind of prison and the only person she could ever have considered as a husband was Lytton. But if she married Ralph, that would be ruled out, while if she did not marry him he might fulfil his threat and leave and then Lytton might give up Tidmarsh and return to London.

She wrote: 'Do you know, I sometimes feel like flying out with my paint boxes and leaving all these complications and simply changing my life and settling at Yegen ... Of all the mortals I have yet met you are the most sympathetic to me.'

That autumn Ralph took a job at the Hogarth Press as Leonard Woolf's secretary. Carrington therefore agreed to live with him at 41 Gorden Square for the winter as a test of how they got on. It was only fair, she said, that, as she was making him so unhappy, she should do this, but it would not be easy for her because, while Lytton never tried to control her or to intrude into her life, Ralph did.

Then she wrote of her awful childhood. She had loved her father, who had just died at the age of 85 – leaving her all she would ever have, £120 a year – but had not got on with her ex-governess mother who had tried to pry into her life in order to control her. 'Honestly when I escaped and came to London at the age of 17 I couldn't speak the truth even if I wanted to. I had acquired such an art of self-protection that even to Ralph I find that I can never completely give myself away.'

All that winter Ralph kept up the pressure on her to marry him. She resisted. 'I hate these little self-centred worlds which married people live in.' Then how could one be a woman artist and have children? Her day-dream was once again of leaving everything and coming out to Yegen. Why didn't I write more often? But at length in the spring of 1921 she gave way. Her great friend Alix Sargant-Florence, with whom she had a compact that they should never marry anyone, had recently married James Strachey and gone out with him to see Freud in Vienna and be trained as a psychoanalyst. So she married Ralph on May 21st, 1921 and they spent their honeymoon with Lytton at Venice. When Gertler heard of it he attempted to commit suicide.

Meanwhile I had been getting desperately tired of my solitary life at Yegen. I had been there for two and a half years entirely alone. I craved for people, friends, conversation, laughter. But now my mother wanted to see me and my father agreed to pay my fare to England. Since my great-aunt had made me her heir he had ceased to fear that he might someday have to support me and this made him prepared to help me in minor ways. So in great excitement I made my preparations for leaving.

I arrived in London on June 23rd, 1921, and after spending a few days there with my great-aunt went on to my parents' house on the Cotswolds. I was looking forward of course to seeing Ralph and Carrington, but our long correspondence had not clarified my feelings about her. I had greatly enjoyed getting her letters and had been flattered by her confidences, but I had had very little experience of women and it had never crossed my mind that she might have any special inclination for me that went beyond friendship. Yet I had been tantalized by her suggestion that she might come out and live with me at Yegen. Only the month before I had written to her:

> You said that you could live with me here and that we should never love one another. Maybe that is true. Yet you are one of the very few young ladies I have met whom I might have fallen in love with had I met you earlier. But now you belong in my mind to R.P. I shall never disassociate you from him even if you quarrel and that somehow makes falling in love almost impossible.

What I meant was, not simply that the thought of betraying my friend was abhorrent to me, but that her connection with him put her in a class that was physically taboo. For I am by nature exogamous and the only women, Carrington apart, to whom I have ever been amorously drawn have been those who came from well outside the circle of my friends.

It was in this state of mind – unconsciously attracted yet on the surface completely blocked – that I went down to Tidmarsh for the night. A few days later I got a letter from Carrington asking me to join her on a picnic at White Horse Hill above Uffington on July 7th. She would be alone, she said, as Ralph had to go up to London. Although I had some doubts in my mind about the advisability of accepting, I went. We met on our bicycles at

the inn and, after climbing to the earth-works, sat down to eat our sandwiches behind a little copse on the forward slope. Then – I do not remember exactly how it came about – we kissed. She returned my kisses warmly
and I held her hand, but it was getting late and we set off for the station to
catch our separate trains. As I rode along watching the rich green country
slide by I thought about what had happened. To me the kisses had meant
very little, but I felt that I had acted irresponsibly and made up my mind
that I would not do so again.

A fortnight passed and I went over to Tidmarsh for a couple of nights.
Most of this visit is a blank in my mind, but one immense thing stands out.
I was sitting in an armchair in the sitting room when Carrington passed
across in front of the window, outlined against the setting sun. She just
passed across and all at once something overturned inside me and I felt that
I was deeply, irretrievably in love.

An avalanche of feelings followed, unlike anything I had ever experienced before. In that quarter of a minute the whole orientation of my life,
all the thoughts in my head had been changed. Like a Pacific Islander who
succumbs to an attack of flu brought in by a foreign sailor, I was struck
down and overwhelmed. Nothing had happened to prepare me for such a
situation and I sat there helpless, dazed by the welter of new emotions that
flooded over me.

What private meetings followed this I do not know. They have gone out
of my mind. All I remember is that we discussed whether or not we should
tell Ralph. I was in favour of telling him, but Carrington was not, saying
that since he would never understand the innocence of our feelings for one
another, he would be deeply disturbed and hurt. Some day she would be
able to tell him and then he would realize that this love that had suddenly
broken out between us had really brought both of us closer to him. But I
can see now that, quite apart from her fear that his jealousy would restrict
our meetings or even put an end to them altogether, she felt that if our new
feelings for one another were known to him and subjected to his interro-
gations, they would be spoiled and vulgarized. She liked to keep the essential part of her intimate attachments to herself and did not consider that
anyone had the right to probe into them.

Our love letters to one another begin from this moment. I had to reply
more cautiously unless I knew that Ralph was away from home because he
always asked to read what I had written. But, present or absent, he was
very much on our minds. As a concession to his feelings both of us denied
being in love because that would suggest that we were either having or
wishing to have an affair. The word Carrington used was 'fondness'. She
insisted once again that she could not tell him what we felt for one another
because 'he is such a dear creature that it would be wicked blackness to

hurt him'. Besides her feelings for me were 'so pure and full of deeper affection that if he could see into her head he would not mind but would be pleased'. Although, she said, she lived with Ralph 'for friendship and not for passions', she believed his existence in our life to be essential.

I had already written to her that I did not think it mattered how fond we were of one another so long as we remembered that one way was closed to us.

> I have even stronger reasons than you have why we should consider Ralph, for friendship, being founded on reasonable affections and not on passions, has more rigid principles than wifely love. I have never found him so charming as this last time nor felt so fond of him and I want to be perfectly open with him. In fact I must be so: friendship would cease to be anything if it were not. I don't even like writing letters to you that he will not read, but that cannot be helped because I could not write to you like this if I felt that anyone else might read my letter ... Still we ought to conceal nothing from him but actual words written or spoken, which depend for their very existence on being overheard by nobody.

But I said nothing about kisses. We were whirling down a slope which, unless I returned very soon to Spain, could only have one end.

A week later, on August 4th, we met in London. I had invited my brother Blair to dine with us and when he left I went back with Carrington to the dusty, half-empty rooms at 8 Fitzroy Street which my friend Hope had lent me. I will quote from a letter I wrote to her a few days afterwards but did not send off:

> I remember every moment of these two days perfectly. First there was that dinner with Blair presiding, a little vague and drugged and with a charming smile on his face. He looked from one to the other of us and at one moment he appeared young and boyish and at the next he was an old man full of wisdom and tolerance who saw us not as his elders, but as two children. His glances threw us together, didn't they? and seemed to say, 'You are not two, but one'. And then he was carried off in the train and we were left alone behind, and at once we both said, 'Now what shall we do?'
>
> Then back in those rooms you sat on my knee and we kissed without stopping for hour after hour. It was from then that you became dangerous to me. I realized that I should not easily let you go.
>
> Of the next day I shall soon have forgotten everything that preceded the theatre. I was glad that the play was so absurd because it left me free to look at you. I wanted to stuff your face into my mind

so that long after you had gone I might still be seeing you.

But do you know what it was that most touched me? It was when we came back together to my rooms. I lit the gas and went out into the passage and when I returned you had put a match to the stove and were setting out the cups. Then as you made tea the true picture of my life rose before me in all its barbarity, its loneliness and its dullness, and the only conceivable way of living seemed to be with a girl who in the evening should put the kettle on the fire and pour out one's cup. For the first time since I was eighteen it seemed to me enough to desire to be a man and to lead the ordinary life of men in town or country, following their ordinary professions and reaping their corresponding rewards. And it seemed to me an aberration to suppose that I was born to do anything rarer or more difficult. Then I forgot all this with your face held close to mine – there was no time nor room to think any more. If there can be happiness where there is not satisfaction, then I was beyond all measure happy. And the cup so overflowing was the next moment upset – the bright light quite put out.

On the morning after this Lytton and Carrington took the train for Keswick in the Lake District. They were to spend a month at Watendlath Farm, where Ralph would join them, while I prepared to return to Spain in the company of my friend Hope-Johnstone, who had just ceased to be the editor of *The Burlington*. I spent a couple of days helping him to pack the cases of books he was taking out and then went to stay with an aunt in Suffolk. On my return I paid a visit to the flat in Fitzroy Street where I had spent those two evenings with Carrington. It was cold and empty: our cups still stood unwashed on the table, but the cat had been shut in and had made such messes that the smell drove me out.

I was now staying with my great-aunt in her large, unswept, undusted flat in Ashley Place, off Victoria Street. She was in her eighties, a little midget of a woman who dressed in Victorian clothes and had been stone deaf since childhood. Later in this book I shall draw a full-length portrait of her, but all I need to say now is that she was the most restless creature I have ever known and that she never for a moment stopped talking. I had a heavy cold and, sitting up with two candles after she had gone to bed, I poured out my anguish and exasperation in two letters to Carrington.

My last night at my great-aunt's flat almost ended in catastrophe. I was sleeping on a camp bed in the dining room, for the spare room was full of trunks and boxes, when I awoke in the night with a violent headache. There was a strong smell of gas in the air and I got up reeling and threw open the window. The flat was lit with gas, for my great-aunt regarded electric light

both for Carrington and for myself, especially after Ralph, suddenly turning a corner, almost caught us kissing. So I drew lots whether to go or to stay, and went. We met again briefly in London, which gave us an opportunity to exchange the letters we had written, and on September 8th I took the boat from Newhaven.

Since these twelve days, in spite of or perhaps because of the absence from them of all sexual feelings, make up the most intense and deeply felt passage of my long and chequered relations with Carrington, I will give two extracts from our letters which – dead though all words become when once the situation that evoked them vanishes – describe the cruel nature of our predicament better than anything I can now put down. Carrington's letter first:

Dear, you can't think how I minded your going away, but I felt a shiver when Ralph suddenly came round that mound. It seemed a warning from the Heights. I think one can't keep things at a certain pressure indefinitely. The whole relation was shifting to trying to escape alone. But you must know that my heart was almost breaking and my eyes crying when you left. Ralph unfortunately made it worse. He became instantly very depressed. He clung to me and burst out, 'I always feel that something may happen to Gerald and that perhaps we shall never see him again'. I think he thought of Michael Davies [J. M. Barrie's adopted son] who was drowned. He suddenly became so sweet and lovely and talked of no one but you and of how he cared for you all the way back. Then he turned on me and said it was *my* fault because I had made you go by not persuading you to stay and if anything happened to you he would never forgive me and said it was my selfishness that had made you go. It was dreadful because I couldn't tell him I cared fifty times more than he did that you should have gone. Yet now I feel it was best. All the same I think it is about as fine a torture as could be invented to force a loved one to leave when there was no necessity for a departure .. You mustn't think ever I do not care as much as you do.

And my answer:

I had hoped at first, you know, to turn my feeling for you into something quieter and steadier. I had imagined a kind of Platonic attachment ... Unless I had thought this I should not have come up to the Lakes to see you. But it was a mirage – as I saw almost from the first evening, for when you are by me everything else is driven out of my head, and I am like a person drowned and overwhelmed in a sea.

What you said about Ralph touched me. After you, there is no one

I care for so much as him – will you tell him I said this? Yes, it is the most fiendish torture that could be devised, for you as well as for me, that he should reproach *you* for sending me away, and that I should love *his* wife more than anyone else in the world: God knows how it happened. I do not think I ever encouraged myself – certainly I never dreamed of this coming to pass. I had lived twenty-seven years in the world free, and known you for two years, and all at once, within a few days, I was taken captive. And now, at every moment, I find myself behaving badly – intending perhaps worse. And treachery to such a friend as Ralph, whom I every day grow to love better, is the blackest crime.

To these things passions lead us. I blame myself, and I do not blame myself, for it seems to me that whatever I do, I do horribly, and there is no right course. To give up loving and desiring you, or to try to give these up, would be a worse crime, for there is no part of my nature whence I could draw the force necessary to make me do this. Only from you could such a force come, for I will always do whatever you tell me.

The thought of Ralph pains me so much – how generous, how frank, how charming he is! His trust in me is a little terrible – why could he not be jealous, rude, suspicious? I can call up now with great vividness that last half-hour we were together. He leant over into your face with the gayest expression and sang that song – 'And where are the dancers, the dancers all in yellow?' You sat there like some enchanting creature, half wild, half tame, your dress was of green silk, your legs were white, your brown hands lay stretched over your knees. You sat there on the river bank, under the green wood, and the water splashed over the stones. The rocks rose up above the trees and the sunlight sparkled on the water. And Ralph sang all the time so gaily as he leaned towards you, and the song was so magical that it all seemed to be a repetition of something done long ago. It was like a dream that one feels has been dreamed before and that had therefore a double sweetness.

My God, that was beautiful. Everything that is beautiful and sad seemed crowded into that moment of our lives. And then a cloud came across the sun, the song stopped, and I hardly dared any longer to look up at your face. The golden bowl was broken, the music stopped, the light put out ... It was so really. I knew it had happened although I lingered on. You held my hand, do you remember, as we went along the road. And it became unendurable when Ralph said, 'let the lady give the gentleman a kiss'. I had feared that, and when I was round the corner, I took my heels and ran.

33

Personal Record

It had been settled that on my way through France I was to spend a week with the Bollards at their house at Ardoise in the Pyrenees, while Hope went on to Madrid. Clare Bollard was the latest of Carrington's particular friends and she wanted me to meet her. To persuade me to go she had praised her beauty and her adventurous, gay and melancholy character and also, because she knew how much listening to singing moved me, her marvellous voice and large repertory of songs.

I walked up the valley beside the tumbling mountain stream till I came to the village, which was situated perhaps a couple of thousand feet below the crest. The Bollards welcomed me warmly to their comfortable house and I took an immediate liking to both of them. Septimus, whom Carrington had described to me as a neutral sort of person, struck me a sensible and friendly man with something in his bearing of the professional soldier and something of the don. He was now on his way to becoming a man of letters with a special interest in Elizabethan tragedy. One could not say that he had any brilliance, but he was serious and modest and devoted to literature and I liked the way in which he would go out at a set hour every evening and dig in his cabbage garden. His wife could not have been more different. She was a handsome woman with jet black hair that hung in a straight fringe round her neck, dark flashing eyes and a soft, white, rather plump body. I found it hard to believe that she was English because she looked so utterly Italian – sensual, passionate, moody and yet capable and full of energy.

The days passed enjoyably. We went for walks and expeditions in the smooth green valleys where the beech trees were hung with beards of grey lichen and the mushrooms were as large as dinner plates. We ate our lunch by the waterfalls, planned to fish but did not and bathed naked in the icy stream. Our evening meals were delicious for Clare was an excellent cook. I often went out for walks alone with her while the industrious Septimus was busy at his books and she talked very unreservedly about herself. She told me that she had started her artistic career as a pupil of Derain's and I thought that her paintings had caught something of his dashing, romantic style. She had also had a number of love affairs while her husband was in Mesopotamia, serving in the war, which he appeared to tolerate. Janko Varda, John Rodker and Mark Gertler were names that often came up in her conversation and Gertler was a close friend with whom she still corresponded. I could not help wondering, with a little envy perhaps of her liberty, what sort of marriage this could be. Septimus struck me as being a good, somewhat pedestrian man who had caught a wild and self-willed beauty whom he could not control. He loved her enough to give her her head when she wanted it and she responded to his love by always, after every affair, going back to him because she needed his support. I thought it a true and touching marriage, each of them satisfying the other's need, and was only surprised that such an apparently conventional man as he was could show so much understanding and tolerance.

Carrington's description of Clare, which she sent me a few weeks later, gives a fuller picture of her:

> I admire the way in which she has no preconceived conception of how a woman and an artist has to live. She is worldly when she feels worldly, is business-like and generous, gay and very melancholy, un-principled though virtuous, and does not think it wrong to bake good cakes or trim a hat with ribbons, yet paints five hours a day and will not be interrupted for all the men in the world.

But she did not paint anything while I was with her except a portrait of myself, possibly because a young man she liked turned up to stay with them. And she did not sing either, declaring that she was not in the mood.

I spent ten days at Ardoise and after getting her promise to pay me a return visit that winter at Yegen, left for Madrid. Here I rejoined Hope and, after a halt to see the Prado, we took the night train south to Guadix. The carriage was packed, the air bad, the fleas numerous and since people kept getting in and out all night we could not sleep. When late in the after-noon we reached our destination we were both tired. But I was in a hurry to get home and read the letter that would be waiting for me from Carring-ton, so on the following day we set out at dawn for Yegen by the Puerto del Lobo, which is the highest of the passes over the Sierra Nevada. It was a long walk – at least thirty miles, with a climb of 6,000 feet above the Guadix valley – and Hope, who was eleven years older than I was and out of training, found it almost too much for him.

3

My breach with Ralph

I was now back in my mountain village, a very different person from what I had been when I had left it three months before. I was glad to be there again because the strain of the past three weeks had been great and, though I missed Carrington, I had her letters to look forward to. They were wonderful letters – one might almost say the best part of herself. Always scribbled off in a hurry, they reveal her way of feeling and seeing things with complete naturalness and spontaneity. But they were no longer love letters. Although she was very constant in her affection, her life revolved round Ralph and Lytton and was filled with activities and social engagements in which I played no part. My role could best be described as that of a troubadour who must supply his absent lady with verses and letters and provide her with a romantic figure – the Spanish landscape and the distance from England made me that – to dream about and pour out her feelings to. It was a role that I accepted gladly because on the whole it suited me, and I felt no jealousy either of Lytton or of Ralph because I knew that my position in the *troika* was assured. Carrington never gave up anyone she had once loved unless, as had been the case with Gertler, he became too demanding.

When today I read through the letters I wrote her – and in the four-and-a-half years I spent at Yegen these total more than 300,000 words – I get a fair impression of what my mental life was like at different periods. My first letters about finding and moving into my house were vivid, but then as I settled down to my hermit's existence they became more and more tedious and prolix. Having nothing else to write about, I filled them with long disquisitions on the books I was reading and on the thoughts and feelings that passed through my head with only an occasional passage that struck a different note. Yet though I passed so much of my life with books, the critical remarks I threw out on them were almost invariably boring and stupid. I only wrote well when something was happening that interested me. Then suddenly, from the moment that I went to England, my letters

became more lively and better expressed and this improvement continued
after I returned to Spain. My love for Carrington had evidently raised me
to a higher mental level, besides which I was no longer alone, bombinating
in a void, but had Hope to talk to. Yet the occasional literary prose pieces
I wrote during this time are very bad indeed. I became an articulate letter
writer many years before I could compose a tolerable paragraph – I imagine
because I found it easier to communicate what I felt to a person I wished to
amuse and please than to compose something of an impersonal sort for a
faceless public.

All this time I was living with Hope. It had been agreed between us
during the last months of the war that he should join me in Spain as soon as
he had saved enough money and that later, at some indefinite date, we
should take up our old plan of travelling together in the East. But he had
been enjoying his (as I called it) Capuan existence in London too much to
wish to change it and he had not of course saved any money. He was exiling
himself to Spain only because Roger Fry had sacked him from his editorship of *The Burlington Magazine* on the grounds that he was hardly ever to be
found in his office, and because he was being so dunned for his debts he
felt it expedient to be out of England for a period. He had therefore
brought with him barely enough money to support himself. However he
had extensive plans for reading and so had shipped out to Almeria several
heavy cases of books, a hundred of which were on Higher Mathematics. It
was also his intention to master the art of photography, which meant that
other cases containing cameras and photographic chemicals and equipment
had been sent off too. Most precious of all were some boxes containing
thousands of small cardboard sheets, each of a scientifically graded shade of
colour, which he intended to use for experiments in colour theory. He had
bought them for £50 in Germany in depreciated marks – a great bargain,
he declared, for their real value was four times that amount – but needless
to say they were never used but, after being brought down in 1934 to my
present house near Malaga, allowed to moulder away quietly in a cupboard
till they had to be thrown out.

The big cases reached Almeria in November and we went down to get
them through the customs. To my consternation I found that Hope had
ordered several hundredweight of photographic materials, including I do
not know how many jars of alum, which could be bought cheaply on the
spot. We had to pay heavy duties on all these materials so that when we got
back to Yegen we found that we should have less than £100 between us to
live on for a year.

But these were mishaps inseparable from any dealings with Hope and to
make up I found him a delightful companion. He spent most of the days
reading, leaving me to go for walks alone, but we also found time to do a

good deal of talking. Given the right audience, he was an admirable conversationalist, for there was no subject that he was not familiar with, from literature and Higher Mathematics to horse racing, bridge, astrology, where to buy smart clothes or how to make paper boats or juggle with coins to amuse children. He was at his best with a younger man, for he loved imparting knowledge, which he did in a cool, impersonal way without a trace of superiority. He could be witty too and had a fund of amusing anecdotes which in course of time, for their number was limited, I came to know almost by heart. His mind, it is true, was a negative one, with only a thin streak of originality, but the range of his knowledge was huge. Every subject that was taught at universities or that could be picked up in the smart or slightly crooked world he had mixed with interested him and his taste in the arts was good and very much his own. I thought of him as a Leonardo da Vinci, lacking only in creative talent, and became infected by his zeal for knowledge. No doubt this was unfortunate, for I lacked his clear mind and his excellent memory. My talents, such as they were, were intuitive and I might have become a better writer if I had mixed in the world more and read less.

Hope's reading habits used to amuse me. Although he read steadily from breakfast till midnight he never stuck to any book for more than an hour. After that he would put it away on a special shelf to be taken up on a later occasion. The result of this was that by the end of a couple of months a whole bookcase would be filled with the volumes he had started to read but not finished. That winter he was particularly engrossed in the Symbolic Logicians – Peano, Frege, Cantor and Bertrand Russell – and in his tutorial way he liked to expatiate on them and their problems. But, although I listened attentively, I could never understand what they were trying to do. Nor was I able to discuss any scientific or philosophic subject with him without getting tied into knots. His hard, clear, logical brain and his perfect memory would reduce me to despair, for my mind is not of the kind that can deal with abstract ideas and when I try to discuss them I become confused. He therefore found me a poor foil for his arguments. Thus it came about that from having once thought I was a genius, he was led to conclude that I was a simpleton, and when in the fifties I produced books on Spanish subjects that were praised, he was angry and jealous and refused to read them, in spite of his great interest in Spain at that time. For how could a person who was as woolly-minded as I was possibly have anything sensible to say or any power of explaining it well?

On the other hand I came to be more and more struck by his lack of antennae. He presented a hard, glossy surface to the world and had very little notion of what other people were thinking or feeling. The cynical tone he often fell into when speaking of them was the result of many failures and disappointments, which his vanity made particularly painful. He looked on me as an innocent because I was frank and unguarded in my dealings with people I liked, but although there was some truth in this, he had the much greater and more incurable innocence of the hard boiled. Thus our relation was that of associate and partner rather than of friends. We got on well, but there was little warmth or affection between us because he had none to give. He was always trying to draw in his limits, to squeeze himself into a hard ball that would both repel enemies and ward off the intimacy of friends and there was nothing he despised more than what he called the adhesiveness of human beings. Even his feelings for girls had to be one-sided, for he dropped them the moment he thought they were becoming emotional about him or demanding his sympathy.

It was now the end of January. We were in the middle of building a chimney in the *granero* or granary, which we were converting into a sitting room, when we heard that Clare and Septimus Bollard were on their way to see us. I met them at Órgiva and brought them up the river valley on mules. I was delighted to have them to stay with me and found that I liked them even better than before. We spent the time talking and going for walks and in the evenings after dinner Clare sang for us. She had a beautiful and well-trained voice and unlike most good singers she did not insist on an accompaniment. The songs she sang were in English, French and Italian and as I listened to her I felt that I had not experienced such intense pleasure since I had left Watendlath. Two in particular I remember – an old eighteenth-century French song which began *Il y avait dix filles dans un pré* and an aria by Alessandro Scarlatti called *Il sole de Gange*.

Clare was very anxious that in the spring Lytton, Ralph and Carrington should visit her at Ardoise and that I should join them there. To persuade me to agree, she promised to take Ralph off my hands so that I could sometimes be alone with Carrington. For we had both talked to her about our feelings for one another and she sympathized all the more with our difficulties because she had been given a hostile account of Ralph's 'tyranny' by Gertler. But she evidently did not believe me when I insisted that there could be no question of our having an affair because in her view love or even mere sexual attraction were things that overrode marital obligations. So I promised her that I would go, though on thinking it over I felt that it might be difficult for me to raise the £12 needed for the double journey. I therefore wrote to Carrington, explaining this to her and begging her to come on to Yegen with Ralph as had previously been agreed between us.

A few days after the Bollards' departure Robin John, one of Augustus John's sons, arrived from Granada on a mule. His father had asked if Robin could spend a few months with us to recover his health and to learn Spanish, and Hope had consented. Nothing had been said about a contribution towards his keep and he arrived with only a couple of pounds in his pocket. Augustus, who had no means of knowing how short of cash we were, sent nothing and Hope declared that he could not explain this to him because he had stayed so often at his house in the past. This meant that our diet became more limited than ever.

Robin was a tall, very good looking boy of seventeen and from the first he fitted well into our life. He was lethargic, no doubt because he had grown too fast, and used to lie for hours on his bed strumming on a guitar he had bought but which he never learned to play. Although he had ambitious plans for educating himself – after he had left I came across a programme he had drawn up in which he set himself the task of mastering philosophy, mathematics and all the sciences with the whole of French and English literature and the theoretical background of music and painting – he did not succeed in making much progress. Indeed the only book I ever saw him open was Casanova's *Mémoires* and even in that he never got beyond the first volume. Yet he was by no means stupid and picked up Spanish with extraordinary rapidity and entirely by ear. At the end of a few months he was talking it more fluently and with a better accent than I was.

There was a melancholy streak in Robin's character which was partly inherited and partly caused by something I did not learn about till many years later. A pretty and lively girl of sixteen had turned up at Chelsea parties and Robin had fallen in love with her. Then he found that his father was having an affair with her. He sank into a decline and was sent out to Spain to recover.

Hope and Robin spent a good deal of their time photographing one another in becoming poses. Hope was then a slim, sleek man with a small head and delicate features, glossy black hair and a very white skin, while Robin was tall and languid with large, dark expressive eyes and a soft rounded face that gave him an almost girlish beauty. Since they were both rightly pleased with their appearance, they enjoyed having photographs taken of it. I, not being good looking, was left out of this ritual and when one day Carrington asked me to send her a photograph of myself, I had to exert some pressure before I could persuade Hope to comply with my request. Then he produced the most wooden likeness I have ever had. Most of the photos he took with such care and preparation faded away at the end of a few months because he omitted to fix them properly. Even in his photographic work he was negative and self-destructive.

However, perhaps because I was so much nearer Robin's age than Hope was, I got on better with him than he did. United over photography, they were at odds over everything else and inclined to wrangle at meals. Robin had developed a strong liking for Spain and for our Yegen mode of life and to provoke Hope, who he thought was lukewarm in his appreciation of its merits, would single out as the thing most to be commended about it – the food. Much of this, as I have already said, was deplorable and Hope was a gourmet, whose mouth watered at the thought of French cooking, so that passionate arguments between them would break out. In these Robin would declare that anyone who could not see that Spanish bread and olive oil and lentil pottage and stews of salt cod and potato omelets were better than roast beef and *sole meunière* and *steak au poivre* was a degenerate who did not understand the true values of life, while Hope, his voice rising in pitch and his forehead wrinkling with irritation and disgust at the thought of such ignorance and philistinism, would reply in a torrent of sharp, hard, trenchant words. When he once got launched on an argument it was difficult to stop him and Robin, satisfied with having roused him, did not try to.

But I was getting bored with this exclusively masculine society. I wrote to Carrington:

I am tired from excess of asceticism and would like some amusing debauch. Last night I dreamed of flaring lights, pools of wine that looked like blood and large purple petals dropping from the air. And if at sunset I look up onto the clouds I see masses of flame and through them, far beyond, a small patch of distant, pale blue sky where I should like to be. And my head is full of plans which all centre round the word Constantinople, of the life people lead there, of the *cafés chantants* and dancing, and lights, and boats, and wine and women. Yes, women, and fearful incredible gaiety. What do you think of that? And will you and Ralph still go on living like farm yard birds, like poultry in hen houses, in that tame domesticated country, if I am in Constantinople, in Rome, in Alexandria? ...

It is Carnival here. Yesterday a lot of men and girls, all dressed up, came in and played the guitar. In the evening we gave a dance. I didn't dance – these Spaniards dance so well that I was ashamed to, but I made every vow and resolution I could think of to be a good dancer before I am thirty. Robin John was too shy – so was H.J. Isn't that incredible, not to dance when one is able to? Three such idiots as we made I never saw before. Oh, dreadful, awful to be an idiot of that description. I felt terribly ashamed of myself. We crowded into one corner to give ourselves some sort of face, like three Fitzroy-Bloomsbury apes with the dust engrained on their faces – the dust of hopeless and irreparable dullness. Oh, how I have seen people like that in London, artists and so on, and hated them with all my heart and soul for their revolting dullness and lack of spirit. And here we were, like those three holy men of God, Shadrach, Meshach and Abednego, walking in the flames and yet not burnt. It was then that

I said to myself the magic word 'Constantinople' and thought of Ralph.

How wonderful and delightful it is to see anything done perfectly. To see men and women moving to perfect time, in perfect balance: ... As they dance a kind of powder rises from the playing instruments and dancing figures and fills the room. It unites everyone present. The men and girls dance and dangle their legs and arms: two old men play: a little boy sits in a corner and leans his forehead on his hands: drawing up his whole face in a kind of snarl, he sings a *copla* and the whole room thrills and vibrates as though a very loud cricket was singing. Old women sit round and smile, and even they cannot smile out of time.

How good it all is, how solid, how earthly! It is pleasant to think about it. The smell of sweat, the heat, the high, piercing erotic scents of the women, the wonderful smell of their hair: the smell really maddens one. The singing, dancing, stamping, laughing, shouting and the faces of every age gleaming in the oil lights. And then, when it is all over, they will go home to their houses and lying in heaps on their dirty beds, full of fleas and sodden with sweat, will sleep together. Now that's just what I like, that's what I call life. At these moments I really love human beings.

The love of human beings – I see what that is. It is not the love of their souls nor of their amiable qualities. It begins by love of the human face, the human body – even the ugliest faces and bodies. And it is only when one is oneself happy that one loves them. Now I see that I love human beings and have always loved them, even more than I hate them. They are the nicest sort of animal, and almost the most animal-like. And that's a great charm in them.

One woman who was here last night was the village tart. She was dressed up as a little girl and looked charming. At first I didn't recognize her. She has a very clear complexion and beautiful ears and neck. Then she has very bright, gay eyes like a bird, and she sings and dances and laughs and talks with wonderful gaiety. How I admire such people. I felt sorry that she is supposed to have syphilis ...

P.S. But I won't stand up for this letter. The moments when one thinks like this are transitory. I have been reading Euclid all this morning in Heath's big annotated edition and that is something better than drinking and whoring. Mathematics is better than literature – I wish I had more sense for it.

In March Alix Strachey fell very ill in Vienna and Carrington went out to help nurse her. From there she wrote that she would meet me at Ardoise in April. Ralph, she said, was unwilling to come to Yegen as he did not get on with Hope. At the same time Augustus John wrote that he would like to come out and stay with us for a couple of months. Since he could be relied upon to pay all expenses while he was there, I would be able to draw enough money from the common fund to get me to the Pyrenees.

I left on April 5th. I was carrying on my back a small tent and a kapok sleeping bag as well as a load of pottery and silk and cotton head handkerchiefs as a present for Carrington. Four days took me to Pamplona. Here I started walking and, after a time came to the foot of the pass I must take. Here on the edge of a beech forest I found a large farmhouse of the chålet type that took in guests and was given a comfortable bed and a delicious stew of *cabra montés*, or wild mountain goat. But I could not pay the bill because I had spent too much on buying antique pottery at Granada, so I had to leave my tent and presents behind me as a guarantee that I would return later.

Next morning early I set off by a track through the beech forest. The pale silky leaves were just beginning to appear and long beards of grey lichen hung down from the branches like Spanish moss. As I climbed towards the col the snow became deeper and I began to fear that I should have to turn back. However when I emerged into the open I found that it did not reach above my knees and with a struggle I got through.

I found Lytton, Ralph and Carrington already established in the Bollards' house. Although the mountain air encouraged an atmosphere of heartiness I soon became aware of a tension underneath. Clare's father, a retired general, was staying with them and on his account the rule had been made that the Bollards should dress for dinner. This produced some jeers from Ralph and myself. The old gentleman had some rather long stories to tell about his military service in Kashmir and a collection of photographs to illustrate them which he invited us to look at, but our principal trial was that every evening we had to listen to Septimus reading aloud to us a biography he was writing of Thomas Dekker, the Elizabethan playwright. His text was punctured by exclamations such as 'Prithee, my lord' and 'How, now, sirrah', which made Lytton groan, though he said that the book was worth writing because it contained some new material.

But other things were wrong too. Ralph had taken a violent dislike to Clare which he made no attempt to conceal, while Carrington seemed less pleased to see me than I had expected. How could this be? I asked myself. Were we not in love with one another? It was not till many years later that she told me that she had been distracted by a Lesbian feeling for Clare, which had made her temporarily less inclined to me. However the weather was fine. The lilacs in the gardens were in full bloom, daffodils peered up through the grass and after a short walk together we made it up and she began a portrait of me in the attic.

Lytton wanted to see Pau, so Clare offered to drive him there. Carrington and I went along too, but Ralph refused to accompany us out of his dislike for Clare's company. Then on the way back the engine of the car seized up for lack of oil. We walked a couple of miles to a town and took rooms at the hotel for the night.

This seemed a heaven-sent opportunity for two lovers. We had dinner and went up to our rooms. Mine was immediately above Carrington's, looking out onto the river, which, full to the brim with melted snow, rushed tumultuously past in a yellow flood. As I stood by the window I could hear Carrington calling 'Cuckoo' to show that she was expecting me, but I could neither go to her room nor answer her. Since the Watendlath days my feelings for her had been sexless and chaste because of the guilt I felt about Ralph. Now, though I longed above everything in the world to join her and was not withheld by any conscious scruples from doing so, I could not because I knew that I would be impotent. A terrible shame weighed down on me. I walked up and down my room. I went out onto the landing and down the stairs as far as her door, but dared not open it. It seemed to me that if I should get into bed with her and fail to make love to her effectively, I should die of the disgrace. All night therefore I paced up and down my room while the moon shone brightly outside and the torrent rushed and roared, and through its noise I could hear her at intervals calling to me. This was the worst night of my life.

Then, as the day began to dawn, I came to a decision. Since sooner or later an explanation would be needed, I would go down to her room now and make a clean breast of my situation. I went and found her awake, for like me she had not slept. Sitting on the edge of the bed I told her why I had not come before and, kissing me, she reproached me for having been so foolish, since I ought to have known that all she had wanted had been to spend the night by my side. Scarcely had she finished saying this when the door opened and Clare came in. Evidently she had been burning with curiosity to know whether or not we had slept together and now she thought she had discovered that we had.

After breakfast we took a taxi back to Ardoise, where we found Ralph waiting for us in an exasperated frame of mind. His evening alone with Septimus and Sir Roger had not amused him and he made some cutting remarks about Clare's stupidity. Later in the day it came on to snow and we awoke next morning to find the village streets and roofs as well as the green hills that rose above them buried under a thick blanket of white. The lilac bushes, with their flowers and leaves fully out, were bent down under the weight. Carrington painted a picture of the church from the attic window while I sat and talked to her, for the fiasco at the hotel had brought us closer together. Then a very surprising thing happened. Ralph and Clare, who till now had been like cat and dog together, suddenly developed a violent crush on one another. The change was startling, all the more as Ralph, completely turning round, directed the aggressiveness he had previously shown for her on to Carrington and myself. He and Clare shut themselves up in her studio, but either because the term of their visit was coming to an end or because Septimus made objections, the three Tidmarshians set off two days later for England.

Before this happened it had been settled that I would go back with them and that they would lend me the money for my ticket. But I had to fetch the tent and pottery I had left in the farm beyond the mountains and, since the recent snowfall had blocked the pass, I should have to go more than seventy miles round by Saint Jean Pied-de-Port and Roncesvalles. Clare offered to drive me if I would stay on with her for a few days, but after being very friendly and singing her most melancholy songs for my benefit, she suddenly, for what reason I do not know, turned against me and dropped me only a dozen miles along my road. From there it took me six days to collect my things and reach London.

After a brief call at Tidmarsh I went straight to my parents' house at Edgeworth, which I reached on May 1st. They both received me very kindly and my father gave me a cheque to pay for my journey and current expenses. However I had a heavy cold in the head and this and the continual rain depressed me. Then my cold receded, the rain stopped and my normal good spirits returned.

I wrote to Carrington:

The country has all day been so ravishingly lovely that if you had been here to enjoy its beauty with me I should have been completely happy. I got up very early and went with my mother to Communion Service. The birds were singing everywhere as we walked through the woods and fields. The grass of the hill slopes was very rich and brilliant, and as soft as some rare texture. The black trunks and branches of the tall trees made a tracery in front of it. In the recesses of the woods the leaves of laurel trees and of holly, still wet from the dew, shone like silver disks and the young opening leaves of other bushes made a pale green mist that covered them in some places.

Inside the church one could hear the birds singing and see the branches of trees pressed against the windows. The wonderful beauty of the language, recited in a half whisper, the smell of mould and of wet masonry, the mysterious titles of God repeated in the *Gloria* and above all the sweet taste of the wine, taken fasting, combined to throw me into a condition when my senses seemed unusually sharpened and my receptivity to what is beautiful greatly increased. I walked home feeling very happy, hearing the cuckoos on every side and wishing that you were there also.

I went to Church again after breakfast. This service always pleases me and makes me gay. All the time one is getting up and kneeling down and opening and shutting books. Does anything, I wonder, present the essence of English country life better than the morning service? It is so absurdly incongruous, it is at the same time monotonous and varied, insipid and gay. I let my thoughts follow their own course, but when every now and then my attention was arrested by some extraordinary phrase, I wanted to clap my hands and to shout out in delight, 'Why this is Russian!'

We had the Litany, where at every moment one says 'Good Lord, deliver us!' I used to hate it as a child because it was so long, but today I found it fascinating to listen to the catalogue of things from which one had to ask to be delivered. What wonderful children the English are – But all the time you are exclaiming at my superstition.

Here I should say that I had not been a believer since the age of sixteen and that I only went to Communion service because it would have deeply hurt my mother had I not done so. Yet I also felt an attachment to the Anglican Church with the stately language of its services and the long tradition of English life which it incorporated, and was inclined to regard the idea of a God, in the metaphysical sense in which Plato regarded his forms, as a necessary idea. Or at least as a finger-post pointing in a necessary direction. For if, I sometimes argued, one rejected the religion of one's country completely, was one not rejecting the element that had created its culture and the pattern of its life and allowing them to freewheel on without any power behind them? And to whom, if not to God, could one pour out one's gratitude for the gift of life? I did not want to pray to him, I wanted to praise him. Yet there were aspects of Christianity that I very much disliked – the gulf it had fixed between Man and Nature, its narrowness about sex, its false promise of a future life with the consequent downgrading of this one. I could never make up my mind about it – sometimes drawn to it under the influence of a poem or picture or of religious music, but at other times indifferent or repelled. Only the teaching of Jesus made a fixed impression on me, although it seemed to come from very far away and from such a different world to ours. Thus I have wavered all my life about religion, without seeing any reason for taking up a definite attitude. I am not a rationalist, but I am both too sceptical and too changeable to commit myself permanently to more than a few simple moral ideas. The rest seems to me to be myth, significant and psychologically valid, created by human minds to suit human conditions, yet surely not to be believed in literally in these days.

On May 11th I went to Tidmarsh and remained there till June 1st. Clare arrived in England and Ralph went up to London to see her. They were having an affair and he, far from being more considerate to Carrington on that account, treated her *de haut en bas* as though he were paying her out for something. It was as if he were saying to her that, whereas she had never responded to his love-making as he had wished, he had now found a beautiful and fascinating woman who did respond to it and who was in every way his sexual equal. As was to be expected, his behaviour led to a change in my way of thinking. If he could display his physical passion for Clare so ostentatiously and arrogantly, I saw no reason why I should not be allowed to make love quietly to Carrington, and at that thought all my guilt feelings and with them my sexual inhibitions melted away. She felt as I did and when he went up to London to see his mistress she came to my room when I was in bed and got in beside me. Yet she was uneasy. She insisted that she was not jealous, that she was a person who did not have possessive feelings, but said that she mistrusted Clare because she could see that Clare was trying to prejudice Ralph against her. This impression was confirmed when she went up to London and lunched with her, for Clare did not trouble to conceal her delight in her triumph. Yet she did not think that she would dare to tell Ralph of our love for one another because she would be afraid of her revealing to Gertler what was going on. For Gertler, who hated Ralph, was Clare's best friend.

So the weeks passed. It was the season when the bluebells spread through the woods like a tide and the dandelions extend their brief empire over the fields, and Carrington and I would go off on our bicycles and picnic among them. I went to London on her suggestion to meet Gertler, and Virginia and Leonard Woolf came down to Tidmarsh for a weekend. I had not met them before, but they were very friendly and invited me to spend a weekend with them at Richmond. Morgan Forster also came down for a few days and, though I did not like his novels, I was drawn to his curiously precise, old-maidish character. But Carrington's moods of preoccupation, caused by her uneasiness at the hold Clare was acquiring over Ralph, showed no sign of diminishing and sometimes fell like a shadow between us. A certain strain was appearing in our relation and on June 1st, to avoid meeting Clare, I returned to Edgeworth.

Carrington and I were planning to spend a weekend in some village in Sussex, after which I would return to Spain. All I asked, I wrote to her, was that we should pass a few perfect days alone together. I did not want either to have our relation debased by familiarity or to take from her more than she could willingly give. For she had her life, I mine: one yearly meeting followed by letter writing would give us the best of one another. These may seem poor ambitions for a man who was as deeply in love as I was, but the weeks I had spent at Tidmarsh had shown me that it would be a mistake to get too entangled in her affairs and that our love would only be preserved in its purity if I kept my distance. I imagined that Ralph, who though possessive was also just, would someday allow me the small share of her life that I asked for. But our last day together had been partly spoiled by her moods and anxieties, so when I reached Edgeworth I wrote her a two-edged letter.

I am writing in the drawing-room after dinner – to whom? To you. To you, who sit far off, across fields, across flowers, across rivers, who sit in a garden among ducks and weeds and apple trees with Lytton and say – 'What a relief to be alone! To be alone at last!' The south wind brought me your words, whispered them softly in my ear. I heard them – oh yes, I heard them.

The lamps are lit, there are yellow roses on the walls, pink roses on the chintzes, blood red roses on the curtains. On the Manchester–Indian carpets lie lilies, blue lotus lilies, exotic flowers. Pale yellow dust floats between the walls, and polished wood and gilt mirrors shine far offly through it. Watercolours in gold frames, silver, china, glass gleam vaguely, brightly, softly.

The air is heavy with the scent of flowers. Yes, and the clock goes tic a tic, tic a tic, tic a tac. In the deepest armchair I see my father's pink crumpled face and round agate eyes over the top of a newspaper. Struck ten. At Tidmarsh you sit on a low chair – Lytton reads to you. 'The worst of Gerald is … ' That's what they say in Georgia.

I am not going to Sussex on Wednesday. It is mad, I say mad … I shall remain here till – till – I go back to Spain – one evening, suddenly, secretly, without telling you, two thousand miles, all in a flash, in the corner of a third class carriage, dirt, babies, fleas, all horrors: yes, I shan't perhaps give you even the chance of betraying me. Stop. What are you thinking of? Tell me, *immediately immediately*.

Of chickens, of dear little Annie, of dear, dear Clare, of – , or are you thinking of all these things at once? I bet, of Clare, that sheep in wolf's clothing. She said, he said, I said – . But I said, and Brett said. It is all unconscious – a dangerous woman. *Une femme fatale*, who has got the innocent Ralph into her clutches. A poisoner.

In the garden darkness is coming on. A thrush still sings. Thrush or nightingale? The trees bend and shake and rustle, yellow flowers lie among the dark green grass. Golden flowers, weeds, yet still bright golden flowers.

My breach with Ralph

Through the plate-glass window I see the blackish blue sky and the trees, which are like pale green flames, slowly waving. Mists, clouds or flames and a million million million leaves and sharp eyed insects that live among the leaves.

In an orchard by the River Pang are pale green apple trees, mayflies that dance under them – all things that I shall not see again. And someone whom perhaps I shall not see again, who once put scent on her hair. Night-scented stock, was it? Here in this garden when pacing the lawn its piercing sweetness surprised me.

And there? Oh no, no, no, I will not meet you again unless for a day, for an evening you can forget everything but me. I will not have less – I do not ask for more. At Watendlath, the day I left you, I did not have less.

Two days later I wrote Carrington another letter, begging her to forgive me for this one and suggesting that we should go to Sussex immediately after my forthcoming weekend with the Woolfs at Richmond. But on the day on which this reached her all our hopes and plans for the future were dashed to the ground. Ralph had brought Clare down to Tidmarsh for lunch and after it they left in the car Lytton had recently bought him for Marlborough, where they were to spend a few days in a hotel. There on the morning of their second night she told him that I had for the past year been having an affair with Carrington and that everyone knew it except him. Also that our meeting at Ardoise had been the result of a plot between myself and her, in which she had promised to take Ralph off our hands so that Carrington and I could be alone together. On hearing this Ralph jumped into his car and, taking a bottle of whisky with him, drove back to Tidmarsh. He arrived, apparently drunk, and had a very violent scene in the garden with Carrington. That evening I got two telegrams, one from Ralph asking me to meet him on the following day at the Hogarth Press at Richmond and the other from Carrington, begging me not to give her away.

I went. As the train took me through the green, elm-leafy countryside past White Horse Hill, past Pangbourne station, I considered what I should say. A strong instinct told me that I must make a clean breast of everything that had happened because it would be a terrible thing to lie in such circumstances to one's best friend. Yet if I did so I would be betraying Carrington, to whom my first duty lay. I decided therefore that I would tell everything that had happened up to three weeks ago, but say nothing of our lovemaking since then. The whole horror of our deception, which Ralph's affair with Clare had made me temporarily lose sight of, rose up in my mind. At the very moment when he was most in love with Carrington and when he was also so full of affection for me, we had been going off into corners to kiss and embrace. That was how he would see it. Had he been in my position and I in his, he would have told me at once, whatever objections Carrington made, because he was a man who hated every form of deceit. I felt weighed down with guilt and yet I could not tell him the whole truth, as to salve my conscience I longed to do, because that would be an even worse betrayal.

I arrived at Hogarth House and Ralph led me into the office. Here I told him the whole story of my love for Carrington down to my last visit to Tidmarsh. He began to press me on certain physical details – had I put my hand down the front of her dress and so forth? I could see that they were of immense importance to him. If I had told him that I had, I felt that he would have been overcome with loathing for her and would almost certainly have refused to go back to her. But, keeping my mind firmly on what had happened between us at Watendlath and Ardoise, I could assure him truthfully that I had done nothing of the sort, and he appeared to believe me. Luckily for me he asked no questions about our recent relations at Tidmarsh, since in that case I should have had to lie to him. Then the story of the supposed plot with Clare came up. Every ten minutes he left the room and went upstairs to consult with her about what I had said. That, at least, was what he told me, though I have since gathered that it was a hoax and that she was not there. At the end he said that he would have to consider what he would do and whether he would return to live with Carrington or not.

Next morning I took an early train to Pangbourne and waited at the tea-shop till I got word that I could go on to Tidmarsh. When I arrived I told Carrington what I had said to Ralph and she replied that she had always known she could rely on me. The lunch that followed was like a funeral meal. Lytton sat, grave and gentle, at the head of the table and we talked indifferently, but I remember that I was in such a state of emotion that my hands trembled so that I could scarcely hold my knife and fork. For I knew of course that this was the end of my relation with Carrington. I must bury myself in Spain because her position with Ralph and therefore perhaps with Lytton was at stake and so we must stop writing to one another. This was what Lytton had advised and I accepted my sentence without protest. What else could I do? I had nothing to offer her that could possibly make up for the loss of her present civilized mode of life. We might be 'in love' with one another, but in her deeply rooted situation at Tidmarsh such love was not enough. Lytton came for her before everyone. Nor did I believe that we should get on for long if she came out to live with me at Yegen, for I knew that our love was an *amor de lonh* as the Troubadours had called it, nourished chiefly on absence and letters, and that she would never be able to endure the isolation of my Spanish village. It was the total breach, not the return to Yegen for a year or two, that seemed like a sentence of death.

I took the afternoon train to Cirencester and walked home across Lord Bathurst's park. On the way I tried to work out how I could kill myself, but the longer I thought about it the more difficult it seemed if I wished to do it smoothly and decently. I have not a suicidal temperament – I love life far too much – but at that moment I needed something to plan for because I had suddenly lost my future. Then, since I could not conceal the state I was in, I had to give a brief explanation to my parents of what had happened. They both treated me with unexpected tact and sympathy and allowed me to go to bed at once and remain in bed for most of the next day. In their Spartan regime this was a great concession and I have since wondered whether they did not feel a certain relief that I was in love with a girl, because my running away from home with Hope ten years before and my continuing devotion to him had probably made them think I might be a homosexual.

The next few days brought me four letters from Carrington:

Five minutes after you have left. – I cry so much I can hardly sec. Oh, Gerald, I saw you thought I didn't care ... I couldn't trust myself to talk to you of myself and you because I only cry when I think of you away from me and this end to our happiness. But *you* mustn't be unhappy. Remember that even if I can't write to you I am your fonesdt friend and that all I ever said and felt towards you *was* true and that nothing that was between us wasn't real. I have not slept since Tuesday and have hardly eaten anything so you must forgive me if this afternoon I was so unhappy and did not show much feeling. I could not dare to let myself talk of you much. It broke my heart completely and made awful moments of despair and misgivings rise up. Lytton has been our only true and great friend ... I shall to my dying day thank you for the one great thing you did for me. Forgive me if for a few moments in my despair I thought you had ... but I can't write more.

Next day came another long and affectionate letter. Lytton had been touched by the way I had behaved.

Oh Gerald, please remember how I cared and still care. That you alone acted as in the worst moments I knew and wished you would act has been my only happiness in this nightmare. You alone did think of me and remembered that a friendship was worth more than anything else ...

Oh Gerald, I moon in the orchard looking at the seat where we two sat, at the flattened grass where you lay .. You mustn't think it wasn't worth while, for you know it was. That I mind so terribly is awful. That you care even more is worse still. The irony of it was that no good could come of it. I was tied. I could not leave with you. I should have felt for ever an exile with a ghost between us. I couldn't have left with that face in the orchard distorted with rage and horrid threats of murder. – *Our* relation was so perfect. It was never marred by callousness or too much intimacy. It never faded into something carnal. Every day I learned to be more fond of you and found new pleasures. That no one now will notice what I wear or how I feel, that I shall no longer rush down to get letters from the post, that no longer can I plan to see you in Spain is more awful to me than to any-one else.

I also had a letter from Ralph:

I have not yet come to any decision as to what I shall eventually do. I am tormented by the most horrible dilemma and confusion of feeling. In my real character I am utterly different from you and her – I feel, when I do feel, with such overwhelming intensity that my feelings are master of my behaviour. As a friend I cannot love her because we both put no trust in the other, as a wife she is so tainted to me so that all my love has been changed to loathing. And yet she has been three-quarters of my life to me for many years and I cannot operate on myself for the removal of such a vital portion without intolerable pain. Then there is Lytton, whom I love for his real character, not for being a great man.

He added that he was sorry she wouldn't go away with me, but that that was a purely selfish feeling as she would have made me even more un-happy if she had.

Lytton wrote me a kind letter too and I sent him one to hand to Carring-ton, if he thought that right. Clare also wrote to me asking me to come and see her, but, acting on Carrington's express wishes, I did not answer. Only one thing puzzled me about these letters. The possibility that Carrington would come away with me had never crossed my mind because I had always accepted her life with Lytton and Ralph as a fixed and unalterable thing. I had no claims over more than a small corner of her life and that was why I had never felt any rivalry with Ralph. Surely that might have been better understood.

Then on June 14th I left for Spain. As I passed through Madrid I caught sight of Augustus John sitting in a café and we spent the afternoon to-gether as he has described with some embellishments in his autobiography.

4

Yegen, Seville and Morocco

I arrived back at Yegen to find Hope and Robin John living in a state of disorder and confusion. Our servant Maria had just given birth to a child which she declared was by her former lover, the landlord of our house, though it later transpired that its real father was a pompous young man who the year before had bored me with his frequent visits. The baby had been born two months before its time in dirt and secrecy and its minute, red, wizened face stared angrily out of the old black shawl it had been wrapped in. Its mother crawled about the house, looking like a torpid, half dead winter fly, one dangling udder showing through her blouse, her complexion yellow, her voice plaintive, her stench overpowering. Pausing in the middle of the kitchen she would look round her at the uncleared table, the unswept floor, the places where the cat had made a mess and let out a solemn gurk. Then she would totter off to her own house next door, groaning as she went.

To escape from this scene we hired a small donkey, loaded it with blankets and sleeping bags and made our way to a place called El Horcajo, or the Big Fork, high in the Sierra Nevada above Trevélez and which I knew because I had camped there before. Here we dossed down in a shallow cave, which gave us protection from the violent winds that swept down every evening at sunset from the snow summits that stood not far above us, and ate at the small farm close by. They gave us milk, hasty pudding (made of wheat flour and boiling water) and fresh curds, supplemented at midday by beans cooked with garlic and herbs, while for dessert we had the dried figs and fresh apricots we had brought with us. When at the end of a few weeks of this pastoral life we returned to Yegen, we found Maria restored to health and everything in order.

Hope, who had by this time had enough of primitive life, returned to England at the end of August. Compton Mackenzie, under whom he had served in the Aegean during the war, had offered him the assistant editorship of a magazine he was founding called *The Gramophone*, and he went to live with him at Herm, the Channel Island where he had made his home. Robin also went back to England, so I was left to my own resources.

All this time I was completely in the dark as to what was happening to Ralph and Carrington. That autumn she began to write me a journal letter, but she did not send it to me till a year or more later. From this it appears that all through June and July Ralph was seeing Clare continually. Clare was doing everything she could to keep him in love with her and to make him dislike and despise his wife, and for that purpose she kept inventing new and false stories about Carrington and myself. Ralph had become completely hard and cynical with Carrington and treated her as a sort of imbecile. Then at the end of July Clare returned to Ardoise with Gertler, telling Ralph that she would not write to him for six weeks so that he could give his marriage a trial. However in spite of this she wrote to him every day.

In August Lytton, Carrington and Ralph went on a holiday to Wales. There were quarrels all the time. Carrington said that she could not bear to have Clare mixed up in her life because she turned Ralph against her and that since she had broken with me, who had always been his friend, he ought to break with Clare. Ralph replied that he had no objection to Carrington keeping in with me and that this was a deprivation she had imposed on herself. However by the end of the month they were getting on a little better and Ralph wrote to me that he had recovered from the passion of hatred he had felt against both of us and that he intended to continue living with Carrington. Later on he might come out and visit me, with or without her.

Three days after this, Clare returned to England with Gertler. Ralph now said that he was no longer in love with her, but that he intended to keep in with her as a friend. However Clare was not satisfied with this, so that when she returned to Ardoise in October Ralph decided that he must give her up entirely. His decision was clinched when Septimus wrote him a letter, requesting him to stop troubling his wife. Her mental health, he said, was not strong and if Ralph continued doing so, there was a danger that she might have a break-down.

Ralph now gave up Clare, but with the warning to Carrington that if she resumed relations with me, he would resume them with Clare. 'You say you mistrust Clare and think she is wicked. I tell you that I mistrust Gerald and think that, not from wickedness but from thoughtlessness and vagueness, he may hurt my happiness.' She replied, 'Since you feel like that I shall not resume relations with Gerald.' Then, addressing me in her journal letter, she said, 'Either one lives decently or not at all. I *won't* have a less perfect relation with you. I prefer to wait till that is possible.'

The great explosion caused by Ralph's violent passion for Clare and by his discovery of our deceit was now over. The air was clearing. Carrington had found that, as I had always told her, she loved Ralph more than she had supposed. She had also, I think, become fonder of me because in the crisis I had put her interests before what she seemed to regard as my own. But above everything there was Lytton and the civilized life of Tidmarsh. Ralph was an indispensable part of that and I was not, though unlike Clare I was not hostile to it. It was this life too that had in the last resort decided his choice between Clare and Carrington. All through these stormy months Lytton had played a crucial part. Ralph was devoted to him and it was more than anything else his patience, gentleness and wisdom that had brought Ralph back.

And Clare? At the time both Carrington and I thought she had behaved with deliberate falseness and treachery. Today I no longer believe this. She had apparently fallen so violently in love with Ralph that she had been ready to leave Septimus to marry him and in such situations passionate women are apt to lose all control over their words and actions. And Ralph, once his suspicions were aroused, would have put pressure on her to tell everything.

That autumn I began a correspondence with Ralph. I admitted no guilt because I maintained that I had never conspired against him and that Carrington had not loved him one particle less because she loved me. If there had been deception that was solely because, since he held different views on the permissibility of love to what she and I did, he could not be told. He would have been furiously jealous and such jealousy would have been irrational as well as harmful to us all because I was not his rival and had no wish to take her from him. I did not hold, I said, to the notion by which a husband possesses or owns his wife. What he owns is not a body but something mental – the affection that she has for him. As an example of how Ralph had been included in my love for her as well as in her love for me I reminded him of the last hour I had spent at Watendlath, when he had sung for us. That, I said, had been for me the highest point in those ten days. Evidently he believed what I said for soon after getting my letter he allowed Carrington and myself to begin writing to one another again, only making it a condition that he read our letters. Today I judge my conduct more severely, for such deception of a friend is inexcusable.

So after six months' interval our old correspondence was resumed. Carrington was still shattered by the storms she had been through and by the feelings of guilt which Ralph's anger and contempt had aroused in her, so that out of fear of saying more than she ought her letters were timid and restrained. She had also taken to hating herself.

I see myself growing misshapen and lumpish, tongue-tied or else garrulous, disliked because in order to appear clever I imitate people like Virginia and make cynical remarks, selfish and bad tempered, lazy and more and more untidy in my habits every day. I often creep off to my room in order to conceal myself from human eyes lest they should suddenly see me as I am and turn from me in disgust ... And I hardly do any painting because I am so disgusted with what I paint.

My letters on the other hand were inordinately long because I suffered from loneliness and the need to communicate, yet had little outside my own thoughts to convey. A new tone comes into some of them, a tone that could almost be called resentful. This was because, now that it was all over, I felt that I had been treated unjustly. Then, going back in my mind over Carrington's behaviour at Ardoise and later at Tidmarsh, I realized how capricious and unreliable she had been. At one moment she loved me, at the next she did not. She had not thought of my feelings when she had broken her promise to spend the day alone with me, but had followed her own mood of the moment in everything. So, though I still loved her deeply, I began to question the genuineness of her feelings for me as well as the advisability of renewing our old relations. Yet in my letters to her I made no reproaches, but continued to dwell on the injustice of the law that separated us. I wrote:

I am designing a new copy-book for infants which will say:
  'You must not like nougat *and* toffee.
  It is not allowed to enjoy eating *and* drinking.
  It is forbidden to play hopscotch *and* marbles.
  If you like Mary you must give up Jane.'
  And so on through twenty pages, for children are slow to learn the sublime truths of morality, till on the last page:
  'Unless you are a citizen of Avalon, of
  Tir-na-nogue, of Cockaigne, of the Hesperides, of Georgia.'

For Georgia was the country to which, I had said, Carrington and I belonged and we used one or two Georgian words in our letters.

That Christmas and the whole of January I spent in Granada. A very kind old lady, Mrs Wood, whom I have described in *South from Granada*, had invited me to stay with her on the Alhambra hill and through her I met the Temples, who had built themselves a house a little higher up near the cemetery. Temple was an impressive man who had explored the Gran Chaco in Paraguay and afterwards been Governor of Northern Nigeria. His wife, who was remarkable too, was a daughter of The Macleod of Dunvegan Castle in Skye. I led a very social life, going to parties and dances and making friends with two brothers, the Rodriguez Acostas, who belonged to a local banking family and were interested in the arts. Indeed one of them was a painter and it was at his studio that I met Federico García Lorca, who was just beginning his career as a poet. But most of my time was given up to a flirtation with an American girl from Buffalo. We used to sit and kiss by moonlight in the Alhambra Park and I would feel how wasted all that romantic background was because I was not in the smallest degree in love with her. One evening she asked me if I was an idealist. I supposed at first, for she had had a certain amount of education, that she was referring to the philosophy of Berkeley, but it turned out that she meant did I believe in keeping sexual advances out of flirtation? She did, and I began to take less interest in her.

I should have liked to remain on for longer in Granada, where I was amusing myself, but I was forced to return to Yegen because my money ran out. Mrs Wood used sometimes to press a little into my hand to pay for my casual expenses, but when the sole of one of my shoes fell off and I had not enough to buy another pair, I decided that it was time to leave.

I got home in February – this was now 1923 – to find that I had hurt Carrington by something I had said in a letter to Ralph and also by not having written to her for some time when she had begged me to write every week. All my love for her welled up in the remorse I felt. But I never concealed from her my interest in girls, though I treated the subject with appropriate lightness. Thus, when Mrs Wood sent me a present of butter, I wrote to her:

I discover that there are two things necessary for my happiness:
1. the company of women.
2. butter.
or else
1. butter.
2. women.
I can't decide on the order.

That spring Katherine Mansfield died. Carrington, who had once shared rooms with her, wrote to me that her stories were the least interesting part of her. She was an extraordinary woman, witty and courageous, very much an adventuress and with the language of a fish-wife in Wapping. But Middleton Murry ate the soul out of her.

Morgan Forster had proposed coming out to see me that spring, but I discouraged him. Although I liked him as a man, I could not bear his novels which I thought were woolly and sentimental, though, like his conversation, with sharp passages in them. I was still a good deal of a prig and would fly into rages against writers whose works I disapproved of. So Forster did not come and instead I had Leonard and Virginia Woolf, both of whom I liked and admired enormously.

I have described the Woolfs' visit in *South from Granada* so I shall say no more about it here. But there was a sequel. Leonard wished to return by the east-coast route and so, because he spoke little Spanish, he pressed me to accompany them as far as Valencia. There was always a risk to be taken in travelling with Virginia because if she got overtired or did not sleep at nights she was apt to fall ill. We set off therefore by bus for Almeria and next morning took another bus which connected with the train to Murcia at Huercal Overa. Leonard and I sat on the roof, holding on tight to keep our seats as the clumsy conveyance lurched about, while Virginia sat inside, choking in the clouds of dust that we churned up. It was a wonderful drive through a desert landscape, either corrugated and ravined like the face of the moon or else rimmed by delicate rose and ochre hills as sharp and bare as the skeletons of animals – then suddenly interrupted by plunges into shallow, cliff-bordered valleys where the sickly scent of orange blossom saturated the air and tall palm trees rose out of green fields of alfalfa. Leonard appeared to enjoy it immensely and I was only sorry that Virginia should see so little. We slept in Murcia, where a strong stench of drains mingled poetically with the scent of orange and lemon blossom, and on the following day we continued to Valencia. Here I left them and started on my way back.

It was now April and my parents were coming out to see me. I met them at Granada where I introduced them to the Temples, who said many things to them in my favour because they thought the young should be adventurous. Then we took the bus to Órgiva and next day made the long journey on mule-back up the river bed. My mother was past sixty and had a delicate stomach, but in spite of the foreign food and the olive oil, which upset her a good deal, she enjoyed every minute of her visit. Both she and my father were impressed by the order and civilization I had introduced into my remote mountain home and realized, for the first time I think, that I was in my own queer way a serious person. They stayed a week and then I took them on mules over the Puerto del Lobo to Guadix and put them on the train for Madrid. It had been a great adventure for them and when he got home my father wrote offering me an allowance of £100 a year, on the condition that I returned every twelve months to see them in England. So my days of real poverty were over.

I had been getting pessimistic about my relation with Carrington. Ralph was now having an affair with a woman he had met at a party, yet, though we were allowed to correspond, his prohibition against my seeing Carrington remained. There would therefore be no point in my returning that year to England. But when I broached my discouragement to her, I got an immediate reply.

The reason why your friendship matters to me is that you are nearer to me in spirit than anyone else. I agree so closely with your views on life. They give me a support and a feeling of self respect. Lytton has the effect of making me feel stupid and hopeless about myself. It isn't that he thinks this about me, it is that his standards are so far out of my reach. Ralph has the opposite effect, but when I read your letters I feel clearer and less gloomy about myself.

In June Saxon Sydney-Turner came out to visit me. He was one of the Cambridge Apostles and a member of 'Bloomsbury', and Leonard Woolf has drawn a portrait of him in the first volume of his autobiography. He was a curious, perverse creature and one of the greatest bores I have ever known. Something, evidently an attack of schizophrenia, had happened to him when he was young which had killed all that was human and vital in his mind and left only the machine. In the course of time I got to know him pretty well and came to see that he was not only aware that he was a bore but that he was proud of being one and enjoyed dealing out his death packets to other people, whose vital qualities he despised. On this visit I had looked forward to talking to him about the Greek dramatists whose works I was reading in Leconte de Lisle's translation. I knew that he was a first-rate classical scholar, but what I had not been told was that he would never discuss literature and in fact all I could get out of him was a long, dry exposition of the intricacies of the Greek accent, which naturally was of no interest at all to a person who could not read Greek. Many years later he took to going every summer to Finland, coming back each time with a collection of snapshots that showed nothing but fir trees of varying heights and small railway stations. When he arrived at Lytton's house for the week-end he would bring these photographs with him and one dreaded the moment when he would fetch them out and display them one by one, very slowly, in that muffled yet persistent voice of his, with brief comments: 'I took that one of a railway station in the tundra because when I first went to Finland it had not been built.'

Saxon throws an interesting light on the mores of Bloomsbury. In that circle, which lived and met for good conversation, to be a bore was the worst accusation that could be levelled at anyone. Yet because he had been an Apostle, loyalty required that he should be frequently asked down for weekends by both Lytton Strachey and the Woolfs. Nothing, I think, shows better how rooted they were in that little Cambridge society. For Arthur Waley, though not an Apostle, had been at Cambridge at the same time as Lytton and Leonard. He lived in Gordon Square, next door to the Stracheys and three minutes' walk from the Woolfs, and was not only one of the most intelligent of men, but a fine prose writer and the best translator of poetry England has had since the Elizabethan Age. Yet because he was a little too obsessed with Chinese things to suit many people, he was put down as a bore and more or less excluded from their society. Why then was Saxon preferred to him? I can only conjecture that every group or society feels the need for a private bore of its own, who belongs solely to them. His death-dealing visits, the awful discomfort and agony he causes provide a subject for wonder and humorous self-commiseration. A pride is felt in him, he is regarded as a perverse family pet who must be tolerated and cherished. If that is so, no one could have been found who was more suited to the role than Saxon.

I was now to discover that early Jewish or rather Hebrew history is fascinating. In order to concentrate better on it I took to working by night, sitting up till sunrise and then going for a short walk before retiring to bed. The consequence of this was that, since my oil lamp gave a poor light, I strained my eyesight and had to stop reading till I could be fitted with glasses. I therefore went down to Almeria in September to get this done.

This town provided a girl, Antonia Fuentes, the daughter of a retired bullfighter, whose beauty laid a spell on me and whom I courted without success. Although I bought a new suit to impress her, I could make no progress. She would talk to me while we were swimming, but back on land she refused to look at me. So I hung about the fishing quarter, went out at night with the fishermen and then, finding that this led nowhere, set off for Seville, which I had never seen before.

Seville was in those days, before it became overgrown and tourist-ridden, an earthy paradise where the air one breathed seemed all gaiety and happiness. My first week there led to an explosion of euphoria which expressed itself in the writing of a sheaf of poems. I used to go every evening to the Kursaal, a large dancing hall in the Calle Sierpes that had a stage at one end. Here one could watch a programme of flamenco dancing and singing which ended with a superb presentation of the *Cuadro Flamenco*. The audience sat on chairs in the gallery while the waiters served them with drinks and in between the turns there was ballroom dancing on the circular floor below. Twenty or more girls, the *tanguistas*, provided the partners and if one pleased them one could sleep with them for a small sum so long as one of their regular lovers was not in need of their services. I got interested in the leading *bailarina*, a young girl from Triana called Lolita Beltrán who came on in a blue silk dress, rattling her castanets in front of a back drop of the moon rising over the Torre del Oro. In the hopes of getting to know her I took a room in her hotel, a grubby old-fashioned place called El Continental, frequented in spite of its bugs and mosquitoes by theatrical people, and tried to arrange my time so as to run into her as often as possible.

At the Kursaal I made friends with an Englishman called Durrell who worked in the orange trade. He was a man in his early forties with a red face, white hair and protruding sensual lips who, though of good family, felt an irresistible attraction to low life. He was bored by women of his own class, found even actresses too respectable and felt at home only with whores. As if to suit them, his conversation, both in English and Spanish, was interlarded with obscene words. But he was not promiscuous. He shared one of the *tanguistas* with a rich Spaniard who lived in Madrid, and was faithful to her. It was a convenient arrangement for him since the Spaniard paid all the expenses while he slept with the girl.

I had hoped that by being seen every night at the Kursaal with Durrell, his friend the British Consul and various titled members of the smart Labradores Club, I might end by making some impression on Lolita. But she continued to walk past me six times a day without a glance in my direction. Her faint, ethereal smile, which I admired so much when she danced in the blue artificial moonlight, was kept for the dark-haired Sevillian youths who followed her about. When I consulted the Consul as to what I ought to do about it he said that I must begin with an expensive present, but that if after that she came to like me she would expect nothing more. Further enquiries brought the information that she was childish, vain and capricious as well as still a virgin and that an admirer had given her a diamond crucifix worth £100 without getting more than a few words of thanks. I decided therefore to stop thinking about her.

A young Englishman just out of his public school had joined our party and one night Durrell suggested that we should take him on a round of the brothels. The first we called at was full, but at the second three big girls, dressed in either black or mauve silk, rushed on us and seized us, crying out as they did so *O mi marido! Qué guapo es mi marido!* They were all under twenty and wore no make-up, but I did not find any of them attractive. However the ex-public school boy retired with one of them while Durrell and I went into the patio and ordered beer. The madame, a big fat woman with cold eyes and a hawk-like nose, was sitting there in a cane chair and at once started on a long complaint of how the trade was being ruined. The season was dead, she had never had worse girls and then the pay they asked! If this went on she would have to go out of business. Then suddenly a door opened and a very pretty young girl, dressed in a white embroidered chemise, appeared, smiling and putting out her tongue at me. She was enchanting. I jumped up to seize her, but the madame called me back. 'You can't have her now,' she said. 'She's with a man.' But she came out, saying that her *marido* or husband had fallen asleep, and Durrell pulled her on to his lap. She was very young – just seventeen she declared – and as slim as a lizard. But what was most striking about her was her liveliness. Her face

nymphs were disporting themselves in the water as in Borrow's time and in any case it was already November. I therefore went on to Cadiz and from there via Algeciras to Ceuta, where I took the little train to Tetuan.

I had never been in a Moslem country before and Tetuan delighted me. It was still an eastern city with few European buildings in it and the Moors had not yet given up their native costumes. In the cafés one sat cross-legged on a low dais and drank mint tea while a musician played on a stringed instrument and sometimes burst into a melancholy song. I bought a *sibssa* or pipe and learned to smoke *kif* – that is hashish. Then on my second day there I made friends with a good-looking young Moor called Hamid Benamar, who spoke fluent French. We took to going for walks together through the olive groves down to the river, holding hands as friends in Morocco usually do. I found him very charming and more deli-cate and refined than are most Europeans. One day he introduced me to his uncle, el Hadj, a tall grey-bearded man who had made the pilgrimage to Mecca five times and who spoke English fluently but with a detestable accent. The Hadj was very friendly and invited us both to dinner in his house that evening. Hamid led the way through the narrow, covered streets of the medina to a little green door and then up a staircase into a small windowless room. Its walls were hung with scarlet damask and round three of the sides were mattresses covered with yellow cloth and heaped with silk cushions. A joss-stick burning in a vase gave off an aromatic smell. I took off my shoes and my coat, put on a white *djellaba* which Hamid held out for me and the three of us sat down cross-legged to drink wine and smoke our pipes of *kif*. So on my third day in Africa I was the guest of two Moors in a Moroccan house! The doors to the East had opened.

Hamid brought round bowls of water for washing our hands and em-broidered towels to dry them on, after which he served a ragout of chicken flavoured with saffron which we ate with our fingers. For the second course there were dried figs and grapes. We went on drinking and smoking. The effect of the *kif* was to make everything seem remote and strange. Then the Hadj brought up the subject of sodomy and said that many Moors pre-ferred men to women. It was a more refined taste. I said that some of my English friends were of the same way of thinking. Many Spaniards, he went on, especially army officers, were sodomites, but he did not like them because they did not wash their bodies. 'That surprises me,' I said. 'Usually Spaniards are very clean.' 'Not so clean as the English,' he said. Meanwhile he had taken my hand and was kissing it and I noticed through the haze of *kif* and alcohol that Hamid had left the room. 'To make coffee,' the Hadj explained, but he was beginning to edge closer to me and I was beginning to take a dislike to him. Still I was in no hurry to throw away this key I had found to a new and strange mode of life. Then suddenly he seized my *djel-laba* and said, 'Why don't you take off those trousers?' I think it was not so much his words as his ugly pronunciation that offended me, for in such a setting everything ought to be beautiful, but anyhow I got up, put on my coat and shoes and left without a word. I found Hamid waiting in the street and, taking my hand, he led me back to my *fondak*.

Next morning I awoke sober but in a state of deep shame and self disgust. I could not think of the Hadj's having kissed my hand or turned his lustful glances on me without a feeling of repulsion and when I caught sight of him sitting in a café I shuddered and hurried off. I felt like a girl of fourteen who has had an indecent proposal made to her by an elderly man and the strength of my feeling surprised me because it seemed to go beyond the bounds of reason, since after all nothing had happened.

For a day or two more I lingered in Tetuan, seeing a good deal of Hamid, but my evening with the Hadj had poisoned the place for me so I decided to go on to Xauen, forty miles inland on the edge of the Spanish zone. This was a so-called holy city which had been occupied for the first time by the Spanish army three years before. Till then no European except Foucauld, travelling in disguise, had visited it.

I left in a car with two women, both of them whores, a couple of Spaniards and a Moor. The road was patrolled every day by the cavalry, for without their protection anyone travelling along it would have been shot by the unsubdued tribesmen in the farms. Before we got there it came on to rain. I took a room at the *fondak*, or inn, which was also a general store, and there I remained for four days, unable to leave because of the ceaseless deluge that poured down.

I had never seen such rain before. In the square it fell in long perpendicular lines like pencils and poured off the roof in rods that were as thick as walking sticks. The patio of the *fondak* was flooded to the depth of a foot and the covered stalls round the sides, in which Spanish and Jewish hucksters sold everything from meat and bread to scent, boots, wine and whiskey, steamed like a hot bath. Upstairs, next to the bedrooms, there was a large saloon containing a billiard table which had lost half its cloth. The rain came in through its roof so that most of the floor was an inch deep in water. Only in the centre there was a little mound that rose like a Mesopotamian *tell* out of the flood, and here I established myself. Outside on the square there were two cafés, one packed with Spanish and Jewish whores of the most repulsive kind drinking and playing cards with slovenly looking soldiers, and the other occupied by white and brown-robed Moors seated cross-legged round the walls. I took off my shoes and socks and waded through the mud and water to reach the Moorish café and spent much of my time there sipping mint tea and smoking *kif* and listening to the small orchestra of lutes and cymbals. Now and then one of the musicians stood up and either sang or told amusing stories.

On my second day at Xauen the rain held off for a couple of hours and I went out to see the town. A mountain rose four thousand feet immediately above it and at its foot there was a spring from which the water welled out in prodigious quantities and irrigated the olive groves and the gardens below. The houses were roofed as at Granada with red tiles and there were a dozen mosques whose pale, rose-coloured minarets stood up like the ghosts of towers in the damp grey air. In all the streets and outskirts I met soldiers slouching sulkily along, but their control did not extend to more than a mile outside the town. Beyond that the tribesmen took over.

I was getting worried because I was running short of money. The *fondak* was expensive, so that I should have to leave on the following morning whatever the weather, though if it was wet I stood a good chance of never reaching Tetuan because the patrols did not come out when it was raining. I was therefore glad when I woke at dawn to see that the clouds had lifted. I took my seat in the car, but when a couple of miles on we reached the river we found that the bridge had been swept away and that the car would have to turn back. However there was a cavalry patrol waiting on the further bank, so I took off my shoes and trousers and forded it. The patrol then began to withdraw. Catching hold of one of the men's stirrups I ran beside his horse, which had broken into a trot. For some miles I kept this up and then, getting out of breath, I fell behind and continued at a walk. At one point I saw a Moor come out of his farm with a gun and look at me, but the patrol was within hearing distance and he did not shoot. By midday I had reached Zoco el Arbaa, fifteen miles from Xauen, where the Spanish troops had a large camp. By that time my trousers were coated with mud up to the knees and the patent leather shoes I had bought in Seville to impress Lolita were coming to pieces.

Fifteen years later I met in England a Spanish writer called Arturo Barea. He was a good writer as well as a splendid man and we became friends. As a youth he had been recruited into the army, had risen to be a sergeant in the engineers and had been with the troops who had first occupied Xauen. He told me that it had been he and his section who had built the bridge that had been swept away and that the reason for that having happened was that the contractor had supplied bad cement. The Spanish army in those days was rife with corruption.

There was no *fondak* at Zoco but the sergeants' canteen took me in. They could offer nothing to eat but one fried egg and as many tins as I wanted of *pâté de foie gras*. This had to be consumed without bread because the flour had got soaked, but to make up there was plenty of wine and cognac. They tried to frighten me by telling me that a horse had been killed and a man

66

wounded on the road I had come by the evening before, and that I was lucky to have got in alive, but I was not unduly impressed as people always tell one such things. A violent wind had now got up and was whistling through the joins in the corrugated iron walls, but at nightfall it turned to rain which, besides beating with a deafening sound on the roof, came in wherever it could find a crack. The only dry place except the bar was a small doorless alcove filled by a gigantic bed. Two whores, a sergeant and a child had claims to it, but they generously allowed me a share and later in the night two more whores and another sergeant appeared and crammed in too. Then at three in the morning I was awakened by a terrible noise that came from under the bed. It appeared that they had put coops of cocks and hens there to keep them dry and now the cocks were crowing.

Soon after reveille next morning I got a seat in a car to Tetuan and on the following evening reached Granada. In this I was luckier than the Spanish troops I had left behind. The Moroccan war was becoming too expensive in lives and General Primo de Rivera, who had just made himself dictator, had decided to end it by withdrawing to the coast. Therefore a few months after I left, Xauen was evacuated by the Spaniards. Then came the turn of Zoco el Arbaa, but the tribesmen under Abd-el-Krim and el Raisuli were by now closing in on all sides and the Spanish troops were demoralized, so that there was very fierce fighting before they could break through the narrow pass behind the camp and reach the temporary safety of Tetuan. But for the courage of two colonels, Franco and Millán Astray, who under heavy fire rallied the Foreign Legion and cleared the way for the rest of the division, not a man would have escaped. As it was, the withdrawal cost the army 16,000 casualties.

At Granada I found some money awaiting me and also a letter from Carrington in which she announced that she and Ralph would be coming out to spend Christmas with me at Yegen. Lytton had at first been opposed to their doing so because with his usual caution he feared that it would start up our old relation again, but in the end he had given his consent.

Three weeks later I met them both at the Posada de los Pescadores at Órgiva. On seeing Carrington I felt nothing. All my old feelings for her seemed to have ebbed away. We sat round the open fire after supper and on going up to bed the flaxen-haired young chambermaid, whom I had flirted with earlier in the day, came into my room and gave me a hug and a kiss.

Next morning we set off for Yegen, taking a roundabout route along the ridge of the Sierra la Contraviesa to Cádiar and getting in by moonlight. I walked with Ralph while Carrington rode behind on mule-back and found that I got on with him well. All my old affection for him came surging back and he told me of the brief affairs he had had with Marjorie Joad and with a woman called Ines. Now he was interested in a very pretty girl called

Frances Marshall who worked in Birrell and Garnett's bookshop. Her sister Ray had just married David Garnett.

The days at Yegen passed in walks and expeditions and sometimes we gave dances in the evenings. I was uncertain what I felt for Carrington. Afraid of Ralph's jealousy and weighed down by her guilt for the past, she kept me at a distance and avoided being left alone with me. Finally, after getting Ralph's permission, she agreed to come on a short walk. Hurt by her reserve, I told her that I thought it was pointless for us to continue our special relation. She at once became very agitated. We sat down in a poplar grove and held hands and she said, 'Speak to Ralph. Tell him that we desire the same relation that he has with Frances – that is, liberty to go about together and to kiss.'

After lunch I took Ralph for a walk and told him what Carrington had said. At the same time I made it clear that I was no longer in love with her, but only very fond of her. He replied with great cordiality that he had no objection whatever to our going about together or kissing. Yet when a few evenings later he went to bed early and she sat up talking to me, he took it badly.

So the days flew by. I went for walks with Ralph while Carrington painted. Then I went out alone with her to carry her easel and for the first time since her arrival we kissed. But her kisses were timid ones. Strongly subject as she was to guilt feelings, Ralph's conduct during the past eighteen months had got her down. Her old feeling of independence seemed to have gone for ever.

After a fortnight of this quiet life at Yegen we left for Granada. Here it came on to rain in torrents and we all got depressed. I found myself becoming more and more unnerved by this situation à trois, while Carrington was several times on the verge of tears. It was easy to see that she was as much attached to me as ever, though in a different way, as a person who had been through a great deal with her. Then early one morning they left.

Lytton, Ralph and Carrington had bought a country house called Ham Spray a few miles to the north of Hungerford and were moving into it that summer. I had decided to leave Yegen a few months earlier and settle in England, where my great-aunt was very anxious to have me, and Carrington suggested that I should rent a cottage on the Downs close to them. I got a sad letter from her written in Paris where Frances Marshall had met them and where she had to trail around with the two lovers. 'All I long for in this world,' she wrote, 'is to pass unnoticed,' but she added that Ralph had told her that he would probably not mind her sometimes going away with me for the weekend. It was clear that he balanced me against his new love. As his courtship with her progressed, he would allow Carrington more liberty. But although her letters show how much she was coming to rely on me, she was also worried because she did not want to lose him. Frances was a young, beautiful and intelligent girl who had many admirers and if she fell in love with Ralph she would surely expect him to divorce Carrington and marry her.

A week after this David and Ray Garnett arrived at Yegen on their honeymoon. Then in March I left Yegen and after spending a few days at Avignon with Hope reached London early in April. Carrington was at Victoria Station to meet me.

I settle in London

I was just thirty when early in April 1924 I arrived in London. I was greeted by a letter from my father in which he made it clear that he was not prepared to continue my allowance unless I found a job. As an example of his epistolary style I will quote it here:

> My dear Gerald – I see from your letter to your mother that you are arriving in London any day, still with the idea of continuing your idle wanderings in spite, not only of what you know my ideas would be, but also of the warnings I have given you. I am writing now to advise you that you had better employ your time in London in finding some employment or in rearranging your plans for the future to something of which I am likely to approve.
>
> You can come down to visit us here and we shall enjoy seeing you again, but unless your account of how you have employed your time and the assistance I have given you since we last parted in Spain and of your plans for the future are very different from what I have understood from your letters, I am certainly not going to help you in any way or to acquiesce in your continuing that life.
>
> I hope I may be mistaken in what I have understood. As I told you the last time I wrote on this subject, I am not going on all my life giving you these warnings. You know my views, but I'm writing this once more in the hope that you may be able to use your time in London to some effect.

Although the tone of my father's letter was not exactly cordial, I agreed in the main with what he said. My period of self-education and of trying things out was over and it was time that I settled down to write a book. But what sort of a book? The only prose writings I had done at Yegen had been a satire on the operations of the Black and Tans in Ireland, owing much to Swift's *Modest Proposal*, and a collection of short pieces entitled *The Bestiary*. This was a satire too, but not on a political subject. Leonard

Woolf had liked it and had published selections from it in *The Nation* under the title of *Natural Histories*.

But what I had really wanted was to be not a prose writer but a poet. Since the age of seventeen I had written verses. During the war these had been influenced first by Jules Laforgue and after that by Rimbaud, poets who were at that time very little known in England. But from the time of my settling in Yegen I took for my models the Elizabethan and seventeenth-century poets whom I had begun to read systematically. I knew that the verses that spilt from my pen were little more than pastiches, but I was training my ear while I sought for a way of writing poetry that would incorporate some of the aural properties of the Elizabethans and something of the tighter baroque style of Góngora, and yet be modern. Then when I was in Seville I wrote some sonnets that seemed to show an advance in that direction. No doubt they could not by any standard be described as good for they flowed awkwardly, yet I felt that they contained the promise of something better. But who could give me an opinion on that?

'For what one has to judge', I wrote to Carrington, 'is whether a melody which in one's head is attached to certain lines has really been put into them so that it exists quite objectively and may be experienced by all properly attuned persons, or whether it is a phantom which lies only in one's own mind, an echo of some other poet which has been too weak to mould the words to its own shape. And the difficulty is increased because this properly attuned audience does not exist for the new poet: it is he who must create it.'

For I thought then, as I still do today, that the basic element in poetry is the rhythm or melody and that it is only through this that the poem becomes alive.

But I found two obstacles to my hope of becoming a poet. One was that I could only write verse at certain periods of excitement which came at long intervals and the other was that I could not expect either to earn my living by it or to satisfy my father. I needed for my moral health something at which I could work for four or five hours every day and, since I had not had enough experience of the world to write a novel and was quite incapable of reviewing books, this must be a biography. But of whom? I had recently read the autobiography of Santa Teresa and had been impressed by it. An account of her later life which I read soon after showed me that she would be a good subject because there was so much published material on her, so I decided to try my hand on her. I convinced my father of the seriousness of my intentions – what else could the poor man do but believe me and hope for the best? – joined the London Library and procured a ticket for the British Museum Reading Room.

At the same time I came to a firm resolution not to write any more verses and to make it easier for me to keep this I decided that I would also give up reading poetry – or at least English poetry. I observed this rule I had made so well that, except once on a short holiday in Cornwall in 1944 and again a little later, I wrote no more verse till, in the summer of 1957, something overflowed inside me and I spent two or three months doing nothing else. If this act of abnegation seems strange I would say that I regarded poetry as such a difficult and important thing that I believed that no one should set himself up as a poet unless he was prepared to give his whole time and thought to it. I was tired of being an amateur and of writing only what came into my head at moments of excitement.

My decision to write a life of Santa Teresa required that I should settle in London, so I took a room at 10 Millman Street. There, as I wrote to Carrington, I had blue panelling on the walls, an eighteenth-century fireplace full of mousetraps, a wash-hand-stand in a cupboard, a sofa and a sofa-bed, a gas ring and an Adams bath. My landlady, the humble and obliging Mrs Veitch, who had gone a little hard of hearing, was ready to cook me an excellent meal for 1s 6d.

But I will quote from one of my letters:

I called on Mrs Veitch today and got from her an account of my house companions. On the ground floor there is a Cingalese gentleman who came to Europe to study philosophy, married an Englishwoman and has now altered his mind about things and keeps a garage. Next to him is a young widow who studied mathematics at Oxford and got a degree – as a preliminary to managing a greengrocer's establishment. On my floor there is a Danish student who has decorated his room with art hangings from Lapland. Then there is Mr V. himself who is out all day but in the evenings listens in, being very fond of good music. Mrs Vetch or Veitch received a polishing education at Dresden sufficient to enable her to read Stevenson and Charlotte Brontë: she has the innocence of many deaf people – but where did she discover her interest in cottage furniture?

Two ominous figures inhabit the top floor – a widow and her beautiful daughter – bitterest enemies of Mr V., who cannot get rid of them, because these rooms do not belong to him. They listen on landings and suck the secrets of 10 Millman Street into their vampirish hearts.

It is Mr Veitch, I gather, who has all the opinions; Mrs Veitch all the feelings and sentiments. Even these cannot be expressed directly, but only in the form 'Mr Veitch says that I have a dislike of glaring colours.' Are all married couples alike? I see a resemblance here to Leonard and Virginia, even to R. and ——. But I am joking.

I settle in London

Since I was finding it hard to get along on £12 a month, I decided to advertise in the papers for pupils who wished to learn Spanish, but no answers came in. Then I started to translate a play of Calderón's which was to be put on by the Cambridge Dramatic Society, only to learn that J. B. Trend, who was professor of Spanish there, had been given the assignment. And now everything began to go wrong in my life. I was so short of money that I often had to miss a meal and was forced to give up seeing my friends because if I went out with them I would not be able to pay my share. Then both my eyes and my teeth started to give trouble and I had to visit an oculist and a dentist. But worse than any of these were the attacks of nerves that would come over me. I had never suffered from anything of that sort before, but now my pulse was very fast and I could not bear to be alone in the evenings. As I sat in my room my agitation would go on rising and increasing until by five o'clock it was quite unendurable. I could not read because I was in a continual state of expectancy, yet what I was expecting I did not know. Time had slowed down so much that I could hear an appreciable interval between the ticks of my watch, while a man walking on the pavement seemed to take an age to pass my window. The doctor I consulted prescribed tranquillizers, but they had very little effect and alcohol was ruled out because I could not afford even a couple of beers. Then the long evenings would come on with the voices of children playing in the street, their key mounting as the light diminished, till I wanted to scream. Worst of all were the dead, empty Sundays. I felt more lonely in London, I declared, than I should have felt in Tibet and got my only peace and stability from working at *Santa Teresa*. Yet when these attacks of nerves came over me, I could not focus my mind on it.

The chief cause of these distressing states I got into was, I imagine, that I was in love with Carrington and that every cell in my body was demanding that I should settle down and live with her. Since that was not possible, we wrote to one another almost every day and later with Ralph's consent spent occasional nights in London together. Now and then I went down to Tidmarsh for the weekend or else we would go to Kew Gardens and walk about hand in hand under the flowering trees in a state of perfect happiness. Yet in my unsettled and neurotic condition these things were not enough for me and I would press her to come up to see me more often and became hurt or angry when she wouldn't. Then, upset by my reproaches, she would write me a long letter of justification.

You have a magnetism over me that always makes it impossible for me to be indifferent to you. But I have at the same time this slight dread of becoming too involved. I have a shrinking from pain and think I can detect its presence by a feeling in the air. Oh why didn't we meet years ago when I was 23? ... You never knew and will never know how much pain I suffered that summer. Sometimes I simply wish to avoid any emotion again. But of course ... this is only sometimes. Yet you feel I give you very little? But surely you know I would not spend a whole day with you if I did not love you rather more than anyone else in London? I thought you knew that. But at the same time I will admit that you are a life-exhausting friend. Partly because your moods are so violent that they project themselves into me as though they were my own feelings ... But, amigo mio, I can't bear to think of life without you. It is just knowing that you are in London, that tomorrow there may be a letter from you, that fills me with secret happiness .. I worry, I am perverse, a shellfish, even a bore, but then are you not sometimes bad tempered, vain, changeable, vague, bitter, stupid, indiscreet? ... But *constantly* I am fond of you. I think of you and I care for you very much in a proper way. But we are neither of us in love with one another now? That is true. And that at moments one regrets. It is outside our province. One can wish for everything else and obtain it except that.

This letter gives a very exact picture of our relation. Carrington's only error lay in her saying that we were not in love with one another. I was of course deeply in love with her, though by a long established custom between us, due to Ralph's insistence on his right to read our letters – a right he still claimed – I only used the terms affection and fondness. These were the terms appropriate to her present feelings for me. Yet there was a depth and quality in Carrington's 'fondness' which I have never come across in anyone else. She could love several people deeply at the same time without feeling possessive about them and she was, as she said, very constant.

Her strictures on me were only too deserved. Although I think that I was not as vain or as irritable as she suggests, my moods have always been violent and submerge me completely while they last and I was also changeable, insensitive to her feelings, indiscreet and above all egotistic. I took little account of the difficult situation she was going through as Ralph became more and more involved with Frances Marshall. Since she was very prone to guilt feelings and had little pride, she had come to love him more since he had broken her spirit, and then, as he had ceased to be physically attracted to her, a long-standing bone of contention between them had been removed. She therefore loved him more than ever and, not only on Lytton's account, was afraid of losing him. In these circumstances my role required me to show patience and consideration and take care not to make too many demands, and I was not playing it well. I made a great fuss about my own attacks of nerves and forgot the headaches, nightmares and insomnia, as well as the continual noises in her ears, from which she had suffered since the Clare episode. Yet we must often have been happy together since most of my letters were gay and affectionate.

Now the move from Tidmarsh Mill to Ham Spray House began. Carrington was in a very excited state about it for she had found the place herself and immediately fallen in love with it. It was a large mid-Victorian farmhouse, not unlike a rectory to look at, standing about a mile from the tiny village of Ham. From its glass-fronted verandah one looked out over a small lawn and a park-like expanse of grass at the steep green slope of Inkpen Down. Not another house was within sight. Not a sound to be heard but the cawing of rooks and the mooing of cows. A few yards from its end wall there rose an enormous poplar tree in which an owl nested and beyond that there was a tiny pond inhabited by a family of moor-hens. The train service from Hungerford, five miles away, was excellent.

The move into the new house naturally kept Carrington very busy so that she had less time to spare on visits to me. But other things too had occurred which were to affect my relations with her. Towards the end of May a beautiful and dynamic American girl, Henrietta Bingham, had turned up in the company of Stephen Tomlin. Henrietta was the daughter of Judge Bingham, a Kentucky millionaire who was said to have murdered his wife, and who some years later was appointed ambassador in London by President Roosevelt. Although she sometimes had affairs with men, as she was doing now, she was mainly a Lesbian. Stephen Tomlin, or Tommy as he was always called, I shall describe later. Enough to say now that he was a young man of around twenty-three, the son of an English judge, who had been discovered by David Garnett and was soon to become a frequent visitor at Ham Spray.

Carrington was fascinated by Henrietta with her pure oval face, long-lashed blue eyes and low husky Southern voice and some time that summer they had an affair. It was the only Lesbian affair of her life and it did not last long since Henrietta changed her lovers often. I did not feel jealous and not only offered them my room for their meetings, but said that I would give up my claim to seeing Carrington when she came up to town if that meant that she could spend her time with her friend. What I did not then know was that Carrington was basically a Lesbian too and that her affair with Henrietta would affect her physical relations with me by giving her a feeling of guilt which made her react against me afterwards. I was to pay dearly for her having met this American girl.

Meanwhile Hope had returned from Herm. He had a load of grievances to unpack against Compton Mackenzie and his family who, according to him, were trying to cut him out of the profits of *The Gramophone* and he had also arrived without any money because what he had earned during the past eight months was tied up in some complicated financial transaction. I had therefore to put him up in my room and give him meals, in return for which he introduced me to some of his friends. One of these was a beautiful girl called Dorothy Varda, who had recently married and then separated from a Greek painter, Janko Varda, Clare Bollard's old lover, who lived at Cassis near Toulon and later became a good friend of mine. Dorothy Varda was so lovely that she was then appearing, billed as *The Beautiful Varda*, in Cochran's variety show at the London Pavilion. Since she could neither act nor dance, she merely walked slowly and fully dressed across the stage. Hope, who hung around Margaret Morris's ballet school in Chelsea, always knew the most beautiful girls though he never made up to them. His vanity was satisfied if people saw him going about in their company and he found no difficulty in passing me on to Dorothy because he had decided that he did not like her on account of her peevish and dissatisfied temperament. I ended by thinking the same, but not before I had taken her down for the day to Windsor Park when Carrington had first promised and then refused to go there with me. I wrote her a teasing poem on this.

Hope also introduced me to a circle of occultists with Gnostic leanings who followed a Serbian seer called Mitrinovitch. He was a tall, heavily built man of around forty with a large fat head studded with black bristles and built up like a raspberry into a number of slight protuberances. He was invariably dressed in a frock coat and striped trousers with boots stained in two colours to imitate spats and in the street he wore a top hat. A kind-hearted young music teacher called Valerie Cooper paid his rent and board, but got no return for her sacrifices because the Master made a point of consorting only with prostitutes. The meetings of the circle took place in her large studio in Charlotte Street and as a rule half a dozen or more people were present. The regulars comprised a certain Dr Young, very learned on occult matters, a Russian zoologist called Professor Schmertyi-koff, another Russian who was a dentist, Alan Porter, the literary editor of the *Spectator*, Blundell, a psychic who trembled all over and had visions, a very humble man called Campbell and lastly the beautiful Madame Agafo-novna, who only turned up on special occasions. The audience reclined comfortably on cushions and divans while grapes and vermouth were handed round and Mitrinovitch either talked or read aloud from the *Pistis Sophia*, the most unintelligible of all the Gnostic scriptures, and commented on it. When he talked he did so slowly and distinctly, with long silences every few sentences, on such subjects as the meaning of the universe, the pleroma, thesis and antithesis, creation and always God – Father, Son and Holy Ghost. Dr Young evidently understood this lingo, which seemed to be an amalgam of Hegel with Greek Orthodox mystical theology, and sometimes asked a question such as 'Do you mean Modality?' or 'Are we in Father now or in Holy Ghost?' A general discussion would follow and Mr Campbell would sit crushed into his chair by its sublimity.

I gathered that the great enemy of the sect was a rival seer called Rudolph Steiner, who was Jew, Pig and Satan – words which the Master spat out with great venom. Then, while the talk drifted on to Swedenborg and Blake, Blundell would lean tremblingly across and ask me if I had ever been crucified or had my will-power broken in two. When I told him that I had not he would go on to talk of planes of vibration, thought transference and circles of future existence. Like most of the others he believed that Mitrinovitch had superhuman powers.

Some evenings however were different. One went in and found everyone drunk and singing Russian songs. Mitrinovitch ceased to be the calm and impassive Buddha: his powerful personality broke out and dominated his feeble followers as he waved a glass in the air and led the chorus, while Madame Agafonovna, lying back on the couch, smiled encouragement at him. I must say that I liked him and often found him interesting to talk to. He made no secret of his eagerness to draw into his group as many rich or intellectually respectable people as possible and for that reason he made a great set at Hope, who he thought could be useful to him through his social connections. He was astute enough to see that he would never be able to convert him to his ideas, but he angled for his partnership, whispering to him confidentially that there was money in it. He treated me differently, telling me that I flirted with serious things, but that some day I would find that I would not be able to flirt any longer but would have to make up my mind.

Meanwhile I had left Mrs Veitch's cosy rooms at 10 Millman Street and rented a studio from Roger Fry for 15s a week at 18 Fitzroy Street. It was on the top or attic floor and consisted of a fair-sized room with a tiny bedroom opening off it. There was a gas ring but no kitchen or bathroom and the only lavatory was on the stairs and had to be shared with the people on the floor below. The furniture was not unattractive, but showed signs of Nina Hamnett's previous tenancy in the wine and grease stains that covered the carpet and upholstery. Across the beams overhead had been laid a thick pile of Roger Fry's canvases and when I looked up I saw ugly women painted in depressing colours gazing stonily down at me. But over the fireplace there was a copy by Duncan Grant of Duccio's *Three Women at the Sepulchre* and that was a wonderful picture to live with.

During these summer months I led a pretty full life. I read all day at the British Museum and often in the evenings as well with books I had drawn from the London Library. I lunched with my great-aunt every Thursday at the Grosvenor Hotel, met Carrington in London and in the country, consoled myself for her absence with other girls, went to an occasional party and made a number of new friends. The set I moved in, which centred round that small group of older people later known as the 'Bloomsbury Group', had certain things in common. They had all of them been at either Oxford or Cambridge, they were much better off than I was and they had none of them fought in the war. Some had been medically unfit, others pacifists, one had served in the Red Cross, others were too young to have been called up. For many years I met no one except Ralph who had been at the front. Not only did the war seem to have been entirely forgotten, but those who had fought in it were slightly looked down on as people who had taken part in a shabby and barbarous enterprise. I on the other hand was proud of having been through it and felt that there was something thin and unreal about those who had not done so. They had missed the great experience of the age and that, I said to myself when I was in a priggish mood, was one of the reasons for their futility. Their comfortable incomes, their cliquishness, their suspicion of new adventures in literature, their lack of any connections with the larger world made me feel that, much as I liked and admired many of them, it would not do for me as a writer to get too involved with them. I wanted to have my own life, not to move in a small literary set or to become anyone's disciple. Yet, bound to Carrington as I was, I was becoming partly absorbed by them.

The ones among them I most admired were Leonard and Virginia Woolf. I was seeing them fairly often that summer so I will quote two extracts from my letters to Carrington that relate to them. The first is dated May 6th, 1924.

> I saw Virginia last night, sitting in her dressing gown and looking rather ruffled and stormtossed, like a bird that has just crossed the sea in a gale. She was very nice and asked me to come to her parties in the evenings. I said I would like to come if I need not talk. 'But really, Gerald, you know you are a perfect chatterbox.' I walked round the square with Leonard and came home and read for *Teresa*.

I have described in *South from Granada* these Bloomsbury after-dinner gatherings at the Woolfs' house, so now I will quote from my second letter, dated June 3rd.

> I went to see Virginia. Mrs Joad [who acted as their secretary] was there and Adrian Stephen and George Sanger. Leonard now takes pleasure in putting me through various tests as though I were some new and quaint form of animal. When he opened the street door he quickly stepped behind it. But I saw him and asked him why he did that. 'To see what you would do,' he said. I see now that his treatment of me and possibly of all new people consists in a series of

elaborately arranged tests or experiments, from each of which he draws some conclusion. No doubt he arranges them in a kind of series, like those keys for discovering the names of flowers at the beginning of botany books: one is sifted from genus to sub-genus, and as each experiment is supposed to be conclusive and irrevocable, the result is at last a pure fantasy. Far from resenting this, I find it gives me pleasure. Leonard's unflattering remarks could offend nobody, and every time I see him I like him better.

When you told me that he liked cactuses, you threw a great deal of light on his character, for what interests him in men is what they share with these plants – variety, quaintness, hard-cut outlines, immobility.

Virginia was discussing her favourite subject – the difference between the younger and the older generations. 'Look at Gerald ...', she began. 'Gerald', said Leonard, 'is completely disoriented – he lives upside down on his head.' Though I did not agree, I thought I could guess what he meant, but he went on, 'All the younger generation are like him. Marjorie (Mrs Joad) is just the same. They are all disoriented.' And then I understood nothing. For that the quality (invisible to me) which I have in common with Mrs Joad and Ralph and many others should be called 'disorientation' was quite incomprehensible.

'They are less subtle, less sensitive, but more downright and more intelligent,' went on Virginia. 'As for intelligence,' said Leonard, 'I would back myself against all of them.'

Leonard, I thought to myself, will always be, wherever he is, the most intelligent person in the room, even when Roger Fry or Bertie Russell are present. And this is because, having a head so clear that no one could have a clearer, he has energy to spare for watching and comparing the speakers and their psychological motives: that is to say, he is detached and this gives him a feeling of superiority, of being in some sense more intelligent than even people like B.R., whose mental capacity he sums up under the rather disparaging word 'brilliant'.

Sanger gave us a long and very amusing account of Bertie's life and marriages. One thing I remember. When Bertie lay desperately ill in Pekin in high delirium and it seemed impossible that he would recover, a learned Chinese deputation arrived at his house and wished to ascend en masse to his bedroom in order to watch the last moments of the great philosopher, to catch his dying words and record them for future generations and at last to bury him in a special and very honourable tomb by the side of the Northern Lake. With difficulty Mrs Russell prevented them.

6

New Romney and the Anreps

At the beginning of August I went down to Kent to spend the summer holidays with Boris and Helen Anrep at their beach cottage on Romney Marsh. I had only met them twice before this, but they needed someone who would give a few hours' lessons to their children, and Carrington, who was a friend of theirs, had suggested me. Boris was at this time beginning to be known as the leading mosaic artist in Europe, the reviver of a long-forgotten tradition: he had already decorated a chapel in the Byzantine style for Westminster Cathedral and was soon to provide a more modern example of his work in the floor of the entrance hall of the National Gallery. He was a fascinating man to meet, full of Russian originality and charm, a genial talker whose picturesque idiom gave a novelty and freshness to everything he said. His wife however was very different. Born Helen Maitland, of a Scottish father who had died in her childhood, she had lived with her mother first in California and then in France and Italy. In Paris she had fallen in love with a handsome young painter, Henry Lamb, and had had an affair with him. He was a twisted, neurotic character and had made her very unhappy, but through him she had got to know Dorelia, the wife of Augustus John, who became her best friend, and also Boris, whom she had ended by marrying.

Helen was a small, fair woman with very fine bones, blue eyes and a skin so clear and elastic that it never showed lines or wrinkles. She was, I think, the only woman I have known whose beauty increased with age and who looked her best after her hair had turned white. But at this time her face when seen in repose seemed hard. She was a person of strong character with great pride and dignity and her husband's recent conduct had embittered her. To begin with he had taken into his house a Russian girl of eighteen called Maroussa who was a distant relative of his. She was a very lovely girl in the Circassian style with dark eyes and hair and a creamy complexion, but she was both indolent and unintelligent, though as she grew older she developed into a genuine and original person with a taste for finance. He made her his mistress and seemed to think it quite proper for him, as a Russian aristocrat and artist, to keep a concubine on the premises and that Helen, who had a Victorian distaste for sex, could have no reason for objecting. She accepted the situation without protest and was always kind to Maroussa, but still it rankled. However this was not the only thing she had against him. Boris was greatly sought after as a talker and when he went to dine with Ethel Sands, that old American friend of Henry James, or with Lady Colefax or other well-known hostesses, he left his wife behind him. This, he declared, was the Russian custom – wives stayed at home with the children – though it was also followed by that even more brilliant conversationalist, Desmond MacCarthy. Helen, who had been brought up by her mother to a belief in women's equality with men and was also well aware of her own social gifts, resented this deeply and showed it in the bitterness of her conversation.

Their cottage, Warren's End, at once took my fancy. It was very small even as Kentish cottages go and stood right on the edge of the beach – so close indeed that the pebbles had piled up in a heap against the back end. It was said to have once belonged to smugglers and after them to coast-guards, but now it was habitable only in the finer months because in winter storms the sea poured in and flooded it to a depth of several feet. Perhaps on that account the furniture was very primitive, the beds being mere wooden frames covered with wire netting and fixed to the walls, with thin, lumpy mattresses laid over them. The point of the place lay in its proximity to the sea. All day and night, breaking through the conversation, infiltering one's sleep, one heard the waves crashing on the pebbles and then sucking them back with a long, rasping sound. The noise filled one's ears, the salt smell saturated one's nostrils, so that the sea seemed to have entered into one's head and to be giving to one's thoughts and feelings its rhythm and colour. One became possessed by it.

During the week Boris worked in his studio in Hampstead and came down to the cottage on Fridays. I used to look forward to his arrival. He was very charming in a clumsy, bearish sort of way, very proud of his few yards of landed property, very positive and emphatic, and he told fascinating stories about his early life and of his passion for his Scottish governess which led him later to study art at Edinburgh rather than at Paris. Then when the war broke out he had returned to Russia and served in the cavalry, after which he was appointed military attaché in London. In this way he missed the revolution.

Meanwhile I was spending my days and half my nights talking to Helen. She was an admirable *causeuse*, her sentences tripping out of one another in a loose, disconnected way and taking any direction. Although she could rouse herself to cook, which she did very well, and usually had a piece of sewing on her lap, she seemed to have been born with a greater gift for leisure than other people, so that every evening we sat talking over cups of china tea till the small hours. I had never yet spoken to anyone except Ralph about my relations with Carrington, but now I began to unbosom myself to her. The truth is that I badly needed a confidant. The course of my love was so uneven, so full of checks and disappointments, that I was making myself ill by bottling up my reactions within myself. The tone I adopted was ironical as that seemed the best one for handling my often violent feelings and it suited Helen too for that was the one in which she usually talked herself. Indeed a lightly ironical tone was the current style of conversation in Bloomsbury circles. Today I admire her patience. She seemed never to get tired of listening while I poured out my hopes and fears and rages and she gave me good advice on how I should behave. Then she began to talk a little about herself. It seemed that Roger Fry had fallen in love with her and wanted her to leave Boris and live with him. Although he was twenty years older than she was, this offered her a new and much more satisfying life and she appeared to be inclined to accept his proposal.

Before long I began to notice that Boris's friendliness towards me was changing to hostility. I was not very perceptive about people in those days and so I was unable to understand the reason for it. But it seems, though I only learned this forty years later from his son, that, on seeing Helen and myself laughing and talking together, he imagined that we were having an affair. He knew, of course, that I was deeply involved with Carrington, but this only made him put me down as one of those 'Bloomsbury seducers' with whom no married woman was safe. Later, after Helen had left him, he supposed that I had been an emissary of Roger Fry's. In fact I hardly knew Roger at that time and felt little sympathy for her projected change of husband because I liked the whole Anrep family so much. However, he had perhaps a little reason on his side for on the last occasion on which I saw Helen, a few months before her death in 1965, she told me that she had once been a little in love with me. I had never even remotely suspected that, but Boris may well have noticed some sign of it. At all events I have never seen him since that date. He forgave Helen, but never Roger or myself.

Every morning I gave Igor and Anastasia, or Baba as she was then called, a lesson. Igor, though he was twelve and obviously not at all stupid, had never learned to read. I discovered that the reason for this was that he had arranged the letters of the alphabet in a certain hierarchy in his head and when he came to a word tried to read them in that order. When I pointed this out to him, he corrected himself and before I had returned to London he was reading fluently. Anastasia, unlike her brother, was a simple and somewhat retarded girl and did not make so much progress. But she had a Russian freshness and naïveté and a way of saying original things that made it a pleasure to teach her.

I spent the afternoons walking up and down the sea wall that led to Dymchurch, conning a Portuguese grammar. I did not have to spend many hours on it before I could enjoy the early Galician *cantigas de amigo* with their slowly unwinding, repetitive movement that suggested to me the returning, ever returning and breaking waves on the beach. From them I went on to Camoens. If one excepts *The Ancient Mariner*, there is no poetry that conveys so well as the *Lusiads* the immensity and melancholy of the sea or the thrill and excitement of adventuring over it. Since I was a child I had never spent much time by it and now it was so close and present that it seemed to be seeping into me.

Before going down to Warren End I had spent a weekend at Ham Spray. Stephen Tomlin and Henrietta Bingham had both been there and I had felt neglected. On getting back to London therefore I had written Carrington a letter in which I said that, since she seemed to have so little room in her life for me, it might be better if we broke off our relations. After carrying this letter about for days I posted it at the station and lived in agony till I got her reply, in which she begged me to go on writing to her and excused herself for her changeability.

'You see only a small portion of it,' she wrote, 'and find it insupportable. Imagine living inside that muddle day after day.'

Heaven knows I was changeable and moody too, but, though I often wished to put her out of my life in order to get some rest from agitation, I was becoming all the time more chained to her. Every morning from seven on I lay listening for the postman's knock and if a letter did not come or it was not sufficiently affectionate, I would go back to bed and sob on my pillow. I had never cried since my first years at my prep school, for I am a fairly stoical person, but love breaks the most stolid natures down.

On September 8th Carrington arrived at Warren End on a long-promised visit. The evening passed pleasantly, for she liked and admired Helen, and we went early to bed. I shall never forget that night. The mattress was thin and narrow and the mosquitoes hummed and bit, but I made love to her again and again and in between lay awake, listening to the waves breaking on the pebbles, in a state of near ecstasy. When at length I fell asleep I dreamed that we were two drowned bodies drifting through green fathomless seas, clutched tightly together, and that this was the end I desired, the supreme and ultimate happiness. At dawn I got up, leaving her asleep, and walked for a couple of hours along the flat, wave-resounding beach. My body felt so light that I seemed to be treading on air and as the brightness in the sky increased and the sea turned pale and the waves changed their note, I was filled with such an incredible and over-powering happiness that it seemed to me that I should never die since through my love for her and her love for me we had drunk the divine nectar and been raised to a state of immortality.

Then the awakening came. All through breakfast, irritated by my look of happiness, Carrington was snubbing me and picking holes in what I said. She spent the rest of the morning doing what she could to charm Helen. Then, lunch over, when we set out together along the sea wall for Dymchurch, she was so scolding and censorious that I scarcely dared to open my mouth. How little she was enjoying her visit was made clear when she informed me that such meetings as this would in future be few and far between. This was the first time we had ever been alone together on neutral ground yet I could see she was counting the hours before she could get back to Ham Spray. She left after breakfast next morning and a few days later the postman handed me a cold and distant letter. There was another much warmer and more affectionate one for Helen in which she alluded to me as 'that ridiculous Brenan'. Such was, though I did not understand it at the time, the effect of her recent affair with Henrietta. Reactions against going to bed with a man, a deep sense of guilt following it and a Lesbian wish to make up to Helen and win her from me.

We made it up, I forget how. Then on October 8th I returned to London where she had promised to meet me, dine at my rooms and make love, but not stay the night. I was greatly put out by this last limitation for I wanted to spend the whole night with her and dream again of our being corpses rolled round and round in the sea, so I wrote that if she did not agree to this I would prefer not to see her. She replied that she could not bear to sleep in my rooms because they were dirty, noisy and smelt of cats. It would make her ill to do that, but she would spend the whole evening with me if I wished it and return to Hampstead, where Ralph was staying, at midnight.

My response to this very reasonable objection was perverse and absurd, probably because I was jealous of the way in which she had begun to cling on to Ralph. I decided that I would buy the most delicious foods at Fortnum and Mason, buy wine, buy flowers, buy fruit and lay them out ostentatiously on my table. I would then telephone her, invite her to dine with me at a good restaurant such as the Étoile, be very gay, not allude to our disagreement and see her to the tube station. When she came to call for me she would notice my preparations and draw her own conclusions. But things did not work out like that. She arrived early while I was still laying out the supper things and we sat on the sofa and argued dismally. Then 'Let's go out' I said and went into my bedroom to wash my hands. She followed me, kissed me and drew me on to the bed – a happy reconciliation. It was entirely characteristic that she wanted me when I did not appear to want her and if I had only been able to act a part I would have taken care never to let her see that I wanted her. But I have never been good at concealing my feelings.

Next morning she came round again, but withdrew her promise to go to Kew with me because she had arranged to have lunch with someone else. However she would come to tea. I was already depressed at having spent the night alone and replied that there was no point in that. I was feeling gloomy and did not want to make her gloomy too. So nothing was decided. I lunched with my great-aunt and returned to my rooms at four. Would she come or not? Convinced that she would not I lay down on my bed and began to sob desperately, wishing that I was dead since I could neither live with her nor without her. Then at 5.10 I heard a knock on my door – she had come. Such transitions from despair to complete happiness do not often occur in a lifetime. She sat on my bed, wished to explain, to apologize: I would not hear of it and implored her forgiveness for my perversity. For two weeks after this I was happy.

These quarrels and reconciliations continued throughout the autumn, increasing in violence every time. One reason for them was the irregularity and infrequency of her visits to London. She had promised to come up every fortnight, but sometimes she made it three weeks because she was working. I could not object to that for I believed that work should come before everything, and yet the effect on me was shattering. Then when she did come up there was the question of when and how soon we should make love. From the moment that she entered the room, dressed in her rather absurd and ugly London clothes – for no formal clothes became her – and carrying a bunch of garden flowers and a home-made cake or pot of jam, her whole face irradiated by her honeyed smile, I was thinking only of that and could listen to nothing she said until the matter had been decided. This was not because my physical urge was so great, but because making love had become the proof that she still loved me. Into those few minutes I could crowd my whole soul. However she sometimes came up resolved to offer herself as a sacrifice to my desires in spite of her lack of inclination and though, even when I saw through this, I could not resist accepting, I dreaded these occasions because I knew that afterwards she would pay me back with her distance and coldness. In her sexual feelings she was unpredictable.

She saw the falling off of our old relation of easy companionship as clearly as I did although she did not understand the reason for it.

'I get on your nerves,' she wrote in November. 'No one else does. You can talk and be happy with other people far easier than with me. It is not even your fault. In spite of our great affection for one another there is something that produces unhappiness between us. I think that what you say is true – I mean, that I do not care enough.'

85

And I would ask Helen ironically whether it was always true that the person one was in love with bored one. For Carrington did bore me with her chatter about life at Ham Spray. I was always waiting for her to say or do something else.

Yet though, as she said, she did not love me enough to satisfy me, she needed me.

'I am always divided,' she wrote, 'between feelings of loneliness and isolation with a craving to see people and have relations with them, and feelings of terror at being involved with them because of my character and my complexes about secrecy and then my general selfishness which always ends in disasters and sometimes makes me long *never* to see anyone again.'

But it wasn't selfishness she suffered from. Rather she was torn by violent conflicts within her own character. She was also becoming more and more preoccupied by Ralph's growing passion for Frances and this constant anxiety, which she never spoke of, left her with less feeling to spare for me. I saw it only too clearly and how incumbent it was on me to show patience and understanding, but I couldn't manage it.

Our dissensions came to a head in late November, and we agreed to stop meeting and corresponding for a time till we should both feel calmer. Next day I wrote her an affectionate letter confirming this and she sent a telegram to thank me. And then in my madness I telephoned her to say that I must see her again if only for an hour – could she come up on Friday? Across sixty miles of country, across brown leafless woods and squelching fields, across smoking chimneys and crowded streets, her voice came back to me saying, no, no she could not. She would not see me or write to me again till the New Year.

7

Some portraits

All this autumn I had been reading steadily for my biography of Santa Teresa. The world of Catholic mysticism was new to me, so to arrive at a better understanding of it I had to dip into the more outstanding mystics of the past to get the hang of it. They led me on to general histories of the Church with its popes and councils and from them to the rich and luxuriant field of hagiography. The range of what I needed to know before I could begin to write seemed limitless.

After reading steadily for eight months I felt that I must make a start on the first chapters. But before doing this I had to fix on a suitable style. I wanted a flowing, spontaneous mode of writing that would be plastic enough to allow me some excursions into a more coloured or baroque manner, but I also wanted a capacity for tautness and brevity. These were opposite qualities, so I decided that I would every day read two authors, each of whom exemplified one of these qualities. Every morning therefore after breakfast I read a page or two of Tacitus in Latin, using a crib to help me with the sense, and every evening I read a chapter of the Duc de Saint Simon's *Mémoires*. Both of these were favourite writers of mine and I hoped that the opposition between their styles would help me to obtain the result I wanted.

Later, after I had covered about 150 sheets of foolscap, I showed what I had written to David Garnett. His comment was that, though some of the passages were vivid and showed that I had a feeling for language, they weren't English. In this he was right. However, a prose style was not a thing that came to me naturally, so that perhaps my struggle to impose my mode of feeling on the language was not entirely wasted.

Since the autumn of 1924 I had been living in a small flat at the top of 18 Fitzroy Street. Here I spent most of my evenings, either reading or arranging my notes in front of the coal fire. In the course of time I got to know the other tenants of the house. They were all people whose characters had been warped by poverty and bad luck, but they were so peculiar that they deserve a brief description.

Immediately below me, occupying a single room, lived an elderly Danish lady called Miss Jensen. She earned her living by cutting out and sewing the cloth backs of men's evening waistcoats, but to add to the small income she derived from this she took in cats while their owners were away. They were always enormous cats, very fat and furry, and they kept up a continual miaowing. She herself was a quiet woman, rather thin and shrunken, and under her polite manner a bit dotty. Her story was that some thirty years before this her fiancé had been lost at sea and as she lay on her bed at night she would imagine that she heard him calling to her. 'Mees Jensen, Mees Jensen,' the voice would say in a plaintive tone, 'Where are you?' And she would get up and look out of the window into the dark courtyard below and say, 'This is Mees Jensen. Please, who is calling?' But there was no answer. Then she would go back to bed only to hear half an hour later the voice calling to her again. She also imagined that people were turning rays on her and magnetizing her and every now and then she would put on her black hat and coat and knock at the door of a neighbouring house where she could hear the radio and beg them politely to desist from doing so. Anyone who was called Johnson was sure of a visit from her.

Below this sad spinster there lived a middle-aged Italian in a room that was cluttered with dark, heavy furniture. He suffered from kidney trouble, cooked his own food on a gas ring and for the sake of company kept two large, black, oily-skinned dogs that were always trying to escape. Since he rarely went out they got no exercise. The room below him was occupied by a Jewish artist who sat glued all day to his easel, painting pictures in chocolate and dark green tints with Cubist distortions. He was as gloomy as his paintings and too absorbed in his own thoughts to take notice of anyone. But our most spectacular resident was a German who rented a small room on the ground floor which he stocked with skeletons. He imported them from Belgium – it was said that they had once belonged to soldiers killed in the war – and sold them to hospitals and to anyone who had a taste for them. His door usually stood open and as one passed one saw them dangling from the cords that he had stretched from wall to wall, with the bed on which he slept set up under them. He told me that he found their company *sehr gemütlich* – very cheerful.

The most touching family however in No. 18 lived in the basement. These were Mr and Mrs Dalton, she a tall, gentle woman of around thirty-five and he a small, dark, secretive man who looked ten years older. Mr Dalton was a scene-shifter at a West End theatre, but he was so neurotic that he could not go out alone on the streets after dark and his wife had therefore to call for him at the stage door every evening and escort him home. They had a pretty daughter called Dorothy, aged about nine, who lived in a perpetual state of ecstasy, dancing and singing and laughing all day long without any apparent reason for her happiness. Then one day she was taken to the hospital with an inoperable tumour on the brain. When I went to see her there she was still smiling, but a few days later she died and her parents were overwhelmed because she had been the one ray of sunshine in their life. I got to know a good deal about this family because Mrs Dalton's mother, Mrs Langsforth, did my room every morning. She was an old lady who had grown up in a country village and her sense of respectability was outraged by the life she had to lead in a dark, damp basement and among people of foreign origin whose ways she disapproved of. She liked me because she could place me – I might have been the vicar's son – and one day she confided to me in a shocked whisper that her daughter was not married to Mr Dalton but had left her real husband to live in sin with him and that it was to be feared that the death of little Dorothy might be her punishment for that.

Fitzroy Street and its continuation, Charlotte Street, though they still retained a few houses let out by floors to residents and an occasional artist's studio as a reminder of better days, were in the process of being taken over by the Jewish-owned tailoring industry. Looking out across the deep trench from my flat I could see the windows opposite me occupied by girls cutting and sewing. They were there when I got up in the morning and till long after the street lamps came on, for this was a sweated industry with little or no limit to the hours worked and very low wages. But there was money in those dark, solemn houses as well as poverty. For this reason on every week-day a band of out-of-work ex-combatants, their medals pinned to their worn blue serge suits, would slowly and depressingly make their way down it, stopping every few hundred yards to play their wind instruments and collect the pennies thrown at them from the windows. Then on Sundays we had the street singers, croaking in harsh raucous voices because the worse they sang the more they took, and after them there came a Salvation Army band and procession. One took these things for granted as a normal feature of London life and in fact there had been little change since Victorian times. England was still a country of low wages, high unemployment and depressing poverty and only those who remember the misery and sordidness of the 'twenties know how much we have to be thankful for today.

All through that summer and autumn I was spending weekends at Tidmarsh and after that at Ham Spray. This meant that I was seeing a good deal of Lytton Strachey. In *South from Granada* I have described the startling and even grotesque impression he first made on me, but as I got to know him better I lost my sense of his strangeness and was struck rather by his elegance. It was an elegance of mind as well as of body, of conversation as well as of face. However I did not find him easy to talk to. He made no efforts to communicate with those who could not tune in to his wavelength. I was one of these for, though I never felt that he disliked me, he had nothing to say to me because, like many other people, I was tongue-tied in his presence. Still, I could watch him and listen to him. His conversation, with its sudden drops in the voice, its strong stress accents, its variations of tone and its unfinished sentences was unlike anyone else's. There was something theatrical about the emphasis he put on certain words and there was also something one could call feminine, yet the mind behind this curious, wavering utterance was exceptionally clear and well ordered. Only the mood was unpredictable. Lytton talked in a great variety of styles – gentle and persuasive with those he liked, calm and dispassionate when engaged in a discussion, fantastic or melodramatic if in high spirits, cryptic or cynical in moments of pessimism. And he was often silent. But the overriding impression that I got from listening to him was of his maturity.

This could in part be accounted for by his delicate health, which had given him leisure for reading and reflecting, as well as by his saturation in seventeenth- and eighteenth-century French literature. From these he had acquired a good judgement, a strong vein of scepticism and a distaste for dogmatic opinions. He had no patience with those who saw the world in sharply contrasting colours. His bent was for psychological interpretations rather than for moral ones – indeed one might cite him as an illustration of what Pascal calls *esprit de finesse*. Thus there was subtlety and discrimination in his conversation, as well as sometimes a hesitation to commit himself, which I find blunted in his books, chiefly because he was not a spontaneous writer. For this reason his rather set and formal paragraphs, which were composed in his head before he began to write and never altered afterwards, fail to take on the colour of his mind. He defended his use of clichés, but too many of these give a book a mechanical air.

Yet there was, I would say, one serious limitation to Lytton's mind. He was so strongly imbued with the views of Gibbon and Voltaire that he could not come to any kind of terms with historical Christianity, but regarded it as an unpleasant and monstrous superstition and nothing else. This meant that when he read Donne or Blake he was unable to enter sympathetically into what they said or find in his own mind an equivalent for their religious feelings and idiom. Although he admired them, he could only do so by separating the content of their verse from 'the poetry'. Thus he was in the same position as those Greek philosophers who accused Homer of having taught false and evil doctrines when he had represented the Gods as having human faces and passions. Lacking, as their age did, a sense for history, these men could not see that Homer's anthropomorphism had been a victory over the faceless and terror-striking *numina* of the

Mediterranean peasants and thus a powerful contribution to the rise of Greek humanism. But Lytton lived in a history-conscious age and was himself a historian. Yet he had imprisoned himself so rigidly and dogmatically in the rationalism of the eighteenth century that he was unable to make the imaginative effort necessary to take over temporarily the mode of feeling of a poet who wrote out of his religious convictions. All religion was to him pernicious nonsense so that when *The Waste Land* and *Ash-Wednesday* came out he could find nothing to admire in them.

But I can see that in my brief sketch of Lytton's character I have failed to give a picture of what he was like to meet. His charm when he felt attracted to anyone, his aloofness when he was not, his long silences, his gift for intimacy with chosen people, his love of rhetorical exaggeration and melodrama, his irritability when he was not well, his gentleness at other times, his wit which one had to listen for, his mature judgement, his knowledge of the world and of the heart – all these elude description. Enclosing those perpetually changing and varying things, his moods, there was a definite face and voice and style of speech and gesture that fix and pin down one's impressions and which nothing but an album of snapshots and a recording of his conversation can suggest. I can therefore only say that, in spite of his having a core of clear and definite beliefs and a well-ordered mind, he was, in Montaigne's phrase, a man of *diverse et ondoyant* constitution.

Lytton's younger brother James was, next to Carrington, the person he was most closely attached to. This feeling was reciprocated, for James regarded Lytton as a hero only to be compared to his master Freud. In character he was a softer and milder man than his elder brother. His nose was Russian not Roman, his eyes were smaller and less expressive, his forehead was lower, his beard bushier, his face rounder, his sense of humour gentler and his whole nature easier and more tolerant. His way of speaking, with its strong emphasis on certain syllables, was similar since all the Stracheys had it. Altogether he was a pleasant, likeable man, devoted to his work and to the study of the odder sides of human nature and, except to attend concerts, going out little and seeing few people except his family and his close friends. He had married Alix Sargant-Florence, who was Carrington's best woman friend, indeed the only one she had not given up, apart from the tenacious Barbara Bagenal, when she had left Gertler to live with Lytton.

Alix was a remarkable character. Captain of the hockey team at her school, she looked till she was well on in life the type of pure-minded, athletic virgin. However she was not only very handsome but a born intellectual. She had married James, who had for a long time been in love with Noel Olivier, somewhat against his will: according to the story, she had sat for two days and nights at the door of his parents' house nourishing herself on chocolate till he gave in. But their marriage turned out to be a close and happy one. She went with him to Vienna, was analysed by Freud and returned to London a practising psychoanalyst like her husband. She threw herself into this with energy: detached, cool, ironic, impossible to surprise or ruffle, she was everything a woman doctor of minds ought to be. Then suddenly in the mid-'twenties a change came over her. A passion for dancing had been sweeping through London since the war and she got caught up in it. From now on she took to spending every afternoon and evening in one public dancing hall or other with a gigolo for partner. For some years this completely absorbed her till, getting tired of it, she went back with equal suddenness to psychoanalysis.

Both James and Alix were a warning that being analysed by Freud does not free one from having inconvenient complexes. Alix developed such a strong one about lavatories that she could not go abroad unless she could have a private loo off her bedroom. In those days these only existed in a very few hotels. Then both she and James developed such a neurotic dread of cold that they kept their flat in Gordon Square heated day and night to a temperature of over 80° Fahrenheit, which few of their friends, dressed in their winter clothes, could stand. This was a pity, for their company was delightful, though Alix's detached and ironic air used to intimidate me. The rational approach to life always remained very strong with both of them. The austere furniture of their flat and their spare, nutritious, calorie-calculated meals, which were taken without wine or beer because alcohol clouds the mind, were examples of this. Another was seen during the war when Alix made a point of never leaving the house without a satchel containing a first-aid kit complete with morphia and a syringe in case she was wounded by a bomb. Armed with this she had no fears of air raids.

My principal friends at this time were Francis Birrell, Arthur Waley and David Garnett. I have already drawn a portrait of David, or Bunny, as he was always called, in *South from Granada*, so all I need say now is that he was the most delightful of companions, slow and leisurely in mind, but with an endless number of stories about the literary world, in which he knew everyone. I felt especially drawn to him because he was a man of courage and independence who got on well with people of every class and condition. He was not intellectual, but he had a great experience of life and one could trust his judgement on everything from literature to practical affairs and politics. But he rarely came to Ham Spray at this time because Ralph was jealous of him, so that what he had said in his autobiography about my rivalry with Ralph over Carrington in 1919 is incorrect because he had only hearsay to go on. We were never rivals.

I had known Frankie Birrell since 1913 through my vague, muddled but saintly friend Reynolds Ball who had died of the plague in Poland in 1919.

Some portraits

He was the son of Augustine Birrell, a Liberal politician and essay writer who had been Secretary for Ireland up to the time of the Easter Rising. He had won a scholarship at Eton and during the war had served with a Quaker ambulance in France where he had made himself immensely popular with the French peasants. In appearance he was rather short with a very large head and a pair of little screwed up eyes that were half hidden behind thick, steel-rimmed glasses. Since his nose was small and his mouth large he was far from good looking, but this was redeemed by his beaming, affectionate smile. He talked incessantly in a loud rapid voice that could make it embarrassing to dine with him in a restaurant because he put no check on what he said. Since he talked well and was completely immune to shyness, he was popular both in Bloomsbury circles and with society hostesses such as Lady Colefax and Mrs Lowinsky. Wherever he went he made friends, especially among women, for he was so completely lacking in envy, conceit, vanity, ill-feeling and egoism and indeed, as his rumpled clothes and hair showed, so totally unworldly that it was difficult not to feel drawn to him. Like his friend Ball, he had the innocence of those who are little troubled by sex, but unlike him, he had – as David Garnett, who has described him better than I can, says – a sparkling intelligence, a strong sense of humour not unmixed with malice, a quick wit and an endless stream of rapid, amusing conversation. His malice, which was purely verbal, came from his inability to take either himself or anyone else very seriously. He noticed people's less attractive sides, but floated over them as he floated over everything. He never stopped to go down to the roots. But his sympathy and affection were given freely and he himself was incapable of being offended by anything that was said. He didn't have to forgive, he forgot, carried away by the heady, rose-coloured stream of his own conversation.

As an odd trait about Frankie, he once told me that his most common day-dream was that he was marching at the head of a column of soldiers beating a drum. In such an unmilitary person this vision of himself seems astonishing, and I can only suppose that his loud, incessant talk was for him a sort of drum beating.

Such was the man of whom D. H. Lawrence said that he made him dream of black beetles. If an insect symbol had to be found, I should prefer that of a bumble-bee, but he was much too warm and human a person to be given an entomological label. The only comparison that seems to me apt is to Mr Pickwick.

Frankie was an omnivorous reader, but was too much taken up by the bookshop he ran with David Garnett and by his many social engagements to have much leisure for writing. However he produced a translation of Plato's *Symposium* which it was a pleasure to read after Jowett's, as well as a little anthology of 'last words', and he might, I think, have written a biography of Napoleon III had he lived longer. But in 1934 he developed an abcess on the brain and after an unsuccessful operation died of it, very calmly and stoically. I have never known anyone whose death was so deeply felt by so many people.

I first met Arthur Waley in 1913 through my friend Reynolds Ball. He was at that time known as Arthur Schloss, but when the war came and a hysteria against everything German-sounding swept over the country he dropped it and took his mother's name, which was more euphonious. As I remember him then, he was a haughty young man with a high, thin, cutting voice and a refined and intellectual face. He was working in the Print Room of the British Museum and had not yet begun to study Chinese, but his air of superiority was so crushing that I did not feel at ease with him. After this I saw little of him till 1924, when something happened to make us friends.

He had quoted in his introduction to a collection of Chinese poems a four-lined Spanish verse or *copla* which, he said, bore a close similarity in style to the popular Chinese poems of the third century Chin dynasty. The comparison was apt, but in the translation that he gave of the Spanish verse there were three mistakes. I pointed this out to a friend, observing rather maliciously that if this was how he translated from an easy language like Spanish, it was not likely that his Chinese translations bore much resemblance to the originals. Someone repeated this to him and he at once came round to see me. I showed him where he had gone wrong and I think it says a great deal for his character that this conversation was the beginning of a friendship that lasted till his death.

At this time Arthur was living in a very small flat at the top of a house in Russell Square with a woman ten years older than himself called Beryl de Zoete. Their liaison, which had begun some years before, appeared to have settled into a steady relation, although there was something so ascetic about him and so erotically equivocal about her that many people believed that there was no physical link between them. Beryl, as I remember her then, was a woman with dark hair and refined features who looked a good deal younger than her real age, which was well past forty. She had a youthful figure and very white teeth which flashed when she laughed and an air that it was difficult to define of being Jewish. However she claimed to be of pure Dutch descent and I once dropped a brick by asking her if she had been brought up to go to synagogue. This drew on me the indignant reply that both her parents had been High Church Anglicans, domiciled in Bournemouth.

Yet Jewish or not, she was still an attractive woman and one could see that, as Bertrand Russell said to me, when she was young she had been beautiful. One day she told me the story of her early life. Her first love affair took place when she was around eighteen. The young man was a year or two older and the procedure they adopted was to take off their clothes and, quite naked, climb two adjacent poplar trees. When they were as high as they could get they would make them swing till their branches touched. They themselves never did so.

Then in her early twenties she married a man called de Selincourt. Before doing so they had agreed that, as sex was so coarse, it should be a platonic marriage, based on a vegetarian diet and on the study of music and literature, but after they had been living together for a few months her husband brought another woman into the house with whom he proceeded to spend his nights while at the same time he switched over from milk and vegetables to beer and beef steaks. Beryl put up with this for a while and then left him.

It must have been soon after this that she agreed to share a flat with my friend John Hope-Johnstone, who was four years younger than herself. This also was to be a chaste relationship sustained on a diet of fruit and yogurt and accompanied by the proviso that each of them would learn to play a musical instrument and take up the study of an Oriental language. Beryl chose the cello and Persian and made some progress in both of them, while Hope chose the recorder and Arabic and made no progress at all. Then one morning, according to her story, as she passed the open door of his room and saw him lying in bed engrossed in a book of mathematics, she stopped on a sudden impulse, went in and kissed him. 'You've broken the agreement,' he exclaimed leaping up and soon after he moved to another flat, leaving her to settle the light bill and the rent out of her own pocket.

These episodes suggest that Beryl suffered from a fastidiousness very common in those days among women, which made normal sexual relations repugnant to her, but I cannot say to what extent these feelings persisted. She took up Dalcroze dancing as a profession and, being both very musical and having a cult for the body, interested herself in ballet, on which she came in time to be an authority. The new friendships she formed were, I gather, with men of greater age and sophistication who were connected with the musical world. Meanwhile the war had broken out. Arthur had moved from the Print Room to the Oriental section of the British Museum where he worked under the poet Lawrence Binyon. He was exempted from military service on account of his blindness in one eye and in 1915 he began to teach himself Chinese. I imagine that his chief impulse to do this had come from his reading Ezra Pound's free translations of Chinese poetry, which were published in that year under the title of *Cathay*. He was seeing a good deal of Pound at that time and I remember him saying to me that he had never heard anyone talk better on the making of poetry than Pound.

Arthur's first book of translations, *170 Chinese Poems*, came out in 1918 when he was just under thirty and won immediate recognition. The speed with which he had mastered such a difficult language seems incredible, and he was now starting to teach himself Japanese. It was at this moment of incipient fame that he met Beryl de Zoete. She must have seen in him the man she had been looking for over so many years, for from their first meeting at a party she made a dead set at him. She even pursued him into his sanctum at the British Museum and did not relax her pressure till he had fallen in love with her. Yet she refused to marry him in spite of his begging her to do so because she wished to keep her liberty. This created a problem for them since Arthur's mother, to whom he was deeply attached and who did not get on with her, would have disapproved of their living together openly. It was solved by Arthur's taking up a partial residence in the flat in Russell Square which an old lover of Beryl's rented for her, but keeping a room of his own elsewhere. These are things I have only learned recently, for at the time their relations were wrapped in secrecy.

Arthur's attachment to Beryl was always something of a mystery to his friends. Few of them really liked her and even those who did, among whom I count myself, found her intolerable at times. My first impression of her was of an unattached, independent woman of vaguely suburban background who combined an exaggerated refinement about certain things with a schoolgirl gaucherie and lack of tact. Then, as one came to know her better, one became aware of another side to her, which was that of a restless, adventure-seeking person animated by a nervous, spasmodic energy that when foiled became hysterical, and very pushing and thick-skinned in the pursuit of her ends. Yet she possessed certain admirable qualities that must have recommended her to Arthur. She had a strong feeling for literature as well as for music and ballet, she was a good linguist and spoke German, French and Italian with scarcely an accent and, though this puzzled everyone who knew her, she was an excellent translator. Her English versions of Italo Svevo read better than the originals. Then her appetite for life must have been very stimulating to such a withdrawn and studious person as Arthur was. She was always setting off for Salzburg or Italy, for Morocco or Egypt, for Bali or India, as a rule with some male companion of foreign nationality whose artistic accomplishments and power to open locked doors gave him prestige for her. So far as one could judge, Arthur was never jealous and when she returned to him she brought back the stir and excitement of a distant, exotic world. But her chief asset must have been her determination to get him and hold him. He was a man paralysed by his own shyness, especially where young women were concerned. At parties one would see him standing by himself in frozen silence because he had none of the small change of conversation and if one went up to him with a glass in one's hand he would make an intellectual remark which came straight out of the blue or else start talking about Li Po and

Chinese poetry. His mind never relaxed, his standard of conversation never fell, as though that high, thin yet sensitive voice of his was not attuned to pronouncing a light or frivolous sentence. Thus it was that, though women attracted him, he could not make up to them. Only one who was prepared to make all the advances herself stood any chance of getting on to intimate terms with him. Beryl was such a person because, when she really wanted something, she did not know what feminine modesty was.

When they were first together in Russell Square they used sometimes to ask their friends to dine with them. The meal was always the same – a dish of tinned beans heated up in a saucepan followed by apples and hothouse grapes. To compensate for the austerity of this fare there would be a bottle of excellent Moselle. But when later Arthur moved to a small flat at the top of 36 Gordon Square and Beryl lived elsewhere they took to inviting their friends to Italian restaurants. If Beryl issued the invitation one was sure of a decent meal, but Arthur's ingrained asceticism made him reluctant to spend money on food and there have been occasions when I and my wife, who was a great favourite of his, have been taken by him to cheap eating houses where we had eggs fried in a nasty margarine washed down with weak coffee. Yet if Arthur was mean – for after his mother's death he was very well off – this meanness was only one aspect of his concern to waste no time or thought on material things, but like a medieval ascetic devote his whole life to one overriding purpose.

Some time in 1925 he became seriously ill with stomach ulcers and had to spend several months in a clinic in North Wales. His friends thought Beryl very heartless because she chose this moment to go off to Italy with an old lover of hers, but when she got back they appeared to be closer to one another than ever. It was after this that he began to go out every year to Switzerland on a skiing holiday. He told me that this was the only way he could find of stopping his mind from working and no doubt it was his ceaseless intellectual activity and incapacity to relax that had given him his ulcers. He quickly became an exceptionally good skier and would go off alone over the mountain slopes, executing elegant twists and curves for his own delectation and no doubt imagining to himself that he was a reincarnation of Prince Genji. On account of his expertise he was known at the hotel where he stayed as 'The Master'. But this was not the only exercise he took. In the summer he played tennis regularly in Gordon Square and one August at least he went to Majorca to practise high diving – a skill he had acquired at Cambridge. In spite of his frail appearance he was a natural athlete and I have seen him in his late forties vault lightly over a field gate. Then down to the last year or so of his life he would cycle, or even roller-skate, all over London, locking the front wheel of the bicycle to the railings when he arrived at his destination. This had the merit of saving him taxi fares, but it also gave him the exercise he needed without expense of valuable time. For his work so absorbed him that he even brought it down with him on his weekend visits to his friends. I remember one occasion during the war when he came to stay with us at our cottage in Wiltshire. My wife, happening to get up at seven in the morning, found him sitting at a table in the unheated dining-room absorbed in a Chinese book. It was freezing hard outside, but that did not seem to trouble him. His powers of concentration were terrific and neither cold nor noise could disturb him.

Although he was greatly interested in people, though less to understand them than to record their oddities, his only access to natural beauty was through works of art. One spring afternoon I took him to Kew Gardens to show him a Chinese tree, the ginkgo, which was mentioned in a book that he was translating. We found it and then in front of us there was a clump of lilac bushes in full flower. I exclaimed at their beauty and he agreed, but then added that he was really only affected by things in Nature when he read about them in a novel or poem. His mind was exclusively literary and that no doubt was why he never considered going to China to see the country whose literature and history he knew better than any Chinese.

Arthur's character can be summed up in a few words – shyness, truthfulness, obsession with his work and affection for his friends. His shyness was the cause of his sometimes appearing abrupt or rude. My wife was once at Clavadel near Davos with Alyse Gregory, the wife of Llewelyn Powys, and Arthur. Llewelyn's brother from Kenya joined them and Alyse introduced him. Arthur gave no sign of having taken her words in. 'This is Mr Powys,' Alyse repeated in a louder voice. 'I heard you the first time,' said Arthur curtly. He could be gentle with simple people as he was with his friends, but if he was taken aback or if someone present made what he regarded as a stupid remark, he could be cutting. And his mind was as sharp as a knife.

Another anecdote will illustrate his incapacity to deviate in the slightest degree from what he thought. One day in the middle 'twenties I handed him a copy of some verses I had written and asked him to look at them and give me his opinion. The next time I saw him he did not mention them, so I asked if he had read them. 'Yes,' he said, 'I have.' 'I know that they are not good,' I persisted, 'but I would like to know if you think they show any promise.' 'No,' he replied, 'none that I can see,' and began to talk about something else. Yet he did not mean to snub me: his abruptness came from his feeling embarrassed at not having liked them.

Later I came to wonder whether he was really such an infallible judge of verse. He admired Sacheverell Sitwell's poems, which I thought dull and academic, perhaps because he was a little in love with him. Then he could see nothing in Hardy. I remember one evening in Dorset trying to convince him that some of Hardy's poems were good by reading them aloud to him. In every case he found something to criticize, so that by the time he had finished I had lost my belief in them too, though I recovered it later.

Arthur's obsession with his work was very great and overflowed more than one would have wished into his conversation. Although he could make sharp and penetrating remarks on life and books, he would soon return to Chinese poetry where only Sinologists could follow him. Yet how could it have been otherwise? He was the greatest scholar the English-speaking world has produced as well as a very fine translator, and to be this he had had to master two – and indeed four or five – of the most difficult languages. His published work comprises some thirty volumes as well as many reviews and learned articles. It is hardly surprising therefore that his thoughts should have continued to run on Chinese and Japanese subjects after he left his study. Yet in fact he had many other interests. He was extremely musical, went assiduously to concerts and picture galleries and kept in touch with what was being done in anthropology and psychology as well as in literature. He also found time to see a fair number of people of all kinds and never missed a party to which he was invited. His closest friends when I first knew him were Frankie Birrell and the three Sitwells, but he also saw a good deal of Roger Fry, James Strachey and Bertrand Russell, to mention only those whom I knew.

This is not the place to speak of his translations. I will merely say that those in verse seem to me to be as good as literal renderings of poetry can ever be. But for him what would one know of Chinese poetry? Then in the *Tale of Genji* and the *Pillow Book* he has given us two masterpieces that make our literature seem crude and barbarous, while his last book, *Yüän Mei,* is very delightful and written in the purest and most sensitive prose. However I have never shared his enthusiasm for *Monkey*, which he once read aloud to my wife and myself from the manuscript. Indeed it sent me to sleep.

I have still to complete my portrait of Beryl de Zoete. In manner she was both impulsive and undecided, moving in little jumps and starts, beginning to speak and then changing her mind. She knew that she must keep a watch on herself, for when she did not she would come out with things that would have been better left unsaid. Where the arts were concerned, she had the bump of veneration developed to excess. This could make her tiresome, as Catholic ladies who use a special tone for talking of their priests are tiresome, but in general she was easy-going and pleasant to be with and, though she did not have much sense of humour, given to laughing very freely. Yet when she wanted anything – and like a child she often wanted things badly – she could be totally insensitive to other people's interests. Helen Anrep and Molly MacCarthy had a number of stories to tell of her lack of tact and consideration when she stayed with them in the country – of how, for example, when asked to be careful of water during a drought, she would run her bath twice a day full to the brim, or, on another occasion, sunbathe on the lawn where all the passers-by could see her, clad in ugly grey combinations and looking more indecent than if she had been naked. Then the Berensons complained that she would turn up uninvited with her suitcases at their house near Florence and stay on impervious to all hints that her room was required. This happened at other houses too so that tales of her obtuseness and of her conversational *gaffes* became a general currency. But what I found most trying about her was her sham refinement. When invited to tea with her at Gordon Square one would be offered a weak jasmin-scented beverage in a very thin porcelain cup and after it a herb cigarette that gave out an odour of thyme and wet hay. If one said that one preferred to smoke one's own, a pained expression would come over her face and she would say that, if one did not mind, she could not bear the smell of tobacco. Then one noticed the bowls of pot-pourri scattered about the room and realized that to smoke a cigarette in such a temple of the muses would be an outrage.

As she grew older, Beryl's face, though scarcely wrinkled, took on an extraordinary look of age, like that of a gipsy fortune-teller. Her hair, dyed a rusty black, and her youthful style of dress only strengthened this impression, so that people joked about her being a hundred when she was barely seventy. But her figure remained young and her voice, which was low-pitched and musical, was pleasant to the ear. She read poetry well and her laugh was attractive. Poor Beryl, she could in her bad moments be sillier and clumsier and more insensitive and selfish than most people I have known, yet I have good memories of her because she was generous and kind as well as loyal to her friends. She could irritate, but she could not hurt because there was no malice in her. And surely her adventurous spirit and her great love of life and art should count in her favour.

8

Myself and Carrington

I must now leave portraits and return to my own life, which at this time means my tormented, obsessional love affair with Carrington. After an interval of a month or two during which we had agreed to stop seeing or writing to one another we met by accident at Helen Anrep's house in Hampstead and decided to renew our relations. This was in January 1925. She promised to come up every fortnight and spend an afternoon and a night with me and I agreed to go down sometimes to Ham Spray. But of what use were promises when it was her mood and feeling as much as her bodily presence that mattered?

The chief stumbling-block was once again the question of bed. Here Carrington was contrariness itself. If she saw that I wanted to make love to her, as I always did, she would be disinclined to do so and, though to please me she might fall in with my wishes, would turn against me and escape from me afterwards. But if I concealed my feelings and appeared to be indifferent, then she would draw me to the couch. Whenever the impulse came from her, she enjoyed love-making, but when it came from me she was apt to say that she hated being loved for her body. All the difficulties of her relation with Mark Gertler, she would add, had been caused by that. But no one had ever wanted Carrington 'for her body'. They had wanted her because they were in love with her and the more she had resisted their demands the more in love they had been.

Nor did we always get on well in other ways.

'I think', she wrote after a meeting which had gone off badly, 'that, as Leonard says, you are sometimes very on the spot and intelligent about people, but at other times hopelessly stupid and tiresome in not under- standing. That to my mind is the most interesting thing about your character. I mean, that one brain should contain such intelligence and such stupidity.'

But although it is true that the degree of my intelligence varies a great deal and that I am frequently confused and dull and unable to express my thoughts clearly, it is also true that Carrington did not stimulate me mentally. Often I was too obsessed by my desire to make love to her to take in what she was saying. Then she was very secretive about herself and her Ham Spray life and her chatter, chatter, chatter about other people all in that flat, rapid little voice of hers was apt to get on my nerves. She had none of Helen Anrep's gift for putting one at ease and making the conversation flow. What she was best at was telling an amusing story or making gay or sprightly comments in a general conversation. At other times her mind would jump about like a bird's, caught by something which her extraordinarily sharp and active eyes had just noticed. But driven as I was by my obsession for her, by my insistant longing to possess her more completely, none of this interested me. What I wanted was a more direct and personal kind of communication, leading to a greater mental intimacy.

When recently I read Mark Gertler's letters I felt that everything he had written to or about Carrington might have been written by myself. She had brought out in each of us the same agony of mind, the same baffled exasperation. 'I am always nervous and tongue-tied in your presence,' he had written. That had sometimes been the case with me, but now more often than not it was boredom that I felt, mixed with impatience. Not that I thought her intrinsically boring, for she was far too vital and original to be that, but that we did not seem to be conversationally attuned to one another.

My own relations with her were deeper and more involved than Gertler's had ever been. She had once been in love with me, as she never quite was with him, and she was still more attached to me than to anyone except Lytton and Ralph. She did not want to give me up because, her affection for me apart, I filled an important place in her life. When the atmosphere at Ham Spray became too dense or ingrown, I provided her with an outlet. But both the tone and the substance of Gertler's complaints were identical with mine. In the diary that I began that August, in my letters to Helen Anrep, in the letters I wrote almost every day to her, one finds the same burden. She was destroying me. My whole nature cried out for peace of mind in which to work and yet I could hardly contemplate the emptiness of a life without her. I asked for what I regarded as very little – two days and two nights a month – but her moods made every meeting a gamble when they should have been a reaffirmation and a certainty.

A month or two before this I had started a light love affair with a girl called Susie Swan whose parents had been neighbours of ours on the Cotswolds. To get away from home she had married when very young a man called Swan, who had run off to America with her jewellery and as much of her money as he could collect. She was now a strongly sexed and rather emotional girl and the ruin of her married life had led her to take refuge in

Catholicism, which of course blocked her only way of escape because it made divorce and remarriage impossible.

In appearance Susie was a big, loose-limbed girl with tow-coloured hair and very large blue eyes. She had round rosy cheeks and a rather piggy face which when she was a child had made people say she would grow up to be plain. But in fact she was attractive, for she had a magnificent body and her loping, lazy, long-strided walk and her large red-lipped mouth and generous, good-natured expression seemed an open invitation. We met several times in the country, and then in November, when my relations with Carrington were suspended, she came up to London and we made love in my flat. But after a few weeks our affair came to an end by mutual consent. Her Catholic conscience gave her scruples and, as soon as I began seeing Carrington again, I lost my physical interest in her. However we continued for some years to meet as friends. Gradually the furrows settled on her forehead as she became more and more sucked into her religion. She brought up her son to be a priest, converted her dour, Presbyterian mother and died prematurely of cancer at the age of fifty. She was a person who was born to be a happy wife and mother, but the cruel breakdown of her marriage and the blocking of her strong sexual instincts turned her in a different direction and she ended up totally absorbed in her substitute faith.

My relations with Carrington improved a little that spring. Ralph was now more than ever taken up with Frances Marshall and, though she still refused to go to bed with him, for the girls of those days did not lightly surrender their virginity, she spent most of her weekends in his company at Ham Spray. Carrington, while always maintaining that she was not jealous, could not help feeling that something had changed. As she heard their shrieks of laughter coming out of the next room, she became aware of a side of Ralph's character that she had no part in and which grated on her. For this house was to her, as houses often are to women, a sacred place. She had chosen its furniture and materials with care and had decorated it herself. She loved its peace and seclusion – the low voices, the subdued gaiety, the close intimacy which allowed its three inmates as well as the most regular of the weekend visitors to communicate by a word. Ralph, though at bottom such a different person, had been drawn into its atmosphere and assimilated, but now Frances, a young girl, intelligent and high spirited but endowed with a different sort of temperament, was bringing out in him a long-buried and discordant strain. This made Carrington turn towards me for, though I did not fit into Ham Spray, I was a person of her own sort who, till I came to live in London, she had believed to be very like herself.

'No one, not even you,' she had written, 'can make me care less for Ralph and Lytton and Ham Spray and my own life: no one but you could make me care as much as I do for a third person.'

Yet the old difficulties remained. She would write that she was coming to see me at a certain hour and then not arrive. At once the orchestra, as I called it, began to play inside me. The feeling of time slowing down, each minute crawling by like an hour, the longing to die and be done with it, sometimes fits of sobbing followed by angry vindictive thoughts and imaginings would pass through me. Then either a telegram would be delivered, saying that she could not come, or she would arrive three or four hours late. If she came I would forget everything in my relief at seeing her. If she didn't I would scribble off an angry letter which, unless I tore it up without posting it, had the worst result.

'Do you know,' she wrote, 'the effect you have on me when you are angry? I simply feel ill inside and my hand trembles so much that I cannot write. Now I shall have to sit on a chair for half an hour and read a book because I feel so agitated ... But I only blame myself.'

This self-blame of hers was a thing I particularly dreaded because it made her wish to avoid me. Inclined as she was to feelings of guilt because of the way in which she had been badgered as a child, always ready to despair of her own character, she would withdraw into herself as soon as she felt she had caused pain to anyone. For the same reason she was much given to little acts of propitiation. Thus she rarely came to see me without bringing me a present, although she must have known that the only present I wanted from her was herself. But it would be very unjust for me to put all the blame on her for our quarrels and dissensions. I was impatient, self-willed and egoistic. My feelings were often too strong to be kept under control. And then I believed that a love such as ours, sealed by so many letters and embraces, purged by so much heart-ache and separation, had in spite of its frustrations something preordained and written-on-the-stars about it and that this gave me rights over her as well as obligations. Could I not truthfully say that for four years the whole of my life had revolved round her? Our love was the thing I was most proud of and with the egocentricity of lovers I assumed that everyone I met knew about it.

Early that May, Carrington suggested that I should take rooms for the summer at the village of Shalbourne, a couple of miles distant from Ham Spray. This would make it possible for us to see one another whenever we wished and so solve the problem that had led to so much friction between us. I agreed with enthusiasm and she found lodgings for me with a small farmer called Levy. So with great hopes on both sides a new phase of our relation began.

At first everything went well. I spent a happy night with her at Ham Spray and on the following morning we took the train to London to see the Chelsea Flower Show for which my great-aunt had given me her member's tickets. Talking of the quarrel we had had last November, when she had promised to come up and see me and then changed her mind, she said: 'I know your character better now. I will never risk our relation in that way again.' Yet this was the last happy moment we spent together.

The fault this time was entirely my own. I was over-excited by a story I was writing, disregarded the anxiety she felt over Lytton being unwell and made a scene about nothing. Then on the following morning, although she had invited me to spend the night with her at Ham Spray, I went up to London and returned directly the same evening to Shalbourne. Next day I was filled with repentance for my stupid fit of pique and rode over on my bicycle to apologize, but she took my explanations coldly. 'She lacks the sense for reconciliations,' I said, not seeing that one does not make too many efforts when one is not in love.

Other scenes followed. She attacked me angrily on a walk over Sheepless Down, ending up characteristically with an admission of her own incapacity for intimate relationships. This alarmed me so much that, though it had been previously agreed that we should spend the following night together, I sent round a note to say that, if that was how she felt, it might be better to put this occasion off since I dreaded the reaction she would be likely to have afterwards. After a sleepless night I got a reply in which she said that she accepted the conclusions of my letter.

From this day something seemed to break inside her. She began avoiding me. I poured out my troubles to Ralph, who had driven over to take me for a walk, and he promised to do what he could to help me. As a start he took me back with him to lunch at Ham Spray and kept me on to supper. Then I began to wonder whether I should stay the night. 'Do as you please,' said Carrington, and I thought this a bad omen, but Ralph said, 'Very likely she wants you to stay. For once in a way don't show pique. Stand out for what you want.' I stayed.

Dinner. General conversation. Night. I went to my room, a large one with a four-poster bed, overlooking the garage. Lytton took an age in going to bed. Eleven o'clock struck. Midnight. Not a sound. So she would not come. Exhausted by a week of violent emotions I sobbed till no more tears came into my eyes. How could I get through the dark hours until tomorrow? I thought I would get up, walk to the canal and drown myself.

At 12.30 she came. My tears, which I could not conceal, made her even colder. She lay there beside me without speaking as though she was tied and bound on an altar for sacrifice. At first I did not want to make love to her, but she insisted. She must carry out her duty. The moment after – 'Have you finished?' And she got up and left the room. Next morning when I went off with Ralph to London, she avoided kissing me goodbye.

Five days later I returned to Shalbourne. I came back full of affectionate and grateful feelings for her and Ralph with presents of plants and pigeons I had brought for both of them, to find that Carrington, who had gone to Cambridge for a couple of nights, had not returned. At once one of my senseless agitations came over me.

I wrote to Helen Anrep a letter that I did not send off:

> I came down here this evening and what has happened? Nothing, and yet at the sight of a letter from D.C. on the table I felt such unbearable pain, such senseless anger that I said 'I will tear it up without reading it'. However I read it – all cold amiability and dull friendliness as I had expected, with a great deal of pleasure expressed at being away and doubt as to what day she should return ...
>
> She has given me a birthday present, two months after my birthday, and since it has been given as a substitute for the affection and responsiveness which I ask for in vain, it would give me great pleasure to send it back to her. Yet if for one moment I indulge my spite and anger I suffer such remorse, so far beyond the consequence and weight of my revenge, that I take back everything, undo everything and promise everything. I punish myself a hundred times for the once that I give her pain. Out of sheer cowardice, therefore, my own anger frightens me ... She will never do enough to make me happy – that is her nature: it is only in her absence and – if she should die – then after her death and in dreams and reconciliations that I love her for herself alone irrespective of how she treats me.
>
> Every contact produces either love or hate, according as to whether she gives or takes away. And she is nearly always taking away – I see her for ever gliding off, turning away, removing something. Good or bad, that is being in love, and I am in love with her and she is not with me, nor ever can be, nor perhaps has ever been except for brief moments with anyone but Lytton.
>
> There is no solution. I cannot go on. For three or four years my life has been more or less this, and during the past year at any rate scarcely a week has passed without my saying 'I must give it up'. Then I could not: now I can. My policy of frivolity and social life will lead me into safety. Still there appears what is almost a moral principle: would it not be a *crime* to give up the only person I have ever loved, and, I begin to believe, shall ever love? It is as though I said – I will never again read English literature before Macaulay. Of course, far, far worse than that.

Such were the feelings that even a slight disappointment could arouse in me. Yet they showed a presentiment of the treatment that I must expect, for when on the following day Carrington returned she clung to Ralph and avoided being left alone with me. This time I was not asked to stay to supper so I spent the evening writing another letter to Helen.

Is it credible the pain one suffers in love? One is a character so hard and indifferent that nothing, it seems, can move one in any direction, and all at once comes an unhappiness so sharp, so unintelligible, so unaccountable that everything else around one melts out of existence. One is astonished that there is room in one for such pure, unmaterial suffering and it puts one at once so far above all other considerations that one feels a superiority that is different from vanity over those who have not got it. I think it is no wonder that those who are unhappily in love invent a variety of passes and lunges, of piques and despairs and rationalizations: by this release of activity they mitigate the pain. If one stops to look the situation in the face, if one dares to put aside all egotism and vanity, one is frozen into a kind of terror.

My first evening with C. and Ralph in the garden has been of this sort: hardly ever have I experienced such acute unhappiness. It is as though one's desires after reaching a certain pitch took physical form and became an actual limb which could be and even was before one's eyes deliberately amputated. In what unknown heaven would their satisfaction at such moments land one? Yet because this pain was not accompanied by the usual horde of false, unreal and egotistic projections I felt a kind of after-pleasure, of distinction: it was the feeling of relief at the plummet's having reached the bottom, of something in the outside world being clearly apprehended. For I have renounced my hopes (rather, my rights, as I used to call them) of any of my desires being fulfilled.

In love one becomes religious. It seems incredible that the immense flood of good will, of devotion, of longing – almost one's whole life – that one throws out like a beam in a certain direction, should be felt to be disagreeable, should be neglected, not wanted, wasted. There *must* be a response: the God *must* pour out for one in gratitude, in duty the cup of immortal life. If one knew by experience what death is as one knows by experience what the unreturn of love is, it would cost one harder to be an atheist. But one never permits oneself to face this blank wall, to take in all the consequences of the words 'not loving', to scrape with one's nails through the padding onto the hard walls of the cell.

Here tonight I saw on the one hand all the happiness that a return of love would give and on the other hand the complete impossibility of any return, certainly now, perhaps for ever. I do not know why it is that at such moments one does not want to end one's life, but certainly one does not. It is false trains of thought, projections, that lead people to suicide, not clear visions of the truth ... Just three years ago I remember feeling exactly as I have felt this evening, except that the obstacles were then external, not these far more cruel and impassable internal ones that are always hidden beneath them. Will there ever be an end to it? When shall I have served my time in this treadmill? And yet to cease to love C., to cease to be affected by all that now affects me in her – horrible, unnatural! It is as though one could contemplate a time when one of the arts that now moves one should cease to be intelligible.

On the following day Ralph went up to London for the night to see Frances, and Carrington, who always hated being left alone, took me over to tea with a painter called Japp who had bought a farm near Hungerford. On the way back she suddenly said, 'Would you care to come to supper?' I hesitated and then said, 'Do you really want me to?' '*I* asked if you wished to come,' she replied. 'Either accept or refuse.' I accepted.

I had never before spent an evening alone with her in the country. The sun set as we ate our meal under the giant poplar tree. A beautiful light lay over the trees and fields. The rooks, cawing loudly, were returning from distant woods to their nests. I thought of the immense happiness that an evening alone with her would have given me a month, even a fortnight earlier. I contrasted my position then with that in which I now found myself. Her cold and angry manner, her marked indifference, the ungracious quality she put into her smallest actions. She seemed to hate me, which was strange when it was she who held me in her power and I who did not dare to ask for anything.

I was perfectly calm. No violence of anger or reproach came to protect me. My head was clear and I was aware of everything that was happening around me. I do not think that at any time in my life I have felt such pain as I did then. At dusk I returned to Shalbourne on my bicycle. I saw the extreme beauty of the trees rooted in the fields over which a white mist had risen and lay like water. Not a leaf in the hedgerows stirred. All Nature seemed to be in suspense and standing still. Inside me as outside me nothing moved. I felt as though everything in me, just at its moment of greatest life, of greatest promise, of greatest vigour had been arrested. I sat down and wrote a letter to Helen Anrep before going to bed.

A change has taken place in my feelings since I have let down my bucket to the bottom of the well and found it empty. Till now every contact with her has produced either love or hate, according to whether she gave or took away, so that each time she gave I felt we should go on for ever together and each time she took away I said 'I must give her up'. Yet whenever I tried to do this one of her forlorn and pathetic letters would arrive, dreams would threaten me, the shortness of life would frighten me, the fear of unhappiness. And when at last, after many attempts, the desert barrier I should have to cross before being free ceased to be impassable, a moral principle leaped up to forbid the journey. Would it not be a crime to sacrifice everything that was good and unselfish in me to what was indifferent and selfish – to give up the only person I have ever deeply loved? But now that I have discovered the real emptiness of the situation, I have no reasonable choice but to break with her.

Next day a girl friend of mine called Freda arrived to spend the weekend with me. As soon as she had left I went over to Ham Spray and once more found Carrington clinging to Ralph in a way that seemed to indicate that they were again lovers. Indeed had they ever stopped being so? When I questioned her about her feelings for me, she said, 'I have lost all physical feelings for the time being. I cannot say how long it will last.'

There seemed no point in my remaining any longer in the country so on the following morning I gave up my rooms and returned to London. But Carrington and I still continued writing in a friendly way to one another. I was getting ready for a final rupture, but before making up my mind to it I wished to feel quite certain that it was necessary. Meanwhile we were seeing one another almost every day, for Lytton's play on the Dowager Empress of China was being put on for a couple of nights at the Scala Theatre and Carrington was in charge of the costumes while I was acting a small part. One evening we even had supper at my rooms and went to see *The Three-Cornered Hat* afterwards, but there was no question of our making love. All that week I kept running into her and Ralph and each time I did so she was hanging onto him in a way that I had never seen before. Since she was so secretive about her Ham Spray life I was unaware that his relations with Frances Marshall were just now approaching a crisis. Had I known that I would certainly have behaved more considerately for I would have seen that her coldness towards me was caused by her fear of Ralph's leaving her, a thing I certainly did not want to happen either for her sake or for my own. Just now she was trying to assure him of her complete devotion to him, which meant that I must be relegated to a distance. Yet with her future so uncertain, she did not want to break with me, only to put our relation into cold storage.

A party was given at the Scala Theatre for the actors. I was in deep gloom because Carrington was avoiding me, so to keep up my end I flirted violently with Marjorie Joad, whom I did not like. At the same time I drank heavily. Then as the party broke up I caught sight of Carrington standing in a corner and, going up to her, began to reproach her. She ran away from me and tried to find Ralph, who had already left. I went out after her into the street. She would not give me the heavy rucksack she was carrying, so I followed her down Tottenham Court Road, saying all the most cruel things that came into my head. 'Go home, go home,' she cried and ran across the street. I left her. But at once I regretted everything. It was two in the morning – she would have to walk a mile to the railway station. I hated myself, I loved her, I only wished to serve her.

I ran after her. 'No, you are tired,' she said. 'You must go home.' She kept on repeating this all the way to King's Cross, her face very pale, her eyes enlarged and fixed in a kind of icy misery. It hurt me so deeply that she would not accept my company and my help in carrying her sack that perhaps then more than at any other moment I decided that I must break with her. There were fifty minutes to wait – we sat on a step at the edge of the pavement. Though dropping with fatigue she would not lean on me. Although we must both of us have known that these scenes could go on no longer, I made her assure me that she would write to me next day and made fresh promises for the future. She agreed that next time everything would be better. Then Ralph appeared and she drew towards him, while I walked home.

All that week I was writing and tearing up letters in which I said that we must break off everything. On Friday I was going to Rodmell near Lewes to stay with Helen Anrep, who had rented Monk's House from Virginia Woolf. I had in my pocket a final letter to Carrington, but should I send it? Just as the train was about to start I ran back onto the platform and slipped it into the pillar box. At once such a feeling of relief came over me that I knew that I had acted rightly. Even when I found two friendly letters waiting for me at Monk's House I did not regret what I had done.

Three days later I received her reply. In it she said that she felt herself utterly unfitted to have a relation with anyone. Her fancies and obsessions bordered on insanity. Then, she went on, I talked about her to Helen and Frances – 'my secretiveness has always been my misery'. That was true, but I would not have done so had she confided in me.

> You think I don't understand your feelings. I understand them only too well. Please do not turn on me. I want your pity more than anything because in agreeing to separate I lose so much and gain nothing. It is always gloomy to be defeated by one's own character. But you have no reason to be sad, you have a great many friends ... Please be a little proud and do not discuss me.

Two days later I got another letter which was more explicit.

If only our feelings for one another coincided more often! You want perpetually from me something which it is not in my power to give and I feel always a sense of guilt and depression because I cannot give it to you ... If only I mattered a little less to you it would be less strained. But of course if I did then probably you wouldn't want to see me. And yet do you know it is more difficult for me to agree not to see you than to do anything else? There is *so much* that I love in you entirely that when one is removed from the physical difficulties one can only feel affections.

It is very hard to be exact. You know I have always hated being a woman ... I am continually depressed by my feminineness. It is true that *au fond* I have a female inside in me, which is proved by my liking to make love, but afterwards a sort of rage fills me because of that. I literally cannot bear to let my mind think of it again. It is partly because Ralph does not any longer treat me like a woman that the strain between us has vanished. All this became clear last summer with Henrietta. I had more ecstasy with her and no feelings of shame afterwards. You pressed me out of myself into a hidden suppressed character, but when I returned I turned against this character and was filled with dread at meeting you again. It is really something unconnected with you, a struggle in myself between two characters ... Probably it would have been easier if I had been completely Lesbian ... In the past everything has gone wrong for this reason – always this struggle between two insides, which makes one disjointed, unreliable and secretive. I find it as difficult as you to bear the strain of our making each other unhappy. Yet I don't see how I can give you up entirely because there is no one who for me can ever be quite the same.

So we agreed to separate, though not for ever, but only till the passage of time should make it possible for us to renew our relation on better terms.

Forty-nine years have passed since that summer and its pains and torments have long ceased to evoke any echo in me. Time destroys everything except the husk of memory. But on reading again through my letters and diaries of these days I have been struck by the force and violence of my feelings. Carrington tore at the roots of my soul in a way that no one else has ever done for the reason that, though she loved me after her own fashion, she was so made that she could not give me what I needed to satisfy me. Thus I sank into a more and more desperate and chaotic state till I could bear it no longer.

111

The normal love affair can be compared to a molecule comprising two atoms which revolve round one another. Its merits are stability, its drawbacks dullness, leading to a loss of tension and to a tendency to drift apart. But the molecule in which I was involved comprised five or, as will later be seen, six or seven components, each of which was perpetually acting on some of the others. At the centre was Carrington, tugged in three different directions, and her worn face showed how severe the strain often was. Yet she did not regard herself as unhappy for her life was a full and intense one and in her house, in her painting and in her relations with Lytton she had great compensations.

9

Ralph and Frances

I have spoken several times of a girl called Frances Marshall with whom Ralph had fallen in love. She was an intelligent girl who had read Moral Philosophy at Cambridge and with her lively brown eyes, well-shaped legs and slim figure she was one of the prettiest girls in London, though she seemed quite unaware of it. Ralph got to know her in the summer or autumn of 1923 and was immediately attracted to her. Soon he was courting her assiduously and she was responding. As a companion she was obviously better suited to him than Carrington was. Besides being young and delightfully gay, she was a normal and dependable person like himself, a good dancer and with no temperamental vagaries to madden him. Then she was able to deal effectively with his most difficult side – his love of arguing. Ralph's usual method of doing this was to attribute to his adversary opinions which he did not hold and then demolish them. This would drive muddle-headed people like Carrington to frenzy, but Frances with her clear head was more than a match for him and was usually able to reduce him to order. Yet, though all that year they were behaving like a pair of lovers, she refused to go to bed with him. Frances was still uncertain of her feelings. This was because she had another admirer.

However the situation was now rapidly approaching a crisis. That autumn of 1925 Frances went with Ralph to the South of Spain. When they returned to England she was in love with him.

The next two months were spent in continual crises. Ralph was more than ever in love with Frances, but did not see how he could abandon Carrington because that would entail the break-up of the Ham Spray *ménage* which meant so much to her. For Lytton, who was in the middle of a passionate love affair with Philip Ritchie, was in a restless frame of mind. If Ralph, he declared, insisted on leaving Carrington for Frances, he would refuse to remain any longer unsupported by a male presence in the country and would settle in London, which offered the advantage of allowing him to see Philip every day. So the moment which Carrington had always dreaded had arrived. She was saved from having to face it by the generosity of Frances, who suggested a compromise. After a good deal of discussion the terms of this were worked out. She and Ralph were to rent a flat in London, but would go down often to Ham Spray.

At the time I knew nothing of all this. Absolute secrecy about Ham Spray affairs was the rule and I had the reputation, which I doubtless deserved, of being indiscreet. Yet I was seeing a good deal of both Ralph and Frances all that year. From being Ralph's best friend I had become a good friend of hers too, chiefly because she was the only person other than Helen Anrep with whom I could talk about Carrington, and we used often to dine out and go to the films together. But I got no confidences. It was not till March, when they settled into rooms in Gordon Square, that Ralph told me that he now regarded himself as married to Frances and that his feelings for Carrington, though very strong, were those of a brother.

The man to whom Frances was linking her life was in many respects a different person from the one who had fallen in love with Carrington seven years before. I have described him as he was then – an extrovert full of confidence in himself, prodigiously gay and high spirited, bursting with a zest for life, but too passionate about his own pursuits to take an interest in the paler secondary world, as Auden calls it, of literature, art or intellectual things. War and women had been the only things that had held his attention up to then, and he was admirably equipped for dealing with both. Yet it was not for nothing that he had been head of the school at Westminster and had won a scholarship from there to Oxford. He was very intelligent, though with the sort of intelligence that shows itself best in a professional career. That is to say, he was a realist about life and lacked the writer's or artist's special sort of imagination. But then Lytton had taken him up, he had delved into literature, history and Freudian psychology and become, what he had not been before, a widely read person with a shrewd judgement on books, people and life. This, it is true, was not the direction that seemed to have been marked out for him. His natural gifts were such that, had he taken up almost any profession, he could have risen high in it. But he was totally unambitious. At Oxford he had lazed away his time, aware that with his great powers of concentration he could easily mug up his subjects in a week and pass his exam with flying colours, but a life of ease and pleasure was what most appealed to him. Thus, when Lytton suggested that he should exchange his law studies for English Literature, he gladly gave up all thought of working for a profession and, when his time at Oxford was over, settled down to live at Tidmarsh, where he found various ways of occupying himself. As he grew older much of the high spirits and ebullience that had so delighted me in his youth abated and he became a quieter and more reflective person, but to the end of his life he remained by a long way my best friend.

I must now go back to the time of my breach with Carrington. My diary, which I began in August, shows my continual obsession with her. I was as deeply in love as ever though, since the state of being in love is at the best of times an intermittent one, there were periods during which I felt free and happy. The best of these occurred when I was writing and I will now describe how one of them began.

One September afternoon, as I sat on the top of a bus on the way to have tea with my great-aunt, I had a strange experience. I found myself occupying the mind of a person who was very different from myself and feeling his thoughts and words pour through me. I got off at Victoria Station, bought an exercise book and a pencil, settled myself on a bench and began to write. I do not know for how many hours I wrote at dictation speed, but when I got back to my flat I had covered a good deal of paper. During the next few days I added more, but by now I had acquired a better notion of what I was doing. I was writing a novel in diary form about a man called Tom Fisher who was spending the summer in precisely that cottage on the Kentish coast where I had stayed the previous year with Boris and Helen Anrep. The other characters were his sister, a dull conventional woman for whom he had once had an incestuous passion, and her husband, a doctor who was slowly going mad.

Since this Tom, whose skin I seemed to have got into, was a very extraordinary man, with an original mind and a mode of thinking of his own, I asked myself how he had come to take his place with such compelling force and vividness in my head. There must surely be a very personal reason for it and I thought I could see that he stood for myself. It was true that he was very unlike me, but could he not be an ironical prefiguration of what I should be in ten years' time when, warped, embittered, forced back into myself, my gifts wasted, I should come into my great-aunt's inheritance? Yet he was also a composite figure. My friend Hope had contributed to his formation. Tom Fisher's bright schoolmasterish manner came from him, while his self-awareness and his egoism were, though not mine, derived from me – mine with a twist, or, shall I say my own thoughts and feelings caricaturing themselves. Yet, whatever his derivation in my unconscious, I did not have to build him up piecemeal as a novelist builds up his characters. He sprang into my head whole and completely formed and was so real to me that I used to talk about him to Helen Anrep as though he really existed.

I worked on my novel for a couple of weeks, and then my fit of composition began to dry up. I felt that I needed a change to the seaside to restore me, so early in October I took the train to Lyme Regis where I found rooms on the port at 8 Marine Parade. Here, as I read Jane Austen, my powers of invention returned with force and I put down on paper those passages on the sea which Arthur Waley, and other people to whom I read them, praised. But I could not go on. Although I realized that I had struck a rich and perversely poetical vein, I found that I had not the experience or the judgement to continue with such a difficult task. So I put it away, although for many years I kept a notebook of Tom Fisher's peculiar thoughts and images, which would come into my head at odd moments. Yet I never abandoned the hope of finishing it. In the summer of 1950 I took it up again and rewrote the first seven chapters. Then I stopped a second time, overcome by my dislike for my egoistic anti-hero whose skin I had to get into every time I sat down to my writing table. Finally in 1956 I made up my mind to go through with it and after many breaks and interruptions, drawing heavily on the notes and passages I had saved, finished it in 1960. Next year it was published by Hamish Hamilton under the title of *A Holiday by the Sea*.

Since with all its faults and excesses it is my most imaginative and ambitious book, I will say a few words about what I was trying to do. Tom Fisher is a Prufrock-like person who suffers from a deep timidity about life. This timidity was the cause of his earlier incestuous relation with his sister because she was the only person he dared to take the risk of loving and it is also the explanation of his enormous, though half assumed and playful, egoism because an excessive interest in oneself is the failing of those who have been thrown back too much into their own minds. It should be remembered too that there had been a fashion among literary people for this sort of egoistic display in the years before the First World War. Tom is a man who, like Hope, had modelled himself upon the previous generation. He is a dandy who wears a mask even to himself and one of the components of that mask is the half-humorous self-advocacy of Shaw and Wilde.

His view of himself is that he is a man who has been turned back and embittered by life – that is by his sister's desertion. Yet once he had a poetic vision of the world. He still remembers the strong romantic feelings that as a child he had had about the sea – at certain moments they come back to him like the recollection of a lost paradise – but his usual attitude towards it now is one of boredom and loathing and he gets a malicious pleasure from jeering at it, finding absurd images for it and generally delighting in its ugliness and stupidity. Yet he cannot forget it. This sea is so constantly present to his mind that it can almost be called a character in the book.

One of the things I set myself to do in this novel was to create a complex, self-aware and very intelligent human being. In most English novels the characters are thin and slightly sketched because they are subordinated to the story or plot and hardly any of them can be described as introspective or intellectual. Only Shakespeare created characters who in range of feeling and intellect approached his own stature. Thus Tom Fisher, with his mind turned back into itself because the outward roads were blocked, is given a role not unlike that of Hamlet. To bring this out better I exhibited him in three different modes – that is, in his conversation, in his musings or soliloquies and (though this, owing to the diary form of the book, was only possible in flashes) as he appeared to other people. For what a person says, what he thinks when he is alone and how he is regarded by others reveal very different aspects of what it is convenient to call an individual. But the other characters are two-dimensional or even less because they are only seen through his eyes. He dominates them with his talk, with his spreading notion of his own personality. In the last resort they are only there to bring him out.

A Holiday by the Sea has many defects. It is too rich, too choked with ideas and images. It is an airless book because the strong obsessionary flavour of the narrator's mind exhausts and stifles one. But I would claim that it is intelligent and well written and shot through with a queer kind of self-awareness and poetry. Only it will never be much read because few people will be able to endure being taken into the confidence of a character whose absorption with himself is so overpowering.

I had been seeing a good deal that past year of a girl called Winifred. She was around twenty-six years old and was a ballet dancer by profession, though she had by now ceased to appear on the stage. Instead she worked at a dancing school, though not I think very regularly because her mother gave her a sufficient allowance to keep her. She was a slim, dark girl with almond-shaped eyes and finely-pencilled eyebrows which gave her a rather Ancient Egyptian look and some people found her beautiful. I did not quite do that, for her very small mouth with its sad, pinched expression detracted from her appearance. She suffered from a deep and congenital depression which even alcohol did little to relieve. This had been increased by an unreturned passion. Some years before my friend Hope had met her and made up to her. She had responded, with the result that he had got frightened, as he always did when girls showed an interest in him, and sheered away. But she was now in love with him and went through a long period of hopeless misery and dejection during which for months on end she never got out of bed before the evening.

When I first got to know Freda, as she was usually called, she was on her way to recovery. But we had both been through or were still going through the same trough of the love disease and on the strength of that we became friends. Unlike most dancers I have known she was intelligent and whenever she was not practising on her cello would sit in her room reading French and English literature. So we saw a good deal of one another and I was glad to have a girl to whom I could pour out all my thoughts and feelings as well as discuss books. Besides she was nearly always free because she went out little and had few friends. Thus it happened that once or twice a week I would either take her out or go round to her rooms. There we would sit and talk or listen to records. She would cook some eggs, we would make tea or open a bottle of wine and then I would stay on and spend the night with her. She had never had a lover before and I do not think that she got more than a vague pleasure from me, but we were company for one another during the long nights. I found too a sensuous pleasure from lying pressed against her naked body, for she had the finest skin I have ever known as well as a good figure. Sleeping with her, I said to myself, was like plunging through the seas clutching a young dolphin, yet because I was not in the least enamoured of her, I sometimes had reactions afterwards, as I think she did too. Indeed, we were never more than friends, drawn together by the loneliness that is the other side of the coin of love.

About a couple of years after this Freda got to know a very neurotic composer who had an addiction to virgins. She fell in love with him and they had an affair, after which I saw no more of her because he was jealous of me and made her promise to avoid my company. Although he was said to be impotent, he made her pregnant and she went down to her mother's house in the country to have her child. Then he committed suicide and I have heard nothing of her since. She was not a person who wrote letters.

10

My parents

Every few months I would go down to spend a few days at my parents' house at Edgeworth on the Cotswolds. No change of scene could possibly have been greater. I would find myself back again in a little world I had long outgrown and where, in spite of my war service, I was regarded as the black sheep of the family. The change of climate and environment was also considerable. From the lawn of our house, a converted Victorian farm, the valley dropped away in a gulf of beechwoods to a stream that meandered and tinkled far below. Seen from above, these tree-tops looked so soft and yielding that one could imagine jumping down onto them and being sustained on their summits. And they were endless. One could walk either up or down the valley for hours without coming out of them or else across Lord Bathurst's park on the other side as far as Cirencester – flat, but trees all the way.

After the din of London the silence was a marvel. By day the only sounds to be heard were the voices of the children coming out of school, the soft thud of someone chopping wood, the songs of the birds or a distant cockcrow. By night there were the hoots of the owls in the woods, the coughing of sheep, the drip of the rain upon the leaves. Whenever the air was still one could hear the whistle of the trains emerging from Sapperton tunnel, sounding from three miles away like the screams of demented animals. Since the village consisted of less than a dozen cottages scattered thinly under the trees and there was no practicable road across the valley, the only mechanical sound to be heard was the soft purr of the baker's van drawing up at the post office every morning.

I loved the place in winter. Feet sank in the carpet of brown leaves and looking up one saw against the blue sky a network of brown interlacing twigs and branches. The edge of the stream would be hung with icicles and if any snow fell one would be amazed to see the number of bird and animal tracks imprinted on its crisp surface. But May was the best month. On fine nights I used to sleep out on the lawn and lie awake listening to the squeaks of the hedgehogs as they scurried round me. Then before dawn I would be awakened by the charm of the birds. Thrushes, blackbirds, robins, linnets, tits, redstarts, blackcaps and chaffinches all nested in our garden or just outside it and sang in the half light with special sweetness. Soon the sun rose and in those empty hours before anyone was awake shy woodland birds such as woodpeckers and tree-creepers would steal unobtrusively in and hunt for insects on the trees. The call of the cuckoo was everywhere.

But in summer I did not like the Cotswolds. The advance of the year had brought all the variously tinted leaves to a common mediocrity of green. One could not go for a walk without waving a branch to keep off the flies that buzzed about one's head. If one wished to enter the woods one had to beat back the nettles that guarded them in thick serrated ranks like German soldiers on parade. One forced a way through and was at once aware of an uncanny silence. This was because the keepers had shot all the woodland birds except for an occasional jay, whose wild screams could be heard in the distance. Every now and then one would come on their gallows, from which the corpses of herons, sparrow-hawks, kestrels, kingfishers, magpies and jays hung in a mouldering line between stoats and weasels. Other signs of decay were there in the soft and squelching fungi, sometimes as large as hats, which grew on the tree trunks and on the rotting leaf mould beneath them, while in the glades the rabbits pullulated in their thousands wherever there was grass for them to eat. And all the time one had a limp feeling in the knee joints as though one's veins contained not blood but bath water and a sensation of heaviness in one's head as though one was digesting one's lunch in it. A cancerous proliferation appeared to be on the march in those millions and millions of small identical leaves, while at night the wild screeching and hooting of the owls seemed to proceed from the spirits of disease and madness.

But October put an end to all this. Then the beech trees turned to gold and copper and the phloxes in my mother's garden gave out their sweet, smoky, slightly incensed smell. Berries gleamed in the hedges and the old man's beard hung in trails of dusty white from every thorn bush. On fine days the sky had a pure transparency, like that of a starling's egg held up to the light.

My father's house was a three-storeyed edifice in grey Cotswold stone that stood up pertly and unashamedly like an out-sized dog kennel in complete disharmony with its surroundings. It was exactly the sort of house he would have designed himself if he had been an architect for, though all its proportions were wrong, it was solidly built, dry and comfortable. When my mother died he sold it to a retired inspector from Scotland Yard. Not long after there was a fire and it was burned out, but the inspector must have approved of its shape for he rebuilt it exactly as it had been before. The only part of it that I liked was the thatched summer-house and here when it was not too cold I used to sit and write every morning.

I must now say something about my father, for he has been with Hope the most important male figure in my life. In *A Life of One's Own* I painted him in somewhat black colours. The truth is that when I was a child I lived in great fear of him and as I entered adolescence he grew in my emotions at least to be a tyrant and despot, the symbol of all the forces that I was fighting. Although I have never in any other respect been inclined to neurosis, my feelings towards him at that time sometimes reached the level of hysteria. So exaggerated were they that when someone said to me, 'He seems a pleasant, brisk little man,' or else, 'Rather an insignificant chap really,' I felt a shock of incredulity. Little? Why he was a figure of enormous proportions, straight out of Tacitus or Dostoievsky.

In my childhood the violence of his behaviour to my mother and the rude, crushing tone in which he had often spoken to her had shocked me deeply. Then in my adolescence I had developed my personal quarrel with him because I was rebelling against everything that he and his class stood for. I think that the war would have put an end to this by making me independent of him, but just at this time his nerves went to pieces because he was suffering from prostate trouble and so he became very irritable. But after his recovery from this I had in fairness to modify my opinion of his character. He had been genial and appreciative when he had come out to see me in Yegen and had acted with tact and sympathy at the time of my breach with Ralph. And now he was giving me an allowance of £100 a year, which was a thing entirely against his principles because he disapproved of my life and thought that a man of my age should be able to support himself. So I felt grateful and did my best to like him better.

He had, I could see, a number of admirable qualities. The first of these was a sense of justice. To give an example of this, he sent back the bounty that he had earned for guarding the London railway lines during the war because he considered that he had not earned it. In reply he got a letter from the appropriate department informing him that since there was no precedent for taking back pay awards he would have to keep it. Then he hated all boastfulness and exaggeration. In the election after the Second World War he took such a dislike to Churchill's talks on the radio that, though he was a dyed-in-the-wool Conservative, he was almost glad when Labour won. Attlee was a man after his own heart, cool, modest and given to understatement. Since he was quite incapable of appreciating genius or imagination, he distrusted Churchill, as so many Conservatives did.

But if in his dealings with the world my father was humane and conscientious, limited of course and inclined to abruptness, but well liked by his neighbours and by the cottagers, he was a difficult man to get on with in the family. His natural impatience was aggravated by his deafness and he was always fighting off boredom because nothing interested him. How to fill in the day was his great problem and he tried to solve it by riding for an hour or two every morning and taking up carpentry in the evenings. This led to a proposal that might have been of help to him. A Swedish master-carpenter had set up a workshop near Sapperton where he employed half a dozen men making beautiful and expensive furniture. My father was fond of calling in and watching him at work and one day this man suggested that they should go into partnership and that he should take over the business side. This would have suited him very well because he had a taste for business, but after considering it for some time he decided to refuse because, as he said, it was not proper for a gentleman to go into trade. I think that a better reason may have been that he could not bear to tie himself down to anything. He wanted to keep his liberty, however much it bored him to have no occupation.

My father's temperament then and lack of profession kept him permanently restless and dissatisfied. Although he made efforts to control himself, he was apt to break out at any moment into some sharp and irritable expression. He needed a whipping-boy to work off his feelings on and my mother usually filled that office for him. But I was on his nerves too because ever since my birth he had been jealous of my mother's love for me and then, as I grew up, had found himself saddled with a son whom he could not understand and to whom he had now been forced into the position of giving an allowance. So I could never go down to Edgeworth without his taking me for a walk in order to tell me that, though he and my mother were always glad to see me, he would not tolerate my coming and settling myself on him. It was an unnecessary warning because I only went there when invited and then solely in order to see my mother, and at the end of a week was glad to get back to London. After that he would give me a lecture on economy and tell me that I ought to put by something every month out of my income. My income of £160 a year!

I felt my position acutely because I hated being dependent on him. I have always been a hard worker and now my whole mind was set on producing a book that would succeed. Yet whatever I took up seemed to go wrong. I had a feeling in my bones that I was a real writer, yet when I looked at what I had written I could see no evidence for it. And naturally enough, as time went by without my finishing anything, my father could see no evidence for it either. He had the habit when he was dressing of talking aloud to himself and as my room was next to his I could hear what he said. As a rule he was complaining of my mother: 'I won't have it. No I won't have it. I'll tell her she can't. She must go back to her family. Yes, she must go back to her family and live with them.'

But sometimes he was talking about me: 'That boy! His friends may think he's a charming fellow, but *I* know what he is. He's a waster – a procrastinating waster. That's it – an *irresolute, procrastinating waster.*'

My dreams today tell me a good deal about the anxieties I suffered from at that time. I rarely dream of Carrington, but I often dream about the difficulties I had in writing and of my uncertainties about myself. It is the problem of every young man who feels he has a vocation for the arts, but it was aggravated by my dependence upon my father and by my wish to show that I deserved the help he was giving me. 'I must make good' – that was a phrase that rang in my head all the time. It was no longer enough for me to taste and enjoy life, I must do something that would justify my existence, both in my own eyes and in those of my parents.

That autumn of 1925, while I was staying at Edgeworth, a big quarrel blew up between my parents. It started with my brother Blair, who was now an announcer in the B.B.C., stationed at Manchester, becoming engaged to his typist. From most points of view it was an acceptable match, for she came from a distinguished Irish family, the Gwynns, and was an intelligent and well-educated girl who had got a degree at Oxford. But she did not have a penny and, though my father raised no objection to that, he asked my brother, who was just twenty-three, to put off getting formally engaged for a year so as to be sure that he knew his own mind. However Rhoda Gwynn's mother, who was a very determined lady, came to see my father and forced him to agree to the marriage taking place within a few months, saying that if it were not her daughter would be compromised.

My father did not like being overruled, especially by women, and besides there was a financial problem. He would have to increase my brother's allowance to £200 a year or more and this at a moment when he was about to buy a second horse and to engage a groom. Not that he was at all short of money. He was in the supertax class, with an income of over £2,000 a year and on top of that living well below his means. But he felt that he had to consider the future. He was a man who worried a great deal about that.

At this moment he had an unpleasant surprise. All my mother's income, which in spite of her father's once considerable wealth amounted to no more than a quarter of my father's, came from the York Street Linen Company of Belfast which had been founded jointly by Lord Dunleath and my grandfather. For some time back my father had been urging her to spread her investments, but she had always refused to do this out of loyalty to her family. Now suddenly it appeared that the firm was in difficulties. Ordinary shares ceased paying and £1,000,000 had to be written off. Although this did not involve a large loss for my mother because all her shares had been in debentures, my father was furious and blamed my uncle

Ogilvie, who was her trustee and a director of the firm, for not having advised her to sell out in time.

Now there was one thing that my mother, who was usually so gentle and submissive, would not stand, and that was an imputation on any member of her family. She was intensely loyal to them all and particularly to my uncle Ogilvie, who was her favourite brother. My father knew this and wished, with one part of his mind, to avoid a painful scene. But with another part he wished to put the blame firmly on her and on my uncle, of whom he was intensely jealous, and to frighten her with a picture of what he called 'our impending ruin,' which would compel them to sell their house and move to a villa. Indeed he had got himself so worked up that he half believed this himself.

A scene then was impending, but so long as my brother's holiday lasted, my father put it off, though keeping my mother in a state of nerves about it by saying at odd moments, 'We've got to talk this over. We've got to have it out together.' He was very given to making remarks of this sort and if one went into his smoking-room suddenly one would some-times hear him muttering them to himself. Grievances and complaints were perpetually accumulating in his mind, but he never came out with them suddenly, but only after long digestion and preparation and then in as formal a way as possible. So this time, when the day for the fatal confron-tation came, he spent an hour at his table preparing what he would say and making notes.

My mother was then invited to come in. 'I think we ought to have a little talk.' With a soothing smile on his face and in a voice that seemed to be reason itself he opened up the subject. But long practice had taught him exactly what to say in order to wear her down and confuse her naturally muddled mind and then, when he had got her to the point of utter pros-tration, he plunged:

'You realize what our situation is. Thanks to your refusing to take my advice about your shares we shall now have to sell this house and move to a small villa in a suburb. You will no longer be able to have a nice garden or to go for walks in the country. You will no longer be able to do parish work. I shall have to give up my horses. That is the penalty we shall both have to pay for your having squandered a large part of our income and of our boys' income after us. And then instead of coming to me and apolo-gizing like a dutiful wife for the injury you have done me, you don't so much as hint that you are sorry but fling your family in my face as though it were I and not they who were responsible.'

My mother was utterly unfit to stand up to this sort of treatment. She felt that she was being unjustly accused for until now York Street had paid a very high dividend. But she also felt to blame and in her confusion and distress, mixed with indignation, she offered to do anything he wanted. But he was not so easily appeased:

'Now listen to me,' he went on. 'I don't want to treat you unkindly. But I've put up with your family for more than thirty years and I'm not going to put up with them any longer.'

'How can you say you put up with them? You refuse to see them.'

'I've had to put up with their influence on you and with your disloyal and undutiful conduct. But now I'm pretty well fed up with it. Here am I – I give up my whole life for you. There is nothing to keep *me* here – I have no interests in this place. I am here simply and solely to make you happy. In return for that I expect you to treat me as every good wife treats her husband. You can see now the effects of preferring your brother Ogilvie's advice to mine. I won't say that he is not in many respects a straightforward man, but I think that he has behaved in this case in a very peculiar manner. I don't wish to say anything against him but clearly – anyone will tell you so – it is not for a business man to entice his family into putting all their money into his firm when he knows it is shaky. As for himself – I know by several things that have been dropped that he will not feel this cut. He has taken good care to feather his own nest and spread his investments. Not that he is not perfectly entitled to do that – but I can't say I call it exactly proper conduct.'

My father had now gone too far. My mother flared up in defence of her brother and did not spare her anger and contempt for her husband. After that she broke out into sobbing and trembling. He, frightened at the state to which he had reduced her and which even after thirty-two years of such scenes appeared to him unexpected and unaccountable, began to speak more kindly. She said her heart hurt her and he offered her a cigarette though she had never smoked in her life. Then, getting up, he said he would not take any steps at present, but that they must talk it over more calmly another time. 'I only wish for your happiness,' he said, taking her to the window. 'Look out there. Everything you see I have made for you and keep up for your sake. My whole life is spent in thinking of your pleasure. How can you say that I worry or ill-treat you?'

When my parents quarrelled I became the peace-maker. I took my mother for a walk and told her that she should not get so excited. He did not really mean what he said. He would certainly not sell the house – that was only said to frighten her.

'I live all the year alone with him. He has taken everything away from me, he is jealous of whatever I have, or whatever I do. I have only to like someone for him to dislike them. Because I enjoyed keeping two cows and some hens, he sold them. All my happiness depends on him and yet I cannot for five minutes trust him. He is charming one moment, then without any reason at all horrid the next.'

'You know that he is very fond of you.'

'A nice kind of fondness! There are two distinct people in your father. He can be perfectly fascinating, but there is something black in him and one never knows when it will come out. He used to have fits of anger – they lasted a few hours or a day or two and were then over, but now he is gloomy for weeks and weeks and so bitter I cannot understand it. What has he got to be so bitter about? Yet sometimes he positively lifts up his lip and sneers at me.'

She went on:

'I am too old for these continual scenes. He is killing me and one day he will give me a stroke that will finish me. He goes on till he has worn me out – nothing less than that will stop him. I would sooner be dead than go on living like this. Just one thing keeps me alive – that is the thought that if I died he would marry again. Oh yes he would. He would pick up some woman or other. That is what he is itching for. But I shall live as long as I am able in order to disappoint him.'

I said this was ridiculous.

'Then what does he sit sighing all day for? For hours he sits shut up in his room groaning and sighing. It's not natural. I'm not accustomed to depressed people. Here we have everything that anyone can desire – riches, health, friends, children. Everyone else is happy and he sits sighing and lamenting like that.'

My father all that day was very restless, gloomy and timid. After lunch he took me for a walk and began in an unhappy and plaintive voice:

'I really do not know what to do about your mother. She is so difficult. I am afraid she is getting old very quickly. I cannot control her any longer: if I say a word to her about money matters, which I must do, she becomes very excited and pours out on me a stream of violent abuse. That's no more than I'm accustomed to. I've had to put up with it all my life, and she is less violent than she used to be. Her illness has softened her, and yet it has left her more touchy than ever. I don't know what to do. I don't want to boast, but I give up endless things for her, I spend half my life trying to make her happy, and yet I know as a positive fact that she tells people here that I ill-treat her.'

This last statement was completely untrue. If my mother was anything, she was loyal and I have often seen her trying to cover up my father's rudeness to her which was apt to break out in public at any time. But his deafness no doubt made him feel suspicious of what she said and the trembling aggrieved voice in which he spoke was pathetic.

I wrote down this scene as it occurred in my diary for I was sitting in the hall outside and could overhear most of what was said and my mother repeated the rest to me afterwards. I have given an abbreviated version of it here because it illustrates my father's character and the terms on which he lived with my mother. And in an autobiography that can only be published posthumously, if indeed at all, the truth must be told unless it is likely to affect people who may still be alive or, in a few cases, their descendants. Thus, though my father exercised an almost total control over my mother, that was not enough for him. He wanted absolute power over her in everything because, like many regular officers of those days, he enjoyed the exercise of power for its own sake. People, especially wives, must be disciplined. And then there was of course his jealousy of her relatives. Because of this it had long rankled with him that under the terms of her marriage settlement he did not have control of her money and that my uncle Ogilvie was her trustee. The failure of York Street thus gave him an opportunity for raising hell about an arrangement that offended his pride. Besides he was always imagining to himself the catastrophes that might occur in the future. 'Supposing', he said to me, 'Blair were to crack up and I should have to support him with his wife and children. I have very great responsibilities and I cannot live up to them unless I have the whole of her income in my hands.' Yet so far was he from being ruined that when my mother died fourteen years later, he was much better off than he had ever been before. He could afford to buy one of the largest houses in Cheltenham, with a small park around it.

As to my mother's fear that he was longing to get rid of her and marry someone else, I would say that there was a certain measure of truth in this. She was eight years older than he was and they had not had marital relations since my brother's birth. Yet what I think weighed more with him than his occasional lust for some younger woman was his chronic restlessness. He was for ever trying to change his life, to sell his house, to get rid of this or that, and yet there was nothing else that he wanted. So far as his nature permitted him to love anyone except himself, he loved my mother and, though many things about her irritated him, he admired her Christian goodness and selflessness. And she, whatever she might say in anger, was all her life in love with him.

A sequel to this quarrel over my uncle Ogilvie took place two years later. My mother used to pay him a brief visit at his house in County Down every three or four years, but neither he nor any of her brothers or sisters were ever invited to stay with us. My father would not have them. Then one summer my uncle and aunt came over to spend a fortnight with some friends of theirs in Oxfordshire, only thirty miles away. My mother therefore approached my father very timidly and asked if they might be invited to lunch one day as they had never seen our house, or alternatively that he should drive her over to lunch there. 'Certainly not,' replied my father. 'I can't have all this indiscriminate coming and going. In any case I consider that the less I see of your family and the less they see of me the better for all of us.'

My mother was put to the deepest distress and embarrassment by this answer, for my uncle Ogilvie knew (or was supposed to know) nothing of the ill feeling my father nursed against him and had written in the most cordial terms suggesting a meeting. As young men he and my father had been good friends and they had never quarrelled. My mother had therefore to write and explain that my father was ill. Then my father announced that he would be obliged to go up to London for the day. This seemed to my mother a heaven-sent opportunity and, sure of a favourable reply, she suggested that her brother could come over to lunch while he was away.

'No one enters my house in my absence,' replied my father, 'who cannot enter it when I am present. I won't have him here.'

A few days later a telegram arrived to say that my uncle was dead. He had had a heart attack. My father was at once stricken with remorse. He drove my mother over to see my aunt Grace and showed the tact and good-feeling of which he was always capable in emergencies. After all, the cause of his jealousy had been removed so that he could well afford it. My mother forgave him as she invariably did and they got on better from then onwards.

I will conclude this portrait of my father by quoting a few of his characteristic sayings. The first that comes into my head is one that I have often heard him use. It is, 'A coat and a skirt and a well ordered mind are all that a woman requires'. On another occasion, after saying that he would like to garden in the summer after dinner but could not because he had to dress, he went on, 'For if one gives up dressing for dinner one will soon find oneself sleeping with one's cook'. Then, after seeing the village bus go by, 'Yes, very useful things. But I'm afraid they are a great temptation to the village people to go down to the pictures and enjoy themselves.' Another of his sayings was: 'Anyone who can't say all he has to say in a quarter of an hour is not worth talking to.' The last that I will quote has a slightly sinister tinge. He once said to my sister-in-law, 'I should like to have a dog for my own purposes.' What he meant, I imagine, was a dog that would come to heel when he called it.

In the manner of Suetonious, when describing one of the Roman emperors, I will give a few of his habits at this time. He rose at eight-thirty and after dressing and saying his prayers, he would take a short trot up and down the drive and eat an apple. Then came breakfast, a less hazardous meal for his family than it had once been, and after that he would read a chapter from one of St Paul's Epistles or else a few pages of a commentary on him that had been recommended by the vicar. What he made of these works I cannot imagine, for his mind was much too limited and matter of fact for him to understand a word of what that subtle and argumentative Apostle to the Gentiles had to say, but he believed that there was an expert on every subject and that the clergy and their precursors the Apostles were the experts on spiritual matters. After that he would attend to business, calculating his monthly expenditure and inditing letters to his stockbroker until the groom brought round his horse and he went off on it, not so much because he liked riding as because he thought it was good for his liver.

In summer he gardened a bit in the afternoons or else went for a walk. He liked to visit the cottagers and chat for a few minutes with the older men. Then tea. About once a week two or three of our neighbours would be invited to this meal and a large assortment of excessively stodgy cakes, baked by our cook Mrs Webb – the Mrs being an honorary title, since she was unmarried – would be laid out before them with, on gala occasions, cucumber sandwiches. In the summer a few small tennis parties would be given at which whisky and soda would be offered to the male players, but only three or four times a year would anyone be invited to lunch. It was not an invitation that can have been accepted with much enthusiasm, for Mrs Webb's cooking was of the plainest kind, and since we had no ice-box and the butcher called only once a week, the meat would not always be fresh. My mother never noticed this because she disliked eating and to my father, who had the digestion of an ostrich, all foods were alike. The only rule he made was that oranges were not to be introduced into the house, because he disliked their smell. He had long ceased to invite any visitors to stay except my brother and his wife and myself, and once a year his sister Maude and her husband for a weekend. So the days passed monotonously, my father going off to his carpentry shop every winter evening after tea and after dinner falling asleep over a light novel, while my mother, who woke very early every morning, dozed in the armchair opposite.

Around this time my father, who had always been a heavy pipe smoker, decided to give up pipes and limit himself to a few cigarettes a day. To help him do this he would cut a cigarette in two with a pair of scissors, take four puffs at it and then start walking up and down his study till the time had elapsed for him to allow himself the other half. I would hear his sharp step – he always hit the ground very hard with his heels – as I sat working in the drawing-room below and it recalled to me John Gabriel Borkman's perpetual pacing up and down in Ibsen's play. I had started smoking too when I settled in London – for before that I did not smoke at all – so, as my father chose to regard the ability to give it up as a sign of having a strong will, I would sometimes say in a casual voice that I had temporarily decided to abstain too. It cost me little effort since I was new to it and did not inhale, but the ease with which I did without it greatly annoyed him since he regarded me as irresolute and weak-willed and my success as a reflection on himself.

As he grew older he adopted a more stoical attitude to life. He knew that what he lacked was self-control and he made great and on the whole successful efforts to attain it. He had a more pressing need of it than most people because he was so often seething with impatience and irritability as well as tormented by fantasies about losing his money. He had besides a mania for giving orders in a sharp, rude voice, for the consciousness of exercising power was his greatest pleasure, and this he endeavoured to check too. In many ways he was a typical example of the infantry officer of the Boer War period. If he had not gone deaf and had to leave the army he would have been one of those irascible colonels I used to run into during the First World War. They were far more despotic than those in the German army, where there was no rule that an officer must not speak to a private except in the presence of an N.C.O. Even then they were anachronisms.

I have much less to say about my mother because I have described her in *A Life of One's Own* at some length. She was a person who loved the sight of the human face, the sound of the human voice, but cared little for social life because she had no gift for it. She knew that her wandering style of conversation bored most of her acquaintances. She was a realist about people and turned a shrewd though kindly eye on them: but a romantic about other things, enjoying the country, foreign travel, new scenes and also books, in so far as her limited faculties, which had been worn down by my father and were circumscribed by her moral and religious views and class upbringing, would allow her. Like so many women of the Victorian Age, she had never got any pleasure from sex and thought that this was a thing that men wanted and that their wives must provide for them. She was very ambitious for her sons and had a snobbish wish for them to have grand friends because that would impress her family who lived on a larger scale than we did. Yet she was totally unsnobbish for herself.

But above everything she was religious. She read the Bible for half an hour in bed every morning and got great consolation from going to church and communion on Sundays. However she was liberal in her religious views. She had strong reservations about the definition of the Trinity in the Nicene Creed because with her natural shrewdness she did not believe that the theologians could know all that they claimed to. Her three rocks of belief were the fatherhood of God, the teaching of the Sermon on the Mount and the future life, and she set little store by Original Sin, the Crucifixion and the Redemption. Although she was steeped in the Old Testament, she regarded it as a mixture of history and fable and by no means inspired, except in brief passages. The history of the Church for her was that of the steady increase of the power of the priesthood, which she disliked. But she lived her religion. That is a thing which very few of even the most pious churchgoers did in those days, and it made a deep impression on me.

My mother had two main occupations. One was gardening and the other was parish work. She loved flowers, both the wild and the garden ones, and remembered their names when she could not remember anything else. She was also exceptionally energetic and active for her age. I have seen her run down the drive when she was well on in her seventies, just for the fun of it, and she was so supple in her joints that to the end of her life she would sit cross-legged on the ground beside the fire. In this I take after her, for at the time of writing I habitually run up and down the stairs. Parish work involved going round the cottages, sometimes providing warm clothes and financial assistance, visiting the sick and above all taking an interest in the children. The revolt of the labouring classes against the gentry had already begun and it required considerable tact to continue making these visits. But my mother was incapable of being patronizing. She felt more at ease with the cottagers than she did with her own class and she adored children and knew how to talk to them. With her cheerful, affectionate smile and her ready flow of conversation she was always welcome. There were two organizations through which she worked – the Women's Institute which got up lectures and private theatricals, and the narrower and more churchy Mothers' Union, both of which had their local headquarters in the neighbouring village of Miserden. From being at one time the president of both of these, she resigned in favour of a working-class woman when she thought that that had become desirable, and served loyally under her. It was not in her nature to boss anyone and yet she could stand up strongly for her principles. Thus when the new, active rector of Miserden tried to compel a girl who had been our housemaid to marry against her wishes the father of her illegitimate child who had jilted her for someone else, my mother defended her unwillingness to do so and my father backed her up. Unlike other pious people of that time she refused to distinguish between married and unmarried mothers for, though extremely prudish herself about sex, she did not think that the aim of Christianity was to achieve respectability.

My own relations with my mother at this time were not always smooth or easy. She disapproved of my choice of profession, not from disparagement of literature, which she thought highly of though she had almost ceased to read it, but because she could not believe that I was likely to succeed in it. The real writers, she thought, were either people of mature years who had acquired experience of life by following some other profession or they were geniuses like Dickens who threw off while still young a book which was an immediate popular success. She did not understand the long apprenticeship that might be needed for writers whose talents were of a modest kind and who had to be given time in which to develop. Then she had a certain irritating way of nagging at me and making indirect allusions to my inability to earn money that had the effect of shutting me up in myself. The gulf too between my life in London and her moral principles with regard to sex was too great to be bridged, so that I could never talk to her about myself or confide in her in any way. But in spite of this we found subjects in common and my affection for her never varied. Her warm welcoming smile, which came out of the deep reserves of her love, was something I could always respond to.

For my father, on the other hand, I had none of these feelings. We had nothing in common. He belonged to an utterly different species of humanity from myself. I could sympathize with his troubles – one of the greatest of which was having a son such as I was – but I could not really like him, much less love him. His friendly moods were too often and too abruptly succeeded by hostile ones. I think that I have never in my life, except perhaps between the ages of twelve and fifteen, got pleasure from his company and I believe that the same can be said of him with regard to myself. We had to make the best of the absurd link that bound us.

I have written at some length about my parents in spite of their being, by the standards of the world, unremarkable. But they had a deep and lasting effect upon my character, so much so that I am often conscious of being made up of little more than a mixture of their qualities. Thus if my love of life and people, with such imagination as I possess, comes from my mother, I owe my self-reliance and my taste for solitude and independence to my father. If too I have learned to restrain my natural exuberance and bent for exaggeration, it is because I hear his stern voice inside me. Besides in this narrative I have set myself to write chiefly on the people who have most influenced me without regard to whether or not they had intelligence or talent. All God's chillun got wings and some of the people I have most liked have belonged to the ordinary run of humanity. If many of my best friends have been writers or intellectuals I do not wish to advance any exaggerated claim for them. It is not they who make the world go round and I trust their judgement on such matters as politics, where common sense is the first requisite, rather less than I do that of the average small shopkeeper or working man.

But now I have to speak of a person who, though little known, was both highly educated and had a good mind. This was the rector of Edgeworth, Frank James.

Parson James, or, as he preferred to be called, Father James, was the brother of the squire, Alfred James, that shy, woman-fearing recluse of the Manor. He was a big, burly man of around sixty with a wife and three grown-up sons. He had been a good Classical scholar at Oxford and had kept up his Latin and Greek so well that he could read Plato fluently without a crib. His chief intellectual interest lay in philosophy, and the philosophers he was most addicted to were Plato, Hegel and, though some way behind these, Bergson. He was besides very musical and spent his evenings playing records while his afternoons were devoted to water-colour painting. In his younger days he used to spend a month every summer in the Alps, for he had an almost religious passion for mountains, was a strong walker and a keen botanist. Now he went to Scotland every August where he made notes and brief sketches which he spent the rest of the year turning into paintings. They were very bad paintings, usually of a piece of moorland with a burn or waterfall in the foreground and blue or lilac mountains rising behind, capped by clouds or vapours, and, since it took him only a couple of hours to paint one, his study was packed with them. He liked to pull them out and show them to visitors, but I think that he regarded them rather as mementoes of the happiest moments of his life than as works of art, for he never visited London or went to picture galleries.

I used to tap on his window two or three times a week and he would let me in himself and we would sit for an hour or two talking in his dark, untidy study, furnished with black horsehair armchairs and thick with tobacco smoke. I enjoyed these conversations. He was a very lovable man with a strong sense of humour and, though he had ceased to read much literature, he retained his old liking for Wordsworth, Shelley and Edward Lear. He was as modest as he was frank and treated me as though I was a man of his own age and attainments, asking my opinion on philosophical matters and speaking of the religious doubts that had assailed him after his ordination. Although he was by no means a hermit like his brother Alfred, he saw as few people as possible outside his own family because the ordinary run of our neighbours bored him. I think that his happiest days had been those he had spent at Oxford where, after coming down, he had held some clerical incumbency until he retired to Edgeworth. All his friends were from there.

The strongest thing in his life was his religion, but it was a kind of religion which I had not met with before and which differed greatly from my mother's. There was no asceticism or self-sacrifice in it, no guilt about possessing money or fellow-feeling for the unemployed or the poor. These things were outside his province and he had probably never spoken to an industrial worker in his life. He was self-indulgent about food, lazy about visiting his parishioners, though they numbered only a couple of dozen, and spoke with impatience of those who thought that the essence of religion lay in doing good. For him it was a matter of attaining spiritual purity and he was so careful about this that when I asked him something about Plato's *Symposium* he replied in a grave voice that he had not read it. To get some idea of his religious feelings one had to see him conducting a service. The warm, humorous, easy-going person that he was in ordinary life became transformed into the priest of God, grave, solemn, dignified, entrusted with the sacred privilege of administering the sacraments. His sermons were always far above the heads of his congregation. Very often they began with the sentence, 'A wise man once said', and that wise man would be either Plato or Hegel. His attitude to religion was, I think, not unlike that of Plotinus – that is, by purifying the mind and the spirit one drew closer to the reality of God, who was to be approached by some inner sense rather than by the reason or the intelligence. Yet the intellectual approach was valuable too and that was why he read the philosophers who could give some support to his beliefs, just as an art lover will read books on aesthetics to show him that his preference for Raphael or Rembrandt to Landseer or Sargent is not just a matter of taste or opinion. His favourite gospel was John and I imagine that he thought poorly of Mark and Matthew, who were my mother's favourites.

But he never discussed religion with me or tried to influence me in any way except by lending me Newman's *Apologia,* whose pure and elegant style enchanted me; or a book by a German theologian on the Numinous. I imagine that with his natural tact he thought that religious belief was a subject too personal to be broached except to those who asked for instruction in it and that if I had it in me to believe I should find my own way there. But my conversations with him did lead to one rather paradoxical result. Up to this time I had taken early communion mainly to please my mother, though I also enjoyed the beauty and solemnity of the service in our little church with its Anglo-Saxon foundations where the trees waved and rustled outside the clear panes of glass. But when I realized the importance that he attached to it, I saw that I had been acting dishonestly and ceased to attend. My mother was so hurt by this that she scarcely spoke to me for a week, but he did not refer to it and treated me exactly as before.

Frank James's wife was a plump, bustling, dressy woman who never opened a book but who must once have been nice-looking. Besides providing a good table, she saw to all the business affairs of the house, for her husband threw every typewritten letter he received unopened into the waste-paper basket, from which they had to be retrieved afterwards. Tax demands, bills, cheques, formal communications from the Bishop of Gloucester, all went into it. She was more socially inclined than he was and twice a week gave a tea party at which he would make a brief appearance. Then after consuming a few slices of her delicious chocolate cake, he would retire again to his study because polite chitter-chatter bored him.

However some time in the late twenties she died of a cancer in the rectum, which she had been too prudish to admit to, and their daughter Margaret came to keep house for her father. She was a tall, willowy girl with large, expressive eyes, very musical, given to folk dancing and singing and to recording bird songs, but I never got to know her because she had an aversion to men. All her friends were young women of her own age. She had become a Catholic like her monkish elder brother John and no doubt her father would now have gone over too if the Roman Church had recognized Anglican orders. But he could not bring himself to admit the invalidity of his priestly functions. Later he developed arthritis and went to live with his son John who ran a preparatory school for Catholic boys in the North of England. Before his death, which occurred not long afterwards, he joined the Roman Church, and the parish of Edgeworth was incorporated with that of Duntisbourne across the valley.

My affection for parson James introduced me to a set of ideas and feelings that were quite new to me – those of the Oxford Movement. They were not ideas that were suited to my temperament, but I was glad to become acquainted with them because they increased my understanding of Anglicanism and of the intellectual and religious depth of which it was capable. Literary people often learn to extend the range of their human sympathies, but respect or understanding for modes of thinking or feeling that are different from their own is not usually one of their qualities. Another thing that he did for me was to encourage my love of botany. By keeping his eyes open on his daily walks he had got to know the locality of every rare or uncommon flower within a range of five or six miles. And our district provided some very rare flowers indeed. But he never got on with my mother, whose religious views were antithetic to his own.

My great-aunt

There was one person with whom I was almost as closely involved at this time as I was with Carrington and whom I saw far more frequently. This was my great-aunt Addie. In conversation with my friends I called her Tiz, which was the Serbian for aunt, because after my return from the Balkans in 1912 I had used code names for my relations in my correspondence with Hope. This name stuck as it seemed to suit her. But her proper appellation was the Baroness von Roeder, since after the death of her first husband, Mr Bower, which took place some time before I was born, she had married an old Prussian junker who was the military attaché at the German embassy in London. I remember seeing him around 1901, a Teutonic giant of a man, very slow in all his movements and wearing a vague, good-natured smile spread over his large face with its dropping white moustaches. She brought him to stay with us in Essex and one day on a short walk he got one leg over a stile and then could not lift the other, while she, a tiny gnat-like creature, so tightly corsetted that she seemed to come almost in two at the waist, buzzed round him screaming instructions.

My great-aunt had been born in 1838, or perhaps even earlier. Her father, Mr Green, had been a London wine merchant, but either because he found London life too expensive or because he wanted to see the world, he set off with his wife and four children to tour Europe in his carriage. Charmed by Vienna, he decided to settle there and so it was in that city and indeed, since he had good introductions, in aristocratic circles, that my great-aunt Adeline grew to womanhood. But the gaiety of Viennese life was offset for the Green family by a succession of tragedies: their only son died, their youngest daughter ran off with a drunkard and died too, while my great-aunt and her younger sister Rose, who later married my grand-father, were both struck deaf – of grief, as my aunt declared, but really after an attack of scarlet fever. My grandmother continued to hear a little with the aid of a long, black, flexible trumpet which she held out to one like a toy snake, but my great-aunt was stone deaf when I first knew her and, lacking as she was in patience, had never learned to lip-read. To communicate with her one had to write on little scraps of paper, but since she never stopped talking for a moment and besides had bad eyesight, by the time she had deciphered the answer one had written to her question, she had forgotten what that question was. All intercourse with her was therefore attended with confusions and misunderstandings, but that did not trouble her because she liked to do all the talking herself.

'Considered wisely,' she would say, 'my deafness has been the greatest blessing of my life because it has saved me from having to listen to other people's foolish nonsense.'

Tiz lived in a large first-floor flat at 23 Ashley Place, opposite the entrance to Westminster Cathedral. Once perhaps comfortable, it now presented the dreariest of aspects, cluttered with heavy Victorian furniture and lit by gas instead of electricity because my aunt regarded this 'new invention' as dangerous. Since the windows were never opened and the gas pipes leaked a little, the air was stale and heavy and since the rooms were never swept, because the servant was in a perpetual state of 'working to rule', a cloud of dust would rise up when one sat down on a chair or sofa. The palms and aspidistras and the spotted-leaved laurels that grew in the window-boxes or in large, hideous china vases on the floor only just managed to keep alive and some of them had in fact died and not been replaced. There was a smell of age and stagnation everywhere.

I used to have tea with my great-aunt one afternoon in every week, as well as take her out to lunch at a restaurant on Sundays. At five o'clock – that is, half an hour late – I would ring the bell of her flat. At once it would be answered from some distant apartment by a sharp, shrill yapping which increased and became sharper and shriller until it was clear that it was just inside. Then the door would be unbolted and opened an inch on the chain, a face would peer through and the chain be removed. A sour, elderly female, clad in a blue and white apron, would say 'Madam is expecting you', while a black smooth-haired dog about the size of a rat, only with thin spindly legs and pointed ears, would retreat, still barking furiously, down the passage. I would take off my hat and overcoat and follow it into the drawing room and there a tiny little woman, dressed in black silk, with her black hair plastered down on either side of her head, would be waiting to embrace me.

'My dear boy, I'm *so* relieved to see you. I was just saying to Eliza that I feared something serious must have happened to you. The streets are so dangerous nowadays. For you know you *promised* to be here at four sharp and now it's past five. My clock, which is *never* fast, says seven minutes past five. But now let's sit down and be cosy. First of all I must tell you that I've found a new, large cream bun at Lyons. Really delicious – only costs 8½d.

137

I'm sure that when you taste it you'll agree with me. And then I have some *very* important things to discuss with you. We'll have our tea first and then go into them calmly and quietly.'

We sat down to nibble a stale Swiss roll and the disgusting cream bun and to drink strong Indian tea. And then the important things we had to discuss would come up. Every week there were some very important things. Often they were to do with the trunks and boxes which filled the small spare bedroom and the bathroom (I doubt if she had had a bath for twenty years) for she was anxious that as her heir I should open them and inspect the treasures she was bequeathing to me. But since they were all locked the first problem was to find the keys that fitted them. She had half a dozen bunches of these, each containing from twenty to thirty, and claimed that she knew most of them – which belonged to that green leather hat-box she had lost at Vienna sixty years before, which to that large black portmanteau that she had left at her bungalow at Dieppe in the 1890s, and she wanted to go through them with me. But for that an entire day would be needed and the servant must be sent out from breakfast to supper so that she should know nothing about what we were doing. At the back of this plan lay her hope of drawing me more closely to herself by interesting me in the inheritance she was leaving me as well as of having me entirely alone with her for the whole day. Every few weeks she would bring her plan up, but I always found some way of postponing it, so that it was not till after her relegation to a home for the senile, when the flat had to be cleared and given up, that I opened them and found them to be full of mouldering mid-Victorian dresses, cutlery, wine glasses and so forth – all things of little or no value.

We did however investigate a few cupboards and in one of these came on half a dozen cases of champagne, for until the First World War my great-aunt had been given to lavish entertainment. She offered them to me and I took them back with me in a taxi, intending to give a party on them, but most of the bottles I found to have gone flat. It used to embarrass me to listen to her telling me what I would inherit on her death and lamenting that she had put so much of her capital into an annuity, and it has only been recently, on passing the age of seventy-five myself, that I have realized that this is one of the subjects that most preoccupies the old. For their future life lies in their heirs and one of their greatest pleasures consists in planning how their death will benefit them.

Every morning of her life, wet or fine, snow or shower, my great-aunt would walk down Victoria Street to the Army and Navy Stores. Here she would remain for about an hour, visiting in turn the different departments, spending perhaps a shilling or two – fourpence on margarine, fourpence on Frankfurter sausages, threepence on soap or matches. She regarded the

Stores as certain pious old women do their church and took the greatest pride in its alterations and improvements. This made her a familiar figure to the liftmen and shop assistants as well as to many of the customers – a tiny, very dignified old lady clad in a short fur coat fringed with twenty cats' tails that bobbed and swayed as she walked, with below it a black or green silk skirt that billowed out till it reached the ground, and, balanced on her head, a large velours hat decorated with a scarlet puff and a plume of green feathers. One day it occurred to her that the scarlet puff might be taken as a sign that she was a communist, so she at once had it dyed black. Certainly no other such strange and antiquated figure was to be seen in the neighbourhood and rumour had it that the reason why her purchases were so trifling was that she was immensely rich and like so many other rich old women a miser. But she had the lack of self-consciousness of the Victorian lady who is sure of her rank in society and with that an indifference to being stared at and an affability that was devoid of condescension to persons in a less fortunate social position. Thus she would stop and speak to anyone – the flower woman and the match-seller in the street, the liftmen and shop assistants at the Stores – and although she could not understand a word they said to her in reply she professed to know all their histories. This readiness to talk to everyone as well as her fantastic appearance made her popular and, except on busy days, when she became a nuisance, she would be greeted with friendly smiles. No doubt they thought of her as the Stores' mascot.

My great-aunt tried hard to entice me to accompany her on these expeditions, for she was very proud of me and wished to show me off to her friends. I hated going out with her because everyone we met turned to stare at her, trotting along with her little flannel-coated dog on a lead, and this made me feel self-conscious and ridiculous. One day however I yielded to her entreaties and agreed to accompany her. My ordeal began at the door, where she introduced me to the doorman and then to the liftman as, 'This is my great-nephew, a very gallant officer who gave his life for his country.' After a few more of these introductions, seasoned with 'twice decorated by the King', I could stand it no longer, but dodged through a door and escaped, excusing myself afterwards for having lost her. A year or two later she forced me to accompany her again, saying that she must have me to escort her while she did her Christmas shopping because the crowds were so great. The grocery counter was indeed packed. People were buying turkeys, plum puddings, pâtés, boxes of preserved fruit and large hampers of delicacies. We queued up, but when my aunt's turn came all she asked for were six eggs and half a pound of margarine, explaining at length to the harassed shopman that she found these foods, when bought at his counter, the most delicious things one could eat – especially when finished off with a

Lyons cream bun.

Her meals were indeed frugal in the extreme. They consisted of either a single boiled egg or a plate of Frankfurter sausages, consumed with bread and margarine and finished off with Swiss rolls and cream buns. One of these last would be put on her bedside table and she would wake up in the night and devour it. Her servant was allowed veal chops, bacon and jam, but nothing else. However once a week my great-aunt would lunch out at the Grosvenor Hotel, next to Victoria Station, and there she would eat lavishly of the full menu and drink a little wine, stoking up for the meagre days ahead. I was expected to accompany her on these outings, because she disliked eating at a restaurant alone.

My great-aunt, unlike her sister, was a woman of immense vitality and of a certain intelligence. She had once been a water-colour painter – her landscapes lined the walls of her flat – and she had written two novels which Fisher Unwin had published. They were both extremely bad. But she had also read a certain amount and I still have the copies of Boswell's *Life of Johnson* and of Jowett's translation of Plato which stood on her shelves. Her favourite book however was John Morley's *On Compromise* which she kept, heavily annotated and underlined, on the table by her bed-side. Prudence, moderation, *savoir vivre* were in her opinion the greatest of the virtues, together with love and friendship. She read French and German fluently and had for many years been engaged on a concordance of the works of Molière. The vast unfinished manuscript was kept in a cupboard and one of her dearest hopes was that I should complete it and that it should be published under our joint names.

As I have said before, she regarded her deafness as a great blessing. 'It has saved me', she would say, quite contrary to the evidence, 'from all kinds of muddles and annoyances. But then I took care – as your father, poor man, did not – to live in my proper station in the world and to avoid eccentricities and queer behaviour. All my friends have been persons highly respected in their own sphere of life and whenever foolish or rubbishy people have come my way, I have been enabled through my deafness to overlook them.' Among these foolish people she included my mother, whose wandering mind and often confused conversation she had taken in immediately, without perceiving her warmth and life-loving qualities. For was she not Irish? To her the inhabitants of that distressful island were all of them crazy and irresponsible, even when like my mother they were of Scottish descent, and she commonly spoke of them as 'the wild Irish'.

Till she was in her late sixties my great-aunt had led a very social life. She would give dinner parties at the Hyde Park Hotel, the Carlton or the Empress Club in Dover Street to twenty or more people, many of whom would be diplomats from the Balkan countries or from China, Japan or

Siam. She would sit at the head of a long table, a band would play to ensure that everyone was as deaf as she was and palms in green tubs would stand around. She also gave light suppers in her flat to fifty or more people at which 'the famous Japanese artist Mr Chu' painted miniatures and 'the great Dr Haydon' played his cello with a tenor and a bass he brought with him. Prince Eitel Friedrich of Prussia would come when he was in London and sometimes a duchess or two, especially the Duchess of Somerset. When I expressed surprise at my aunt's having got her, she said:

'That's nothing. If you offer chicken, good ices and champagne you can get anyone. The difficulty is to keep them away.'

Since she was a Baroness and reputed to be rich she had suitors. She would show me their photographs and their love letters tied up in pink tape. The last of these had been Chedo Mijatovich, the Serbian minister, a stout man with a black bushy beard who after his retirement took a flat at the top of her house and set up as an author. She had flirted with him, but prudently put off accepting him and then one day, despairing of her hand, he married his cook. She never forgave him for this and whenever they met on the stairs she would pass him with a slight bow, but without speaking.

Death had now taken its toll of her older friends. Those that were left were the younger men – 'boys' she called them – in their sixties or seventies. They were all of them Bertie Woosters, 'men about town', as the phrase went, that is bachelors who had never followed any profession. Most of them were confined to their rooms by bad weather or health for a good part of the year, but whenever they were well enough they ventured out, immaculately dressed with gloves and a cane, to pay a round of visits. As my father remarked, 'Whatever one may say of Aunt Addie, her friends are all gentlemen.' But their dullness was overpowering. They would pay two or three social calls in the course of an afternoon in the hope of picking up in one house some piece of gossip which they could pass on at the next. Apart from this their only subject of conversation was their health. My aunt was interested in health too and their stream of platitudes and valetudinarian complaints did not bore her because she could not hear them. The few words they scribbled on her pad told her all she needed to know and she invented the rest. Their dullness too was a guarantee of their steadiness and respectability, which were the qualities she most esteemed in her friends, and when she praised them it would be either for their true loyalty or for their gentlemanly deportment. Indeed I suspect that she regarded dullness and stupidity as necessary and endearing features in any man because they set off her own comparative brilliance. She certainly regarded me in that light. The yawns I stifled when I had tea with her, my wandering thoughts and inattention as she rattled on and on were clear evidence of it. Or when, to save myself the trouble of writing explanations,

I would nod my head in agreement, only to be caught out later contradicting what I had previously assented to. I remember once, when I had gone into the next room to fetch something, hearing her through the open door analysing my character aloud to herself.

'Weak in the head,' she said. 'Decidedly muddled and weak. No experience of the world, but all the same *such* a dear.'

And of my brother Blair, she would say, 'Quite hopelessly vague. I don't believe he understands a word that is said to him. No head at all, but still a dear boy.'

The first of her friends whom I remember was a second cousin of hers called Borodaile, one of the last of a line that traced its descent from a Westmorland dalesman in the fifteenth century. He had never had any profession, but when in 1914 war broke out he pulled himself together and sacrificed himself in patriotic zeal, at much cost to his inner tranquillity, by consenting to run the Essex County Cricket Club. When some years after this he died my great-aunt would declare that he had worn himself out on this arduous task and done as much for the service of his country as any soldier at the front.

Another of her friends whom I remember rather better was Mr Garnett. He was a man who lived for his nose. He had had I do not know how many operations to this organ, which stood up smooth and white like a snow-covered peak out of a red, well-weathered face. For his nose's sake he had abandoned the legal profession almost as soon as he had entered it and since then had spent eight months out of every year either at Aix-les-Bains or at Baden-Baden or on the French Riviera, the quality of the climate being all important for its comfort and efficiency. Indeed it was so sensitive that it could distinguish clearly between the air of Cannes and that of Antibes. Cannes suited it perfectly, but as it moved eastwards it became more and more dispirited, to collapse entirely when it entered Nice, which for other reasons its owner preferred. However in spite of this disability Mr Garnett lived to survive my aunt and to reach, if I remember right, the respectable age of seventy-eight.

The most likeable of her friends – indeed the only one who was endurable – was Colonel Stuart of, I think, the Black Watch. He lived in cheap lodgings in Ebury Street, but as his chest was delicate he could only issue out from them on fine, warm afternoons. His recreation was music. He played no instrument, but he could whistle any tune he had once heard and told me that he used to spend several hours every day whistling to himself. His other occupation was knitting woollen mufflers, mittens and tea-cosies, with the result that all his friends were well supplied with these useful objects.

The only woman to cross my great-aunt's threshold without a previous invitation was a certain Lady Dimsdale, the widow of a mayor of West-minster and a distant relative of hers. Tiz was little inclined at the best of times to her own sex and did not care for this bustling lady whose only reason for visiting her so regularly with gifts of flowers appeared to be her hope of being left something in my great-aunt's will. But of this she never stood a chance.

Servants made up an important part of my aunt's existence. For many years she had been waited on by a crusty but efficient old maid called Emma. After a long and devoted service, which did not exclude frequent, *sotto voce* grumblings about the difficulty of her mistress's character, Emma had retired to her sister's house in the country and then died. My aunt had been annoyed by her retirement, but still more so by her death, which she regarded as a mark of defeatism and moral laxity. She was always put out by the deaths of old or elderly women and when Queen Alexandra died showed great indignation, speaking of her as 'a weak woman' who had given the country a deplorable example. Only men could be allowed to drop off before reaching a ripe old age because they were the feebler sex and thus little in the way of firmness of purpose was to be expected of them. Then of course Emma's retirement had put my aunt in a quandary. Servants were not to be trusted in these days. They were undependable, muddle-headed, scatterbrained creatures and might even, in spite of their coming with the best of references, be in league with burglars. I was there-fore entrusted with the task of finding a new one. I went to an agency and arranged for a succession of elderly women to be sent to my aunt's flat for her to interview. Two difficulties then presented themselves. The first was that few of these women were willing to be shut up with a deaf, restless, eccentric old lady or to content themselves with the very meagre diet which was all that she would provide, even though the work expected of them was minimal. The other was that my aunt took an almost instant dislike to every woman she interviewed and, even when they seemed suitable, found some insurmountable objection to them. This led to a somewhat acri-monious correspondence between us. I had suggested that she should offer more money and she replied that *nothing* could be more foolish since her need was for *servants* and not *adventuresses*. Everyone she had seen had been that. One, 'grinning all the time on her great red face', had been a nursery governess, another fancied herself at cooking – 'as though I wanted any-thing of that sort!' – while a third brought only two dirty, ill-written references with her. The agency had told her that till Easter was passed no properly trained servants would be available.

It soon became clear that my aunt did not want a servant of any kind because she hoped to force me to come and sleep in her maid's room and share her life with her. Living with her, she said, would be a good preparation for marriage. I would learn from her the ways of the world and the work would be trifling as we would either live on boiled eggs and tinned foods or go out to meals and she would do all the dusting that was necessary. She therefore refused the women whom the agency sent her and, since she was afraid of living alone in case she should be burgled or have a stroke, she ended by forcing me to spend a fortnight with her, sleeping in the servant's room, until I put such pressure on her that she yielded and engaged a maid.

Eliza was a plain, squat, surly-faced woman in her late fifties who, as one of her legs was shorter than the other, walked with a pronounced limp. She had a passion for playing on the mandolin, so that service with a deaf mistress held the special attraction for her of allowing her to play it all day long to her heart's content. Since my aunt, who was too restless to sit still for more than ten minutes at a time, had formed the habit of running into the kitchen at all hours to pour out a long stream of conversation, Eliza took to locking the kitchen door. Her mistress would bang and hammer on it without getting any reply, for Eliza would be in her tiny bedroom that opened off it, strumming on her mandolin and pretending not to hear. My aunt ended by accepting this philosophically and would even open the front door herself to visitors when her maid, rapt in her music, failed to hear the bell.

An indispensable auxiliary in Tiz's lonely life was provided by her dog Mimi. She was devoted to animals and in her time had kept and buried a great many of them, not only dogs but cats, parrots and monkeys of various descriptions. She spoke of them with sadness and affection and when her last husband, the Baron, lay dying he had had to share his bed with a pet monkey which was dying too. When I first knew her she showed me a correspondence she had had with Prince Eitel Friedrich, the Kaiser's second son, which took the form of an exchange of letters between their lap dogs, Fifi and Mignon. During the war I tried to get hold of it and publish it, partly because of its absurdity, but also to reveal the downright childishness and silliness of the Prussian Royal Family who were then being held up in the press as ogres who had deliberately deluged the world in blood. But I found that my aunt had destroyed it. As an enemy alien, one of whose stepsons was chamberlain at the Kaiser's court while the other commanded a battalion of the Prussian Royal Guard, she had become suspect to the Home Office and was for a time forbidden to leave London and in danger of being interned. This led her to reclaim her British citizenship and renounce her German relatives and altogether to assume an intensely patriotic attitude to the war.

But to return to the subject of her pets, the only one left of a long line was Mimi. She was a nasty little animal with legs too long and thin for her body and black oily hair. She was jealous and bad tempered and although an utter coward was given to taking little nips with her sharp teeth at one's leg if she thought it safe to do so. Her usual station was between my aunt's skirt and her petticoats, where she lay swaddled in a red flannel cloth, and from this hiding place she exercised the office of sentinel, for whenever the front door bell rang she would begin to bark and yap with such fury that the vibration of her body told her mistress that there was someone trying to get in, so that, if it chanced to be Eliza's afternoon out or else she was too drowned in music to hear, my aunt would get up and, after the usual precautions, open the door herself. Another dumb friend was a mouse that would appear at tea-time and, sitting up on its hindquarters, beg for crumbs. Mimi was terrified of this mouse and, if she happened to be on the ground lapping her saucer of milk, would jump on to my aunt's lap or hide under her skirts. When she went out on her daily walk she wore a black flannel coat with a monogram stitched in red on it.

Tiz's reminiscences about the past always fascinated me. She possessed several photograph albums of picnics and festivities from her Viennese days, showing elegantly dressed ladies, every one of them a countess, posing in grand style. She claimed as a young girl to have danced with Prince Metternich and had of course been presented to the young Emperor Franz Josef and to his beautiful wife, the Empress Elizabeth. Then she had visited the Great Exhibition of 1851 in Hyde Park, where she had had a good view of 'our dear Queen' and of Prince Albert, and later in 1864 had spent a summer in Paris 'in the time of the Emperor'. It gave me a strange feeling to think that when Rimbaud was still a schoolboy she had been a married woman who shared her bed with a husband and two monkeys.

Her earlier reminiscences were even more interesting. As a girl she used sometimes to ride out with her father to Richmond to breakfast at the Star and Garter. Kensington was then a village. One trotted down the muddy high street and after that came to fields where the road was barred by gates which one had to open with one's riding crop. When once as an old lady she went to have tea with my brother Blair and his young wife in Kensington she said on getting up to leave, 'Now I must go back to London.' But she did not repeat her visit to them because she did not like my sister-in-law nor approve of the marriage. When one day my mother, in an attempt at exculpation, wrote down on the pad, 'Rhoda is very shy', my aunt exclaimed, 'Ah yes, *shy*. One can see it in her face. *Very shy*. Otherwise she would never have managed to catch poor Blair.' And nothing my mother could say would alter this impression.

We used sometimes to hire a car and go on expeditions. One of these was to Kew Gardens which my aunt enjoyed very much, remarking how the trees had grown since she had been there last. Down to her late eighties she was an excellent walker and she swept indefatigably round the gardens, visiting the lake, the beech wood and all the hothouses. On the following day I got a letter telling me how she had enjoyed it, 'especially the extreme beauty of the exquisite ferns – a great art-work of Nature really, though I daresay assisted by the gardener's skill: at first I thought that the network of wire-like rods was wire itself.' On another occasion I took her down the river to Greenwich, where we had lunch and saw over the Hospital, and then at her special request to the Tate Gallery, which she had not seen for some thirty years. She greatly admired the Constables and Turners, recognizing many of them from previous visits, but when we entered the Pre-Raphaelite room she shook her fist angrily at the Rossettis and Burne-Jones, exclaiming in a loud half-shrill, half-hoarse voice, 'Ah, those horrible *modern* paintings! So vulgar, so extremely vulgar! I wonder they dare to exhibit them here.' Yet she showed a deep appreciation of Watts on account of his symbolical representation of moral qualities, and loved Landseer because he painted animals.

I had talked so much about her to my friends that they were all anxious to meet her, so I gave a tea party for her in my Fitzroy Street flat. Arthur Waley, Roger Fry, Helen Anrep, Hope-Johnstone and Ralph Partridge all came. She was perfectly at ease in this intellectual company and chattered away all the time, speaking of the famous painters and writers she had met in the past, hardly any of whom were known even by name to her audience. Roger Fry, with his usual amiability, laid himself out to please her, writing down questions and answers on her pad, but she did not take to him and turned all her attention on the good-looking Arthur Waley, who characteristically replied only with wan smiles. After this she always referred to Roger Fry as Mr Fox, declaring most unjustly that his face and expression suited his name.

But how tedious these weekly or twice weekly meetings with my aunt came to be! All communication with her was attended by the most fearful muddles and confusions. Arriving late as usual, I would scribble down some excuse on her pad, but before she could read it she would need to put on her reading spectacles. Half a dozen pairs lay strewn about the room, but they were not the ones she needed. The bell would be rung for Eliza, the dog would jump down from under skirts and bark and a frantic search would begin. At length they would be found just beside her on the tea tray. The dog would return to its hiding place, Eliza would limp back to her den to resume her mandolin playing and my aunt would take up the pad I offered her.

'But what is all this about?' she would say. 'I can't make out a word of it. *What* bus was held up by *what* fog? I hope it was not a bus on which anything of importance or urgency was travelling. In any case the fogs of today are nothing to what they used to be. I remember coming home with dear Rose from our club in Albemarle Street when in the middle of the day one could not see one's hand in front of one's face. Though when I was a child and we lived in Bury Street we never had any real fogs at all.'

And so the conversation would drift on, my occasional questions and answers reaching her only when she had forgotten what they referred to. Later, after I had gone, she would collect all these little scraps of paper and go over them carefully till she imagined that she understood them. But she hadn't, for as she could not remember the context in which they had been written she never got the meaning right.

Cross-purposes and confusion thus made up the air she breathed, and yet she never put them down to her deafness or to her chronic restlessness and impatience, but to this crazy modern world where everything was at sixes and sevens. She looked back with regret to the time when life had been governed by exact rules and procedures and saw nothing but fuss and frenzy in the present deplorable age. And so she was always seeking for calm and composure. 'We must discuss this question calmly and thoroughly,' she would say, 'bearing in mind all the ifs and ans and pots and pans.' Or else, 'I feel that there are very important decisions we might come to between us if we went about them tranquilly and unhurriedly.' But what these important decisions were never appeared.

Much of my aunt's life resolves itself into a series of anecdotes. There was first of all the story of her spectacles. She had not been to an oculist for as long as she could remember, but used to choose her glasses from a tray at the Army and Navy Stores. Every year she chose a stronger pair but now she found that even with the strongest she could not see to read without tiring her eyes. I insisted that she must consult a Harley Street oculist and chose one called Mr Rugg-Gunn, who later operated on the King and was, I believe, knighted. We arrived and were shewn into his consulting room and the usual ritual for sight testing began. A screen with letters on it – C, X, A, M, D and so forth – was displayed and my aunt was requested to read them. With complete assurance she read off numbers – 7, 4, 9, 6, 3. A good deal of scribbling on her pad was required to explain to her that these were letters not numbers and then the reading began again. But more and more difficulties cropped up, more and more writing on the pad became necessary till at last she said, 'I really can't see the use of this, Mr Gun Rug. All I need is a stronger pair of glasses to read by.' In the end, after examining her eyes, he wrote out a prescription for some spectacles, observing that she was suffering from cataract, but that it was too soon to operate.

The examination had lasted for almost an hour and, tucking her dog under her arm, she got up to leave. With her usual dignity she asked him what she owed him and he replied 'three guineas'. 'But I've only brought with me two pound notes,' she said, 'and some of that I shall need for my taxi.' I promised to send him a cheque, but he wearily waved the whole matter aside and said, 'I'll take a pound'.

'A very difficult man,' she remarked as soon as we were out in the street. 'And with a very unusual name. What has a gun got to do with a rug? One meets with such curious people nowadays.' And when the glasses arrived she said they were not strong enough and refused to use them.

My great-aunt had some very odd habits, but since she was a rationalist she could always provide a good reason for them. For example she wore round her neck a medallion she had bought at a stall outside Westminster Cathedral and which had on it, 'I am a Catholic. If I am injured please send for a priest immediately.' When I asked her why she did this, seeing that she had been brought up as an Anglican, she replied: 'My dear boy, you must realize that, however careful I am, there is always a risk at my age of being knocked down at a street crossing. Now it is well known that the Catholic ambulances and hospitals are better than any others.'

In reality she had no religion, but she would never discuss the question as she regarded all mention of such subjects as being in the worst taste, even more so than speaking of money. Yet she loved to talk about her health. She called her corns 'the victims' or 'the sufferers' and when she described to me how forty years or so before she had had her tonsils out she added with pride, 'And the surgeon said they were the largest tonsils he had ever seen in his life'. She had kept them in spirit in a glass jar on her bedroom mantelpiece till one day Eliza knocked them over and that was the end of them.

There were few limits to my aunt's inventive powers and some of her stories about the past were hard to believe. There was, for example, the sad tale of the death of her first husband, Mr Bower. They had owned a bungalow in the country, I think near Bexhill, where they spent the summers. I used to have a photograph of the two of them having tea in the orchard, waited on by a maid in a white cap and apron. Now it seems that there was an earth closet in a corner of the garden for the use of men, and there Mr Bower used to retire every morning to read *The Times* and smoke a cigar. But one day he dropped a lighted match into the bucket, the paper in it caught fire and he was badly burned before he could get up because he suffered from rheumatism in the knees. His spine was injured and after a long illness in which she nursed him devotedly he died.

The old, when they live by themselves, often lose all sense of modesty. Towards the end of 1925 my aunt fell ill and I had to spend several hours every day with her. She would jump out of bed and run about the room in a skimpy flannel night-dress and I feel sure would have pulled it up on the pretext of showing me her varicose veins had I given her the least encouragement. Then in January she began to recover. Her cough left her, her rheumatism ebbed away and she ate and slept well. But the trouble with her urine remained. Its colour, she declared, was *most* alarming. Every day as soon as I arrived I was given the bulletin. 'My dear boy,' she would say as I entered the drawing-room, 'it has gone back to that dreadful orange. Come at once and see it.' And I had to follow her.

My great-aunt made up her face heavily. She painted in her eyebrows, which had all fallen out, she rouged her cheeks and dyed her thin and skimpy hair, which was plastered down on either side of her head with a parting in the centre and a small knot behind. But as her eyesight grew worse she made up more and more wildly. She would paint one eyebrow high up on her forehead and the other in its proper place but running far down below the eye socket, while the blot of rouge on her right cheek would be larger and redder than that on her left. This gave her a macabre appearance, like that of a clown in pantomime. I had always wondered how she dyed her hair and when her mind began to fail her maid told me. It seems that she would put her hairbrush up the chimney till it was thick with soot and then daub it on. This explained the smudges of black that mottled her forehead and neck. Then the clothes she wore had been made for her around 1900 and even at that time had been highly fantastic, from which one may gather that she presented as extraordinary a spectacle as any that could be seen on the streets of London.

I was anxious to have her appearance recorded and after a good deal of persuasion obtained her consent to having her portrait painted by Carrington. But then I drew back and made an excuse for dropping the plan. For I reflected that she developed an immediate aversion for all young and attractive women and would be deeply suspicious of my acquaintance with one of them, even though she was the wife of my best friend. One of the strongest lessons that her long life had implanted in her was the risk that men – that soft and foolish sex – ran of being caught by a pretty face. They were slow to learn, poor gullible things, that marriages based on youth and good looks were to be avoided at any cost, because in the long run it was only character that counted. 'In my time,' she would declare, 'a proper age for embarking on marriage was the early forties, but in these wild modern days it is not safe for a man to tie himself up before he reaches fifty, and even then he must be careful to choose a mature, steady woman, well experienced in the ways of the world, who is not more than five or six years younger than himself.' So I had to restrain Carrington's longings to meet and paint my great-aunt by writing a description of her myself. Here, to complete my portrait, is one I sent to Carrington in a letter soon after my settling in London:

I worked at Santa Teresa all morning and then lunched with Tiz. How shall I describe her? She swung into the restaurant, a little figure about four foot six high, with her face covered with paint, and a comical expression on it like that of a costermonger. She had on a large black hat, tilted on one side in a Scottish manner, with a giant red puff, the size of a sunflower, on the edge of it. A black silk cloak that hung in a train behind covered a stomacher of rainbow-tinted silk, very bright and rather dirty, and her little ant's head rested on a high white lace tube which was fastened in front with a nickel plate, the size of a saucer. This plate she calls her brooch: it was given her on her marriage by Prince Eitel Friedrich, whose portrait is stamped on it in the uniform of the Prussian Guards. Like Monticelli, she paints thick; where he threw his palette into the canvas, she leaves a long river of white paint, stiff and immobilized like cooled lava, jutting out over one eye, and her soft, clammy, wrinkled cheeks are the colour of fresh blood. The lobster was bad: I sent mine away and watched her fingers, as stiff as a handful of twigs and yet in perpetual jerky motion, plunging a long hook into the claw of the red, stinking fish, breaking it with her artificial teeth, cracking, sucking.

Colonel Scrymgeour-Wedderburn had been to call – such a dear man, a sort of artist person, but oh, not what you think, very much a gentleman. She had told him that her nephew wished to give Spanish lessons in the evenings to rest his nerves worn out by severe literary work and by the terrible life he had led in the war. The Colonel had promised to make every enquiry. No, he himself had no leisure in which to learn Spanish, nor did he think that it would be very useful to him since he would never go to Spain nor even enter business, being seventy-nine years of age and almost a cripple. But he would ask his friends.

'He's a very dear friend', she added, 'though such an old dodderer, and would do anything to oblige me.'

I must tell you how she approached the head shopman at the Book Department of the Army and Navy Stores on this subject. 'I have a nephew,' she said, 'such a dear boy but rather vague and inconsequent, not in the least like his poor father. He is engaged on very important work connected with Spanish history, but he suffers from insomnia and weak eyesight and the doctor will not let him work for more than three hours daily. He is trying to find pupils to whom he may teach Spanish in the evenings, and both his doctor and myself agree that this will be very soothing and stimulating to his nerves. I thought you might recommend him to your clients. There are sure to be some who wish to learn Spanish, which has a very high utility just at present for commerce, with these Spanish American cowboys over here and the King of Spain popping across every month to see us, and all sorts. He speaks four or five languages fluently and then he has been living for four years on a mountain five thousand feet above the sea, in a delicious climate, he tells me, with orange trees in his garden flowering at Christmas. However his nerves are very bad and I am anxious about him for I have suffered all my life from nerves myself, although I haven't the reason that he has, for I was never, as you may suppose, in the trenches. He is at present teaching Mr David Garnett, the nephew of my old friend Richard Garnett whom I knew when I was a reader to Fisher Unwin. You have heard of Fisher Unwin? Such a nice man, I was for two years his reader. Although I am afraid that it is true that he has not a very practical character and is unreliable and unpunctual, one must make every excuse when one thinks of the way his parents brought him up, stuck down there in the country. His father is a most foolish man, very obstinate, who thinks he knows everything but is really completely narrow and in every way petty, and his mother is a mad Irish woman who thinks of nothing but her family. But certainly he is very good at languages – he always was from a child – and he comes to the Army and Navy Stores every time he is in London. So please do what you can for him.'

All this in a very hoarse, loud voice that at moments becomes piercing, and without any possibility of a reply from the shopman, whom for thirty years she has seen and spoken to every day, yet never received any answer from. I have exaggerated nothing, for she herself repeated all this to me and I know she is capable of it.

In another letter I described how I had had dinner with my great-aunt and her lawyer. After the meal we had returned to her flat and sat drinking *crème de menthe* by the fire out of the late Baron's eyebaths.

'I do it in memory of my dear, de-ar husband. He died of influenza without uttering a single complaint. The executioner [undertaker] arranged the most beautiful flowers on his grave. What do you think? When the executioner died during the war I myself took a wreath to the cemetery.'

As a commentary on this letter, I remember my father's account of the Baron's funeral. Prince Eitel Friedrich, if my memory is correct, came over for it and also the Baron's son, Colonel von Roeder. At the lunch afterwards my great-aunt could talk of nothing but the undertaker, whom she always referred to as 'the executioner'. His good looks, his tact in providing mutes who were all black haired and dark eyed, his beautiful manners. She introduced him to the company and after the period of mourning was over continued to see him from time to time.

Unlike my grandmother, my great-aunt was a person whom it was impossible to love. Her fidgetiness, her talkativeness, her weird and far-from clean appearance created a barrier against the growth of the warmer affections. It is true that I could admire her spirited and courageous character and be amused by her eccentricity, but the boredom I suffered from our long and frequent *tête-à-tête* was difficult to endure, all the more as they took me away from my work. The one strong sentiment therefore that bound me to her was gratitude. She had lifted me out of the poverty into which I had sunk and given me the chance to pursue my literary ambitions, for my father would never have offered me an allowance if she had not first provided me with a small one and after that made me her heir. On the contrary he would have tried to starve me into taking a job which would have made writing impossible. Then, as I got to know her better, I came to have a genuine liking and sympathy for her and to be touched by her affection for me. She was of course lonely with the incurable loneliness of old age, which was increased by the fact that she rarely slept for more than a few hours of the night and was too restless to doze off by day. Time therefore hung heavily on her hands, all the more as her failing eyesight made it impossible for her to read. So she clung to me and was continually devising pretexts for inveigling me into seeing her more often. Yet I must say it to her credit that she never used her money to put pressure on me or to insist on more than I was prepared to give, but, when I would not agree to doing what she wanted, accepted my refusal with a good grace. For she was in love with me, with the hopeless love of the old for the young, and that put her in a position of weakness. And though I often showed myself impatient and unreliable, I became in the end sufficiently aware of the pathos of her situation to take her feelings into account and make greater efforts to please her.

12

More portraits

All this winter and spring of 1925–6 I continued living in Roger Fry's studio at 18 Fitzroy Street. I was still working steadily at my biography of Santa Teresa, though occasionally I would take a day or two off to add a page or so to my novel, which interested me more but demanded a special vein of feeling. Every evening I dined, usually alone, at one of two restaurants which stood exactly opposite one another in Charlotte Street. That on the west side was called Bertorelli's. Here one sat at a bare marble-topped table and was served with a substantial plate of appetizing food, followed by an orange. There were no frills and the napkin provided was a paper one. At the other, which was called Vaiani's, a different principle prevailed. Mr Vaiani, a small bird-like Italian, believed that the style in which meals were served was of more importance than the materials of which they were made and thus saw to it that every table should be spread with a spotless white tablecloth, set off with a glass vase of paper flowers, and every cover have an elaborately folded linen napkin and a roll of fresh bread placed beside it. He believed too that his customers liked to be offered rare and exotic foods, with the result that such delicacies as pheasant, grouse and capercailzie figured on his menus. But since his prices had to compete with Bertorelli's, he was obliged to cut down on something, and so the game would have been bought on the cheap when it was half rotten while the sauce on the spaghetti would either be similarly tainted or else consist of nothing but a mulch of tinned tomatoes. It was this aspiring strain in Mr Vaiani that made him such a touching figure. All the creative instincts of the great chef were there, struggling to assert themselves against their economic limitations and now and then bursting out in some surprising invention, as for example in the dish to which he proudly gave the name of Pêche Vaiani. This consisted of tinned peaches with chocolate poured over them.

Certainly one ate better at Bertorelli's, but I found that its long bare tables where one sat cheek by jowl with other eaters cramped the spirit.

Everything about it proclaimed that it was a place without personality, a mere filling station for empty stomachs, and for that reason I was more often drawn to its rival opposite. The way in which Mr Vaiani hovered delicately like a black and white crow around the gleaming tables while his customers were bent over their plates was a pleasure to look at, and then one felt sorry for him because his wife was so dreadful. She was a grim, ponderous Englishwoman of outsize bulk and girth who sat sullenly with a perpetual scowl on her face at the cash desk like a female spider keeping a watchful eye on its mate, and one shuddered to think of the scenes that would break out when the restaurant closed and the two of them were left alone to face their marital problems. I sometimes occupied the next table to the Russian critic, Prince Mirsky, a silent, black-bearded man who ate with a book propped up in front of him, and wondered whether he frequented Mr Vaiani's restaurant for the same reason that I did. But evidently it is the quality of the food and not its glamour that in the long run counts for most in the popular mind, for one day Vaiani's restaurant closed while Bertorelli's, flowering out into white tablecloths and napkins as it was freed from the competition of its rival, remained, its prices a little higher.

I made two friends at about this time – Alec Penrose and Stephen Tomlin. Alec was the eldest of four brothers who came from a family of Quaker bankers, the others being Lionel, Roland and Beakus. Alec became in the course of time one of my best friends. He was good looking and had a rather wistful charm which came from his sense of the ambiguities and uncertainties in his character as well as from the mental blackouts he suffered from. That is, he would begin to say something that was perceptive and intelligent and then a sort of fog would come over his mind and he would get into a tangle and not be able to finish. This confusion in his thoughts led him to be psychoanalysed by James Strachey, but the only result of this was that he was converted to Christianity and became a convinced Anglican. His attempts to write a play having failed, he married a close friend of Frances Marshall, who from having been an ardent atheist soon became converted to Anglicanism too. They settled in great comfort in a Georgian manor in Norfolk, but his fears of being damned after death became such an obsession to him that he came to feel that he could only be saved from it by joining the Catholic Church. But to do this he would have to separate from his wife and admit that his children by her were bastards and while he was hesitating about this he died in 1950 in great distress of mind.

The other friend whom I made at this time was Stephen Tomlin, or, as he was always called, Tommy. But perhaps I should qualify this word friend, since for some reason that I never understood he regarded me as a rival and would attack me at parties. The son of a judge, he had refused to read for law and had become instead a sculptor, though I always felt that he was more of a literary man than of an artist, in spite of the fact that chiselling stone seemed to fulfil some need in his nature. He was ambisexual and though hardly good looking enough to attract men he often produced a great effect upon women. One reason for this was the ease and fluency of his conversation. He could talk to anyone, pouring out a flood of ideas, good, bad and indifferent but always stimulating. For talking was his link with others. He could not bear to be alone, but clung to other people, asserting himself vigorously in their company and yet all the time dependant, lonely, demanding friendship and affection. One felt something chaotic and unhappy under his self-confident air and one also felt that his nature held depths and potentialities that were not shared by the other young men one met in Bloomsbury circles. Yet he was spineless and lacking in a sense of direction. He went to bed with anyone and everyone, often merely for the sake of company, and, though he was supposed to be in love with that beautiful American girl, Henrietta Bingham, I used to wonder what in his case was meant by the words 'being in love'. In his ideas too he could be carried in any direction – even to praising in Lytton's presence that unmentionable thing 'the Christian spirit'. A character from a Russian novel perhaps. One felt his imaginative gifts yet knew that they would come to nothing.

My friends at this time were for the most part Oxford or Cambridge men and they were all of them a good deal better off financially than I was. The older generation had got what were called first-class minds, lucid, reliable and orderly, whereas I had a vague and intermittent one which only became articulate in flashes. I was never able to join in discussions on abstract or philosophic subjects although I could follow them, and generally talked my best with women, whose style of conversation on the whole I preferred. Yet I must have been able to hold my own sometimes, for I was still seeing a certain amount of Leonard and Virginia Woolf and was getting to know Roger Fry pretty well, though this last association was due to my close friendship with Helen Anrep, who left her husband Boris that spring and settled down with Roger in a house in Guilford Street.

My diary does not give much space to Bloomsbury parties or *conversaziones,* but here is a brief account of one which I will quote:

Jan 28. At 10 a small party at Angus Davidson's for conversation. Virginia, Vanessa, Julia Strachey, Mme Raverat, Edith Sitwell and one foreigner: the rest men, for it is not easy to put women in a room with the Stephen sisters. Lytton and his young man Philip Ritchie, Leonard Woolf, Duncan Grant, James and Oliver Strachey, Raymond Mortimer and one or two others. It was amusing. Virginia leaning stiffly sideways attacked the painters: how fantastic they were, how only the smallest details interested them, how they argued about everything. Vanessa and Duncan will talk for an hour on end simply on a cat. 'Only three legs!' 'Yes, and a white spot on its tail.' 'I'm sure I don't know how it catches mice.' 'But it doesn't.' 'Oh, but I've seen it.' 'You're quite wrong about that, Duncan!'

Wherever Virginia goes she undoes a knot like a Lapland witch and lets out a war: an old well-practised war, whose tactics have been polished up by many previous encounters. If it is not the Older Generation v. the Younger, it is Writers v. Painters or even Men v. Women. It is these well-worn topics that produce the most brilliant and fantastic conversation that one can hear anywhere in England.

Another member of Bloomsbury of whom I had seen a certain amount up to now was E. M. Forster or, as his friends called him, Morgan. He was a dry, friendly little man, rather ordinary and insignificant at first sight, with a spinsterish manner which came from his having been brought up at Weybridge by two maiden aunts. If it was difficult to see his distinction, that perhaps was because he was more interested in listening to and sizing up other people than in expressing his own views, which would only appear in some oblique comment. I had read *Howards End* and had not liked it. Then – it must have been in 1924 – he gave me a copy of *A Passage to India* and later came round to my rooms to ask if I had liked it. I had not and felt obliged to say so, with the consequence that I have not seen him since. Today I have changed my mind about this book, which seems to me a masterly production, conveying all the ambiguities which lie in the Indian mind and their clash with English moral positivism as well as Forster's own uncertain and enigmatic views about the Universe. How I can have been so stupid not to see this at once I do not know. All I can say in my excuse is that in those days I was too much glued to the notion of concrete and vivid expression to appreciate a novel written in a quiet tone on a sociological theme.

Morgan's letters, of which I received about a dozen, are characteristic. They are written in a rather mannered style with odd turns of phrase which bring out the elusive and elfish side of his nature. Like his conversation they are dry with now and then little sharp, deflating points in them. When I first knew him his approach to people was impersonal and neutral – it was said because he had not yet faced up to his homosexuality. But this was to change and, according to Lytton Strachey, the increased bite and hardness of *A Passage to India* and its lack of sentimentality are due to his having meanwhile had a love affair with an Indian.

I was always divided in my loyalty to 'Bloomsbury', considered as a group. There could be no doubt about the high level of their intelligence, while their cult of good conversation made them very stimulating people to know. But I thought that Maynard Keynes' description of them as 'water spiders swimming gracefully on the surface of the stream' contained a good deal of truth. Civilized, liberal, agnostic or atheist like their parents before them, they had always stood too far above the life of their day, had been too little exposed to its rough-and-tumble really to belong to it. Thus, though they thought of themselves as new brooms and innovators, they quickly found they were playing the part of a literary establishment. What I chiefly got from them was their respect for the truth. Yet this – they gave the word a capital letter – was defined in a narrow and exclusive way so that anyone who held views that could not be justified rationally was regarded as a wilful cultivator of illusions and therefore as a person who could not be taken seriously. Religion in particular was anathema. The subject was finished, closed, or existed merely as a personal weakness or as a hangover from early associations, like not washing or continuing to play with dolls or tin soldiers. That psychological pressures could drive people to believe things that could not be proved rationally or scientifically was something that they refused to allow. Scepticism was a moral duty. They thus found themselves out of touch both with large areas of the world they lived in and with most of the past. For if history showed, as they thought, a slow progress from superstition to enlightenment, why bother to understand the impulses that drove people to religious belief, much less to communism or Nazism? By saying 'they're so stupid', they imagined that they had disposed of them.

This attitude was illustrated for me by their opinion of Joyce's *Ulysses*. Lytton dismissed it by saying that he could not find a single intelligent sentence in it. Virginia was more hesitant, yet disliked it for being vulgar and lower class. Morgan Forster attacked it as a book that covered the universe with filth and mud. Not one of my friends, except Arthur Waley, had a good word to say for it. Yet for me Joyce was, after Proust, the greatest novelist of the century and their incapacity to see any merit in him showed how conventional their minds were. They lived by good taste and I saw with regret that I was being carried along the same road and being obliged to live by it too.

What I also found lacking in these élite circles was the range and variety of human types which a painter or writer rubs shoulders with in a Bohemian or merely more open world. They all smelt of the University. They had been brain-washed and class-conditioned there. The Johns had once provided a different ambience where talents and opinions of many kinds could show themselves, but they were now becoming respectable and would soon be moving from the caravans and heath ponies of Alderney to a Georgian manor house near Fordingbridge. Only Dorelia John with her liking for the original and unconventional continued to stand for broader values. She was in London for a good part of this winter, the most beautiful woman at any party she attended, yet totally indifferent to the impression she produced. I saw as much as I could of her, for if she did not say anything that could be called clever – she spoke entirely in brief understatements – one was always conscious of her wisdom and understanding.

I had been seeing little of Hope-Johnstone during the past year because he did not get on with my Bloomsbury friends and now he was on the point of sailing for America with the plan of selling old masters to millionaires. The boom for picture buying was just beginning there. He had saved a little money from his collaboration with Compton Mackenzie in founding *The Gramophone* and, as editor of *The Burlington Magazine* just after the war, had picked up a fair amount of information about paintings and made useful contacts in the art dealers' and connoisseurs' world. He therefore hoped to make his fortune by a few big deals and there appeared to be no reason why, as soon as he had learned the ropes, he should not do so. His preparations were, as one would expect, on a grand scale. The better to impress the millionaires, he had decided to assume the role of the cultured English aristocrat, and this demanded a large wardrobe of well-cut clothes. He laid them out on his bed to show them to me – five Savile Row suits, two dozen shirts made to order by Edouard and Robinson, a case of cut-throat razors, ivory hair-brushes with his monogram on them, shoes from Moykoff in Burlington Arcade and pigskin suitcases. Then he took a first-class berth to New York, but before much time had passed his suitcases with all his clothes in them had been stolen. This was so typical of his Charlie Chaplin career that I was scarcely surprised. However he persevered in his task of educating the millionaires and though he made no sensational deals he contrived to keep his head above water.

All this winter and spring I had been avoiding Carrington and when we met accidentally at parties we did not speak to one another. Yet I was still deeply in love with her and knew that she had not ceased to be attached to me. Indeed since Ralph's settling in with Frances her need of me had become greater than ever: our separation had been imposed on us by the conflict between our characters and not by any falling off in affection. The diary I kept at this time is full of anguished passages about her – some of them bitter and satirical, others full of love and remorse. Here is one of them, dated November, which illustrates the general run of my feelings.

I was crossing Tottenham Court Road when I saw Ralph and Carrington coming down the opposite pavement. Very large and tall and wearing a broad-brimmed hat, he looked as if he came from the

Colonies and was a tea planter or a cattle rancher.

Beside him, looking short and squat and dressed in ugly yellowish clothes, came Carrington. Her hair was a yellow mop: her face, as it often does when she is alone, looked anxious and haggard. Her expression was disagreeable, her age might have been forty. As she walked she turned her ankles outwards and kept a pace behind him as though she was an inferior. I could hear their voices as they passed without seeing me: they were arguing. His voice went up every moment into a hoarse squeak: this was the effect of grafting on a man with a naturally deep voice Lytton's peculiar treble. Hers was low and angry.

I saw them perhaps for the first time in my life as strangers see them: a gypsy tinker and his squaw, striding through the London streets. They had for five years lived together and argued, he bullying her, she exasperating him. Although she always got her way, she had paid for it in the loss of her youth and beauty. At the same time they were inseparable. Bad habits attach people to one another as closely as good ones. These two conserved the attachment when they had lost the sentiments of lovers and would no doubt continue to persecute and to irritate and to wear down one another until they were dead.

Yet, as she passed me, I caught sight of her bare hand. It was the same hand on which I had so often fixed my eyes as though all the beauty of the world and all my happiness were contained in it. Now at this moment it seemed to me that nothing had altered, and that this middle-aged, dull-looking married woman was in some way another 'myself' since she carried about in her so large a part of my life. I felt for her as one only feels for oneself, loved her as one only loves other people, and I knew that no alteration in this would ever be possible.

Other passages about my feelings for her are more perverse. My love-hate would take extravagant forms. Often it seemed as though my whole nature, which till now had been relatively simple and naive, was being warped and twisted, turned in on itself and filled with bitter and ironical overtones. The novel I was writing, *A Holiday by the Sea,* as well as my letters to Helen Anrep, are evidence of it.

Yet these were my formative years as a writer. My love for Carrington had bitten deeply into me and broken up my self-sufficiency and egoism. Under all my interests and occupations it ran like a dark river, making everything else unreal in spite of the delight I felt in the immediate moment. A love which, contrary to the course of Dante's *Divina Commedia,* moved from the Paradiso to the Inferno.

In April I decided to go for a few months to the South of France. Inflation was making it the cheapest country in Europe and I needed a change of scene. My father gave his consent and my great-aunt, though far from pleased, raised no objection. I therefore wrote to Carrington, telling her of my intention, and suggesting that we might meet before I left. She agreed at once and we had supper in my rooms and afterwards went to a film about circus life called *Vaudeville* which moved me deeply by providing a catharsis to my feelings that was all the greater because my emotion was shared by her. Back in my rooms again I longed to make love to her but, fearing a refusal, stifled my inclination and instead escorted her quietly to the underground. Two days later I got a letter in which she said that she had wanted to spend the night with me, but had not dared to suggest it. Rather tentatively we agreed to resume our old correspondence.

I did not however leave England for another month. The General Strike and my interest in two girls delayed me. But all the time I was in a hurry to get away for I badly needed to be alone and free from commitments and responsibilities. So at last I tore myself up and took the night boat from Newhaven.

13

Toulon

I reached Paris towards the end of May. The chestnut trees were in flower in the boulevards, the tulips gleamed in the Luxembourg Gardens and wherever one looked one saw young men and girls kissing and holding hands. Everything spoke of love and I felt lost and sad because I had no one. Then suddenly I did have someone. As I was buying a shirt in the Magazin du Louvre an English girl asked me what was the French for button. *Bouton,* I replied, we both laughed and I asked her to lunch. By the time the dessert was served we were kissing like everyone else.

Jean was twenty-four, new to love affairs and engaged to be married to a very correct person, the Hungarian tennis champion. We spent three or four days together, eating delicious meals in the Parc de Montsouris, taking our siestas in my hotel at Montparnasse and finishing the evenings at the Closerie des Lilas. It was the place and the month that had drawn us together and we did not separate till I had spent almost all my money. Then I bought a third-class ticket to Marseilles and travelled all night in a carriage packed with Armenian refugees who seemed to be suffering from a pustular complaint which made them repeatedly sick on the floor.

From Marseilles I went on to Cassis, a small fishing village set among vineyards and pinewoods where a colony of artists had established itself. The leading figure among them was Colonel Teed, late of the Bengal Lancers, who had settled here with the lady of his choice after his wife had refused to divorce him. He was a delightful man, perfectly at ease and happy in this unconventional society and his house with its tapestried rooms, carved staircase, lime walk, Dutch pond, shady plane trees and Aleppo pines provided an ideal setting for his hospitality. He made his own wine and the feast he gave for the vintage was a splendid occasion. After the grapes had been picked and carried in carts to the vats, his guests sat down to a gargantuan meal – fish, turkey, goose, chicken, kid, ham, salad, aubergines, figs – laid out on trestle tables under the lime trees. The dishes were decorated with garlands of zinnias and vine leaves. Conversation buzzed, wine flowed, the sun shone, birds twittered, bees flew out of the pinewoods and back again while thirty people of various nations – Greeks, Hindus, Russians, Italians, French and English – drank and guzzled. Then the Colonel's home-made brandy was passed round and we staggered back at dusk in a pelting storm of rain.

Roland Penrose, Alec's younger brother, had a house just outside the village. He was a gentle, serious, good-looking young man with considerable charm of manner who had recently taken a French wife. Before that he had shared his house with a young Greek painter called Janko Varda. I took a great liking to this man because he had a most original style of conversation in which he made use of the dogmas of the Orthodox Church to illustrate his views on life and art.

He had a great way with young girls. Few could resist him, for he not only amused them with his conversation but charmed them with the delicacy of his advances. It interested me to know that he was a great friend of Clare Bollard. When shortly before the First World War he had left Athens for London his father had warned him not to be taken in by the free-and-easy manners of English girls because underneath these they were as strict in their conduct as Greek girls. He must therefore be careful to comport himself on all occasions like a gentleman. However the first English girl he got to know was Clare, who was then eighteen, and she had different views of how gentlemen should behave. A few years later he met and married the beautiful Dorothy, whom I have spoken of, but they did not get on and at the end of a few months he left her. Varda was not meant for marriage.

In the late 'thirties he emigrated to America and took up his residence in a boat in San Francisco harbour. I used to hear of him through friends. Then one day in the spring of 1966 he turned up at my house near Malaga after a visit to Robert Graves. But instead of the slim, faun-like Adonis I had known forty years before I was amazed to see a short, stoutish old gentleman with drooping white moustaches. No doubt he got a similar shock on seeing me. But his powers of fascinating young women had evidently not left him for he came accompanied by an attractive and delightful girl of twenty-three who was driving him round Europe in her car and, since he never had any money, was presumably paying his expenses. She could hardly have found a better cicerone, for he knew the art world well and had friends wherever he went. Also he had become an even more entertaining talker than he had been before.

One of the more noteworthy members of Cassis society was an English woman of around forty called Miss Sellers. She was a pleasant, cheerful person who, clad in her invariable brown tweed suit, would have passed unnoticed in any village in England if her mode of life had not contradicted her air of respectability. For she was a Lesbian who paraded her propensities by sharing her little house on the port with a flashy and much-bedizened prostitute from Marseilles. Her sense of incongruity had led her to drape a Union Jack over her bed and to hang another from her balcony, on which at any hour of the day her painted friend could be seen looking down like Jezebel into the street below. To supplement her small private means Britannia, as she liked to be called, drove a taxi and one of her specialities was a conducted tour of the Marseilles brothels. Any friend of Roland Penrose could visit them free of charge, for as it happened the owner of the principal chain of houses had been a Belgian refugee in England during the war and in that capacity had been taken in by the Penrose parents and lodged in all innocence in their house. When some years later he had run into Roland in the Canebière he had been moved by the impulse to return this hospitality and so had offered him and his friends the free run of his establishments and of all the girls in them. Neither Roland nor Varda were the sort of people to avail themselves of this offer, but my curiosity led me to accompany Britannia on one of her tours and to see a blue film which disgusted me. After this we visited that notorious quarter of the Vieux Port where old, hideous and diseased whores stood each outside the door of her tiny bedroom and by snatching at the hats of passers-by tried to oblige them to enter their dens. I noticed that over each bed there hung a coloured lithograph of the Virgin which I was told they turned to face the wall whenever they secured a client. No more horrifying spectacle of vice and squalor could exist anywhere and perhaps the only good thing the Nazis ever did was to dynamite this whole bug-ridden quarter.

After a week or two at Cassis I moved on to Toulon. I found this to be a place completely after my own heart. The port with its jostling fishing boats was as pretty as a port could be and I took at once to the old quarter of the town with its narrow streets and high houses hung with brightly coloured washing in the Neapolitan manner. There was a row of brothels marked by red lights, but it was dangerous to walk alone here after dark because every week someone was knifed.

The summer was now in full swing. The sun blazed down from the sky, drenching the white walls of the houses and the green leaves of the trees with its dazzling light. The girls had all come out in their summer frocks. They were prettier than they are in the north, some of them being really beautiful, and as I walked along the street or stood next to them in a crowded tram, with their heady scents filling my nostrils and their dark eyes sometimes catching mine, I felt almost overpowered. It seemed impossible to speak to any of them and yet I wished to speak to them all.

One afternoon as I was taking a stroll over the quay I noticed a girl with a flat basket on her arm heaped with cream buns which she was selling to sailors. She was about eighteen, with clear eyes, a finely-cut mouth, an olive skin and a serious expression that was almost hard in its lack of sensuality. I had seen such faces before in Florentine paintings. The only way of attracting her attention was to buy one of her buns. So long as one munched she would laugh and talk, but as soon as one's jaws ceased moving she would relapse into silence and look in another direction. Unfortunately the buns were disgusting, for she had bought them at a cheap confectioner's after all hope of selling them across the counter had gone, with the result that they were stale and fly-blown and their cream rancid. However there she was, the only girl in the town I could talk to, so I began to build up a day-dream life around her. I would marry her and either settle down among the fishermen or buy a caravan and a coconut-shy and move from fair to fair through the beautiful land of Provence. But when I spoke to her of this she only laughed at me, perhaps unable to believe that I was serious in what I said. I was still hoping to persuade her when my digestion gave way from all the buns I had been eating and I had to stop buying them.

I now moved out to Mourillon, a mile or so to the east of the town, and took a room at the Hotel de la Réserve, overlooking the Rade. How blue, how calm, how mild and pond-like was that sea! The beach was heaped with squelchy seaweeds that had been washed up by the tide and were alive with sand-hoppers, but when I got into the water I found it as tepid as a bath. A rickety wooden pier had been built out over it and at the end there was a tiny glass-enclosed restaurant. Here one could sit and eat grilled sole or red mullet as one watched the brown bodies of the bathers swimming below. Beyond lay the pine woods, silent in the heat and giving out their resinous smell, and under them men and girls sat about in their underclothes, flirting and drinking.

Every morning when I came downstairs I noticed a strange young woman, heavily made up and perfumed and dressed in the smartest frocks, who sat alone in a corner of the balcony and spoke to no one. I imagined that she must be a dancer or singer, but when I enquired I was told that she was the daughter of the hotel proprietress and by profession an actress. I soon got to know her and to learn more of her history. Her father had been the manager of the railway buffet at St Etienne and on his death M. Herriot, who was then prime minister, had offered to take her to Paris and to launch her on a theatrical career. He put her in the Odéon and she became his mistress. But then his government fell and she was dismissed. Herriot, who now had another mistress whom he liked better, sent her back to her mother's hotel at Toulon to await his return to office, when he promised to reinstate her in the Comédie Française.

Toulon

Her character was a disagreeable one, peevish, sulky and with such an insatiable thirst for flattery that her conversation consisted almost entirely in an open fishing and pestering for compliments. She would shut herself up in her room all day, thrumming on the piano, reciting her parts and playing with a savage fox terrier. Then she would come out and sit on the balcony, watching and waiting for something that never happened. Bad health made her ill-tempered, yet every now and then she would come up to me, smiling all over and purring like a cat that asks to have its back scratched. She wanted compliments. If I forgot to say at once, 'Comme vous êtes ravissante ce matin, Mlle Marguérite!' she would not be ashamed to ask, 'Comment me trouvez-vous aujourd'hui?' And when reassured on this point, she would add, 'Et mes oreilles?' For the great Valentino had once said to her, 'Mademoiselle, you have the most beautiful ears in France.'

A scandal with an admiral had shut her out of Toulon society, which as an actress and the best-dressed woman in the town she might otherwise have been admitted to. For that reason she preferred to know no one. When she went out at four o'clock to buy flowers, visit her modiste and drink tea in the fashionable tea shop, she went by herself. Twice a week she crossed the harbour to play at the Casino at Tamaris. At night she would have a secret meeting with a naval officer in a dark lane or at her *garçonnière* in the town. To console herself for her isolation she would boast of her friends and of what they were going to do for her. They had got her an invitation to play at Monte Carlo, they were taking her on a yachting cruise to Greece, she was to sit for the greatest painter of the Salon and be filmed for both Mary Magdalene and La Gioconda. But none of these day-dreams ever came true.

One evening as I leaned on the balcony of the terrace watching the moon rise over the sea, Marguérite came and stood beside me. We talked for a little, then walked down to the beach. Here we sat on a heap of dried seaweed at the edge of the slip-slopping water and as she bent over towards me her scent (she drenched herself in three different kinds, one for her face, one for her hands and one for her breasts and body) rose and intoxicated me. I forgot my aversion for her and kissed her.

This led to her inviting me to go to her *garçonnière*. It was an invitation that appealed less to my senses than to my vanity. Had she not known and – or so she said – refused Valentino? For two days I was excited by the prospect, yet there was something about her that repelled me and though I kept the appointment I could not bring myself to make love to her. After this we never met without bickering.

I had made friends with a retired *professeur de lycée*, M. Bordier, and his wife, who lived close by. He was a man in the mould of Anatole France, a good bourgeois with a veneer of wit and scepticism, and when I left Toulon we agreed to write to one another. It was he who a couple of years later told me of Marguérite Duchesne's end. It seems that her mother, getting tired of running a hotel, had retired to the country to cultivate her kitchen garden and Marguérite became bored. She left for Paris, alleging that she was to work on a film, and after drawing her mother's savings, which amounted to 200,000 francs, from the bank, proceeded to live on a luxurious scale till in a few months' time they were exhausted. She then took veronal and died while her mother was left with nothing to support herself on.

At the end of August I went for a few days to the mountains to escape the heat. Here is a letter I wrote from there to Carrington which shows a different and healthier side of my character.

Colmars, where I am, is a little XVI century fortress with five shops, a fountain, a square and an immense number of cocks and hens. Round the battlements is a walk planted with walnuts and horse-chestnuts, where peasant women in wide black skirts and spreading straw hats sit gravely and young men play bowls. The whole town, with its double fortifications, sallyports and towers is no bigger than the tail end of Ham Village.

I arrived here after two days of travel in great heat … I am at 4,000 feet above the sea and very happy. The Alps of white and rose lime-stone tower overhead. Orange clouds like feather beds pass by, the air is cool. I sit outside my hotel drinking tea.

Nowadays no one of course dares to like Alpine scenery. I am simple enough to find great pleasure in it, in the streams and woods and meadows and hayfields and in the innumerable flowers. 'The arrangement of the masses', you say, 'how is that?' Not, I am afraid, very good. But as I'm a mere writer I must be allowed sometimes to escape into pine woods, to pick gentians and vetches and hawk bits, to rub my face and hands in the damp fresh moss and eat delicious wild strawberries. After the sea and the heat this plunge into a northern climate sets me living and feeling again in all kinds of forgotten ways. Tomorrow I shall go to the lake at Allos, which is nearly 7,000 feet above the sea, and perhaps sleep there. I wish that you were with me, but no, it is Sunday afternoon and you are playing badminton with Prince Bismarck or being cross-questioned by Lady Oxford or repeating your dreams to Tommy and thinking of everyone in the world except Mr Crusoe, who makes his appearance, I'm afraid, only when you've exhausted everyone else and are completely bored and at a loose end. Then you remember his existence and the odd fact that he is always ready to answer your letters (which no one else does) – but visit him on one of his islands? What nonsense! It is rather impertinent of him even to suggest it.

I am now two days older than when I began this letter and my hair is two days thinner and greyer and my fountain pen rustier and scratchier. I set off at five yesterday morning, climbed to a little lake, ascended a peak, visited another lake, climbed another peak and returned home at 10 o'clock at night. I am delighted to find myself so strong and active. I was scarcely content with walking: up the steepest slopes I ran and scrambled and then tumbled down a thousand feet in a few minutes. I reached the châlet of the lake of Allos at noon – and famishing. I eat a plate of ham, two trout, nearly half a chicken, a whole loaf of bread, a bowl of curds and drank almost two bottles of wine. Then I fell onto the ground feeling like the wolf in the nursery tale who had stones sewn up in its stomach. At three I went on and with each hour that passed I seemed to walk faster and to feel stronger. And although my activity as a walker does not help me to write my novel, or to live more cheaply, or to persuade you to visit me or to be more constant in your affections, it does give me a greatly increased feeling of self-confidence, which extends even to these things. Yes, if I ever have money, I shall have a try at climbing with ropes and picks. But then one cannot go alone. To get full pleasure from the conquest of Nature one must be without any companion. These painters that give laws to our taste have robbed us of half the pleasures of life. The world of significant appearance is not the only one nor the most interesting. It is the fields, the stacks of corn, the gardens, the horses, the wild flowers that excite me more each year – everything that is connected with some possible form of life. When next I have a house in the country, I shall work the garden myself and learn something of farming.

Your conception of country life is so different to mine – perhaps that is why Ham Spray does not move my imagination. First I should like to be connected with a village – to know all that goes on in it, to meet all the people and to see the cows, the horses, the carts coming and going and the harvest and vintage carried on. And I should like myself to have cows, horses, hens, ducks, pigs, everything. If I had the money I should certainly start thinking of marriage and then I should want children for just the same reason that I would like to have dogs and horses and pigs. I have passed my youth in day-dreams – now I should like to live as full and as real a life as possible. Unfortunately I am not likely ever to live in this manner – it's merely another dream.

There is really something extraordinary about this mountain air.

The sound of the rivers at night, by day of cocks crowing, of a man sawing wood, of children playing fill me with ecstasy. It is a long time since I have been so happy. The restless state of mind I am generally in is gone: I feel deliciously contented. How suffer from depression when one is always, as it were, eating a meal? For the sight of the thick sprouting grass, of the struggling plants and flowers, the sound of the crowing cocks and the streams, the smell of the beech woods and of the wet grass are by themselves food and nourishment.

On my return to Toulon I took a room in the Rue Courbet between the Place d'Armes and the prison. It was a short street of run-down, decaying houses which had acquired a bad name because a certain amount of opium smoking, introduced by the French sailors from Annam, went on in it, but I liked my room which was large and dark and shabby with a double bed of black oak, a full-length mirror and a sombre red wallpaper. The flat above me was occupied by a retired Parisian cocotte called Madame Georgette who was learning English in order to read Conrad because his novels and those of Pierre Louÿs were the favourite literature of the young naval officers, back from service in the South China Seas. She engaged me to give her lessons and I used to sit in her little salon stuffed with hideous *chinoiserie,* speculating on whether she had known the original of Odette de Crécy. She also introduced me to opium, of which she smoked a pipe or two every evening as soon as the sun had gone down, for then the police had no authority to enter. But I did not persevere with this since I got no dreams from it and was afraid of getting hooked.

As usual I lived very quietly, spending most of my time at the Café Brasserie du Coq Hardi in the main boulevard, working alternatively at my novel and at my life of Santa Teresa or else reading Proust. I had got to know some of the girls who frequented the café – Zizi, Youyou, who was later stabbed to death by her *maquereau,* and a very louche English girl called Lulu. She was said to be a spy because she had a sufficient income to live on and yet was not, like the others, a tart. I used to go to her villa sometimes, but only for conversation. The world of vice interested me and she knew more about it and about the seamier side of sex than anyone I had previously met. As she was completely uninhibited, and indeed usually received me in her bath, she talked about it freely though she was reserved about her own life. One day she took me to a voyeur's establishment. We went in by the back door to a cheap sailors' brothel and looked through a pane of glass into a tiny room in which there stood a girl in a dirty chemise beside a bed. She was probably not more than twenty-two or three, but her face was worn and haggard. Every five or ten minutes a sailor came in, for it was Saturday night and a queue was drawn up outside. I had never understood what lust was before. The scene was sordid, pitiful, cruel and very Toulouse-Lautrec. I imagine that by taking me here Lulu had hoped to excite me to make love to her, but it had the opposite effect, for it put me against sexual relations for some time just as the blue film I had seen at Marseilles had done and left me with a strong feeling that brothels were iniquitous places and ought to be abolished.

In a letter to Helen Anrep I gave a rather more Byronic account of my way of life. After speaking of my acquaintances at the Coq Hardi I went on:

> As a writer this world interests me though in itself it is no more interesting than a world of nursery governesses and clergymen. When I am melancholy and cynical, as I often am, I find in the rapidity and inanity of a life of debauchery a certain satisfaction. Under the music and the embraces, lies the skull. Beauty is shorter, love is shorter, life is shorter among these people who live for pleasure without ever obtaining any. I make my incursions into this world and retire again, more sober and more sensible, into myself. It is an exercise that everyone might derive some advantage from ...
>
> I am slipping into a more and more degraded life: it's my own form of chastity. When one reduces love to a habit and an absurdity, one has no illusions about what one is missing and life becomes more endurable. I do not wish to be tormented any longer by ideas of lost or missing happiness. Besides, low love-affairs are a means to the satisfaction of one of my chief instincts – curiosity. With their light I explore certain caves and dungeons of the world which would otherwise be closed to me.

A little later I was writing to Helen again in a state of deep depression:

> What is a very bad sign with me, I have lost my power of laughing at myself: you, if you were here, would restore it to me. Without that I am like a tortoise which because it has rheumatism in the neck cannot stretch its head out of its shell.
>
> Then there are other complications which I cannot explain at present. Indeed I don't pretend to be able to relate anything in this letter – only enough to implore your succour, your prayers, your rogations, your intercessions, that is to say your ironical glances, your sarcasms and all the apparatus of your deadly armoury.

At about this time I got to know a young lieutenant in the Submarine Service called Arar who lodged in my house.

His parents were wealthy Parisians of I think Jewish or Armenian stock and he introduced me to some of his friends in the service, who came from aristocratic families. One, whom I lunched with, was a prince and a duke. Arar was uncommonly good looking and so strongly sexed that he required, he told me, a woman every day, while at sea he made use of his sailor servant. He was also very attractive to the opposite sex and I remember one day when I was out with him his running across the street to accost a pretty and well-dressed young woman and telling me when he returned that he had made an assignation with her. While I admired him for his success with women, he professed an equal admiration for me, partly because I was so dedicated to my work, but also because I was reading Proust in French, a thing that he had supposed no Anglo-Saxon was capable of, seeing that his novel embodies all that is most subtle and refined in the French spirit. He was still more amazed when I told him that I had read more than half of the *Mémoires* of the Duc de Saint Simon and that I knew Baudelaire and Rimbaud well, but he could not understand my being so poorly versed in Corneille or regarding Lamartine and Hugo as bores. He found only one thing to criticize in me – that I had no sexual life. How was it that though the Coq Hardi was frequented by *filles* I had never engaged the services of any of them? For 500 francs a month I could have a regular mistress. Then it must have occurred to him that I could not afford to pay so much, for he came out with a solution of his own.

'Why don't you take Marie?' he said. She was the servant who made our beds, a big, stolid peasant girl of around twenty-four. I knew already that she had been brought up in an orphanage and had then been in a brothel, which she had left to marry a soldier. But this had not lasted, so she had come to work in our house. She always wore the same flimsy cotton dress with bedroom slippers on her feet, never went out and talked little. She appeared to have a passion for washing floors and dusting and gave the impression of being a bit simple.

'You've only got to call her', Arar said, 'at any hour of the day or night and she'll be happy to oblige. Don't give her money as she has no use for it, but give her caramels. She is mad about caramels and sucking sweets.'

I replied that I was afraid of venereal disease.

'Don't worry about that,' he said. 'I've had her examined by a doctor. Only J. (another naval officer who lodged in the house) and I ever sleep with her. And he hardly ever does so as he's religious and suffers from guilt afterwards. You know that she never goes out because the streets frighten her. She has the temperament of a nun.'

I resisted his suggestion for some time because I found it impossible to make a conversational bridge to her, but then gradually her silent love of washing floors and her strong body began to make an impression on me. She really was nun-like. So one hot afternoon after lunch when I found her doing my room I said to her, 'Come on, get into bed.' Without a word she pulled off her dress and got in naked as she wore nothing under it. Her body was hard and firm and strong and smelt of wet earth like a garden after rain. She knew a lot about making love, whereas I knew little, and she enjoyed it, though I think more out of a wish to be serviceable than from sensuality or the urge to get pleasure for herself. She was humble and silent and practical and I felt touched by something in her willingness and enjoyed the feel of her strong, earthy body next to mine. What she gave me was a simple physical satisfaction – no complication with minds. I felt that our contact was wholesome and pure and yet I was also ashamed of it and for that reason did not record it in my diary. For ought not every sexual rela-tion to be also a relation between persons?

My real life was spent at the Coq Hardi, reading and writing. I toiled on at Santa Teresa, getting more and more bored with it and I also worked at my novel, which had begun to go wrong. Then I started a picaresque story about a commercial traveller, but it went badly. While I was still struggling with it Ralph Partridge and Frances Marshall came out to visit me and, seeing my difficulties, they urged me to drop all these books which I found so difficult to write, and embark on something easier. Yes – but what? I was reading a little volume of Quevedo's prose at this time and came on a satirical piece in the style of popular almanacs. Swift read it later and made use of it in his famous spoof prophecy of the death of the astrologer and almanac writer, John Partridge. At the same time Quevedo's *Sueños* had been making a deep impression on me by the splendid sonority of their language and these works, together with my friends' advice, were at the back of my mind when one evening at the Coq Hardi I began to write, without any previous plan or intention and almost as though the words were dictated to me, a piece that as it got down on paper became *Dr Partridge's Almanack*. It started off with an introduction written in grandiloquent prose, full of archaisms in the manner of Quevedo and Sir Thomas Browne, in which Partridge's death and recent return from the grave are described by a friend and disciple of his. This was followed by a summary of his message to mankind. Life being such a tormented, inco-herent and fatuous thing, so full of pain and disappointment, the only rational course was to put an end to it. Indeed, stirred by the rain of bodies that had fallen into death during the war, the astrologer had risen from his tomb expressly to urge this. After this follow the predictions of the almanac, Partridge's aim in offering them being, as he said, 'to introduce into this fever called life some of the order and certainty of the grave', and thus gradually to wean men from their love of it.

In these two prefaces my memories of the war, together with the bitterness I felt over Carrington and some rather inappropriate Old Testa-ment imagery, combined to set up an atmosphere of horror, disgust for life and melancholy that is so far-fetched that it is always on the point of toppling over into absurdity. The predictions, which consist of short paragraphs often devoted to the saints or pseudo-saints of particular days, drawn from my studies of hagiography but sometimes influenced by Edward Lear, continue the same mixed strain. One could describe the book as a celebration of the death instinct and therefore absurd because we none of us really want to die. Thus it also celebrates life, though at the same time satirizing it. I sat up writing *Dr Partridge* till four in the morning and continued it next day. By nightfall I had finished it but for a page or two where my inspiration ran out. Then I put it aside till in 1934 Chatto and Windus published it in a handsome format under the nom de plume of George Beaton. It fell dead in spite of a glowing review by David Garnett, but I keep a warm feeling for it because it displays, I think, a certain command of language as well as a pessimism that seems to forecast the days of Stalin, Hitler and the atom bomb.

Ever since my arrival in Toulon I had been corresponding regularly with Carrington. I was still obsessed by her, but, mixed with my feelings of love and affection there were pockets of resentment that kept breaking out in reproaches and recriminations. Why did she always have to behave so perversely?

Nearly a year before, at the time of our first breach, she had offered an explanation:

'I do not believe that it was any particular circumstances that made our relation impossible; it was my predestined inability to have intimate relations with anyone. I believe that I am a perfect combination of a nymphomaniac and a wood nymph. I hanker after intimacies, which another side of my nature is perpetually at war against. Lately, removed from any intimacies, causing no one unhappiness and having no sense of guilt, I have felt more at peace with myself than I have ever felt before.'

But just now she was going through a different phase. Faced with the need to console herself for Ralph's absorption in Frances, she had adopted the plan of spreading her interests and affections over as many people as possible. She was also seeing a good deal of Tommy (Stephen Tomlin) who was spending the summer at Ham Spray. As I gathered later, he was being tried out as a substitute for Ralph, to form the third leg of the tripod, but this broke down because, much though he liked Lytton, he could never be tied for long to any one person or place. In July she wrote to me about her friendship with him and at first I was sympathetic. She felt a complete ease, she said, in talking to him, and I could understand that for he was the most congenial of companions. But then, as she went on to tell me of the long midnight walks on the Downs that she was taking with him and of the weekend excursions they made, I began to feel jealous, as no doubt she intended me to be. For even in the time of my closest intimacy with her I had never been allowed these things. I replied by teasing her about Bertha. This pretty and lively girl had just left her husband for another man, whom she later married. But meanwhile she was on holiday. Before leaving for France I had had a mild flirtation with her in my rooms and now she came to spend a few days with me in the Rue Courbet, after which I went back with her to Cassis for the vintage celebrations. Her lover, a tolerant man who habitually travelled about with an ugly ex-wife and two rather less ugly ex-mistresses – each of them, like a succession of cars from Baby Austins to Rolls Royces, marking a higher stage in his amorous progress – raised no objection to her staying with me, in spite of the fact that he was in love with her.

My first letters to Carrington that summer contained the simple suggestion that we should renew our old correspondence.

> I only ask of you a little more of your famous invention – the tele-friendship. For I've become wise, and even this Love-at-a-distance, when it flowers among the leaves of your letters, has enough charm and perfume to be worth picking and wearing. I'm not so rich in friends, nor so popular, nor so happy as to neglect even the daisies and chick-weeds you send me.

But before long I was suggesting a full renewal of our old relation. If we could forget the painful memories of past quarrels and refrain from the angry expressions that came to our lips or pens when we felt hurt, we might be able, I said, to achieve this. But mutual recriminations kept on cropping up in our letters. I complained that she had developed the habit of paying out the frustrations of her life on me. 'You have three or four close friends, but only one scapegoat.' She complained of my continually criticizing her. 'You say now', I replied, 'that if I did not observe, measure and react from all your actions so closely, we should get on better. But there it is! To all other signals I am dumb, but one little bell tinkling in your head sets a whole belfry rocking in mine.'

Then in a long letter she accused me of having a malicious hatred of her. In a reply which I did not send off I said that between irony and malice there was a world of difference and that her misfortunes would always move me.

> On the contrary I would say that in your voice there came to be an almost perpetual grudge and hatred: *you* hated *me* and only in my absence were able to veer back to affection. Of course I understand the reason: my love seemed a menace to your liberty.
> So why then do you say that you fear to meet me on account of my

irony or my hatred? Last time we met I had no other emotion than surprise that after all I should love you so deeply. Your voice opened up cave after cave, corridor after corridor – a whole story buried and hidden from the light whose existence I had almost forgotten – and echoed through them. How then was there room for the faintest ray of irony? No, it was for other reasons that you did not wish to see me, for those same reasons that have operated a thousand times in the past to unstitch the seam of our friendship.

Do you wish us to be friends? Then you must learn to sew, not always to pull apart. If you were not by nature so perverse and gifted with so few instincts for success and happiness, you would have seen that my last week in England was one of those occasions such as occur few times in a life for mutual forgiveness and reconciliation. There is, dear amiga, something inhuman and maniacal in your contrariness. Had you felt indifferent towards me, it would have been sensible not to have come. Had you not wished us to be friends, sensible also. But to wish to come and not to——! It is people like yourself who turn the world into the torture chamber and mad-house one so often finds it.

I said I often bore resentments against you: it is precisely on this account that I bear them. Not because you have grown tired of me, nor because you care more for others – these things I can accept with resignation. They are wounds which heal quickly. But that during the time when we were lovers you never did anything for our joint happiness – that you showed yourself always stingy, grudging, even spiteful – I forgive that with greater difficulty. The more I see of other women and the more I see of the love affairs of others, the more cruel and tormenting your conduct appears to me ...

Such were the feelings that in black moments I nursed to myself. But Carrington was now, she wrote, leading a dissipated life, going out night after night to parties and returning home to Gordon Square at three in the morning. I remonstrated rather priggishly with her over this, telling her she was a person who could only live by her heart and never by frivolity or light affairs. She should choose people who had serious qualities and stick to them.

In my eyes all this falling in and out and in and out of love is incomprehensible ... I've never grown tired of anyone yet. My feeling for you never has, never will, never could alter, not if I lived for forty years ... I can no more cease to love the people I do love than I can cease to enjoy Shakespeare and Milton.

Toulon

She was sleeping badly, as she often did, and I advised her to try a
country remedy, a pillow stuffed with hops. She was also getting a new
pleasure from riding over the Downs on the white horse, Belle, which she
had just bought, so I asked for a photograph of her on it.

I carry your last photograph everywhere with me – in my pocket?
round my neck? in my boot? in my heart? Never mind where so long
as I carry it, but perhaps you will send me another to leave in my
room and spread a benign influence.

I was now trying to persuade her to come out and visit me, as Ralph and
Frances were about to do, but after hesitating for some time she said that
she could not get away. This provoked a bitter reply from me – it was the
mood that had led me to write *Dr Partridge's Almanack*.

You once had it in your power to make of me what you pleased: my
character, hesitating at the crossroads, might have taken any direction. This is what you have made of me – someone who still loves you
and is not essentially unkind, but who, under his ordinary façades, is
as embittered at heart as if he had been born with a hump on his back.

Then suddenly she changed her mind. I was due to return to London in
the middle of November and she agreed to meet me in Paris. She arrived,
then I saw that she had really come to see her friend Lucy de V., a beautiful
cocotte who had married a French marquis. I was not well-dressed or
fashionable enough to be taken to call on her, so I spent the day walking
about the streets by myself. That evening she did her best to atone for this,
but underneath there was a feeling of strain. Then when we reached Calais
she insisted that we must separate on the boat because in a sudden access of
respectability she feared that I might be taken as her lover. It was the old
story, only more crudely expressed than before, that after spending a night
with me her guilty feelings would make her wish to avoid me. Although it
did not augur well for the future of our relations, I tried to pretend that
nothing had happened.

14

London again

On reaching London I found that Roger Fry was giving up his studio at 18 Fitzroy Street, which meant that I should have at once to find other quarters. However Freda offered to lend me her rooms, so, while waiting for them to be free, I went down to visit my parents on the Cotswolds. Here my father received me in a more friendly way than usual and I spent a pleasant week walking in the dripping beech woods and talking to my mother. What one likes about one's parents is that they never seem to change.

On returning to London I set about looking for a flat and soon found an attractive one on the top floor of 14 Great James Street. The rent was two guineas a week but my aunt offered to increase my allowance so I took it for three years from the first week in February as it was not available till then. But hardly was Christmas passed when Freda wanted her flat back again. Since there was no time to look round I took a bedroom on the top floor of Vaiani's Restaurant in Charlotte Street.

It was a large bare room with no other furniture than a chair, a double bed and a gas fire that was out of order. Next door to me lived two slatternly prostitutes, just back from Port Said, who would come in drunk at one in the morning. In their room there was a new deal wardrobe with a mirror set in it which had the habit of suddenly swinging open of its own accord. This put it into their heads that it was haunted. Every time it did so they would give a shriek, run into my room in their filthy nightdresses and try to get into bed with me. After this had happened twice I fixed a lock on the door, but this only led to their hammering on it so that I was obliged to complain to Mr Vaiani, who turned them out.

I had not been here more than a few days when the weather turned bitterly cold. Snow fell and lay in the streets and after it came a yellow fog. At the same time I went down with a severe attack of flu. For a week I lay in bed without seeing anyone but the little waitress who brought me my meals so that I almost regretted losing the company of the girls next door.

Then, as I was slowly recovering, Carrington arrived. It was evening. The lamplight from the street threw the shadow of the dingy lace curtains on to the opposite wall where they trembled slightly like the shadow of a trellised vine. Since it was too cold to sit in the room she got into bed beside me and we lay watching them. As I was still feeling very weak I had no wish to make love, but this unusual disposition on my part excited her and, for the first time since our meeting in Paris, we did so. The next day I felt worse.

I was barely up and about again when she fell off her horse in Richmond Park and ricked her back. She was taken to Ralph's flat at 41 Gordon Square where she lay unable to move and in a good deal of pain. Although I telephoned frequently for news I did not go to see her because I was not asked to. In a fit of absurd jealousy of Ralph I preferred to stand on my pride and so naturally hurt her feelings. When she was not wounding me I was wounding her.

Soon after this I began to move into my new flat. Great James Street, which dates from the reign of Queen Anne, is with its continuation Bedford Row the most beautiful street in London. The staircases and the main rooms are panelled and, though my attic floor lacked this and its rooms were low and rather small, it was well proportioned. I had a sitting-room, a kitchen and a bathroom with at the back a bedroom which gave on to a small balcony from which one looked out onto a large plane tree. One of my pleasures lay in lying in bed in the early mornings resting my eyes on its dense sea of leaves, but before the end of the year the landlord, with characteristic philistinism, had it cut down, saying that trees produced damp.

Carrington showed a great interest in my flat and, since her back was now better, helped me to paint it and to choose furniture for it. After all, I had taken it largely on her account. Remembering the complaints she had once made of the squalor of my Fitzroy Street rooms, I thought that if I got others that really appealed to her she would come to see me more often, especially since Lytton had taken to spending most of the week in London. But although she would sometimes pass the night with me because she found it convenient to do so, we were not getting on well. I regarded our relation as being that of established lovers and supposed that this must entail mutual adjustments to please one another, but she would accept no limits to her freedom. She came and went as she pleased and preserved an absolute secrecy about her other engagements. In a letter written that March she outlined her attitude sharply and clearly:

You will never know the whole of my life. Every time you put me under inquisitions and cross-questionings I feel you are trying to separate me from myself. Pulling the bark off my tree. I shall come and stay with you when I want to, but, if I should choose to sleep at Alix's, I resent not being able to without implying a lack of affection for you. Of all characteristics in human beings I dread jealousy and possessiveness most.

I was now much less in love with Carrington than I had been and therefore I was not demanding so much of her nor making emotional scenes when she let me down. But my moderation failed to stabilize our relations as I had hoped it would because she had become much more perverse and withdrawn. Her secrecy about her most ordinary actions was now psychopathic. Four months before in Paris she had issued a declaration in which she had claimed the right to have secrets, carry on love affairs and tell lies, but now she was going even further. Other people noticed this too: for example Topsy Lucas, meeting her in Cambridge, remarked that she was 'maddeningly secretive about things that didn't matter, like meeting people in the street'. When I protested about this she appealed to her peculiar, unalterable character to which everyone else must conform. She would offer me no concessions – it was I who must adapt myself to her. I tried to argue with her about this, but it was useless.

Early in May our relations reached a crisis. She had promised to come and stay with me and then put me off, saying that she was going to visit a certain young man whom she did not name in Cambridge. He was, I later learned, not a potential lover as she had insinuated but a homosexual, so that she had deliberately tried to make me jealous. In a moment all the old agony and torment, which I thought I had left behind me, surged up, and with them anger: I even had day-dreams of shooting her. I wrote to her that she must come and see me or I would break with her. Three days later, after reading a few pages of Voltaire's *Diatribe du Docteur Akakia,* I began a short *conte* or novel in the same style, or rather in that of *Candide,* which I called the *History of Poor Robinson*. It ran to 24,000 words and was a satire, both cruel and comic, of my long love affair with Carrington. All the chief actors, as well as my friend Hope, were represented in it and, after following the actual course of events pretty closely, it came to an appropriate though fictitious end. I showed it to no one and it lay among my papers till 1965, when I corrected it and had it typed. Although it has no pretensions to literary value, since it was written solely to relieve my feelings, the three people who have seen it have found it amusing. Its patterned style, full of parallels and antitheses, takes it out of actuality and makes it move rapidly.

Meanwhile our quarrel had been made up. Carrington spent a night with me on her return journey from Cambridge. Although she was no longer in the least in love with me, she did not want to lose me. I was one of the fixed properties of her life, like her house and her white horse Belle, and her link with me was important to her. At the end of the month therefore she asked me down to Ham Spray for the weekend. It was a couple of years since I had stayed there because Lytton had come to regard me as a disturbing influence, but this time he would not be there and the only visitors would be Ralph and Frances. I therefore went down in good spirits, determined to be as agreeable as possible.

Saturday passed off well but on Sunday evening an argument sprang up on the nature and value of art. Ralph and Frances took their usual ultra-rationalist view: the value of a work of art was purely subjective and depended on the amount of pleasure it gave one. I contended that when one said Milton was a better poet than Robert Bridges one was making a judgement that would not be invalidated even if one happened to prefer the poetry of Bridges. Feeling ran high on both sides when, to my surprise and annoyance, Carrington, who had hitherto, like G. E. Moore and Lytton and indeed all artists and writers, held absolute views on art, sided with them against me. Clearly this came simply from her desire to antagonize me and no doubt was left in my mind when, on our retiring rather late, she said that she was too tired to sleep with me. The result was that I lay awake till daylight in a state of agitation and left early next morning without saying goodbye to her. As usual, whenever I raised the courage to pay her back, this petty retaliation was followed by days of nervous exhaustion and misery.

Again we made it up and she came several times to see me in London and spent the night, but without allowing me to make love to her. I had by now learned to take this philosophically and offered no reproaches. But our relation was evidently petering out. Love is a sugar that turns in the end into an acid, hate, and I was beginning to consider how I could escape from her. Then, just when we had planned to meet on White Horse Hill to celebrate the sixth anniversary of our love, she went off for a fortnight to Munich without letting me know. On her return in August she did not come to see me and, in reply to my letter, broke off our relationship.

In the following spring, that is in February 1928, there was an epilogue. Carrington left some flowers at my flat and in reply to my letter of thanks said that she would always be ready to see me and to renew our friendship. I replied cautiously, saying that, though I felt it would be useless for us to try to do that, we might meet occasionally for lunch or tea, since it was better that we should be on good terms than on bad ones. Then in March she rang up to ask if she could come and see me. She came, stayed half an hour and left. A letter followed in which she said how much she had enjoyed seeing me and that she would have written sooner to propose a meeting if she had not feared my irony or my hatred. I replied that she had no need to fear that since a grain of kindness from her always had the power to move me and indeed that, when I had heard her voice on the telephone, I had had no other emotion but one of surprise that after all that had happened I should still love her so deeply. How then could I show the faintest tinge of irony? But because I thought that she might take this letter as a sign that I wished to return to our former relations and so feel strong enough to rebuff me, I did not send it off. That is, I feared her even more than she feared me.

A few weeks after this I met her by chance in Ralph's flat and invited her to dine with me at Gennaro's. She accepted. We were just beginning to break the ice when she said, 'I'm afraid I shall have to go in five minutes. I promised Alix to listen to her new loud-speaker at half past eight.' I said nothing. We drank our coffee in a hurry and went out. But when she kissed me goodbye in the taxi she put her tongue in my mouth.

For an hour or two I walked the streets in a state of rage. Then I picked up a girl, an Arab as it happened, and took her back to my flat, half hoping that I should catch a disease. How black the account against Carrington would then be! That disease would be the outward and tangible sign of the fact that she had ruined my life.

The anger and pain I felt at this typical rebuff showed me one thing – that I had been rash enough to open a little door, to indulge once again in hope. So long as I had hopes and she knew it she would find the means to making me suffer. Yet I had not really been hoping for the restoration of our old relation. The most I wanted was that perhaps once a year, perhaps once in every two years we could pass an evening and a night together. For after all, I said to myself, our love for one another had not so much died as been buried under a deposit formed by our quarrels and resentments, so that it might be possible for us to dig down like archaeologists to the original floor and for a few hours revive the past. But now I realized that even this was an illusion and that everything was over.

Throughout that summer we continued to see one another occasionally, though only in the presence of other people. Then in September I began a mild flirtation with Poppet John, a lovely and amorous girl of sixteen who was going through the stage of having a crush on a new young man every few weeks. Carrington was also attracted to her and had become her friend and confidante and I had annoyed her by telling Poppet that she was cruel. At a party to which we were all invited she refused to speak to me, so to pay her out I told her quite untruthfully that I was taking Poppet home with me afterwards. Since Carrington was supposed to be putting her up for the night she took this as a challenge.

The riposte soon came. A few days later I got a letter from Carrington in which she offered me one of Lytton's old suits and some ties that he had no further use for. A feeling of rage out of all proportion to the provocation came over me on reading this. I was no longer so poor that I could not dress decently and I bought my ties – very special ones of Madras cotton – at Rose's in Burlington Arcade. Was Lytton such a sacred person that even his cast-off clothes brought honour to those who donned them? However I overcame my annoyance and wrote a polite letter of refusal. To this I added what was in fact, if not in form, a question. It happened that the day before I had seen Frances wearing a silk neck handkerchief I had given Carrington in our early days together and which she used to value particularly. She attached, I knew, even more importance to such remembrances than I did, so that if she had really given it away it meant that she had renounced not only me but the whole of our past connection. I therefore added to my letter, though without mentioning the handkerchief, the rider that she must be very angry with me to give away my presents.

In reply came a very characteristic letter, enclosing some ties of Lytton's which I knew she must consider vulgar ones and admitting that she had given away two of my presents, but not from hatred, oh no! but on account of the pure pain they gave her. Since her character, she said, was quite different to mine she did not feel resentments and hatreds.

The admission that she had given away my presents, the parcel of ties, most of all the hypocrisy of her tone so enraged me that I forgot all my resolutions to behave with self control and decency. I determined to end everything at once and in such a way that there could be no renewal of our friendship and so I packed all the presents she had given me, and they were many, into a parcel and left them at 41 Gordon Square with a letter which, it seemed to me, would make it impossible for us ever to meet again. This happened on Nov 22, 1928. A day or two later I learned that, whatever presents of mine she had given away, it had not been the handkerchief, which had been borrowed without her knowledge by Frances. It was the same misapprehension which had led Othello to kill Desdemona and had I known it before I should certainly not have acted with such anger and violence. Thus, in a dispute over Lytton's old ties, ended my once rapturous, then tormenting and always unstable and seesaw relation with Carrington which had begun almost imperceptibly by her making up to me nearly ten years before.

In every age the form taken by love affairs is different. In the 'twenties the tendency was for A to love B, for B to love C, for C to love D and so on. Long chains of attached atoms were formed because the magnetic current flowed only in one direction. None was double bonded. Horace describes a similar situation in one of his *Odes* (L, *36*), echoing perhaps the Greek Sicilian poet Moschus who appends the moral that if you would be happy you should continue to love those that love you. The Moslem poet al-Ashè comments on the same phenomenon of lovers' perversity. But today, I fancy, the pattern has changed. Love affairs are more lightly undertaken and, unless they end in marriage, much sooner over and this has led to the contemporary obsession with sex and sexual techniques, which are coming, especially among the beats and hippies, to take the place of love. That is to say it is the act that has become important rather than the human relation, so that the lives of the young tend to be spent in brief affairs that lead to disillusion and emotional instability because they debase the currency. Tangled as our affairs often were in the 'twenties, they were generated and kept going by love rather than by purely sexual urges or by passing infatuations and that is why, in spite of all the obstacles and difficulties, they lasted so long.

But my case was of course a special one because I had been caught by a girl who could neither satisfy her lovers nor give them up. Without intending it, she played with them and thus I, like Gertler and Ralph Partridge before me, became involved in an experience that convulsed me to the depths of my being. It was not an arrow that she had planted in me but a barbed harpoon that tore the flesh when I tried to tear it out and that was why I continued to cling to our relation long after it had ceased to cause me anything but pain. For there was really little in Carrington's appearance or gifts to elicit such passionate devotion. In nightmares and insomnias she had lost most of her looks by the time she was thirty and even before that few men had found her sexually attractive. Her intelligence was not remarkable and her conversation a flat patter that too often echoed other people's ideas. Although she was generally liked, she did not make a strong impression on most people because she preferred to keep in the background. Yet for those who got to know her well she had a peculiar and unforgettable charm. Now coaxing and cajoling, now elusive, at one moment melancholy, gay and radiant at the next, she was completely herself all the time. Every movement, word and gesture displayed her idiosyncrasy. The intensity of her feelings and enthusiasms, though revealed only to her intimate friends, if indeed to them, was greater than I have seen in any other person and one can say the same of the strength and constancy of her affection for those she loved. Yet the state of mental and emotional conflict in which she lived made all decisions difficult for her. She was torn this way and that by contrary impulses. Her frequent changes of mood, her need to follow her feeling of the moment, her neurotic love of secrecy, her repressions over sex prevented her from maintaining intimate relations with anyone for more than short periods. If she got on so well with Lytton that was because he never wanted anything of her except some nursing when he was not well. So in the end I see her as a deeply tragic figure, thwarted in the main aspiration of her life, which was to marry him, and compelled by the contradictions in her character to wear down and destroy those who loved her and whom she never ceased in her own erratic way to love too.

Carrington made me suffer more pain than I have had to endure at any time in my life except during my first years at my prep school, yet since most of that pain came from her unwillingness to give me up, I have never except for brief periods borne her a grudge on account of it. And today I can see that by breaking down the hard shell of my egoism – all those stubborn and self-protective features that during my life of poverty and isolation had grown over me – she did a great deal to make me a richer and more evolved human being.

The end of a long love affair leaves a horrid void behind it. Instinctively I sought to fill it with some other attachment. But where were the girls? Middle-class girls in those days did not have affairs – that was left to married women and the only ones I knew who were available were those dreary specimens who in every literary society make the rounds of the younger men so as to give themselves the feeling of 'belonging'. I have never, or hardly ever, been able to combine bed with friendship and, since my relation with Carrington had left me with strongly exogamous feelings, I needed to find my girls among those who were not known to my friends.

There were two or three young women with whom I used at this time to go about. The one I liked best was a tall, handsome, Viking type of blonde called Marion who was the daughter of a well-known engineer. She was engaged to a man in the Middle East about whom she had ambiguous feelings, but there was no question of my flirting with her. She was not the sort of girl for that because, like Mlle de la Mole in *Le Rouge et le Noir,* her erotic feelings, which she did not conceal, were balanced by a pride that would have made even a kiss seem a degradation. Thus, though I found her very attractive, her energetic character, her pride in her body and her neurotic obsession with purity intimidated me. When in the end she got married the scale of her preparations in the way of embroidered underclothes and nightdresses and fine cambric sheets was overwhelming, yet by a strange contradiction in her nature she got a perverse pleasure from supposing that her fiancé spent his evenings in Eastern brothels and was riddled with syphilis.

Then in the autumn of 1928, just after my final breach with Carrington, I met at a party a young woman called Vivien. She came from a family which had lived in the same house since the thirteenth century and her brother held a post at Court. She was a singularly lovely girl of around twenty-eight, small, slight and dark with fine bones and a complexion so delicate that it seemed to be transparent. Her sensitivity of mind matched her face and she had a feeling for poetry. Besides this she was a flirt who cultivated the society of young actors, but gave them nothing.

I soon found myself imagining that I was in love with her. Her air of purity and refinement cast a spell over me and I began to conceive a horror of the light affairs with working-class girls whom I had been in the habit of picking up to console me for the misery and despair into which Carrington so often threw me. But what Vivien wanted from me was not love. She liked me because, as she wrote, 'I can talk to you without the hundred and one reservations I make with other people and you can do the same with me. And then because when you read me your things I lose myself entirely and that is a state I am always craving to reach – to get out of my body.' In fact when one day I read her the Introduction to my *Dr Partridge's Almanack* she went into a sort of trance because the idea of death excited her. I gave her the key to my flat and she used to steal in without a word and sit quietly in a corner while I was writing. 'I think I could promise you almost anything,' she wrote, 'if you make me part of your work.'

We came to be on kissing terms: we discussed what we would do if we got married, how many children we would have and so forth – pure day-dreaming on both sides for she was not physically attracted to me and I had no wish to marry her and be absorbed in her upper-class set. And then everything collapsed. By March it was over. It had been a soap bubble blown up into the air by both of us and had no body of serious feelings to sustain it. I had been too deeply stamped by the image of Carrington to be capable of falling in love with anyone and was soon to become involved with girls of another sort. But before speaking of them I will say something of the other sides of my life – of those which are concerned with friendship.

It was about this time that I got to know Desmond MacCarthy and his wife Molly. Desmond was the editor of *Life and Letters,* the chief literary magazine of the day, and he was also one of the original members of 'Bloomsbury'. As a literary critic he was sensible without being inspiring and I never saw in him any trace of those imaginative gifts which, according to Leonard Woolf, he had possessed at Cambridge. But then Leonard has always confused the brilliance of mind that counts at universities with those exploratory faculties that nourish literary talent. In my opinion Desmond simply did not have in him the stuff of a writer.

As a talker, however, it was very different, for his conversation was the most entrancing I have ever listened to. To begin with he always had the air of being completely relaxed and at ease in company. He could talk to anyone and, what was more difficult, make them talk back. He once told me that the reason for his being invited to political luncheons was that he was the only man in England who could draw out Mrs Baldwin. However that may be, shyness and constraint vanished from the room when he opened his mouth. He had a beautiful voice and his timing was perfect. Everything he said was adjusted to the capacities and interests of his audience. One listened and was charmed, without knowing exactly why, for he was discursive rather than witty and never rose to those flights of fancy which his future secretary Cyril Connolly is apt to break into. But Desmond had another string to his bow for, with Compton Mackenzie, he was the best raconteur I have ever heard. I shall never forget his account of a conversation he had overheard at his club between Yeats and that ultra-rationalist zoologist, Ray Lankester, in which Yeats had described his encounters with fairies. I have also heard him give imitations of Henry James's conversation which told one more about that novelist's circumlocutory style of writing and thinking and his neurotic terror of committing himself to a statement of fact than several volumes of criticism could do.

There is one other thing that I should like to say about him, because it has not always been recognized. He could be direct and forthright in expressing his opinions and had little tolerance for what he regarded as nonsense and pretentiousness in contemporary writing – and this included most *avant-garde* prose and poetry – but he was never malicious. When people talk as well as he did they do not have to amuse at the expense of other people's lives and characters.

Desmond's wife Molly was as delightful to meet as he was and I came in time to know her a good deal better. She was a plump, warm-hearted, motherly woman who lived in a cloud of vagueness and indecision, out of which she would emerge in short, erratic flights of wit and fancy which ended, like a hedge sparrow's song, suddenly. Her husband, as was the custom for social entertainers in those days, would accept invitations to lunch and dinner in which she was not included, but she did not appear to feel any resentment at this, perhaps because she was so diffident of her own capacities. Then she became deaf and wore a hearing aid which she would switch off when the conversation bored her. During the 'thirties my wife and I saw a good deal of her – that is, whenever we were in England – and we both became very attached to her. She was a better writer than her husband, for all his greater range of mind, and one of her books, *A Nineteenth Century Childhood,* is a little masterpiece.

It was when I was spending a weekend at Shulebrede Priory near Haslemere, which had been lent for the summer to the MacCarthys, that I first met Cyril Connolly. He was then acting as secretary to Logan Pearsall Smith and was beginning, after coming down from Oxford, to show an interest in girls. He appeared to have selected Rachel, the MacCarthys' quiet and rather old-fashioned daughter, as the object of his first courtship, and made a sulky scene because I talked to her for a few minutes in the garden. Molly, though she liked him, complained that he was 'difficult'. One of these 'difficulties' lay in the high standard of sympathy and loyalty he demanded of his friends. Since he suffered from perpetual doubt as to whether he was really loved, he would impose severe tests on them. Yet if they satisfied these tests, he might turn away from them, for his love, at least where girls were concerned, fed on his uncertainty.

He was at this time sharing a flat with Patrick Balfour, later Lord Kinross, a journalist and travel-writer who has since become well known for his books on Turkey. He seemed to think that I knew something about low life, so I introduced him to a girl called Lily of whom I shall later have something to say. She was a fascinating girl with a music-hall style of wit and it particularly intrigued him that her married name was Connolly.

My first recollections of him are somewhat indefinite. He was often very silent, and silent men, when I know that they are intelligent, alarm me because I feel that I am boring them. His face too, except when he was talking, had no expression on it, although when he was in a good mood or wished to please, it would light up with a smile that revealed an unexpected sweetness. But, though I liked him, I did not feel at ease with him. For this reason I did not try to get in touch with him during the war years, when I was often in London, though at his request I wrote two articles for *Horizon*, that brilliant literary journal which he edited. It was not therefore till the 'fifties that I got to know him at all well. I was then living near Malaga and he would come to stay with his sister-in-law Annie Davis whose large country house stood only a few hundred yards away from mine. This covered the period of the breakdown of his second marriage to Barbara Skelton and, as it was so much on his mind, he talked freely about it with his usual lack of reserve.

I hesitate to attempt a portrait of Cyril because I have never known him intimately and, like all people who hate themselves, he is a man of great complexity of character. But I will make the effort because he is one of the most brilliant literary figures of the post-war years. In his deeper layers he is a romantic, but shot through with the sort of psychological realism that an Englishman can only acquire by reading and assimilating French literature. Say a disciple of Baudelaire, La Rochefoucauld and Stendhal. Then he is a narcissist, filled with a love-hate for himself. Guilt therefore plays a large part in his writings, just as boredom does in his life. After this one must put his much vaunted taste for luxury which has often made enemies for him in the literary world, where few writers have private means. 'One of Nature's Rothschilds', as he once called himself, frequenting Palace Hotels whenever he could afford them and demanding in the house where he stays V.I.P. treatment. His hosts must show their regard for him. With this goes a love of food and especially of sea-food and exotic fruit, for greed is a normal compensation for not having been loved enough as a child, and these foods appeal to his romantic imagination. Thus during the 'thirties a frown might appear on his face if he was not offered avocado pears when invited to a meal, although at that time they were an expensive luxury which few English people had acquired a taste for. Readers of his finest and most revealing book, *The Unquiet Grave,* will remember the sensuousness with which he has written of fruit, shellfish and vegetables, for there is a side to his nature which has an affinity to Colette's.

But perhaps Cyril's most productive gift has been his curiosity. He has spent a good part of his life studying other men's talents, experiences, characters, faces, possessions, and this has led him, as it did Boswell, to a quest for outstanding and original people, both in the world of art and outside it, as well as to a certain contempt and indifference for those who do not possess these qualities. Till he was near forty he was a hero-worshipper in search of a hero, yet demanding nothing from him when found but the enrichment of his own mind by the experience of knowing him. Thus his interest has always been of an appreciative and admiring sort – what on the analogy of magic I would call 'white envy' – and I can think of no literary man who has shown himself more generous in praising his fellow writers, whether they were his friends or not.

He is of course selfish. He puts his own comfort and convenience high and his intellectual needs above everything. There was, I think, a time when he liked to be invited to the houses of the more intelligent of the rich where the food and service were good and where he was treated in the style he expects. Yet under his worldly and rather pampered exterior his only real concern has always been with the things of the mind, of which literature, art, travel and the enjoyment of natural scenery and of the animal and vegetable kingdoms come first. To this list I should add girls – the first stage always in *la chasse au bonheur*. I have heard him described as malicious, which he certainly is not, though since malice is the occupational vice of wits, he can say things which if repeated would give pain to others. However, when his feelings are hurt, as they easily are, he can react viciously and wound back.

As he says of himself, he is lazy. After publishing five short books – two of them collections of essays – he stopped. But that is understandable in a man who is neither a poet nor a novelist, but an inspirational writer who can let himself go only when a window opens for him. He had his period, the late 'thirties and early 'forties, when he wrote chiefly as a recorder and analyst of literary trends, inspired perhaps by Edmund Wilson's *Axel's Castle,* but writing with greater brilliance than Wilson though with less solidarity. His only subjects have been social satire, literary criticism (often in the form of parody) and of course himself. If he did not follow up the first of these lines as Waugh did, that is, I think, because the literary tempo of the novelist, the slow development of a situation, do not accord with his temperament. His mind works too quickly, he has to sparkle in every sentence. But now the age he understood so well has passed: a new generation that he is less in touch with has appeared on the scene and he feels his path blocked. Since he is not ambitious and lacks the professional writer's compulsion to go on writing after he has ceased to have anything to say, I do not think that that that worries him too much. Today he writes to earn his living, labouring over his *Sunday Times* reviews in the expectation of some happy moment when his mind will catch fire and throw up a brilliant and witty passage. His own explanation of his indolence used to be that it was due to his guilt at not having used his talents better. But all writers feel that guilt and work harder than ever on account of it. And so in the end Cyril has been obliged by his past extravagance to work extremely hard, turning out a long review every week and publishing three other books of a critical sort.

Among his friends Cyril has always stood out by his conversational powers. He has a very quick mind and an extremely retentive memory, but it is less in the give and take of general conversation that his wit shows itself than in those flights of fancy that he is liable to break into at any moment, whatever his audience may be. Like the best passages in his books, and especially the parodies, they are the result of inspiration and leave all other forms of eloquence that I have heard far behind. Yet he cannot exactly be called, as Desmond MacCarthy was, a good talker. He is a solo performer and his presence does not help the conversation to flow. Indeed if often blocks it. There he sits with his heavy, expressionless face exuding boredom, waiting, it would seem, for the witty remark from one of the company that does not come. For Cyril is like a child, utterly sunk in his mood of the moment and determined to impress it on everyone else. When he is happy, no one knows better how to please, but when he feels bored or irritable, as he often does, he makes no effort to conceal it – indeed rather the contrary. He can kill a dinner party dead. But bait him with a girl whom he finds attractive and no one can show greater charm or persuasiveness.

Today he lives at Eastbourne, collects first editions, adores his young son and daughter and goes only once a week to London. Age has softened and matured him. But he has still after Auden the most brilliant mind in contemporary English literature.

A certain part of my interest in Cyril has lain in the parallel his life has had to mine. We both of us have Celtic Irish names derived from ancestors in the Pale who emigrated to England in the eighteenth century and married into rich families – that is, not Wild Geese but tame ones who were ready to change their religion in order to better themselves. Most of their descendants went into either the Army or the Navy and both Cyril's father and mine were military authoritarians. Then we both of us spent our early childhood in South Africa, where the flowers and the landscape were the first things to stir our imagination and to implant in us an image of a lost Paradise. After this there were visits to relatives who occupied large houses in Ireland, which provided romance, and more prosaic days in England, he in Bath, I on the nearby Cotswolds. Finally as we entered adolescence we each in turn discovered the Mediterranean, which came to be our spiritual home, and found in French literature a sense of order and a psychological penetration which the more imaginative literature of England lacks.

Here the similarities end and the contrast begins. But our differences of temperament as well as our degrees of talent are too obvious to need enunciation, not to speak of the divergent paths our lives have followed.

I have already spoken of my friend Hope-Johnstone's setting out for the United States in 1926 with the aim of making his fortune by selling pictures, and now a year later he was back in London again. Through the influence of a newspaper proprietor called Robert Booth he had obtained a job at the newly created Museum of Art at Detroit. But Booth soon lost interest in him, no doubt because he failed to conceal his lack of enthusiasm for any work of a public kind, and then he offended Detroit society, which seems to have been particularly crude, by a remark he made at a dinner party. The woman who sat next to him was telling him about local conditions:

'The worst of it is that there are so many social climbers.'

'Surely you don't have them here!'

'Indeed we do – quantities.'

'But where do they climb to?'

This repartee was published in the local papers and for six months Hope did not receive another invitation.

In April 1924 he returned first class on a boat with a thousand pounds in his pocket. He made me a present of fifty pounds as I had helped him with small sums before. Then he went off to Italy and Austria on a picture hunting quest, which he followed up with another short visit to the States. A few months later he was back in London again, confident that he had prepared the ground and that on his next visit he would really make his pile.

But now, as invariably happened to Hope, disaster fell on him from an unexpected quarter. Some years before he had met an Italian girl called Mireille and had fallen a little in love with her. She had all the qualities he demanded in his girls – an outer hardness combined with an inner pathos due to her poverty and considerable beauty. Later he had spent a few days with her in Paris, where they lay on a bed and petted, for she was what was called a *demi-vierge* while he was never in a hurry to push physical love to its extremes. After this he put her out of his mind and was extremely surprised

189

when, just as he was about to sail to America, she arrived in London and suggested that he should take her with him.

He asked my advice about it. Since he was no longer in love with her I advised him not to do so, at all events till he had made enough money to support her decently. But his vanity overcame his better judgement. She was a beautiful girl whose photograph had recently appeared in the *Tatler* and he saw himself cutting a figure with her on his arm. So he agreed to do what she asked.

The consequences for Hope were tragic. He had taken a flat in New York, but she would not let him touch her and refused even to go out with him and meet his friends. So he slept on the sofa and had a nervous breakdown. He failed to sell any pictures and six months later the market for them, which had been booming, collapsed and the great slump which was to bring Hitler into power in Germany began. He returned alone to London, knowing that his last chance of making a fortune was gone.

Hope never quite recovered from this fiasco. Although he had saved enough to live on cheaply for a time and was further helped to the tune of a thousand pounds by his banker friends, the Stoops, he gave up thinking about girls and a year later wrote to me that he still suffered from 'a loneliness that was like toothache.'

He was my oldest though no longer my best friend. I had known him since I was fifteen, from which time he had been both my mentor and my partner, introducing me to the wide range of subjects that he devoted his life to studying, from the arts on the one hand to philosophy and mathematics on the other. There was no branch of knowledge that he had not done his best to acquire, for like Aldous Huxley, whom in many ways he resembled, he had the intellectual curiosity and the passion for self-culture of the Renaissance man. Yet his mind, though not totally unoriginal, was negative and uncreative. He could neither write nor lecture nor paint nor, in spite of his continual efforts, play tolerably on any musical instrument, and although he could talk with great lucidity on almost any subject, his love of showing off caused him to be regarded as a bore by literary people. Others were repelled by his veneer of cynicism or by his seeming to be too much on the make, so that in the end he got on better with simple people who were easy to impress. Only for the young who, like myself, suffered from a thirst for knowledge, he was a marvellous companion.

Many years after this I wrote for my own amusement an account of his character which I called 'A Theory of Hope'. Since he has played such an important part in my life I will quote it.

His policy in life is defensive. He occupies a strongly fortified and guarded castle in the middle of which there is an ivory tower, built of poetry and mathematics and recollections of travel. Here he dwells alone like a Byzantine princess. Yet he is not anti-social – quite the contrary. Often, especially when a good lunch or dinner is in prospect, he will sally forth to the house of one of his neighbours and meet them there under a flag of truce. But no one is ever admitted to his intimacy. Although he likes to have acquaintances, he dreads friendship and almost the strongest word of praise he finds for anyone is 'very civil'. Even love is for him chiefly a form of day-dreaming. His girls are the Pre-Raphaelite maidens whom he watches bathing in the water-meadows from the summit of his battlements, but he can never give himself to any of them, much less allow them to cross his drawbridge. This is why he has come to find the society of children, who cannot love back, safer.

Yet his expeditions into the outer world are fraught with danger. Since he lacks antennae, he never knows what other people are thinking or feeling and so is continually getting trapped. This is especially the case when he is engaged on one of his cattle-lifting raids – that is, is in quest of money. Mathematician that he is, he plans and calculates his steps beforehand, yet since his calculations leave out of account the human factor, they are continually going wrong. To rectify this he relies on a series of maxims, compiled out of his past experiences of guile, assault and treachery. Some of these maxims have their point, but others are the mere textbook rules which every tyro adopts, coloured by an adolescent cynicism.

Having the nature of a cat, he does not understand dog feelings. Thus he has no sense of solidity with his own species. When once I said to him of his work on *The Burlington Magazine*, 'Anyhow you can feel it is useful,' he turned on me in fury: 'Useful? Am I here to be useful?' On another occasion he said to me, 'I look on the whole world and all its culture and science as though it was made for me and my enjoyment.' His favourite philosopher is Yang Chu, who said, 'I would not give one hair of my head to save the world.' Yet on other occasions he can discuss socialism or the condition of the poor or the wickedness of politicians on a theoretical basis and even with a certain fervour, though always on the condition that he shall not be asked to do anything about them. That is to say he lives for his own material and spiritual ends and thinks that anyone who gives time or thought to public affairs is either a fool or a hypocrite, unless he is well paid to do so. It has never occurred to him that is is precisely this exclusive concern for number one which he does not trouble to conceal that has prevented him from making his way in the world or even from being trusted. Thus when he filches, as he often does, a book or a

191

drawing from the house of a friend he is innocent enough to suppose that its loss will not be noticed and is surprised when on his next visit he is received coldly.

His repeated failures in life have left him with a tendency to paranoia which has increased with age. When I first got to know him I used to be struck by the frequency with which he would allude to his enemies. Then one of his favourite words became 'jeer'. If one believed him, people in his social world were continually jeering at one another. A little later I began to notice in him a tendency not so much to jeer as to sneer, choosing for his target anyone, other than the few poets and artists whom he really admired, who was successful or famous. These sneers were clearly prompted by envy and were directed at people whom he did not know or knew very little. Indeed it was always the unknown enemies who loomed largest for him and as a rule they were enemies of a more or less ideological kind – that is, people whose opinions he disliked. It was against them that he tilted in his argumentative moods, as that other paranoiac Don Quixote had tilted at windmills, and this brings me to a new and very exasperating feature in his character.

He has always been a terrible arguer. He likes to take up some trifling point that interests no one but himself – a misquotation in a book or a false train of reasoning – and though no one present breathes a word in disagreement, he will hold forth about it and the stupidity of the misguided author for an hour on end. With the passage of time the points that arouse his annoyance have become more and more trivial. Thus when, during the war, he lived next door to my wife and myself in an annexe to our Wiltshire cottage, the chief target of his wrath would be the B.B.C., whose announcer he would accuse either of mispronouncing a word or of using a false quantity in a Latin quotation. It would usually be at breakfast, as we were quietly reading the paper, that he would make his appearance in the doorway and break out with 'What do you think that man said last night?' Then in his hard mechanical voice – all real arguers have the delivery of a road drill – he would launch out on his account of the crime, his speed getting faster as he went along. Stuttering from indignation, his face tied up in knots and convulsed with rage, he would attack those desecrators of the language, those scandalous ignoramuses who dared to hold forth on the air about things of which they knew nothing, till his voice rose to a scream. Then, as we usually said nothing, the fit would subside and he would return to his normal state and talk quietly and pleasantly.

It was of course only too understandable. Hope was not attacking his real enemies, if indeed he had any, but those unseen, omnipresent adversaries of the human race, the Powers and Dominations – the faceless creatures who, like the Jews or the bankers or the freemasons to fascist-minded groups, had prevented him, an exceptionally intelligent and cultivated man, from acquiring the income and status to which both his birth and his mental endowments entitled him. For poor Hope, who loved all the things that money can buy – clothes, good food, nice rooms, books, works of art – had been obliged to pass most of his life either as a suitor to the rich or as an impoverished scholar. Given a moderate income he would have been a far more likeable and generous person, for his small meannesses and subterfuges about money had been forced on him by his indigence, or rather by the gap that separated his desires, which he regarded as his rights, from his income, and did not accord with his true character.

15

Winny and Lily

During the course of my affair with Carrington I had from time to time picked up girls in the street and taken them home with me. Loneliness, that other side of the coin of love, much more than sexual urge had been my motive, and the girls I accosted were never prostitutes but either out-of-work shopgirls or teenagers who had left their homes and were drifting about the streets, relying on any men they got off with to provide them with a meal and a bed. My first pick-up was a girl of nineteen whom I had met in April 1925 while watching the fire in which Madame Tussaud's was burned to the ground. There was a terrific blaze and the spectacle of the firemen in their brass helmets ascending on their ladders to the top floors through the surging clouds of smoke and descending again with wax queens and princesses in their arms was very dramatic. As I stood there jammed in the crowd I asked the girl beside me with whom I had begun a conversation her name. 'Ann Moore,' she replied and, struck by the fact that this had been the name of John Donne's wife, I invited her back to my rooms for supper and spent the night with her. She was a tall, loosely built girl whose dark eyes swam in a mist of day-dreams which prevented her from taking in much of the outer world, but we had one taste in common. This was to go for long walks through the London streets after dark, eating apples or chocolates as we went and stopping for coffee in the cabmen's shelters. One night I remember we made our way out through the City as far as Limehouse, getting back to my rooms at three in the morning to tumble exhausted into bed. Ann had a long soft body of the consistency of a ripe plum and when she let down her black hair over her shoulders the contrast it made with her white skin and moist dreamy eyes called up for me the image of a Persian or Syrian odalisque. This fantasy image was reciprocated in a different style by her, for she told me that when I made love to her she imagined to herself that she was in the arms of the Prince of Wales. However she soon began to bore me and the return of Carrington to my life put an end to our meetings.

Winny and Lily

My flirtation with Vivien put an end to my night-time forays in the streets, but as soon as it ended they broke out again with renewed vehemence. Their source lay, as I have said, in loneliness – that erotic loneliness that cannot be relieved by the company of friends, but requires the presence of a girl every evening to allay it. No sooner did the light begin to fade and the voices of the children in the street to rise into a higher key than I found it impossible to remain any longer in my rooms and was forced to sally out and comb the pavements. Sometimes I would walk for hours before finding a girl whose looks I liked. Then if I felt doubts about her I would invite her to a glass of beer in a pub and, if I still fancied her, would ask her to come home with me. She always did so, for these girls were as lonely as I was and were glad to sit for a few hours over a cup of tea and perhaps a couple of fried eggs and talk. They were willing to go to bed with me too if I suggested it, but I by no means always did. The mere fact that they were there, ready to be made love to if I wanted it, was often enough to kill my feeling of loneliness. As time went on this search for girls became an obsession. I refused all social invitations that interfered with it and went off on my rounds of the streets every evening. There was something of the excitement of gambling about it for I never knew what I would find. At any moment I might light on a girl who would be quite extraordinary, whom I might fall in love with and even marry. Yet, though I was always on the look out for this extraordinary girl, those whom in fact I met and took back with me were merely working-class girls who as a rule were out of a job. While some of them were not unattractive to look at, their chief appeal lay in their youth. They were all under twenty-four and most of them were still in their teens.

But the quest for a girl with whom I could assuage my loneliness was by no means my only incentive in these excursions. I was exploring a new stratum of society. I have always resented being confined to a middle-class environment and eager to escape, if only for short periods, into another. But in those days the gulf between the classes was almost unbridgeable. Only sexual attraction, that great leveller, made it to some extent possible. Taken for itself alone sex is a pretty trivial thing which can easily leave a bad taste behind it, but it acquires another dimension if it is used to explore the personalities and lives of others. It then becomes a breaker-down of barriers as well as a medicine for the loneliness in which, if we have no one to love, we are compelled to drag out our days in a state of emotional stagnation. Thus, though the physical pleasure I got from these girls was slight, I enjoyed their company and often admired their courage and high spirits and that adventurous feeling for life which the middle-class girls of those days lacked so conspicuously. And then were they not the poor, the lonely, the deprived? That was in many ways my condition too and it was partly on this no doubt sentimental ground that we met.

My nightly perambulations of the streets ended in August when a girl called Winny Stafford came to live with me. I had first met her some months before and liked her, but since I could not afford to keep her had encouraged her to take a job at a Lyons restaurant as a nippy or waitress. Roger Fry lent me a room in Lamb's Conduit Street in which he stored canvases and she settled down there, often dropping in to see me in the evenings. Then she got tired of the long hours and low pay, I pawned a ring of my great-aunt's and she came to live in my flat. She was just nineteen, a well-built girl with large brown eyes that had very clear whites; not pretty exactly but with a look of health and youth. Her story was that of most of the other girls who found themselves adrift in London. She was the eldest of seven children and had been brought up in a slum in Bermondsey. Her father got drunk every Saturday night and beat his wife so, when her Jewish boyfriend quarrelled with her and left London, she decided to run away from home, even though this meant leaving her mother, whom she was fond of, to look after her small brothers and sisters. For a year she had lived on the streets, always on the edge of becoming a prostitute, though, since she was very clever at getting men to offer her meals without giving anything back, she had been able to avoid going over entirely. On some occasions she had been driven to pinching wallets, but men who try to buy girls' bodies must risk being tricked and underneath she remained decent and honest. What I liked best about her was her high spirits. With this went a complete self-confidence in being able to deal with any situation she might find herself in as well as a strong curiosity as to what went on around her. There were no flies on her and she was very observant. She was also a tremendous talker and would pour out her experiences by the hour, repeating almost word for word the conversation of the men who got off with her in bars and took her out to meals. This flow of chatter amused me.

As a mistress there was less to be said for her. She was both in love with her absent Jewish boy and repressed about sex, so I soon gave up expecting much of that sort from her. I liked her chiefly as a companion and friend. For one thing I could trust her absolutely. She never tried to get me to spend money on her and was scrupulously honest with me in every way. Our plan of life soon became fairly regular. Every morning she went out around ten so that I could work, picked up some man at the Trocadero to give her lunch and came home after spending an hour or two at a tea-dancing establishment in Oxford Street. She was never late and that was something that was very important to me because I would get into a state of agitation if I had to sit waiting for her key to turn in the lock. As soon as she got in she would start on an account of her adventures, mimicking the usually dreadful man she had found and perhaps producing a bottle of scent or a pair of gloves which she had wheedled out of him. I never knew whether to believe her story that she had given him nothing back in exchange, but I was certain that she would have done her best to avoid it. Once when I was broke she offered me a couple of pounds, but although I felt flattered at being treated as her ponce, I refused. In all my relations with women I have to be the giver.

Sometimes however we would go out together in the afternoon, either to row on the river at Richmond or to the Zoo or the Tower. On other occasions we would call on friends. I introduced her to David Garnett, who was not impressed by her, and took her several times to tea with Roger Fry and Helen Anrep. As she was totally devoid of shyness she prattled away to them in her usual style and I think that that amused them. On Sundays she would cook a dish of steak and onions for lunch and after that we would pay a formal visit to one of her friends. For this I had to put on my best suit and don the bowler hat I had bought for my great-uncle Byron's funeral. I enjoy disguising myself and these expeditions gave me a pleasant feeling of being a small tradesman who had recently got married. One of Winny's friends was a girl who lived with a successful burglar in Bethnal Green while another was married to a fence or receiver of stolen goods, and I was surprised to see the respectability of their houses – the Nottingham lace curtains on the windows, the well-washed aspidistras in their pots and the canary in its cage – and to listen to their conversation which ran either on football or racing or on the correct feeding and management of pets – anything in fact but their professional activities. We also paid a visit to a girl called Lucile, whom both Winny and I knew. I will tell a short story about her. She was a thin, dark, lizard-like girl of French descent and a contortionist by profession. I had picked her up one evening in Piccadilly Circus and taken her to one of those cheap hotels, called cases or casos, where rooms are let by the hour. We had not been long in bed when we heard a furious barking coming from the next room. A double door divided us from it and in it several eyeholes had been cut, so we jumped up and peered through them. Then we saw a strange and grotesque sight. A man and a woman were lying naked on a double bed. Their bodies were hidden from us, but we could see a large, hairy pair of legs and another smooth, fat pair clasped round them. A few yards away there was an Alsatian bitch which had been tied by a leash to a wardrobe. It was barking furiously and by straining at its leash had succeeded in dragging the wardrobe forward till it was only a few feet from the bed. The woman had begun to screech and then we saw the man get up, pat the dog on the head and push the wardrobe back to its place. He was a very ugly man in his late forties, with a black moustache and bald head while his body was covered with black hairs. On a chair hung his cheap pin-stripe suit and a bowler hat. Then, having calmed the dog, he got back into bed, but no sooner was he in position again than Wow, Wow, Wow the dog began to bark and to strain at its leash. This happened several times till the woman would stand it no longer, but got up in a temper and dressed. We saw her – a heavy, coarse looking tart – and a dispute at once began as to how much the man should pay her.

Winny also knew Lucile and, happening to run into her one day, learned that she was living with a ventriloquist at Peckham. On being told that Winny was living with me, Lucile invited us both to tea with them so, after dressing up in our usual way – Winny in her beige two-piece suit and I wearing my bowler hat – we set off. The tea was lavish, with muffins and several plates of cream cakes, but how these had been paid for we could not guess for the ventriloquist was out of a job. As soon as we had finished eating he put on an exhibition of his art and then we saw the reason for this, because, although technically his ventriloquism was adequate, he had no sense of humour and so the patter of his dummies was lifeless and boring. After we had finished applauding him, Lucile, who wanted to be admired too, threw off her clothes and began to go through her contortionist tricks on the floor. Winny, who was prudish, at once became uneasy and when Lucile suggested that we might like to see her and her ventriloquist boyfriend give a sexual exhibition in a new style they had invented, she made an excuse of being in a hurry and we left.

Winny was a complete Cockney. She had never been out of London. To show her the sea I took her down one Saturday for the weekend to Bognor. The view from the train amazed her. So many fields, so many woods and trees – she had always supposed that the country was full of people and dogs and football fields like Regent's Park. Then there were the animals. She knew sheep and rabbits and hens, but had never seen cows or ducks or geese before. She was like a child seeing an elephant at the zoo for the first time and comparing it mentally with the drawings in her picture book. And the sea of course filled her with astonishment and in the end frightened her because, brought up as she had been in crowded rooms and streets, she could not bear the idea of so much emptiness. Another of her simplicities was her belief that the English middle-class accent was an affectation put on to make them feel superior. 'Why don't yer drop it,' she would say, 'and talk natural?' No doubt there was some historical truth in her view, but I had been brought up to talk as I did and could not suddenly switch into a Cockney accent.

One day Winny told me that her boyfriend had turned up unexpectedly so I lent them my flat for the evening. He was a huckster who toured the country in a van selling carpets and perfumery and when I re-entered my bedroom that night it reeked of cheap scent. Then around Christmas she

decided to set up with him, but as he went out to work every day she got
bored sitting by herself and would come back to spend the day in my flat.
Then they quarrelled – apparently over me – and she left him and returned
to her Lamb's Conduit Street room. I now had another girl living with me,
a dark, clinging, willowy creature I nicknamed the Rosebud, who had a
weakness for policemen and guardsmen, and Winny became jealous of her.
For the first time since I had known her she made amorous advances to me
and then, deciding that her room was not ready for habitation, dossed down
on my sofa. On the following night she moved into my bed. I now had two
girls sleeping with me and, although I enjoyed this rivalry in a sultan-like
way, it meant that I could make love to neither of them. Decidedly things
were going too far, all the more since I had in the offing a girl I was a little
in love with, ready in a week's time to take their place.

On my return from Toulon I had put aside the two books I was writing,
that is the biography of Santa Teresa and the novel later called *A Holiday
by the Sea* – both of which I was badly bogged down in – and begun a novel
of a different kind. Since I did not feel I had enough experience to write one
of those that deal with social life, I chose the picaresque form. This demands
a succession of characters, appearing in turn and then vanishing, and not
reacting upon one another. I took as my model the Spanish picaresque
novels of the sixteenth century in which a boy runs away from home and
has adventures with tramps and people in the underworld. I felt that I had
some imaginative insight into that sort of life, but unfortunately I knew
nothing of the sort of people whom such a boy would be likely to encounter in England. I began therefore by reading up the literature on
tramps and vagabonds in the British Museum. After this I started, cudgel-
ling my flagging powers of invention, and drawing on such odd down-
and-outs as I had run into. But the only characters I could think of were
such stupendous bores that after a little I took my young hero to London,
whose low life I was more familiar with. Here my long night walks had
brought me into contact with some extraordinary creatures: a woman who
dressed in newspapers pinned together, came out of her lair at two every
morning and collected her food from the dustbins set up outside restaurants; a man of middle-class origin who lived the life of a medieval hermit
in a tiny hut in the railway yards, was clothed in sacking and had a pessimistic philosophy. These I could make use of and besides there was Lily,
whom I will speak of later and of whom I drew a romanticized portrait.

The first half of my novel, which dealt with tramps and country scenes,
was written in a simple style with a certain amount of description in which
I tried to convey my love of the English landscape, but in the second half
the sentences became longer and the style more involved and loaded with
parentheses. The reason for this was that I had been soaking myself in

Proust, that writer whom no novelist under forty should allow himself to read, and had been conditioned by him both to feel and to write in that way. So I let myself go in mystical and philosophical passages, which perfectly represented my mode of experiencing life at that time, but were out of key with the earlier part of the book. I had not yet learned how to separate the needs of a novel from spiritual autobiography.

My novel, which was much admired by David Garnett, was, thanks to his recommendation, published by Chatto and Windus in 1933 with the title of *Jack Robinson* and under the meaningless pseudonym of George Beaton. It got very good reviews because for a first novel it was well written and its romantic subject and treatment suited the mood of the 'twenties. But today there is no book of mine that I dislike more.

Soon after my return from Toulon my great-aunt's mind started to go. She had a stroke and after that, though she remained as active as ever, she began to suffer from delusions. The most persistent of these was that she owned and lived in two flats. The first of these was her present flat while the other was one which she had occupied at a previous period of her life and believed that she was still responsible for. She was obliged therefore to transfer herself at frequent intervals from one to the other. Yet there was a difficulty about this because, owing to 'the confusions of this crazy modern age', they had now exactly the same address as well of course as the same furniture. Every morning therefore she would walk to the nearest taxi rank, say 'Drive me to 23 Ashley Place,' and in two minutes be back at the flat she had just left, believing it to be 'the other one'. These imaginary changes of residence left her in great confusion of mind because she could not decide which of the two similarly named and furnished flats she was in and when I went to see her she would ask me to help her puzzle it out. It was a metaphysical problem really, involving subtle distinctions, and I was unable to solve it for her.

She also lost her sense of time. One night she rang my door bell at 3 a.m. when I was in bed with Winny. I let her in and found that she believed it to be three in the afternoon and that the darkness was due to a London fog – 'so much worse in these modern times than they used to be'. Her powers of rationalization had been developed to an extraordinary degree because she had for so long been cut off by her deafness from communication with other people. I made her a cup of tea and asked her if there was anything I could do for her. 'Yes, my dear boy. I would like you to tell me what day of the week it is.' She had driven all the way from Victoria Street to ask me that.

She was now drawing cheques almost every morning from her bank and leaving the money in the taxi, so that it was evident that she was no longer fit to look after herself. I wrote to my father who came up and we had her certified. The problem then was to find a mental home where she would be well looked after. I visited half the private asylums in London and found them every one of them unsuitable. That is to say, they were both expensive and nasty. Then I came on a small house near Denmark Hill that was run by Catholic sisters and which I liked the look of. I took my aunt there as though for tea, left the room quietly and made off. When I returned three days later I found her sitting bolt upright in the hall in her fur cape and plumed hat, waiting for me to come back and take her home. The sister who was in charge of her told me that she had insisted on remaining there every day from breakfast till dark. Her reproaches, though made with her usual dignity, were painful to bear, for after all I had betrayed her and was about to do so again. But on my next visit a few weeks later I found that she had settled down happily and indeed hardly recognized me. Her mind had gone back to the distant past and the sister told me that she had evolved the idea that her parents lived on the first floor and her grandparents above them on the top floor and that she spent a large part of her time going upstairs to visit them and returning again to the ground floor perfectly satisfied. I would like to say how deeply impressed I was by the goodness and patience of these sisters, for my aunt's restlessness made her a maddening person to look after and she was no longer able to go upstairs or downstairs by herself. I could see that they really liked her and appreciated her eccentricity and when she died they adopted her nasty little dog. Only Catholic nuns with their sense of dedication are capable of such devotion and whenever I have felt irritated by certain manifestations of Catholicism I have remembered these nuns, as well as others I have known.

My next step was to terminate the lease of my aunt's flat and sell her furniture. I gave Winny as much of it as she could take and she was especially delighted by a mahogany cabinet inlaid with blue faience and decorated with gilt scrolls that had come from the Great Exhibition of 1851. She stored them in Roger Fry's room in Lamb's Conduit Street until her boyfriend should have saved enough money to marry her.

I must now bring my life in London to a close with an account of my affair, if that is the word to call it, with Lily Holder or Connolly. One evening in March 1927 I had seen standing in a doorway in Greek Street a girl whose appearance struck me. She was slim with rather short light brown hair and under her cloche hat a pair of blue eyes stared out into the street without any expression in them. It was clear that, though she made no attempt to attract passers-by, she was a prostitute and I never picked up girls of that sort. But this time I was so affected by something at once sad and enigmatic in her face that I spoke to her and took her back in a taxi to my flat. When she undressed I saw that she had a perfectly proportioned body with small though firm breasts, yet her voice was so slow and her eyes

shone in such a fixed stare that I guessed that she was taking cocaine. After
this I lost sight of her and then in June I ran into her again. She was more
lively this time and I took her back twice to my flat, liking her better on
each occasion. Then she once more vanished and though I searched the
streets for her and made enquiries of other girls who were 'on the game', I
could find no trace of her.

Nine months passed before I rediscovered her and after that I began to
see her fairly frequently. She would take me into Allen's or Cap'un's, two
minute tea shops off Gerrard Street where the tarts sat and chatted in
between their rounds. Here she introduced me to her friends and I came
to know some of the girls of the quarter and their peculiarities. They were
not all of the sort that one would expect. One had a wooden leg on which
she stumped round the streets while another was got up to look like the
primmest of Edwardian governesses and wore gold pince-nez on her thin
nose. She had a brisk, businesslike walk, kept a cane in her flat and made a
lot of money which she paid into her bank every Monday morning.

I enjoyed these evenings with Lily very much. She was beginning to
obsess me as none of my other girls since Carrington had done. As I lay
awake at night listening to the melancholy hoots of the trains shunting in
the railway yards – those owls of the great London rain forest – I would
long to have her in bed beside me. But this I could not often afford to do
and then I knew that I did not get on with her as well as I did with Winny.
I was never quite at ease with her and felt that I often bored her.

Lily was a country girl from a village near Ipswich. On her mother's
death she had come up to London and gone into service as a housemaid.
Then one day she had dropped a valuable piece of china and broken it. Her
mistress, the Hon. Mrs A., had scolded her so she had at once packed her
bag and left. No more menial jobs for her – she meant to be her own mistress. After living for a time with a man, she had drifted on to the streets
and become a prostitute. She enjoyed the life. Her professional duties did
not disturb her unduly for they soon became mechanical and then she often
liked her clients, especially when they amused her or took her dancing.
She told me that she did not mind how ugly men were if they were gay and
made her laugh. As she was a really beautiful girl she could easily have bet-
tered herself by setting up in a suburban flat as a call girl, but she enjoyed
the life of a West End tart; the talk and gossip in the small tea shops with
the other girls and their ponces, the visits to pubs and above all the feeling
of absolute liberty. She never saved anything and if she was doing well
would either spend her money on clothes or give it away. For there were
two kinds of girls on the West End game. Some were just wage earners,
working hard every evening with their eyes on their mounting bank
balances and hurrying their clients along with a 'Have a quick one, darling'

or 'I can't waste my time any longer', while the others were Bohemians, living in the moment and enjoying the variety and the up-and-downness of their lives. Lily belonged to this second class. Yet she had also a deep sense of guilt about her profession because she had been brought up by her mother to be religious. Once she had lived with a ponce and she told me that what she had most liked about that was to wake up in the morning and see beside her a man who was even lower and more degraded than herself.

Sometimes her conversation was fascinating. She had a strain of wit and could be wildly gay and amusing in a style that came straight from the music hall tradition of Little Tich and Nellie Wallace. But as she had no resources in herself she suffered acutely from boredom and would then become gloomy and silent. She needed to be amused all the time and Cyril Connolly, to whom I introduced her, must have pleased her more than I did, though in general she did not care about educated people because her instincts, like mine at this time, were all for low life. But whereas I was trying to purify myself from middle-class ways of thinking and feeling and from the slow stain that having money gives, she was indulging her deep-seated self-destructiveness.

Now that my great-aunt was happily settled in her asylum and the sale of her furniture completed there was nothing to keep me any longer in London. Besides, reduced as I now was within the strict limits of my allowance, I could not afford to remain there any longer, all the more as I was mixed up with so many girls. I therefore decided to return to Yegen in the spring and live quietly and economically there until my aunt's death provided me with a larger income. But then in January 1929 Lily fell ill and was taken to hospital to have her ovaries removed. For some days it seemed doubtful whether she would get over the operation, but then she began to recover though she continued to suffer great pain. I visited her every day. In the dim light of cold, foggy afternoons I would take a bus down the Harrow Road to the Paddington Infirmary. I brought her flowers and, defying the regulations, food, for she disliked the sops they gave her and had an inordinate craving for cheese and tinned salmon. Then she passed out of danger, was taken off the day list and could only be visited once a week.

On April 2nd Lily left hospital and on the following day I took her out in a boat on the river at Richmond. For three months she had not been out of doors. The sky was blue, a pale sun shone, the first buds of the poplars and hawthorns were coming out. She lay back on the cushions, one curl of her brown hair that had come loose dangling against her neck, her eyes glittering and dancing with happiness. For once she had entirely forgotten herself and was given up to ecstasy.

Lily was now living in my flat and a life that was entirely delightful began for me. She did not get up till two or three: then at six we went out, dined, bought tickets to the theatre or the cinema and after that went to the supper room of the Queens' in Leicester Square where we drank till midnight. By this time we had usually got down a good deal – she Bass, for she never drank anything else, and I wine or brandy. After this to Allen's or Cap'un's tea rooms to sit there among the tarts and their ponces till one or two o'clock, when we went home and sat drinking Bass till three. It was only late at nights that she had those flights of fancy where wit, bawdry and a tragic feeling about life were intermingled in an indescribable way. At such times she came out of herself, whereas during the rest of the day she would be wondering whether she was looking well, deciding she was not and then considering what she should do, where to go, whom meet to get her out of her despondency and uncertainty. For she was one of those people who live only for the high moments of life – for what she called 'merriment'. Yet on any fancied slight being offered her she would flare up in a moment, for she was spirited and pugnacious.

I began to think that my life with Lily would go on till my money ran out when she told me that she had found a 'business flat' off Regent Street at a rent of £5 a week. She wanted to move into it at once and nothing that I could say would persuade her to defer it.

'But I shall come back,' she declared, 'and sleep one last night with you.'

On the following day I gave her £10 to pay the rent and we went off to look for a new dress she wanted. I had told her that I could only afford £6 for this, but at such a price no sufficiently attractive one could be found. At last at Mentone's we came on a cherry coloured serge costume with a white ermine collar, flounced sleeves, a bow at the waist – a 'Paris creation'. She longed to have it and looked so well in it that I bought it for ten guineas. From there she took me to see her flat – a large bedroom with a double bed, thick dingy curtains, tall gloomy mirrors and a sitting room next door that was obviously not made for use. No bathroom. It was a prostitute's apartment and the rent was on that account twice what it would otherwise have been. Then she put on her new dress and we went out. She had been off the streets for five months and now she must start again. Her lizard-skin shoes drew her feet so that she could hardly walk and she trembled with nervousness. On seeing a man standing at a corner she imagined he must be a 'bogie' – that is a policeman. To calm her I took her into a pub for a drink and then, still nervous and hesitating, like a schooner before the wind catches its sails, led her out into Regent Street and left her. And then I knew from the familiar pain I felt as I walked away that I was in love. Some of the feeling I had once had for Carrington had spilled over on to her.

I went back to my rooms and began to pack. Then at 3 a.m. a phone message. 'I can't come. There's a man here who must stay till five. But I'll be round for breakfast.' Breakfast for Lily meant two in the afternoon and half an hour after that she phoned me to meet her at Denman's café at five. I met her and we went on to Allen's. But I was now 'in love': my gloomy, anxious face betrayed it. I wanted something from her and that, by all the rules of love as I knew them, was a reason for her not to give it. Besides, craving all the time as she did for release and 'merriment', she hated despondency and gloom because she was so subject to them herself. While she had been living with me I had never taken her dancing, I had been dull, I had bored her with my attentions and my devotion. She felt grateful and a little touched, but she had now had enough of me for she was a girl who demanded continual change and excitement. Sitting next to us there was a smartly dressed girl called Molly who was her special friend of the moment so we all three went off to have a drink. In the pub I took Lily aside and said, 'Promise to come tonight.' She replied, 'I promise, Gerald,' but her face expressed her irritation and I knew that she would not come. I lay awake till daylight.

On the following evening I searched the cafés for her without success, but decided against going to her flat as she would only be there if she was with a man. Then I picked up a girl of nineteen called Rose Dillon and took her home with me. She was a really pretty girl with thick fair hair and a pale oval face, intelligent and anxious to educate herself. She worked in a cinema and was half Jewish, though she did not look it. We undressed and made love – she told me it was the second time she had done so – and she seemed to like me for she told me that though she could not stay the night she would come and live with me if I wished it and contribute to our expenses by going on working. This was a tempting offer, but I could not accept it as I had already sublet my flat. I therefore dropped her at her rooms at midnight and took a taxi on to the West End. Opening the hood I drove round the empty streets, lit up by their coloured signs, but could catch no sight of a cherry coloured dress. So, remembering that Lily still had a duplicate of my keys, I thought this a good excuse for calling at her flat. A light was burning in the window and I knocked loudly. She came down. 'My keys,' I said. 'There's a man up there,' she answered. 'Wait till he leaves.' I waited and after a little saw a man come out wearing a bowler hat and smoking a cigar. Then she appeared, looking tired and anxious, holding the keys.

'Why do you add to my difficulties?' she said in an irritable voice. 'I'm not making enough money. I need £15 a week to live at all and you come and beat on my door like that.'

'Come and have something to eat,' I said and we went together to the bar of the Continental.

She sat there talking to a girl friend without once looking at me. When we came out it was half-past one.

'Lily,' I said, 'I want you to sleep in my rooms for the last time. I'll give you whatever a client would give you. Come home with me now and have a good sleep.'

'I'm expecting a phone call tomorrow morning.'

'Treat me fairly,' I said. 'You've promised twice – won't you come?'

'I'll just walk round once more,' she said. 'Go back and at half-past two I swear I'll come.'

'You've told me that before,' I said. 'It's for the last time – I'm leaving England.'

'This time I'll really come. On my mother's grave, Gerald, I swear it.'

I went home and lay awake till five, but she never came.

The following day was her twenty-fifth birthday. I bought her a bunch of lilies at the florist's and at four o'clock rang her bell. She came down in her pyjamas. She appeared touched by my offering. 'What, flowers for a girl like me!' she said. 'No one's ever given me flowers before.' But a man was there, so I could not go up – she would meet me at Denman's café at five. I went and waited till seven, but she did not turn up.

That evening I had dinner with my brother, giving him and my sister-in-law a full account of the past week. They advised me on no account to pursue Lily any longer, but to leave for Spain next morning. My luggage was already packed. Nothing remained to be done. So, after telling the telephone exchange to call me at seven, I went to bed. Next morning I drove through the sleeping streets, bathed in a pale golden sunlight, and caught the train for Folkestone. Thirty-six hours later I was in Avila where, in the city of Santa Teresa, I wrote down in my diary an account of my last weeks in London.

16

A year at Yegen

I reached Almeria on April 30th, 1929. For the first few days I took in nothing of my surroundings. The town, so appealing in its run-down way, and which in the past I had loved so much, now appeared unrelated to anything else in my life. The sunsets, the sea, the bare plantless mountains, the herds of black goats driven up the dry river-bed, the girls leaning out of windows with flowers in their hair, made no impression on me. Yet an illustration of Piccadilly Circus in a Spanish newspaper almost brought tears to my eyes. Then after a few days of emptiness and boredom I suddenly began to write and, sitting in the Café de Viena in the main avenue, got down in three days some sixty pages of my picaresque novel, discharging into them the feeling that had been accumulating over these last months from my relations with Lily. Only the onset of an attack of food poisoning prevented me from finishing the book.

A day or two later, a little after midnight, I arrived at Yegen. It was just five years since I had seen it last. The babies had grown into children, the children had become young women and the young women had got married. The house, the furniture, the books were there precisely as I remembered them – and yet there was a strangeness about them due to the fact that I had changed.

There was however a more objective difference. Maria, my black witch of a servant, had recently inherited from her sister a small piece of property worth about a hundred pounds and this had completely turned her head. She was now claiming that my ex-landlord Don Fernando, who had been her lover, had left her his house when he had died seven years before and that I was therefore her tenant. She was also engaged in a lawsuit over a cow and some goats which had belonged to her sister but which had apparently been omitted from her will. This alteration in her disposition should not have taken me by surprise because the previous summer I had sublet my house to a tough, middle-aged woman who had complained bitterly of her. Now I could verify the truth of her account of Maria for myself. Alternately raging and whining, obsequious and grasping, obsessed by her lawsuit with the Ayuntamiento, she paced about the house in her dingy black skirt and bodice, her features haggard, her complexion yellow, her expression cunning, and giving out all the time a nauseating smell. The kitchen reverberated from morning to night with the loud voice of her legal adviser, a small farmer called Cecilio, while the patio and stables were overrun with her hens and goats, a donkey brayed under the floor of my bedroom and a plague of flies invaded the rooms.

The work of the house was carried out by her elder daughter Angela, a prettyish but sickly-looking girl of seventeen whose father had been my late landlord and whom I had once sat on my knee and taught to read. She was deeply ashamed of her scheming mother and had taken for her *novio* a silent, mulish but touchingly defenceless youth called Angel, who also hated his parents for having, as he thought, dissipated their property and on their death left him nothing. His sisters were the illegitimate daughters of my late landlord's father and therefore Angela's aunts, but his own father had been a tough, foul-mouthed old peasant called Maximiliano who had been rewarded for marrying his master's mistress by being appointed bailiff of the property.

And now an event occurred that put me in a painful and embarrassing position. Doña Clara, Don Fernando's widow (in my book *South from Granada* I gave them other names), had often toyed with the idea of adopting Angela, but had never quite got to the point of doing so because of her hatred for Maria, who she feared would maintain some hold over her daughter. The knowledge that the character of her mother was a bar to a rise in her fortunes had naturally embittered the poor girl all the more. It also happened that Doña Clara had from my first coming to Spain shown a marked interest in me. She was a delicate, bird-like creature, rather Japanese in features, with a refined and girlishly romantic disposition, very warm-hearted and given to impulsive acts of generosity. Her life had been a deeply tragic one, for she had lost all her six children before she was forty and can have had little love for her husband. Since 1919 she had been living with her domineering mother and insipid brother in her family house near Granada, but on her husband's death she paid a long visit to Yegen to put her affairs in order and during that time she would spend every evening alone with me. A sympathy sprang up between us and I came to realize that in her loneliness she was developing warm and romantic feelings for myself.

What now happened was that, on learning that I was back at Yegen, she had one of her characteristically generous and hare-brained ideas. She wrote me a letter in which she said that if my affection for Angela, of which I had written to her, were to turn to love I need not hold back from marrying

her out of lack of means because on our wedding day she would make over
to me the whole of her property at Yegen, including the valuable mountain
ranch. The only condition she made was that Maria should never enter my
house again. At the same time she confided her proposal to Araceli, the
wife of her young bailiff Juan, who had once been her maid, so that, as
might have been expected, it was soon known to the entire village. Thus
if I married Angela I would become one of the two principal landowners
in Yegen and, since the possession of property is everything to the peasant
mind, no one imagined that I would refuse. But there could of course be
no question of my accepting. Apart from the fact that I had no wish to
settle permanently in Yegen, Angela did not attract me. Though pleasant
on the surface, she had grown into a typical small shopkeeper's daughter,
narrow in her views, highly strung, and with a shrewishness derived from
her mother which age would develop and bring out. I therefore said nothing
of the offer I had received, though, as it was known to everyone, the tension
that already existed in my household greatly increased. Angela began to
withdraw from her *novio* and to smile at me while Maria became more
frenzied and sycophantic than ever and cut buffoonish capers all over the
place. Only poor Angel, sitting silent by the kitchen fire, sulked and
glowered.

Summer had now come in. The sun, thin and wafer-like, poured down
its rays through the clear mountain air. The wheat on the terraces, taller
and thicker than any English crop, was turning from a deep green to bronze:
the cicadas kept up their loud chirping in the poplar groves while on every
hill slope white streams of water splashed and tumbled between the rocks.

Inside the house, where I had now managed to restore some peace and
order, the cool darkened rooms, the white walls, the pots of tradescantia
trailing from the banisters, the smell of orange flower water sprinkled on
the tiles soothed the senses. All day long as I sat reading or trying to write
I could see the heavy, dark green leaves of a mulberry tree impressed like
a stain on the intense blue of the sky. At night, when I opened the window,
the sound of crickets chirping and of water falling, with now and then the
fluting of a nightingale, poured in and seemed to fill the room. They were
sounds that increased the silence. Yet I soon found that I could not return
to my old quiet life of writing and study. Something was lacking.

This something was a girl. The craving for girls had become part of my
system. Books, writing, walking, talking were now empty and meaningless
operations unless there was a girl in the background. But how was I to
find one at Yegen? Love affairs in Spanish villages are difficult to bring off
because young women are rarely willing to do anything that could prejudice their chances of getting married. The sort of girl I wanted would
have to come from the poorest stratum of village life, not only because

they were the easiest to obtain but because they were the ones who attracted me most. It was they who with their fathers and brothers provided the *copla* singers and guitarists, while the witches and *curanderas*, repositories of a centuries-old folk tradition, were drawn from their mothers. To my mind at least they stood for rural Spain, for that untutored life of the pueblos in which I wished to sink myself, so that in making love to one of these girls I would be drawing closer to what I most admired and loved in this country. To explain better this way of feeling I will quote a passage I wrote in a notebook at this time.

> One is taking things very lightly if the girl one makes love to, but whom one is not actually in love with, is no more than a particular girl with a particular voice and face and mode of feeling. She must, to have elicited a worth-while desire, be a symbol or point of condensation for some traditional form of living which one finds significant or attractive. Ages of beauty and the slow drip of history must be felt to have come together in her face and in her body and movements, or one's feeling for her will be merely what contemporary novels tell us most light love affairs and even marriages are. That is, something commonplace and vulgar, the mere result of propinquity and convenience and lacking in poetic overtones.

I had discovered before, though less from experience than from observation, that if one wishes to attract a girl one has cast one's eye on, it is often a good plan to begin by ignoring her and to make up instead to one of her more admired girl friends. If this friend responds even a little – and she may well do so because she enjoys attention – one's prestige in her group will rise and a certain interest be created. Now at Yegen I had not yet come across any girl that I liked, but I supposed that there might be such a one whom I had not yet seen and so I decided to advertise my existence by paying attention to a girl who came from the right stratum and whose habits and manners were reasonably free. The one I chose was a certain Isabel, famous for her repartee, and from her I switched to her sister Ana, a snake-like creature who had had a gipsy father. These two girls were known, after their mother's *apodo* or nickname, as the Rats and since I have described them in *South from Granada* I will not repeat what I said there. I did not care for either of them and they were in no way drawn to me, but they found the attentions of a young foreigner flattering, which was all that I wanted. Within a week or two my stratagem worked, for they brought to my house a girl whose appearance and manner I took an instant liking to.

Juliana – for that was her name – was the daughter of an old crone who shared a house at the bottom of the village with a man who had once been a shepherd. Her father had died in her early childhood, but she had several half-sisters who had left the village to seek their fortunes in the world. When I first saw her she had just returned from serving as maid in a house in the next village, so, as the only way of seeing much of her was to engage her in the same capacity, I did so at once although there was no work for her to do. She of course understood perfectly the true reason for my taking her on.

At this time she was barely fifteen though, since she was physically well developed, she looked older. Her face, which was indolent and sensual, had a somewhat Slavonic look, but her eyes were Spanish – that is to say large and expressive and with very clear whites. Her neck rose with a graceful sweep from her shoulders and her breasts were full and well formed, but the lower part of her body was dumpy and her legs, like most Spanish legs, were short. Her worst feature was her hair, which was coarse and fuzzy, but to make up for that her skin was exceptionally fine. Even in the heat of summer it remained cool and milky and I was soon to derive a special pleasure from stroking it. The usual expression of her face was soft and gentle, without any of that challenging sparkle so often found in Spanish girls. It was a permissive face, unarmed by pride, while her voice was low with unexpectedly deep tones in it.

In character she was above all emotional. Her moods seemed to change all the time and, though she was good-natured and did not harbour resentment, she was given to fits of sulking which came and went without perceptible reason. No doubt these were in large part due to her youth and to the sudden change in her position and status. Add to this that she was very lazy, very fond of eating and drinking and very susceptible to every hint of love. She could not talk without flirting, but though she had a fair degree of understanding she was not given to the quick give and take in which most Andalusian flirtations are conducted. Her whole style was easy and leisurely and had something of the charm I have met with in coloured girls.

I began my courtship of Juliana by teaching her to read and write. This gave me an excuse for spending the evenings alone with her in the *granero* and, as I provided some love stories to stimulate her interest, she learned quickly. I also taught her a few English phrases after the manner of George Borrow's lessons in Armenian to Belle, making her say things to me that she would not have said in Spanish. I could see that she was perfectly aware that she was going to end by sleeping with me and that her mother knew it too and desired it, and yet for some time she would not let me even kiss her. In this she was following the usual practice of Spanish girls – to raise their value by making themselves appear difficult and at the same time to build up the man's desire for them and keep him on tenterhooks.

Their instinct told them that if they yielded too quickly they would be despised, since the average Spanish boy looks down on any girl he has not had to make great efforts to win. Her plan worked admirably for I soon became quite desperate to have her, all the more as in conversation, where no subject or word was barred, she did her best to excite me. Yet nearly two months passed before I was able to obtain what I wanted.

It happened in this way. Juliana slept with Maria's younger daughter Mercedes in a double bed in my old bedroom and locked the door when she retired. But one night Maria, who knew what was going on, took her child to sleep with her in her own house next door because she intended to set off before daybreak for the market at Ugíjar. On learning this I removed the key of Juliana's door, but she went to bed as usual, though if she had not liked the idea of sleeping alone in an unlocked room she could have gone to her own house. In fact she knew what was going to happen, all the more as we had come near to the point a couple of days before when she had allowed me, with only a show of resistance, to embrace her violently. Spanish girls keep to a schedule and the next step was this.

Around midnight therefore I went into her room and got into bed with her. She was, or appeared to be, plunged in deep sleep. I tried to wake her by shaking her, but failed. I then did what I had come to do – that is, make love to her – while all the time she pretended to be sleeping heavily. She groaned and she sighed and held me tight, but not till it was over did she allow herself to wake. She then sat up abruptly, began to scold and to cry and insisted on my leaving the room. Next morning she was crying again and in the evening she went back to her house and slept there. Rather naively I wondered whether I had not really offended her, but on the following day she reappeared as though nothing had happened and that night I slept with her without any show of reluctance on her part. The formal protest was over. I have described this seduction scene in some detail because it illustrates the intense symbolical feelings that Mediterranean girls attach to virginity. Juliana had wanted to lose hers and, to save her modesty and excuse herself from blame, had simulated sleep while I took it, but the moment it was over she felt that she had lost something very important about which a great fuss must be made. Yet it was not simply an act that she was putting on, but a deep convulsion of her nature welling up from below, a regret for a stage of her life that could never be reversed, and she had to give herself time to recover from it.

A love affair now began for me such as I had never known before. My previous sexual experiences had been by comparison mere dabblings, seated as much in the heart or mind as in the body, but Juliana was a very sensual girl and I became completely obsessed by her. It was the first, and was to be the last, passionately physical affair of my life and yet my mind was involved too for her company charmed me and with every night that I passed beside her I became fonder of her. We made love several times a day and I could hardly see her without wanting to touch her. But all these erotic performances had a devastating effect upon my intellectual and lite- rary life. I ceased to be able to read a book or to write a line, for whatever it is in the mind that drives one to art or literature had sunk into abeyance. I felt as completely drained of imagination as a ship's stoker or a general in the First World War, yet I felt no physical fatigue and when Ralph and Frances came out in the autumn to visit me I found that I could walk twenty miles or more, charge up and down hills and return almost as fresh as when I had started. But I had to finish my novel. Only a few pages re- mained to be written, but they were difficult ones and I felt as incapable of getting them down on paper as I would have been of composing a long poem. In October therefore I set off for Seville, of which I had kept such happy memories, in the hopes of writing them there.

At first my visit looked like turning out well. The Great Exhibition or World Fair that had opened a few months before proved to be delightful. I made friends with a young Arab dancer from Algiers, tall, almond-eyed and elegant as a gazelle, and went about with her, only to discover that she was in love with another woman in the same company, an ugly negress from Martinique who was twelve years older than herself. Nothing was to be done about it and after a little they left. But I had come to Seville to work. Every morning I went to the Café Central with a portfolio under my arm so that the waiters called me *el Ministro*. Every morning I spread out my papers and sat there hour after hour trying to finish my chapter. But it was all useless. For now instead of being obsessed by one girl I was obsessed by all girls. As I walked down the Calle Sierpes in the evening those brown bodies, those gleaming skins, that proud yet gentle carriage of the Sevillanas set my blood on fire and I began to pick up prostitutes as I had never done before at the risk of catching venereal disease. Yet prostitutes give a false and hollow satisfaction so that, as I no longer knew a soul in the city, I began to feel homesick for Yegen and Churriana. I only stayed on because I hoped that suddenly, in that city that charmed me so much, the impulse to write would come over me. Then I left, but to spend a few weeks at Granada with my old friend, Mrs Temple. While I was there I went with Spanish friends to a number of parties and dances. Under that most humane of dictators, General Primo de Rivera, the universities had opened their doors to girls and those I met were all taking, or at least professing to take, Greek and Hebrew. But attractive as many of them were, my usual diffidence as well as my inability to dance prevented me from making friends with any of them.

Now after a couple of months' absence I returned to Yegen, but to a different set up. My servant Maria had made herself so intolerable that before leaving for Seville I had sacked her and sent her back to her own house. On this Angela became reconciled to her mother and turned against me and there was a complete breach between us. In their place I installed another Maria – I called her White Maria to distinguish her from Black Maria – who was as different from her predecessor as it was possible to be. That is to say, she was gentle, dignified and reliable – not beautiful exactly but with something calm and resigned in her face and bearing that, as she sat quietly by the fire, reminded me of certain Flemish Madonnas. Order and peace returned to my house with her arrival.

I now took up again my previous life with Juliana. Once more I became completely obsessed by her and spent much of the day, as well as the whole of the night, in her company. But since we made love too often, the mental lethargy I had suffered from before returned. In the afternoons I used sometimes to go for long walks up the mountain to clear my thoughts. That great empty countryside, with its fields of air spread out below me, still had the power to move me. Not a sound, not the crack of a twig nor the rustle of a leaf except when, as I sat under an ilex tree, the song of a blue tit that with its cheep-cheep-cheep seemed to be sewing together two sheets of silence. I could not live without Juliana, I could not lead a rational life with her – what was I to do?

For, quite apart from the question of our excessive love making, the girl was not easy to live with. Only fifteen, her head, which was never very strong, had been turned by her position. She was continually flying into storms and tantrums, so that it often seemed that we only got on well in bed. When, to keep her amused, I gave a dance she made eyes at the young men who crowded about her like flies round a sugar loaf because, since her relation to me was known, this proclaimed her as easy and therefore fair game to all of them. I was not particularly jealous, for I regarded her attraction to her own age group as natural, but my position required that I should keep a close guard over her as otherwise I should have been looked down on by the village. I was also aware that, if she should snatch a moment to have a brief affair and be made pregnant, the baby would be saddled on me. I therefore saw to it that, when she left the house, she was watched and guarded – my friend Paco, who was my confidant in this business, being kind enough to offer his services. These restrictions produced sulks and storms in Juliana, yet if I had not taken such precautions, she would have thought that I was treating her not as a much-loved mistress but as a *puta* and would have been very indignant. Spanish girls complain of their boyfriends' jealousy, yet would be enraged if they did not show it, and the more violently the better.

She also wanted to be the sole centre of attention. One day I went for a long walk in the sierra, got involved in snow drifts and did not reach home till nearly midnight. I found the house full of people who were anxiously awaiting me since, with the exaggerated dread of the snow that is felt by all Andalusian villagers, they imagined that I was lost and that they would never see me again. But this interest in my fate did not please Juliana. She felt that her sole possession of me was menaced and as soon as the crowd had left she made a jealous scene and went off to her own house for the night. At one time I had had the idea that I might take a flat in Seville and install her in it, but now I saw that such a plan was totally impractical. Not only would she start to have love affairs right and left, but she was quite incapable of keeping house. Lazy and self-indulgent, she had never learned to make even an omelet. Perhaps as she grew older she would change and acquire a normal sense of her interests, but I could not wait for that. Young men and love-making were just now her only concern and I could scarcely complain because it was for that reason that I had won her.

I had always wanted to visit the Sahara so at the end of February I set off, after committing Juliana to the care of my friend Paco. I took the boat from Almeria to Melilla, the bus to Tlemcen, that most beautifully situated of all North African towns, and thence to Oran, which is quite the nastiest. Here I bought a ticket for Beni Ounif, the railway terminus which stands a little way out in the Sahara. But the desert was not looking its usual self, for it was under water. Two days before it had rained for the first time in thirty years and, since there was no natural drainage, all I could see was a shallow lake stretching for miles. But Figuig, an oasis of date palms lying in a cleft of the saharan Atlas, was within a walk and I was able to get down in an army lorry to Colomb-Béchar and thence to Igli, in the dry river valley of the Saura and see the great sand dunes of the Western Erg.

In the small Hotel du Sahara at Beni Ounif there was an elegantly dressed Swedish count who claimed to be a painter. He was a pleasant though decidedly odd man for he lived in such a fear of bacterial infection that he wore grey cotton gloves all the time, not taking them off even when he went to bed. A company of black Senegalese troops was stationed at the *ksar* close by and we were told that in the brothel assigned to them there was some good dancing to be seen. We decided to visit it and were delighted by the spectacle of three or four Berber girls dancing slowly and gracefully each in their turn while two negroes beat time on enormous black drums. An audience of Senegalese troops sat round drinking mint tea and the atmosphere was restrained and decorous. We were then invited to go out with two of the girls and as the count at once agreed to do so I followed him. A row of little whitewashed rooms, furnished with carpets and cushions, opened off a large courtyard. The girl I had chosen, who was as white-skinned as I was, proved to be charming. I was struck by the delicacy of her manners, which contrasted strongly with those of European prostitutes, but the thought of all those huge Senegalese warriors who had regular access to her body prevented me from touching her, much though I should have liked to. When we got back to the hotel I compared notes with the count. He had of course kept on his gloves all the time, but though he had had intercourse with his girl he had not taken the precaution of using a rubber sheath.

I returned by lorry across the high, waterless tableland to Oran and from there made my way by train, bus and boat to Almeria. Paco met me at Ugíjar. He told me that to test Juliana's fidelity to me he had made advances to her and that she had given in at once. Every night therefore he had made love to her on my big chair in the *granero*, though taking precautions not to make her pregnant. I cannot say that I was surprised or indeed greatly upset by this information, since I was not in love with her and had after all had other girls myself while I was in Seville. But I was determined to show her that I knew about it because this would save me once and for all from having any child she might be given by someone else fathered on me. To do this without giving Paco away I resorted to a ruse. As soon as we went to bed that night I began to question her. As she insisted on her innocence, though her whole manner showed that she felt guilt and embarrassment, I told her that I had consulted a *niño dormido*, that is a child who is put into a mesmeric trance by a wise woman and then answers any question that is put to him, and that he had described in detail her dealings with Paco in the *granero*. Juliana, who like all the village women, believed in these soothsayings, burst into a flood of tears. I did everything I could to console her, confessed falsely to having myself been to bed with a Moorish prostitute, but she remained inconsolable. Something in her feeling for me had changed because she had been found out and saw that I would never trust her again.

The passage of a few days showed that Juliana had not been left 'embarrassed', as Spaniards put it, by her affair with Paco, so, as we were now getting on well, she began to press me more strongly than ever to give her a child, which up to this time I had been careful not to do. She wanted one firstly because Spanish girls feel that something is lacking to sexual relations if they do not lead to children, but also because she knew that if she had a child by me I would support both her and it for some time to come. Her mother, I gathered, was urging this on her too: they often went hungry in her family. Then one day as we were having lunch alone together and drinking wine she began to quarrel with me because I would not give her what she wanted and, getting up from the table suddenly, ran off in a rage to our bedroom. I followed, and a little excited by the wine but also wishing to please her, changed my mind.

'All right,' I said. 'I'll give you one. Here and now. But I make it a condition that when the child has been weaned you hand it over to me to bring up in England and I will see that you don't lose by it. And also that till you know you are pregnant you do not leave this house unaccompanied after dark or speak to any young men.'

She promised and the rest followed. Now that I no longer had to use self-restraint I found a renewed zest in making love to her and we did so even more passionately and assiduously than ever. But this excessive eroti-cism proved to be a strain on our tempers and nerves, for we took to quarrelling and I could see that our affair was drawing to its natural end.

It was bound to do so very soon in any case, for my great-aunt had slipped out of life the previous summer and I had only remained on in Spain for the legal business to be settled and to come into my inheritance. This had now happened and I had to return to England at once. So we parted. Juliana left for Motril to visit a sister, knowing that she was with child by me, and I set off for London a couple of days later. I was still very fond of her and sad when she left.

17

My marriage

In May 1930 I arrived in London. After calling on my lawyers I found that I now possessed an income of nearly £350 a year, drawn from some thirty different industrial concerns. These were scattered all over the world from China to Peru in the form of mines, railways, factories, tramways and gas-works, and it amazed me to think that so many different spots on the earth's surface were preparing to support me in comfort. A feeling of gratitude towards these kindly organizations welled up in me, only to be succeeded by others of guilt which prevented me from ever thinking about them again.

In those days £350 a year was a pretty good income for a young un-married man and enough to allow me to do anything I wanted. Had it come a few years earlier I should probably have applied it to carrying out my old day-dreams of travel in the Middle East or in the Sahara, but such things no longer appealed to me because it was women and not deserts that now held my interest. I had contracted what Byron called 'madness of the heart' and wherever I went my mind was filled with images of girls. To spend a night alone in a city had become a torment for me and so I decided that I must on no account settle in London since if I did so I would only go back to my old promiscuous habits. My aim must be marriage – but to whom? I had drifted away from the literary world and except for a few isolated friends I knew no one. If I failed to find a suitable partner there would be nothing left for me but to take a flat in Seville and there lead a debauched sort of existence with one of the semi-prostitutes of the Kursaal. But first I must finish my novel. If that proved a success it would give me new friends among whose daughters or nieces I might meet with the girl I needed. And to finish my novel I must find rooms somewhere in the country.

I looked up Winny, who was on the point of marrying her Jewish boy-friend. The furniture I had given her had apparently helped him to make up his mind, though this did not prevent her from begging me to take her to Paris for a few days, promising me a good time if I did so. But

My marriage

Winny's function for me in the past had been that of a tranquillizer and I was not tempted. I searched for Lily but could not come across any trace of her. These girls are as rootless as gipsies. So I did what any penniless young man does who comes into money – I bought a car. As I wanted a fast one I chose a 24-horse-power Ford coupé, with a canvas hood that could be pulled up and two small dickey seats behind. I had never driven a car before since my father had not allowed me to touch his, but the garage man explained the levers and drove me to the beginning of the Great West Road, where I took over from him. Somehow or other I managed to get down safely to my parents' house in the Cotswolds. After a week of practising on country roads I decided that I knew all about driving and could safely follow my instinct to go as fast as possible. With such a powerful engine I could overtake any car on the road and I made it a point of honour always to do so. In those days there was no speed limit even in built-up areas, but I had a quick reaction and that saved me. I realize now that I was a menace to everyone on the road and, though I never had an accident, I certainly deserved a prison sentence for my recklessness.

Stephen Tomlin had suggested that I should take rooms in a Dorset village called East Chaldon, which lies about a mile from the sea between Lulworth and Weymouth. There was, he said, a novelist called T. F. Powys who lived there and I should enjoy talking to him because he was a man of great originality. I set off therefore on July 9th and took a bedroom and a sitting-room in a new house in the middle of the village. From the first moment I was delighted with the place. A small collection of cottages and farmhouses was scattered over a gentle hollow between cornfields and green hills. There were few trees. The land was poorer, the fields rougher than in Berkshire or Wiltshire, yet the hills kept their shapes and their smooth turf slopes were terraced with linchets. Only one road, skirting a small brook, led to the village and that gave it an air of seclusion.

As soon as I had unpacked and had tea I went out to reconnoitre the place. At the foot of a lane that ran up the hill between overgrown thorn hedges I came to a haystack and here I saw a young woman walking very slowly with her eyes on the ground and stooping every now and then to pick up a flint. I guessed that she must be searching for prehistoric implements and took her to be the Miss Powys I had heard of. Her face struck me by its freshness and beauty, but her slow, lethargic movements and sad, dreamy expression modified this youthful image by introducing a suggestion of old age. There was an air of gentleness and resignation about her that reminded me of my grandmother, whom I had been much attached to, and since my mind was always running on whom I would marry, it occurred to me that she might be the person.

I had written a note to Theodore Powys announcing my arrival and on the following morning I received an invitation to have tea with him. I went, and there was the girl I had seen by the haystack on the previous day and her name was not Miss Powys but Miss Gamel Woolsey and she was an American poetess from South Carolina. I felt immediately drawn to her. She was living in a cottage in the village so I asked her to tea with me on the following day. She accepted and after that we met for lunch or tea on almost every day for some weeks to come.

Before long I had learned her history. Elizabeth Gammell Woolsey had been born in May 1899 at Breeze Hill Plantation near Aiken. Her father, John Woolsey, was a cotton planter who had come south from New York after the Civil War with his wife and three sons, one of whom later became that Federal judge who gave the famous decision that Joyce's *Ulysses* was not an obscene work. After his wife's death he married again, taking a Charleston girl called Elizabeth Gammell who was still in her teens. By her he had two daughters, the eldest of whom was Elizabeth, or, as she was called in the family, Elsa, though since she disliked that name she later changed it to Gamel, which is a Norse name meaning old. Then her father died and after a trip round Europe in 1914 with her mother, the two of them settled down in a house in one of the principal streets of Charleston.

Here Gamel grew up to be a strikingly beautiful girl as well as a very precocious one. By the time she was sixteen she could read French and Latin fluently and was started on a life-long love of poetry. Then she developed tuberculosis and was for a year or more in a sanatorium. The melancholy that, though she could be gay, gave a pronounced cast to her features, seems to date from this period. Then in her early twenties she went up to New York with the vague idea of going on the stage. One reason for her leaving home was that she could no longer get on with her mother, who had taken to fits of heavy drinking.

But she did not become an actress. Instead she met and had an affair with a New Zealand journalist, a tall, fair-haired, handsome man who was a great Don Juan and prided himself on the number of his illegitimate children. He soon made her pregnant and then, seeing that she was a girl who could not fend for herself, he broke his rule of avoiding commitments and married her. However she did not have his child, since, owing to the state of her health, her pregnancy had to be arrested. Soon after this, though she was still far from well, they went on a trip to England. The trip was a failure. She soon found that she had nothing in common with her husband, so, having drifted into her marriage without being in love with him, she proceeded to drift out of it. On her return to America she took a room at Patchin Place in Greenwich Village. Here she met J. C. Powys and later his brother Llewelyn and on their suggestion came to

England and took rooms in a cottage at East Chaldon. She was very poor, for her income was under £120 a year.

As I sat evening after evening talking to Gamel I began to come more and more under her influence. There was her face to begin with. It was a beautiful face, one of those that are built to last because they have a fine bone structure, and it was also a sensitive one. Under her dark hair a pair of calm grey eyes looked out gravely at mine. Her complexion had the sort of transparency that one sometimes finds in consumptive people and her voice was soft yet precise, with only a slight trace of a Southern accent. In her conversation there was a mixture of ingenuousness and quickness of perception and everything she said was clearly and naturally expressed without hurry or hesitation. She seemed so utterly candid and simple and yet there was a mystery about her which appeared chiefly in what she did not say. Why for example had she been living for a whole year in this tiny Dorset village without having ever been to the trouble of unpacking her suitcases? And what was her connection with the Powys family?

I had by this time seen a fair amount of Theodore Powys. He was a man of rather stocky build with a round head covered by a thatch of hair that had already gone almost white in spite of his being only just past fifty. He occupied a solitary brick bungalow called Bethcar whose ugliness he seemed to like and was married to a dark, lively woman by name Violet whom he had taken from an adjacent cottage. He had lived here since 1904 without ever going out of the district except once when Stephen Tomlin had taken him to London for two nights to celebrate the publication of his first novel. Now he rarely left his house except to walk up the valley away from the village, which he refused to enter because he did not like being looked at. By the ideas of today he was a case of religious mania for he was wholly possessed by the conviction, which seems to have come out of his child-hood reading of the Old Testament, that all human beings are irredeemably steeped in sin. More than that, he was sometimes privileged to talk with God, of whom he held a rather poor opinion. He was also, like John Donne, from whom the Powyses were descended, obsessed by death and rarely passed a day without walking round the churchyard, where he would muse lovingly over the tombstones. Yet although his religious obsession was never far below the surface, he did not lack sophistication of a kind. He knew English literature well and had a special partiality for Jane Austen, whom he had read so often that the characters in her novels were more real to him than those of his friends. Then he was a very entertaining talker, though to appreciate his style of conversation one had to have some grasp of his character and way of thinking. Only quotation can convey its quality, which was a mixture of wit, irony and humour with something of the dry, down to earth realism of a Chinese sage. Since he was almost morbidly circumspect and cautious he spoke in understatements, but his sly, pointed remarks, uttered in a tone of great politeness but with a malicious twinkle in his eye, had a flavour that was unlike anything else. Their penetrating quality sprang from his belief in the total depravity of human nature as seen through the eyes of an implacable and possibly wicked God and they were often coloured by a sort of whimsicality which came from his preferring to hint than to speak out. This was no doubt because his deeper thoughts were too dangerous to be uttered. He was indeed a man who had been cast in a different mould to everyone else. Cut off as he was by his life and reading from the contemporary world, he seemed to belong rather to the seventeenth century than to the present age.

The other Powyses were enthusiasts and romantics, celebrators of life each in their own way. But Theodore was afraid of life and deeply pessi-mistic about it. This set him apart from the rest of that close, mutually admiring clan, for though he was attached to them all and enjoyed their company, he was inclined to be ironical about them. Indeed in his cautious, cat-like way he was ironical about everyone, including God. Only the dead held him in total sympathy and loyalty. Another thing that stood out a mile at Bethcar was the incompatability of temperament between him and his wife. Violet was a quick, lively, hospitable woman who had once been pretty, but she had had little education. Naturally she did not understand him, though perhaps it would have been worse if she had, for he was afraid of all women except his sisters and most afraid of educated ones. He even warned me against Gamel, whose company he particularly liked, saying that she moved as stealthily as an American Indian so that one could not hear her coming. His real preference was for little girls up to the age of fifteen and Violet had not been much older when he had married her. Yet they never quarrelled. Although she often showed her impatience she kept a certain respect for him, while he was far too timid to oppose her openly. They therefore led their separate lives in one another's presence with only a faint edge of polite hostility separating them. This underlying discord was symbolized by the fact that they ate separate foods. Violet cooked heavy meals in the English cottage style with a profusion of stodgy cakes and pastries which were set out at tea time, while Theodore lived on milk, boiled eggs, oranges and bread and butter, washed down with tea and a pinch of bicarbonate of soda. Possibly he would have been a little less pessimistic about the world if his wife's cooking had been easier to digest.

There were other Powyses in the neighbourhood besides Theodore. John Cowper had lodgings in two rooms that had been carved out of a derelict farm building called Rat's Barn, but just before my arrival he left for America. However the youngest brother Llewelyn and his American wife Alyse Gregory were still there, installed in one of the coastguard cot-

1 Gerald Brenan in 1922

2 Gerald Brenan and Ralph Partridge at Watendlath, 1921

3 Gerald Brenan and Dora Carrington at Watendlath, 1921

4 Stephen and Julia Tomlin

5 Dora Carrington, Ralph Partridge and Lytton Strachey at Ham Spray

6   Saxon Sydney-Turner and Francis Birrell

7   Ralph Partridge and Frances Marshall

8   Dora Carrington

9   Alix Strachey

10   James Strachey

11 (*left*) Roger Fry
12 (*right*) John
      Hope-Johnstone

13 (*left*) Boris Anrep
14 (*right*) Lily

15 (*left*) Arthur
      Waley
16 (*right*) 'Beakus'
      Penrose

17 The author's father

18 The author's mother

19 Great-aunt Tiz

20 Gamel

21 Llewelyn and John Cowper
Powys in Dorset, 1931

22 Augustus John, Gamel, and
John Hope-Johnstone at
East Lulworth, 1932

23 Gerald Brenan in 1933

24 Yegen from the east

25 (*above*) Joanna Carrington   26 Raymond Mortimer and Gerald Brenan

27 Gerald Brenan in his study at Churriana, about 1960

28 Bertrand Russell, Gerald Brenan and Peter Russell at East Lulworth, August 1934

29 Gerald Brenan with Ralph Partridge, Gamel, and Ronald Duncan at Welcombe, late 1930s

30 Gamel, Gerald Brenan and Ralph Partridge in the *granero* at Yegen, 1937

31 Gamel, Ernest Hemingway, Annie Davis and Gerald Brenan in May 1959

32 Lynda Nicholson Price

tages at White Nothe, half an hour's walk away on the cliff's edge. So far I had only seen him for a few moments – a good looking, prematurely aged man of forty-six who dressed in loose homespun garments that were often surmounted by a long tweed cape. He was in an advanced stage of tuberculosis. Sometimes, I was told, he had to spend whole weeks confined to his bed – then he would feel better and, getting up, go for long walks over the hills till he exhausted himself and the haemorrhages broke out again. The only other Powys to live in the vicinity was Gertrude, who occupied one half of a lonely house called Chydyock that stood high above the village, near to the chalk cliffs. She was the most stable member of the family if one excludes the dull and conventional Littleton, an ex-schoolmaster who lived at Sherborne but often came to Weymouth. She was the nearest in age as well as in character to Theodore – a handsome, rather masculine woman who had kept her loyalty to the Anglican religion while admitting a certain infusion of her brother Llewelyn's flamboyant ideas. For he was one of those religious atheists who deify Nature and his books were passionate tracts, couched in ultra-Romantic and Rabelaisian language and stuffed with archaisms.

After I had been seeing Gamel almost every day for three weeks, she gave me a book of her poems to read entitled *Middle Earth* and also the typescript of an unfinished novel called *One Way of Love*. I did not care much for the poems which, though they showed talent, were in the loose romantic style of the early 'twenties, but I felt differently about the novel. It was an autobiographical novel, describing her marriage and her discovery with her husband of London and of the English countryside. Although it had serious weaknesses of style because she had not learned to co-ordinate her sentences, its best passages showed a freshness of feeling and language that delighted me as well as a very un-American sensitivity to places. There were also descriptions of love-making that by the standards of that time were unusually frank. I felt carried into the interior of her mind and confirmed in the impressions her conversation had made on me, so that as I read it my last doubts vanished and I began to fall in love with her.*

I should have liked to go on for some time in this vague, half dreamy

*The later history of this novel is as follows. It was accepted by Gollancz and set up in 1932. But just as it was about to appear, a book on Lesbian love, *The Well of Loneliness*, by Radclyffe Hall, which Cape had brought out in 1928, was prosecuted and suppressed. Gollancz took fright and decided not to publish Gamel's novel. So far as I know, only two copies of it exist today, one in my possession and one which I sent to the British Museum Reading Room. It was characteristic of Gamel that she gave her heroine the name of Mariana after Tennyson's early poem. That was how she saw herself at the time, waiting for the knight on horseback to appear, despairing of his coming and neglecting the housework.

state without declaring my feelings, but there was a time limit as Gamel was preparing to return to America. I thought that the best way of persuading her to marry me would be to find a house that she would like to live in and on my first attempt to do this I was successful. At Langdon Herring, a few miles beyond Weymouth, I found a small house to let called Ivy Cottage Farm which overlooked the Chesil Beach. It had a walled garden on one side and a flourishing fig tree by the door, while tall grey-leaved ilexes overhung the paddock behind. On the following afternoon I drove Gamel over to see it.

We arrived. The haymakers were at work in the field in front of the house and on going towards them we caught sight below us of the melancholy waters of the Fleet, pale and forbidding like a legendary Arthurian lake and bordered by bullrushes. Floating about on its surface like scraps of white paper there was a flock of wild swans. Beyond it we could see a low pebble belt, the Chesil Beach, that divided it from the sea. Gamel was enchanted by the house and place but alas, on inquiring of a farmer, we learned that it has been let to 'a gentleman from London' a few days before.

In much dejection we walked down the hill to the edge of the water. The bullrushes were sprinkled with swans' down and white feathers. Long strands of briony festooned with scarlet berries and of bindweed with its white trumpet flowers climbed over the thorn bushes and I picked some of them and made a garland for Gamel's hair. Suddenly I found myself in an embarrassing situation. She was standing still with her calm face and eyes turned on me. Moved by a sudden impulse I kissed her. No doubt I appeared to act without conviction, but she did not draw away though she seemed to tremble when I touched her. Everything had gone more rapidly than I had dared to hope.

We had tea at Abbotsbury and supper together in her cottage. She was very tired and her grave face in the lamplight looked almost translucent. I asked her if she would marry me and she replied that she would give me an answer within a few days. That, I thought to myself with my usual optimism, meant yes, so I lay awake half the night in a trance of happiness. Next morning I walked out over the fields. I felt so light that my feet seemed scarcely to touch the ground. The sun was shining, the grass was green and the earth as fresh and new as if it had just been created.

On the following day Gamel set off on an expedition with Llewelyn and on the day after that she went away for the weekend. It had been arranged that I was to drive him and his wife Alyse into Bournemouth. I scarcely knew them, but from Gamel's frequent references to them I gathered that they were in some way mixed up in her life. Immediately the situation became clear to me. Llewelyn was in a state of misery that he scarcely attempted to conceal, while Alyse talked only of jealousy, unhappiness and suicide – in the work of Proust, it is true, but from Proust to one's own condition it is not a long step. On the way back I could see in my mirror Llewelyn's anxious, furrowed features which reminded me in their intensity of an illustration depicting Grief in one of Lavater's or Darwin's books on physiognomy. I guessed at once that he was in love with Gamel, but he seemed so worn and racked by age and sickness that it did not occur to me that she could also be in love with him.

On Monday Gamel returned from her visit and the evident pleasure she showed on seeing me told me what her answer would be, though in fact she said nothing. She spent the following evening and night with Llewelyn and Alyse and after that we set off on a long-planned expedition to Salisbury and Avebury. As we went up to the inn after inspecting the great stones we saw some farmers sitting on a bench by the porch with hooded hawks on their wrists. They had been flying them at skylarks.

On our way back across the Plain we found the Military Tattoo at Tidworth about to commence, so stopped till dark fell to see it. Then as we went on through the night Gamel gave me an account of her life during the past year – her desperate love affair with Llewelyn, the painful situation over Alyse, the child he had wished in spite of her precarious health to give her, the operation that had been necessary to arrest the pregnancy, the prostration that had followed. I felt deeply moved. I stopped the car to kiss her and she told me with the tears streaming down her face that everything was over between her and Llewelyn and that she would *perhaps* – and this *perhaps* clearly meant *certainly* – marry me. But was she considering doing so, I asked myself, merely in order to escape from an impossible situation? On my pressing her she assured me that she was no longer in love with Llewelyn, only very attached to him and concerned about his health. On the following morning she reaffirmed this and I drove up to London, where she agreed to join me in a week's time in a flat I had taken. After that we were to spend our honeymoon on the west coast of Ireland.

Several days passed without my hearing from her and then came a very short letter which mentioned only the weather. After an inconclusive conversation with her on the telephone I drove back to Chaldon. Arriving at tea time, I found her nervous and very tired. She told me that, after a painful scene with Llewelyn, he and Alyse had left for London with the intention of sailing at once for America. The scene, she said, had distressed her very much, all the more as any violent agitation might bring on a haemorrhage which could kill him. While we were talking Gertrude came in and, seeing Gamel looking ill, suggested that she should spend the night with her at Chydyock. This seemed a good plan and I drove them up.

Next day I walked there for tea. I found Gamel in a distressingly weak state. She had never properly recovered from the operation to remove Llewelyn's child and that night she had had a slight haemorrhage and had spat blood. Although she was unwilling to see a doctor I insisted that she must do so and drove off at once to London to fetch a woman doctor whom I knew and had confidence in. I brought her back next afternoon with a hamper of provisions from Fortnum and Mason since the Powyses were vegetarians. After examining Gamel she said that there was no immediate need for anxiety, but prescribed absolute rest for a week and then a visit to a lung specialist in London.

My prospective marriage was turning out very differently from what I had anticipated. In the first place Gamel's attitude towards me had completely changed. She was now distant and constrained, agreed at once with everything I said and made it clear that she preferred to be alone in her room to being with me. Her previous feelings for me had dried up and her only thoughts were for Llewelyn. Knowing her as I do today, I can see that she was benumbed by feelings of guilt, for Llewelyn was not the man to have spared her reproaches. Then the reasons that Gertrude Powys gave me for her state were not reassuring. The love that bound her to Llewelyn, she declared, transcended all other loves. It had something super-natural about it which meant that nothing could ever quench it, not even the grave. No wonder she was ill. But now, thanks to me, she would recover. All would be well and this unseverable link would in due course be restored to what it had been before. It also seemed that the moon played some part in this sacred affinity, since vows had been solemnly made to it which had cemented it.

I saw that I had got myself into a disagreeably false position. I was about to go off with a very sick woman who, whatever she might say, was in love with someone else. My function was to save her from a situation that had become untenable. Llewelyn could not leave Alyse because she alone could provide him with the care and attention he needed. Gamel was far too weak and too unfitted for cooking and housework to do that. Her part must be to play Mary to Alyse's Martha. This meant that I was required to pull the chestnuts out of the fire for them and allow Llewelyn to con-tinue his affair with Gamel later on. After my experiences with Carrington this role was extremely distasteful to me. I wanted a wife for myself.

I also gathered from Gertrude's conversation that Gamel occupied a special niche in the Powys family. She was, one might say, their holy woman, their Muse, their fetish. In this murky pseudo-religious world which as a rationalist, though with Christian leanings, I disliked, she held a peculiar position because she had *mana*. They had adopted her, promoted her to being one of themselves and she with her romantic Southern feeling for the old, the run-down, the ancient family reduced to ruin, felt herself to belong to them all conjointly. That at least was what I not altogether mistakenly suspected.

However my love for Gamel was of too recent a growth for me to throw it over at a moment's notice. I could not dream of abandoning her, ill and deeply distressed in mind as she was. I therefore suppressed the doubts and fears which my self-esteem had prompted and, so as not to think any more about them, busied myself in practical matters. Perhaps everything would work out all right in the end.

Gamel was now feeling stronger so I drove her to London and left her for the night in a nursing home. The lung specialist examined her and declared that it would be taking a great risk for us to spend our honeymoon in Ireland. Instead I must take her to Mundesley Sanatorium in Norfolk.

A heat wave of unprecedented ferocity was now sweeping over England. The temperature in the shade went up to 95°. We set off through the torrid air, hoping it would grow cooler as we went north and on the way stopped for the night at Rodwell near Ipswich where Helen Anrep had settled with Roger Fry. She was not only my best woman friend but the person on whom in all the most serious affairs in life – marriage, sickness, death – I most relied and now I wanted her reassurance. But the moment chosen for our arrival was not a propitious one. The heat had got on everyone's nerves, Molly MacCarthy was staying in the house, the cook was ill, and a luncheon party had been arranged for the following day. Gamel, in a tired and apathetic state and dressed in clothes that did not suit her because we had bought them in a hurry, made a poor impression. I felt that we were not wanted and though Helen made an effort to cover up her lack of appreciation of, as she must have thought, just another of my girls, she did not succeed in blinding me. I felt in a suppressed rage and during the next three days, which we spent in sightseeing, paid off my anger and frustration on my companion.

On the last day of August we arrived at Mundesley where, after leaving her at the sanitorium, I took rooms for myself close by. Next morning the heat wave broke and it began to rain in torrents. Day after day for four entire weeks it continued to pour down from a low grey sky. My thoughts, which had been sullen and resentful before, now took on the colour of the rain and I sank into a deep depression. Gamel, whom I visited every afternoon, was even more dispirited than I was. My whole demeanour told her that I regretted having gone off with her, so that she felt herself caught in a painfully false situation. Her reaction to this was to withdraw into herself, so that all real communication ceased between us.

I can see now how different everything might have been had I shown a little more understanding and patience. Her feelings for me had not been destroyed by the shock that Llewelyn's stormy leave-taking had given her. I still represented for her the promise of a new and happy life, whereas he stood for a sad and painful past to which there could be no return. Had I therefore avoided wounding her acutely sensitive nature she would gradually have come back to me and her old lover would have ceased to be more than a close friend. But my hurt pride and egoism prevented me from seeing this and neither Gertrude nor Helen had helped me.

At this moment I had a rather discreditable adventure. One morning as I was coming out of the sanatorium I gave a lift to a tall, attractive girl who might have been about twenty-six. She was a Chilean and was visiting a much older man whom she spoke of as her protector. I drove her back to her hotel in Cromer and found it a pleasant change to be able to talk Spanish again, for foreign languages release a side of us that is buried when we speak our own. After that I took her to her hotel every day and before long we were on kissing terms. Although she expressed surprise that I should want to make love to her when I was on my honeymoon, she responded warmly and only her fear of being discovered prevented her from going to bed with me. Indeed she at first agreed to my taking a room close to hers at her hotel and only changed her mind because the man at the reception desk stared at us as we came in together. I was of course acting irresponsibly, but the girl's youth and vitality made such a strong contrast to Gamel's despondency and apathy that I was carried away.

On the first of October the head doctor at Mundesley declared that the activity in Gamel's lung had ceased and that she could therefore leave. We moved to a little inn at Trimingham and then to rooms at Wells-next-the-sea. The question of our future relations had now to be decided. Should we continue living together or not? I could see that Gamel had ceased to have any confidence in me. The love which at Chaldon had begun to pierce the crust of her old love for Llewelyn had been arrested if not destroyed. The normal way of restoring it was lacking for I found myself unable to make love to her. At the back of my mind there lay all the time the nagging thought that I had been trapped into going off with a sick, melancholic young woman who was in love with someone else. If so, this was a double calamity, for my past experience told me that the beauty of girls counted for me less than their gaiety and sense for life, while I had had enough experience of three-cornered situations to last me forever. Yet now I had to sit back in silence while fat envelopes with American stamps on them were delivered by the postman and watch Gamel spending the rest of the morning answering them. But if this was hard to bear there were other times when her gentleness, her fine sensibility and her clear and precise intelligence would come out from under the cloud where my doubts and jealousies had hidden them and disarm me. I reflected that she was unhappy and deserved all the patience and affection I could give her.

I realized too that I had been mistaken in attributing to her a sympathy for those half-baked ideas that filled Llewelyn with such vehemence. She had once enjoyed living in New York and going to theatres and cinemas – both things that were anathema to him. However much she felt herself to belong emotionally to his little clan, she turned a cold eye on his beliefs. In nearly all her tastes and interests she was a modern person, who admired writers such as Joyce and Eliot, whom he regarded with disapprobation. I saw that in fact I had a great deal in common with her – more indeed than with any woman I had hitherto met. The only things I did not like in her were her low spirits and a certain passiveness and lack of spring in her disposition, and with time these might change. And what about my own defects?

Gradually then I began to understand that for better or worse our lives were linked together. One look at the chaos and misery of my past life was enough to convince me that I could not go back to that. Nor had Gamel any alternative but to cling to me. Marriages are made as well as born and I saw that if we built up ours with patience and good will we had a fair chance of succeeding. Then one evening the ice between us was broken and we had an explanation. It was brought on by my realization that she was on the point of leaving me and I felt that I could not bear that. My distress convinced her that in spite of all appearances I still loved her and that set her free to begin to love me back, for she was one of those women whose timidity conceals a large measure of pride so that they have to feel that they are loved before they can give affection. Once more she assured me that she was not in love with Llewelyn, merely very attached to him, and, though I took this with a grain of salt, I saw that her best interests and hopes of happiness must tend with the passage to time to draw her away from him towards me. So we agreed to call ourselves married and with my confidence now restored to me I found myself released from the spell of impotence that had fastened on me and able to make love to her Between us we had rounded the bend.

We spent October driving about Norfolk and visiting its great houses and churches in the beautiful autumnal weather. After that we went on a week's tour of the Lakes, spending a couple of nights at Watendlath where I looked again with mixed feelings on the place where my love for Carrington had begun. On our way back we visited Haworth to see the Brontës' house and then began our preparations for wintering near Naples. The first thing to be considered was Gamel's health and I imagined that the drive out in an open car and the good food in the restaurants would do more than anything else to restore it. I was beginning to discover in myself a vein which I had not previously been aware of – the desire to look after and protect someone. In the thirty-eight years of my married life that was the role I took. Gamel needed protection more than any woman I have ever known and I believe that I acquitted myself well in that respect, perhaps because by so doing I was making up for a certain lack of intensity and sharpness in my feelings for her. For I was no longer 'in love' with her – Llewelyn had seen to that – and though with the passage of time we became the best of partners and companions, there was always something lacking in our deeper feelings for one another.

Before starting for Italy I wrote to my father that I was engaged to be married. In the past he had never allowed even jokes on that subject, but now he wrote that he had had a presentiment, which surprised even himself, that my marriage would make for everyone's happiness. But till the divorce had been settled he did not want us to come down to Edgeworth together. His future daughter-in-law's reputation, he declared, must not be tinged by the slightest suspicion, for should anyone at some later date cast a slur upon it, he would be compelled to knock them down. So, as he was not much of a pugilist, he invited her to stay for a few days by herself.

The visit could not have gone off better. From the first moment my father was carried away by Gamel's beauty. 'Centuries of breeding,' he declared, 'must have gone to the making of that mouth and chin.' The same breeding, he added, could be seen in her manners and it amazed him, he told her, thinking it was a compliment, that such refinement should have come out of a new, raw country like America. The only thing he could not understand was how she had consented to marry such a dubious character as myself. So, taking me aside, he said in a stern voice, 'Remember this, my boy. If you ever do anything to upset that splendid girl, I'll never speak to you again.' My mother was equally enthusiastic. Although in principle she disapproved of divorce, in practice she was ready to make exceptions and it especially pleased her that, like her own mother, Gamel was a Southerner. I told them that we were going to Italy with Miss Powys as a chaperone and they accepted that, though I am sure that my mother never believed it.

A week later we crossed the Channel and spent Christmas at Chartres, where the stained-glass windows made a deep impression on me, though one that was perhaps more hypnotic than aesthetic. Then on through Burgundy, eating delicious food in its famous restaurants, to Aix-en-Provence. Here the last crisis in my married life took place. On going one morning into our bedroom I saw on the table an unfinished letter which Gamel had been writing to Llewelyn Powys. On a sudden impulse I read it. As I had expected, it was a love letter. I could put up with that, but what I could not put up with was her saying that she was utterly miserable with me, hating every moment of it and longing only to see him again. That I knew was untrue. Although in the depth of her mind she was no doubt deeply concerned over him, she was enjoying herself immensely as her almost continual good spirits showed. On my confronting her with the letter, she first tried to throw the blame on me by saying, what was true, that I had no right to read her correspondence, then she said that if she had told Llewelyn that she was not happy with me she had only done so because she was afraid that if he felt she was forgetting him he might have a haemorrhage. When I got to know her better I saw that this explanation was largely correct. In contradiction to her invariably high standard of conduct, she had no respect for the truth and believed in telling people not what she herself thought or felt but what they wanted to believe. Indeed it became a sort of joke among our friends that she would agree to every-thing they said even when they knew that she thought differently. On my taxing her with this she would reply that she had so poor a regard for people's opinions that she preferred to save herself trouble by agreeing with them. But the fact was that she did not know how to disagree with anyone without displaying acrimony. With her ultra-sensitive nature any expression of difference seemed to her an act of hostility and therefore to be avoided. In later years, whenever we found that we disagreed on some small point, such as the merits of a particular book, a tone of sharpness would come into her voice which warned me that I must give way if I was not to annoy her. That is to say, she was so totally feminine that she took any difference of opinion as a criticism of herself. But now at Aix I did not understand this. My marriage seemed to have tumbled down like a pack of cards and I felt that no trust or reliance could be placed in any-thing she said. For a whole day I drove along the corniche road to Porto-fino without speaking to her. Then my anger subsided. I never again read her letters or had a serious quarrel with her. When annoyed, I merely with-drew into myself and she did the same.

We drove into Pisa on the following evening with the full moon flood-ing the *duomo* and the group of buildings round it with its enormous light and then continued on our road to Naples, stopping frequently to visit places, but by-passing Florence and Rome. Finally we settled into a small Danish hotel at Capo di Sorrento where I spent two quiet months working at my novel, taking Italian lessons and reading Dante. Maxim Gorky was in residence in a large villa just across the road and every day a limousine would draw up, decorated with a bunch of red carnations, to take him and his large dog for a drive. I should have liked to meet him to tell him how much I admired his portrait of Tolstoy, but I was informed that he spoke no language but Russian.

Towards the end of March we set out again for the south with the intention of exploring Calabria. In those days the temples of Paestum still rose in lonely grandeur from the marshes, for the malaria prevented anyone from living there. The only inn was a wretched, bug-ridden place, but the scene was incomparably more impressive than it is today, crowded as it is with tourist shops and charabancs. Men kill the things they pretend to worship. Then on reaching Lauria we found that we should not have time to explore the toe and instep of Italy, so we turned off and, after putting the car on a railway truck for twenty miles because the road was not yet finished, reached Metaponto, on the site of the city where Pythagoras had spent his last days. The only house in this ugly, malaria-ridden plain was the stationmaster's. We were given a room which was so filthy and bug-infested that we did not dare to undress. As it had no door, goats and hens wandered in during the night and rats scuttled and scampered under the bed. Our supper, eaten by a smoky fire, consisted entirely of beans – this in a place where the founder of Mathematics had said that a man who could eat beans was capable of devouring his grandmother. On the following morning we walked in an icy wind over the bare sherd-strewn fields and I picked up a silver coin with an ear of wheat on it which dated from the time of Pythagoras.

I was discovering that Gamel, in spite of her delicate health, was the perfect travelling companion, for she was enthusiastic not only over the scenery and the paintings but over the historical associations of places, especially when they derived from Greek or Roman times. She was prepared to put up with any hardships and discomforts to see something that moved or interested her and this readiness for adventure continued to the end of her life. Both of us were ardent sightseers and we never got on better together than when we travelled.

We went on through Taranto and the Adriatic coast to Castel del Monte, the castle of the Emperor Frederick II and architecturally the finest castle in the world. Then by Naples again to Rome, where we spent five weeks. Here we went through a marriage ceremony of our own devising. Climbing the steps of the church of Santa Maria d'Aracoeli on the Capitoline hill, which had once been the temple of Juno, we held hands before the altar. Putting a ring on Gamel's finger, I said, 'With this ring I marry you, for better for worse, in sickness and health, till death do us part,' and she repeated the same words. For true marriage, as I understand it, is made in the heart, and to have obtained a divorce she would have had to go to America and spend far more than we could afford. Later she changed her surname by deed-poll to mine.

Soon after this ceremony she had a miscarriage (due to a failure in her contraceptive) which made her feel very ill. I continued sightseeing by myself till she was well enough to resume the journey. Then we drove to

Assisi where we met Roger Fry and Helen Anrep and from there on through Umbria to Ravenna and Padua. The plain of Lombardy was now grilling in a torrid heat so that we were glad to spend a few days in the Alpine coolness of the Dolomites. Bavaria proved to be even more antipathetic and barbarian than I had remembered it and I did not feel safe till we reached Strasbourg with its great cathedral and its excellent restaurants, and heard French spoken. By the middle of June we were back in England.

18

The deaths of Lytton Strachey and Carrington

On landing at Dover we drove straight to East Chaldon and moved into rooms there. Llewelyn Powys and Alyse Gregory had got back from America a few months previously and were living at White Nothe. Gamel lunched with them and afterwards he walked down with her to the village and met me. We talked for a little and then he asked me to accompany him part of his way home. On reaching a gate he turned and with the tears streaming down his cheeks begged me not to separate him from Gamel. He had the most expressive face I have ever seen, registering every emotion with vividness – forehead deeply furrowed when he was troubled and eyes dancing when he was happy. I was touched by his misery and, remembering what I had gone through with Carrington, promised that till we found some permanent home we would rent a cottage close to Chaldon so that he could see her whenever he wanted to. He pressed my hand and said, 'God bless you.' It was my own decision, for Gamel had said nothing to me about wanting to remain in the vicinity. That was her way – to express no preference, to ask for nothing. Many years later she declared that it had been a mistake to settle close to him because it had injured our marriage, but that was certainly not what she had felt at the time and it was not what I felt either, for although I was well aware that Llewelyn's proximity would injure our relations I could not in decency have acted otherwise. Love had its claims which must be respected.

We soon found a house in East Lulworth, a tiny thatched cottage adjoining the Weld Arms Inn, and moved into it. When the furniture we had bought in Italy arrived it completely filled it so that there was scarcely room to turn round, but there was a small beach only a mile away at Arish Mell to bathe from and the woods of Lulworth Castle to walk in. Then four hundred feet above the village stood Rings Hill with its British camp and turfed entrenchments – too steep for Gamel to climb but just what I

234

needed. In the same month Llewelyn and Alyse left White Nothe and moved into the empty half of Gertrude Powys's house at Chydyock. Here the revolving wooden hut in which he slept and never left when he was ill was set up among the cabbages and Alyse carried his trays to and from the kitchen. By taking the bus for a couple of miles we were within half an hour's walk of them.

I soon came to know Llewelyn well and to like him, all the more as he was extremely anxious to please me. Aware as he was that Gamel was a person who shrank from asserting her wishes because she dreaded difficulties of any kind, he felt himself dependent on my good will for seeing her. And I can say that I never did anything to discourage their meetings, in spite of the fact that every time they spent the day together I felt a little estranged from her. Jealousy divides, but that division has to be bridged if some sort of civilized façade is to be maintained and he understood that as well as I did. This led us to cultivate a somewhat uneasy friendship in which we went for walks together and wrote to one another. If there was at times an undercurrent of strain, it was Gamel who bore the brunt of it.

I must try to describe this man whose life had become so involved with my own. Except for Willie, who farmed in Kenya, Llewelyn was the youngest of the six Powys brothers and he had always been a bit spoiled by his family. His appearance was striking: with his deeply furrowed cheeks and grey dishevelled beard and hair he suggested a preacher in some new-fangled religion, while his long cape and broad-brimmed hat bore out this impression. But he looked gay rather than solemn and in the button-hole of his heavy country tweeds he liked to wear a bright flower. Those who met him for the first time were usually captured by his charm, although this could sometimes be a little too mellifluous because he was given to propitiating anyone with whom he did not feel completely at ease. Underneath this there lay an obviously attractive personality, open and spontaneous and endowed with a tremendous zest for life. Enthusiasm flowed out of him, not only for Nature, around which he had built his religion, but for people. He was especially appreciative of those who, however uneducated, showed some originality of speech or character and was inclined to build up his not very interesting friends into types or symbols of philosophic attitudes somewhat as Yeats did in his poetry. Indeed he was more akin in his mode of talking or thinking to the Irish writers of the early years of the century, although he had probably never read them, than to the realistic world of Wells or Dreiser or the academic one of Bloomsbury. Yet his mind was a simple one and his message, that one must enjoy every moment of one's life to the full, left out too much, though it perfectly suited his own sunny nature. Frank and outgoing, compassionate to those in trouble, generous and high-spirited, courageous and affectionate – these are all adjectives one can apply to him. A countryman through and through, mistrustful of those who lived in towns, he belonged to the age of Ruskin and Morris rather than to the 1920s.

Yet I never felt quite at ease with him. There was a little too much sweetness and desire to please in his manner and this led me to pull up my drawbridges. His enthusiasm exhausted mine and made me feel stiff and reserved so that, since we like our friends chiefly for the side they bring out in ourselves, I was prevented from fully warming to him. He was given to holding forth eloquently about life and death and such weighty topics to people who came to see him, introducing quotations from the wisdom writers in the Powys way, but such displays often made me feel uncomfortable. I was made impatient by his actor's facility of speech, by his apparent belief that everything had been solved when it had been put into well-sounding words. He quoted Ecclesiastes, he quoted Montaigne and Nietzsche and yet, because he seemed to float above reality, to lack the capacity for genuinely assimilating experience, the final impression he left on me was one of innocence. The innocence of a child who has picked up a few good phrases and knows that he uses them well, the innocence of a child playing his games with life. Yet this was not the only thing to be said about him. He was sensible in practical matters and, as his letters show, had a shrewd judgement in politics. He could be honest with himself. The difficulty I have in describing him lies in relating the different sides of his character. There was, as ornithologists say of birds, the 'displaying' side, there was the child-like side and there was the honest and common sense one.

In the past his 'let us pretend' notions about the sacredness of the moon and of fairy rings and of standing stones and so forth had irritated me because I feared their influence on Gamel. But now that I realized that she did not share them I became more tolerant. Although there was still something of a rationalist prig about me – for in criticizing Llewelyn I am aware that I am also criticizing myself – I accepted them as a part of his exuberant, paganizing ideology, though I found it embarrassing when he pressed them on me and expected me to respond. Yet although Gamel was as much of a rationalist as I was and even more lacking in religious feelings, it was the child in Llewelyn that drew her to him. She romanticized her own early youth, which she regarded as the one happy period of her life, and had preserved from that time a naive or ingenuous streak as a refuge from the adult world that she could not cope with. Thus she and Llewelyn could sit down under a hedge and talk like two children, admiring the whorl of a snail, watching a caterpillar arch itself and be perfectly happy. Neither I nor Alyse could enter into such states. Yet in another respect they were complete opposites. Llewelyn was wildly forward looking and optimistic and, except when he was in the throes of a haemorrhage, overflowing with the joy of life, whereas Gamel professed to believe that life was an evil and found her deepest happiness in withdrawing from it into her past. Yet since, like many pessimists, she also had a strong faculty for enjoyment, she found in his winning ways and childish enthusiasm an incentive to look at the world more favourably.

One could not imagine Llewelyn without his tuberculosis. It had first attacked him when he was twenty-three and had shaped and drawn out his character ever since, intensifying his love of life and the passionate romanticism he cloaked it in. He enjoyed playing a game with his illness, taking long walks and making exhausting trips to Greece and Palestine and challenging it to do its worst with him. Had he taken more care of himself he could have gone on for many years longer than he did, but he believed in living dangerously because he found that this gave a greater sharpness to things. Besides, he saw himself in a dramatic role, that of a man engaged in a personal combat with death, and he played it with verve and gallantry, like a bullfighter drawing the bull's horns close to him with his *muleta*.

His books give a good picture of him. Although he was a natural writer with an easy and fluent command of English he was unable to restrain his love of archaic and flowery language. One of the marks of a good prose writer lies in his getting the value of words properly adjusted and this in a person of exuberant feeling demands a good deal of restraint and toning down. He must leave something to the reader's imagination and this is best done by understatement; for people, though they enjoy being surprised, do not like being bullied into feeling what the text had not made them feel. But only too often Llewelyn used words and phrases as if they were costumes for a fancy dress party so that in most of his books passages of vivid and straightforward writing alternate with show-off passages where Rabelais, the Elizabethans and Meredith break in disastrously. The worst case of this occurs in his cloyingly romantic novel, *Love and Death,* which he wrote about his love affair with Gamel. She did not like it, nor indeed most of his books, whereas she greatly admired John Cowper Powys's novels. Her love for Llewelyn never prevented her from seeing his defects with a clear eye.

Llewelyn's wife, Alyse Gregory, differed in every way from her husband, except that like him she was a great lover of people and of life. She was a small, fine-boned woman with a high, domed forehead and a stoop in her shoulders which became more accentuated as she grew older. Her hair was fair and her eyes sharp and blue and with her nervous, fidgety movements she suggested a hedgerow bird. But a brave, defiant bird. As a girl she had taken up the cause of women's emancipation with ardour and spoken on tubs and at street corners all over New York. In the course of doing this she had been mobbed and roughly handled by the police. But such things had not discouraged her for she was a person imbued with a life-long hatred of injustice and cruelty and in spite of her gentle and often diffident manner, she had a moral courage that was in inverse proportion to her size. I remember how, after visiting us in Spain, she spent a few days on the way home at the American Embassy in Madrid. They took her to one of the best bullfights of the year and she was deeply shocked by it. That night there was a big dinner to celebrate the occasion and Alyse, a tiny, drably-dressed old woman, so bent as to seem almost a hunchback, was present at it. The conversation turned on Antonio Ordoñez's wonderful work with the *muleta* and then Alyse looked up from her plate and burst out into a denunciation of this cruel, brutal sport and expressed her amazement that any civilized or humane person should wish to look on at it. John Pilcher, the First Councillor at the British Embassy, told me afterwards how splendidly courageous she had been. But then in America it is the women who have moral courage rather than the men.

But hatred of injustice was only one element in Alyse's character. She was a literary woman and had for a certain time been managing editor of *The Dial*, which was the principal *avant-garde* journal of New York. Scofield Thayer, who was both editor and joint proprietor, was an intimate friend of hers. It was while she was working at it that in 1921 she met and fell in love with Llewelyn. They married in 1924 and in the following year crossed to England and settled at White Nothe.

She had now to adjust herself to a life that was unlike anything she had known before. In New York she had lived at the centre of the literary world of her time. She knew French and Italian well – for she had studied music and singing at Paris and Naples – and had an intense admiration for Proust and after him for Rousseau and Diderot. Among English writers her favourite was Henry James. I remember that her formula for what she most admired in literature was 'integrity, intensity and sophistication'. But the Powyses did not read these writers and sophistication was regarded by them as a vice of city life. Nor were any of them musical. So she found herself imprisoned in a close, provincial world that was entirely foreign to her and among people who, her husband alone excepted, regarded her as an outsider.

She was also compelled to sacrifice her feminist principles. On marrying Llewelyn she had refused to change her surname to Powys, but she soon had to give way on a more important matter. One of her chief grievances against the man-made society of those times was that the women became the slaves of their husbands, bound to cook and sweep and wash up for them and in so doing to sacrifice their own identity. Yet she now had to spend most of her day precisely in those activities and to put aside her own projects for writing. For no Powys ever helped in the house. They were

Victorians and Victorians left all such things to their women. Besides Llewelyn was for long periods confined to his bed and needed constant attention. Alyse had therefore to drudge and slave and, as she had no natural capacity for housework, the strain on her nature showed itself in a perpetual agitation and fussiness. Merely to get tea for four people cost her as much effort as it would have taken another woman to prepare a cooked meal. Llewelyn, who, like most invalids, had a fair share of selfishness, took her devotion for granted, thinking her sufficiently rewarded, when she brought his lunch tray out through the rain, with one of his sweet smiles. Yet she could not even wish to escape because she was in love with him. (Mr Malcolm Elwin, the biographer of Llewelyn Powys, writes to me that I am mistaken on two points. Llewelyn had read and admired Henry James in 1910 at Clavadel and J.C.P. had been influenced by him. Then it is not true, as I said, that Llewelyn allowed Alyse to do all the housework. When he was well enough he used to do the washing-up and when he was confined to his bed Gertrude helped Alyse in the job of nursing him. Theodore would chop the kindling wood in the shed and delighted Llewelyn by solemnly telling him that 'chopping sticks can be a very dangerous practise'.)

After much scouring of antique shops to furnish our cottage, Gamel and I settled down quietly for the autumn and winter. Various friends came to visit us – Augustus and Dorelia John, Ralph and Frances, Arthur Waley and Beryl de Zoete. We had a turf fire to sit by and a few hundred books and I finished at last the novel I had begun four years previously. But before continuing to write about my married life I must go back a year and speak of the renewal of my relations with Carrington.

As soon as, early in August, Gamel consented to marry me I wrote to Carrington saying that one of the things I most looked forward to in my marriage was that we should be able to be friends again. She replied and we met briefly in London. Two months later I wrote her a long letter from Watendlath, recalling the happy days we had spent there, and this touched and pleased her so that before we left for Italy she came up to see Gamel and myself. We dined with her and Dorelia John and went to see Albert Chevalier afterwards. After this we continued to write to one another and in one of her letters she told me of a dream she had had which conveyed only too well the feelings she had had about me as our love affair dragged to an end. She had been sitting on my knee at a sort of open-air party because, owing to the branches of the trees and the people moving about, she could find no other seat. Then I had put my arm round her waist and squeezed her so tightly that she could scarcely breathe or answer my questions. On waking half suffocated she had found her arm pressing on her lungs.

Soon after our return to England we went for a weekend to Ham Spray, but the visit was not a success. Gamel was ill at ease and in low spirits because her health was not good so that she made a poor impression, while Carrington was distant and avoided being left alone with me. However she told me of a wedding present she was making for us – a patchwork bed-spread sewn out of pieces cut from the dresses she had worn during the past ten years. Over it, she said, she had muttered spells which would give me strange dreams. A few weeks later it arrived. It was beautiful, but what sort of spells, I wondered, had she laid on it? Then on December 14th I saw in the paper that Garrow Tomlin, Tommy's elder brother, had been killed while flying his plane. He was a good friend of mine who had at one time been my neighbour in Great James Street so I drove down to Kent for his funeral. On my way back I ran into Ralph who told me that Lytton had for some weeks past been suffering from severe diarrhoea and running a temperature. The doctors, who had at first thought he had colitis, now suspected typhoid and Ralph, who had come up with samples for analysis, was very worried.

Lytton continued to grow worse. The analysis had revealed no signs of typhoid so the doctors returned to their first hypothesis that he was suffering from ulcers in the colon.* Then on Christmas Day he sank rapidly and appeared to be dying. Everyone except Carrington gave up hope. However, just when it seemed impossible that he should do so, he rallied. The doctor had spoken to him and told him that, if he could keep alive a little longer, the fever would probably subside. Lytton pulled himself together and took up once more the struggle for his life.

The routine of a long illness now set in. There were three nurses in the house and two general practitioners, as well as three or at one moment four specialists, in attendance. His sister Pippa took turns with Carrington in sitting by his bed while Ralph ran the house and Frances Marshall waited in the village close by. The Bear Hotel at Hungerford was packed with Stracheys and friends come down from London – not of course to see Lytton, but to provide some relief for the three people on whom fell the brunt of the anxiety. For there was no respite. His temperature would soar to 104 and then drop in an hour to 96, while the attacks of diarrhoea were each time more severe and unremitting.

The weeks passed. The heavy frost that had set in before Christmas continued without a break. Every day the sun rose and set in a clear blue sky. The hares, grown tame with the cold, scampered over the field next to the house. The birds, waiting to be fed on crumbs, huddled in the bushes and

*In this account of Lytton's illness and of what follows after it I am transcribing from my diary, which Michael Holroyd also made use of in his biography. Hence the verbal similarities in our two versions.

puffed out their feathers. By night the stars shone fiercely while the tawny owl that nested in the great poplar tree kept up its hooting and the rooks cawed restlessly, unable to sleep. But Lytton seemed to be a little better. By January 15th it was thought that his complaint might be receding although he had by now shrunk to such a shadow of himself that no one who saw him for the first time since his illness began would have supposed that he could recover. His weakness was so extreme that he could scarcely speak, yet the doctors were full of hope as they believed that the ulcerous condition was abating. None of them seems to have thought that he might have something more incurable than colitis, or was it that they were keeping their secret forebodings to themselves? But meanwhile the watchers by the sick-bed were also getting worn out. On learning of this the Woolfs drove down, and on the following day Roger Fry, and took Pippa Strachey out to lunch. Ralph always had Frances waiting in the village near by when he needed her. But Carrington, eaten by a gnawing dread, would not stir beyond the garden or see anyone. At night she scarcely slept or, if she dozed off for a few minutes, would start up suddenly out of a ghastly nightmare. Another support and helper was clearly needed so James Strachey came to live in the house. He was less emotional than Ralph and could be completely relied on in any emergency.

I was now staying with Gamel in London so as to be able to come down at a moment's notice if I was needed. On the 20th Ralph asked for me. He met me at Hungerford and we drove to the top of Rivar Down where, sitting on the turf overlooking Shalbourne and Ham, we ate our sandwiches. He spoke of the utter doubt and uncertainty with which the doctors' bulletins filled him: of the cruel alternatives of hope and despair in which, as symptom followed symptom, they all lived. He did not know whether there were any grounds for hope or not. And now a new anxiety had been added to the previous ones. They had discovered from a letter that Carrington had written and put in a drawer to be opened after her death that, if Lytton should die, she intended to follow him. Ralph had not the slightest doubt that she was set on this and would do it if she could find a way, for she was a person whom nothing ever stopped from carrying out even the least of her desires. He felt sure, however, that she would choose certain means and reject others – those for example that were disfiguring. James had at once accused her of this intention and she had denied it, but her denial meant nothing so they had searched her studio and taken away a medicine that was poisonous.

Carrington had especially asked that I should be brought back to the house for tea as she wished to see me. But as we drove to the door James came out: there had been a crisis and Lytton was sinking fast. Ralph hurried in and I drove to the post office to send off telegrams since they could not use the house telephone for fear of being overheard.

I returned and sat in the dining room. Soon I heard Carrington's low and musical voice, more exquisitely modulated, more caressing than ever, and she came up behind me – for I did not feel able to look at her – and took my hand. Her tone, so flat at ordinary times, a sort of quick patter, took on a wide range of nuances when she was moved. Then she went out. Ralph had already told me that if a crisis occurred he would send for Stephen Tomlin (Tommy) who had already been warned and was standing by. The reason for this was that he was certain that, while he was in the house, Carrington would not take her life. It was a cruel expedient, for its efficacy depended upon Tommy's being so unbalanced and neurotic, so shattered by his brother's recent death, so prone himself to suicide, with his marriage to Julia Strachey, which Carrington had arranged, on the point of breaking down and all his supports in life tottering, that Carrington's sense of responsibility would be aroused and she would pull herself together to look after him. In addition to this there would be the shock to him of Lytton's death. Lytton was one of his most intimate friends and in his close relations with other people there was always a strong element of dependence. But in order to come to this decision Ralph had had to overcome his own prejudices. Jealous of every man who showed signs of being attracted either to Carrington or to Frances, he had some time before conceived an aversion for Tommy. However in this emergency he decided to overlook this and to summon him, and I drove to the station to meet him.

Tommy stepped out of the train looking more than usually pale and undecided and we set off in silence for Ham Spray. But Carrington, though apparently glad to see him, would not hear of his staying in the house, so I took him back to the Bear Inn at Hungerford. Here a family party of Stracheys was assembled, but they went off almost at once to bed while Tommy and I sat up talking and drinking till two in the morning. We had been on somewhat distant terms for several years, but at Garrow's funeral had come together and now I found his company very welcome. So many thoughts and feelings had accumulated in my mind that I was glad to have a person as intelligent and perceptive as he was to air them with. When at last we went upstairs he asked if he could sleep in my room since he could not face the idea of spending the night alone. I said, 'Yes, of course,' but then instead of lying down in the spare bed, to my embarrassment he got into my double one and burst into tears. It was impossible not to be touched by his misery and I regretted that I was not a young woman to be able to console him more effectively.

Next morning there was a telephone message from Ham Spray asking him to come there at once. I was told I could return to London. To pass the time till my train left I took Frances Marshall, who was now staying at the Bear, for a walk along the Kennet Canal. The fine frosty weather that had gone on without a break since Christmas still lasted. A soft golden mist lay over the green meadows and enfolded the elm trees. The sunlight seeping through it seemed to move more slowly, seemed to linger and delay, as if to touch those red-brick walls, that gleaming water, were a pleasure and delight. It was impossible not to contrast the beauty of the weather with Lytton dying or to wonder what consequence might follow for the three, bound together in precarious equilibrium, that he was leaving behind.

I got to London early that afternoon, January 21st, and a few hours later heard on the telephone that Lytton was dead. Next morning after breakfast Frances rang me up and asked me to come as soon as possible to Ham Spray. I found there Ralph, Frances and Tommy, with James about to leave. The body had already been removed to be cremated. There had been an autopsy from which it appeared that the stomach was completely eaten up with cancer and that a perforation had actually been made through the wall into the colon, by which food had been passing. Lytton had therefore never had the slightest chance of recovering and this news had been a relief to Carrington as she had seen in it the hand of fate.

After lunch Ralph took me for a walk. He told me that on the previous afternoon, about an hour before Lytton died, he had missed Carrington. Going out into the garage he had discovered her lying behind the exhaust pipe of the car, with the engine running. She was unconscious. With the assistance of the nurse she soon came round and was able to get up and walk. But had he found her ten minutes later she would have been dead.

It had never occurred to him that she would attempt to kill herself while Lytton was still alive: she would have wished, he had imagined, to be there at all costs till the last moment. It now seemed to him that by some obscure train of reasoning she had hoped to save his life by the offer of hers. Besides she would be well aware that from the moment of his death she would be guarded and that Tommy, waiting a few miles away, would be brought to the house. She had promised him solemnly not to make another attempt at least during the next few days and he believed that she would keep to this.

He then went on, with an emotion he could scarcely control, to describe Lytton's last moments – the extraordinary fragility of his appearance, worn down by the long weeks of illness, his courage and serenity, the crown of evergreens which after his death Carrington had picked and placed on his head. For all his devotion to Lytton it was her feeling for him which seemed to affect him most profoundly.

Meanwhile life went on much as usual in the house: it seemed surprising, after what had happened, that there should still exist in the people assembled here the needs for eating, talking and sleeping. Carrington alone did not come down: she remained in bed where she spent most of the day and night in tears, for even with the strongest sleeping draughts she scarcely slept. Ralph was in and out of her room all day. Tommy too saw her a good deal – she liked him to read her poetry – while Frances found a relief for her feelings in running the house. My function, I soon saw, was to go for walks with Ralph and to sit up talking to Tommy after the others had gone to bed. He could not bring himself to do that before two or three and, though as a rule I cannot bear late hours, the pleasure and distraction of his conversation provided some relief from the prevailing sadness.

On my second day at Ham Spray, Carrington asked to see me. I had been somewhat dreading this for, besides the pain of seeing her in such distress, I guessed beforehand that our past estrangements, recent uneasy terms and above all the fact that it had been chiefly Lytton who had come between us, must make any real communication impossible. Then we now belonged to different countries and had no common language. She was totally unhappy and I was the opposite: Lytton's death meant little to me. I sat on the chair by her bed and she began to question me about my life, about our cottage, about Gamel. Her tone was not unkind or even insincere, but it was very remote, indicating that there was a wide gulf between us that could not be crossed. I asked her about her plans – she answered vaguely. It seemed to me that she was cut off not merely from myself but from everyone and that for the time being neither sympathy nor pity were acceptable.

In the course of our walks Ralph gave me an account of what her life had been since we had broken off relations more than four years before. Until Tommy had given me a brief outline of this at the Bear I had known nothing of it. It seemed that for the past couple of years she had been involved in an affair with a friend of mine called Bernard (Beakus) Penrose. He was a young man who, though enjoying a private income, had served for some years at sea in various capacities and rounded Cape Horn before the mast in the last of the British windjammers. He was attractive to look at with a square muscular body and a brick-red face, but though good-natured and a pleasant companion, he was not interested in literature or in the things of the mind. He had bought himself a Brixham trawler which lay moored to the quay in Falmouth harbour, while it was being refitted for a voyage to the Mediterranean.

It might seem surprising that a young woman who enjoyed Lytton's society should fall in love with a person whose interests were so different, yet in the past all her strongest passions and affections had been attempts to recreate some childish situation. One did not need to have read Freud to know that Lytton took the place of her much-loved father. Similarly her strong feeling for me could be explained as an attempt to find a substitute for her sailor brother Teddy, who had been, or so she chose to believe, drowned at sea during the war. The shock of his loss had been so great that she had thought for a time of killing herself and the myth that she had woven about him, for actually he had died as a soldier on the Somme, is evidence of her refusal to face reality where he was concerned. But if I had been her first substitute for him, Beakus filled the role far better, because he was a real sailor and like Teddy stolid and phlegmatic.

Her feelings for him were all the stronger for being so meagrely returned. Beakus was not in love with her – after all she was ten years older than himself – and he had besides two gay young girlfriends whose remarks on her worn and haggard appearance were repeated back to her. But although this hurt her badly it only increased her desire to hold him. She clung to him with the desperation with which women cling to the man who they know will be their last lover. Besides, she found peace in his company because his silence and indifference allowed her to feel alone and unobserved, free from all reproach and criticism, which she had not been with either Gertler, Ralph or myself. Then in 1931 he left her to get married.

So Carrington was now suffering, not only from the loss of Lytton, on whose existence the whole structure of her chronically unstable life had for years depended, but from a feeling of remorse that she had neglected him in favour of her lover. And this lover too had gone and with him her last link with youth and beauty. She was approaching forty. Old age, which she had always so terribly dreaded, lay before her – wrinkles, sagging cheeks, disease, decay, feebleness – things she held to be far worse than death. Nor could she get any consolation from the thought that she might in time get accustomed to these. She wanted to go on suffering: she could not bear to think that she might live to get over her loss. For not only was this pain the only link she had with Lytton, it was also the punishment imposed on her by her remorse and bad conscience. She had to end it and it was only to please Ralph that she promised to make no other attempt on her life for a month.

I left on the 24th. Before doing so I saw her again for a few moments, but the gulf that separated us remained as unbridgeable as ever. Letters from Ralph and Frances kept me informed of her progress. She visited the Johns at Fryern and then returned to Ham Spray where she reassured everyone by her activity in tidying the house, arranging her books and papers and gardening. The piece of waste land under the ilex tree in front of the house was cleared up: new trees were planted and a seat put up facing the Downs.

She also wrote letters to her friends. Some of these friends had been helpful, others were less so. On occasions like these there are always people who need to find some roundabout vent for the hostile feelings which death arouses in them. One or two found fault with Frances Marshall, whose conduct throughout had been perfect in its tact and selflessness, and declared that 'but for her everything would have been different'. Others insisted that she must at once sell Ham Spray and 'make a fresh start somewhere else', not understanding that in her eyes this would have been equivalent to killing Lytton a second time. A few, among them Desmond MacCarthy, who came down to Ham Spray to see her, tried to interest her in the publication of Lytton's unpublished essays and letters, and this, though premature, was I think a good plan. The letter I wrote her did not please her – how could it since she still bore secret resentments against me? – but she repeated as her own some of the things I had said.

Ralph knew that the main thing was never to allow her to be at Ham Spray by herself, but this was not so easy to arrange. The only people who did not jar on her feelings were Dorelia John, Tommy and his wife Julia. Dorelia was at the moment occupied with Augustus, who was ill, but she had promised to take her abroad in March. Ralph was of course ready to give up his entire time to her, leaving Frances in London, but there were many reasons why he should not be left too much alone with her. There had always been a good deal of strain in their relation, while now his agitation increased her own and his constant watchfulness got on her nerves. It was therefore essential, as the month of promised safety came to an end, that Tommy, with or without Julia, should remain in the house till the time came for her to go abroad with Dorelia. Ralph was the only person who could arrange this, but unfortunately he had come to resent the strong influence that Carrington's former lover was exercising over her. Under the stress of what he was going through his old jealousy of Tommy broke out again and he could scarcely bring himself to speak to him. Nor had Carrington even at this time been able to resist playing on the bad feeling that existed between them (I remembered how in Toulon she had used her brief affair with him to make me jealous) while Tommy's attitude was not exactly mollifying. Thus it came about that Ralph's feelings were too strong to allow him to approach Tommy, explain the situation and ensure however unwillingly (for Tommy was longing to get away) his co-operation.

March came and Ralph wrote to me that he had noticed many signs of improvement in Carrington's condition, and yet he did not trust her. He was certain that she had some secret up her sleeve because she was giving away too many of her possessions. But he had been obliged to agree to leave her alone at Ham Spray for a few days because she had absolutely insisted on it. At the same time he felt considerable anxiety. Then on Friday afternoon, March 11th, I got a telegram to say that she was dead. I hired a car, for my own was being repaired, and reached Ham Spray that evening. When I arrived I learned that she had shot herself early that morning.

It appeared that Ralph had been to a party the night before, drunk a good deal, slept heavily and been awakened by a telephone message giving this news. David Garnett, who was sleeping upstairs, had his car parked outside so he drove him and Frances down. They arrived at about eleven o'clock and found Carrington lying on the floor of her bedroom where she had fallen, still conscious and in spite of the morphia which the doctor had given her, in considerable pain. She said that she only wished to die, that she hated life, but on seeing his distress she changed her story, claimed it had been an accident and promised that she would try, for his sake, to live. As the pain increased, the doctor again injected morphia but toward midday she became unconscious and died shortly after two. Ralph had broken down completely and when I arrived was unable to speak coherently. Bunny Garnett left. Alix Strachey, Carrington's best and oldest friend, came down by train and with her admirable calm and self-possession was as great a support and comfort to all of us as her husband James had been during Lytton's last days.

After a little we began to reconstruct what had happened. Twelve days before, on a visit to Biddesden, Carrington had asked Bryan Guinness if he would lend her a gun to kill the rabbits that were destroying her garden. Ralph was present when she asked him this, but his powers of vigilance had been exhausted by the strain he was continually under and he accepted her explanation. Possibly, as Michael Holroyd has suggested, some unconscious longing to end an intolerable situation to which no solution could be seen was at the back of this most uncharacteristic negligence. Then on the morning of the eleventh she had awoken, as she always did, very early, made herself a cup of tea and eaten an apple. Olive, her cook, was laid up with the flu and had gone home so that no one but herself was sleeping in the house. When the post came, she opened her letters and *The Times*, which she seems to have looked at, for we found it crumpled in the cupboard. After this she put on Lytton's yellow silk dressing gown, which no one had ever seen her wear, and took up the gun. On the lawn beneath her window were walking two partridges, for we saw them every day afterwards at the same hour. It would have been like her to see a joke in shooting not one of them but herself, who was a Partridge too.

She had thought out her preparations carefully. First she moved to another part of the room away from her favourite rug so that it should not be stained by her blood and put in its place another rug to give the impression that she had slipped on it. She next stood with her back to the window facing the tall mirror so that she could check her position in it. Then she put the butt of the gun on the floor and the barrel against her side opposite her heart and pulled the trigger. But since she had forgotten to release the safety catch nothing happened. This must have put her out for when she pulled it again the gun was not pointed correctly and the shot, though taking away part of her side, missed her heart.

The gardener had heard the noise and, coming under her window, could catch what he thought were groans. He hurried to the foot of the stairs and she called out to him, telling him that she had slipped on the mat and shot herself and that he must at once fetch the woman who lived in the lodge at the end of the drive and send for the doctor. When the woman came she repeated the same story to her and told her to telephone Ralph. To the doctor when he arrived she said the same thing and, as she was in great pain, he injected morphia. Since he seemed upset, for he had known her over many years, she sent him to fetch the key of the cellar and help himself to a drink, apologizing at the same time for giving so much trouble. Although he could not examine her for fear of increasing the flow of blood, he saw that she was probably too seriously injured to recover.

Was this act premeditated from the first? She had certainly thought continually of death and had deliberately planned it. No doubt the knowledge that, after getting the gun, she could do it at any moment had been a great consolation to her. But there were also signs – unfinished letters, an engagement book with future entries and so forth – that seemed to indicate that she had intended to go on living. I am inclined to think that she did not make up her mind till the last moment. It must have come over her that if she did not do it then she would not be able to do it for a long time, for Ralph was coming down that evening and on the following week she was going abroad with the Johns. This thought and perhaps some fear of her intentions weakening may have been what brought her to the point.

She left a letter for Ralph in which she said that she hoped he would marry Frances and have children. A long list of presents that she wished to be given to her friends followed and instructions that her ashes were to be buried under the Portuguese laurels and Lytton's, if possible, close by under the ilex. Her activity in the garden, which a few weeks before had so reassured everyone, had thus been a preparation for her grave. She also left Tommy £100 to design her a tombstone, but Ralph suppressed this for the strange reason that he considered it a slight to himself. No doubt too he saw the disadvantages of any monument so close to the house. Her ashes were later buried as she had directed and Lytton's, I believe, were scattered over the Downs – not at all events, as she had wished, close to her own.

I stayed on three days till the inquest was over and came back with Ralph and Frances to Dorset, where we spent a few days together. Before they took her away, I saw her – or rather the terrible changes wrought on her by death. The same hard frost, the same icy weather prevailed as when Lytton had died, seven weeks before. As I lay awake in his room – for they had put me to sleep in his bed – I could hear the rooks calling all through the night among the frozen trees. It was not possible, even by walking into the next room where her body lay, to understand it.

19

Our house near Malaga

Ralph was shattered by Carrington's death. He and Frances went abroad for the summer and on their return got married, but it was not till the end of the year that he began to be himself again. They took up their residence at Ham Spray, where they altered nothing but kept it as a museum dedicated to the past in what some people thought to be a morbid way. Gamel and I meanwhile resumed our quiet life at East Lulworth. Since Gamel's death I have read the letters she wrote to Llewelyn which were returned to her after his death. These were no longer love letters. I was her husband and her loyal acceptance of that fact is evident on every page. Yet she still kept feelings for him which were probably intenser than any she ever felt for me; though as she greatly valued the peace and security of our life together, they were less solidly founded. My opinion of her has, if that were possible, gone up since reading them for they are very wise letters. In some of them she had the difficult task of persuading Llewelyn that, while she still loved him as much as before, he must accept the fact that she was married and that her first obligation must be to her husband. Llewelyn did not always take this change in their relations so easily. He would reproach her and since reproaches were things she could not endure because they exacerbated her natural propensity to feel guilt, this had the effect of alienating her a little from him. So it had once happened between me and Carrington. But then his sunny words and looks would return and, as she was quite lacking in Carrington's neurotic perversity, she would draw towards him again, though on looking back over these years I can see a general tendency for our marriage to become consolidated at his expense. I never reproached her or brought up the subject of her relations with Llewelyn, though the effect they had in inhibiting the deeper levels of my feelings for her did not escape her. Many years later she remarked that our marriage had been a *mariage de convenance,* but then added that such marriages were often the best. I would say that we achieved a very happy and successful marriage, with deep and increasing love on both sides, but that it was one of a rather negative kind. On the deepest level there was some lack of consonance in our characters, besides which our relation lacked the roots which only the feeling of having once been mutually in love can give.

In August Gamel developed a tumour on her breast and had an operation to remove it. I got the best surgeon in London and it was completely successful. But it left her very run down so in October we set out in the car for Yegen, where I thought the sun and mountain air would do her good. Although she found much of the food unpalatable, she fell in love with the village and picked up enough Spanish to understand what was said though, as she was a poor linguist, she never learned to talk it correctly. Juliana was still there, now aged eighteen and more sensually alluring than ever, and with her was her little daughter just beginning to toddle. It was agreed that in another year's time Gamel and I would adopt her.

We had arranged to join Roger Fry and Helen Anrep in March and take them on a motor trip through southern Spain. We met at Gibraltar and drove to Cadiz. Here Roger gave a characteristic example of his readiness to revise in a moment one of his old, long-established opinions. He had always held that Murillo was a bad painter, but in spite of this we went to see his last picture, which hangs in the chapel of the Capuchinos close to the sea wall. It was unfinished because he had fallen off the platform while he was working on it and died of his injuries and thus it lacked that sentimental mistiness and transparency which makes his other pictures so displeasing. Roger looked at it and his eyes lit up. As his excitement mounted he came out in his slow purring voice with his discovery that Murillo was in spite of everything one of the great masters. If his other pictures did not give that impression it must be because he had been compelled to ruin them to conform to the mawkish taste of the Sevillians. It was characteristic of Roger to believe that artists are often corrupted against their will by popular taste, but actually, I believe, his explanation is not correct. It was Murillo's excessive facility and Andalusian indolence that chiefly account for the defects of his pictures. Both in Italy and in Spain the art of painting was in decline and it was the Guido Renis he had seen in the noblemen's houses at Seville rather than the Titians and Tintorettos in the royal palaces at Madrid that had influenced him.

After a night at Ronda, we drove on to Yegen, where we spent a couple of days. 'I was wondering,' said Roger as we stood on the flat roof of my house, looking out over the tangle of red and ochre hills and valleys below us, 'why you had picked on this remote mountain fastness when there are so many more attractive little *pueblos* lower down, but now I understand, you came here because it offers you a *Mapa Mundi*'. This was partly true, but as Roger, who suffered from kidney trouble, could not negotiate steep paths I was unable to show him the richness of the slopes below the village, with their terraces of wheat and beans overhung by huge olive trees. Helen had never been willing to walk more than a few hundred yards except on London pavements, when she could keep going for hours if she was shopping.

From Yegen we went on to Almeria and then through the strange lunar landscape that extends beyond it to Cuevas de Almanzora. Here Roger painted the cave quarter, but when I suggested that we might visit it after supper to see it by the light of the full moon, he demurred. Although he had a highly developed sense for the *genius loci,* Nature did not interest him, he said, after the light failed. What he couldn't paint didn't exist for him. So he spent an absorbed evening at the casino, playing two games of chess with one of the local inhabitants and losing them both. On the following day we continued on our journey to Murcia and from there to Alicante, where he and Helen took the train for Madrid.

I had got to know Roger pretty well over the past eight years and had become very attached to him. He was one of the pure – a man whose whole mind and soul were given to painting and to the arts in general. His selfless devotion to them, his uncompromising honesty, together with a strain of Quakerish austerity that was only contradicted by his love of French cooking, gave him something of the character of a saint. But unlike most saints he had an unusually open mind and, since the natural failing of the open-minded is gullibility, he was continually being taken in by the most extravagant and quackish of notions, much to the delight and amusement of his friends. He would believe it did not matter what absurdity, provided that an ingenious explanation could be given for it, because out of sheer excess of scepticism he felt drawn to any idea, the more paradoxical the better, that would demolish the conventional view. For him the charm of science lay in its being a chain of revolutionary subversion and discovery which proved that nothing was what it seemed. Virginia Woolf in her biography of him has given several examples of his credulity which I will not repeat.

Roger was also a man who lacked the faculty which enables one to understand other people's characters or to see into their minds, so that he needed the assistance of a woman's intuition to explain them to him. There had been altogether three principal women in his life – his wife, who had been languishing in a mental home for some thirty years, Vanessa Bell, with whom he had fallen in love in 1912 and never ceased to regard as a kind of oracle, and Helen Anrep, whose close friendship with me was my passport to him. He found her perverse, provoking, intriguingly feminine and admired her skill in cooking and house management as well as her social gifts. He was also deeply attached to Virginia Woolf, whom he regarded as a pure genius and therefore wayward and capricious in her judgements – a being who lived in a fantasy world of her own and was incapable of real contact with other people. This was the general Bloomsbury view of her, but her *Diary* has shown that it was wrong, for under the glittering and erratic surface of her conversation she was a woman of feeling and understanding, deeply devoted to her friends in spite of the malicious remarks she sometimes made about them. Roger was also drawn to Gamel for her calm beauty and receptive mind, and it was from him that she learned to appreciate painting and to visit picture galleries whenever she had the opportunity.

I have never known anyone whose conversation I enjoyed more than Roger's. He was not a brilliant talker though he possessed a great range of knowledge and information which he could draw on with lucidity and accuracy, enunciating the words in a rich, persuasive voice full of gently ironical inflections. But his special gift lay in getting people to talk better than they were normally capable of doing. Every new idea excited him and, since he treated everyone present as being as intelligent as he was himself, he would seize on some chance remark made in the course of conversation and develop it so that it appeared more interesting than it had really been. This made him, especially for the young, the most stimulating of talkers and there was no subject on which he did not have something to say.

He had taken science both at his public school and at Cambridge and this training in the scientific method gave his mind a clarity and vigour which benefitted his art criticism. Till he began to write, painting had been judged in England mainly by its literary content, but he restored the primacy of purely pictorial values, although in the course of doing so he underrated the literary ones, which had always been stressed by the painters of the past, possibly because no language for expressing pictorial values had then been evolved. Thus he opened the way to abstract painting, of which however he did not approve because he believed that it could only lead to decoration and flatness of surface. Since in his view Cézanne was the greatest of modern painters, he drew the conclusion that the supreme aim of painting must lie in the realization of the third dimension in the picture space.

Roger Fry was also a superb lecturer. During the last years of his life he could hold large audiences. If there is such a widespread interest among English people in painting today, it is chiefly because he did so much to educate public opinion in it. His honesty was only equalled by his politeness. I have listened to him addressing the directors and patrons of a municipal art gallery and making the most devastating comments upon their recent acquisitions – all in the gentlest and most persuasive tone imaginable, which of course only irritated them the more and led to his making many enemies. Yet he did not really enjoy writing or lecturing on art. He undertook it as a duty imposed on him by his high conception of public service, for he thought of himself as a painter rather than as an art critic and was only completely happy when he was at work upon a canvas. It was the great disappointment of his life that his pictures were so little admired.

He never lost his interest in science and, since he had little time for reading books upon it, he liked to have friends who would keep him up to date about its latest discoveries. For this reason one often met Gerald Heard at his house. Heard had been, I believe, a secretary to the Irish poet George Russell (A.E.) and his wide knowledge of the latest scientific developments concealed a substratum of pseudo-mystical or Vedantic notions which in Roger's presence he kept to himself. I found him a rather negative person without any of that charm of conversation for which Irishmen are famous and besides quite sexless. But Roger would not have been aware of that: he liked men less for what they were than for the ideas they expressed. Other people one met at his house were Bertrand Russell, Arthur Waley, Aldous Huxley and Kenneth Clark – all top-rank minds – as well as his old Cambridge friend Goldsworthy Lowes Dickinson, or Goldie as he was always called, whose gentle, woolly high-mindedness and frequent quotations from Goethe I found trying.

I must not end this brief sketch of Roger Fry without mentioning his deep admiration for France and for everything French. This often led him to run down things that were English. I shared this prejudice with him, though less strongly, for at this time I preferred French prose writers to English ones and my favourite poets were Racine and Baudelaire.

Not long after Roger and Helen left for Madrid we had a visit from Bertrand Russell and his new girl, Peter Spence, whom he later married. I had not been anxious for this visit, but Russell had been told by Roger Fry that we were willing to let our house for the summer and so he had written to ask if he could take it. I regarded our primitive village as a very unsuitable place for a distinguished man of over sixty to stay in, especially as he knew no Spanish, but my attempt to dissuade him from coming merely had the effect of making him more insistent. So we agreed to let him the house at a low rent and to remain there till he arrived so that we could show him how to manage.

One day then in May we drove down to Berja to meet him. I had had lunch with him before at Roger's and had been intimidated by the power of his mind, but the man who descended from the bus could not have been more friendly or amiable. He was shorter than I had remembered, red faced, looking with his large nose and jaunty step a little like Mr Punch, and covered with smiles. Peter Spence was a tall, red-headed girl of twenty or twenty-one with a fine white skin and pleasing face.

The two of them settled down very easily. They found fault with nothing, not even with the monotonous food or the unrefined olive oil which upset one's inside, not even with the lumpy flock mattresses or the plague of flies, though Bertie remarked that he really only liked country that had large trees. We went for a few walks together, for they were both very active, and then after providing them with a Spanish dictionary, we left. In the next chapter I shall describe Bertie more fully, for I was to see a great deal of him, so for the present I will merely report a near-disaster which occurred soon after we left. It seems that in spite of our servant's warning he ate a tin of meat which had begun to go bad, developed ptomaine poisoning and ran a high temperature. The doctor was called in and, according to Bertie's story, cured him by giving him a serum taken from horse's blood, to explain which he went down on all fours, neighed and kicked his heels in the air. For Bertie, in spite of the dictionary, had not mastered the Spanish word for horse and Peter was no linguist.

As soon as the Russells had settled in we returned by a devious route to England and to our little thatched cottage at East Lulworth. Then in August Llewelyn had a severe haemorrhage. We went to see him every day, bringing ice and provisions, and gradually he rallied, though from this time on he was a permanent invalid, unable to walk more than a few yards. He had also developed stomach ulcers, which led to his adopting a vege-tarian diet of nuts, cheese and fruit with various special dishes that had to be carefully prepared, so that Alyse, weighed down by continual anxiety as she was, became more of a slave to housework than ever. In the meantime we had come to a big decision, which was to give up our plan of settling in England and make our home on the south coast of Spain in some place that would be more accessible than Yegen. One reason for this was that, although we had combed Wiltshire and Dorset, we had not been able to find a house we liked which was within our means. Then the political situation was disturbing. The unemployment figures were mounting, the Baldwin government was stupid and apathetic and the Nazis had come into power in Germany. The condition of England, drifting and leaderless, had sunk to a very low level. I foresaw bad times ahead with rising prices and inflation and wished to put down roots in some quiet place where we would be able to live on our income and work. Gamel, who had fallen in love with Spain, entirely concurred with me and showed no desire to be chained to Llewelyn.

We had let our house in Yegen that autumn to a young brother and sister, Mark and Angela Culme-Seymour, who had answered an advertise-ment we had put in the *New Statesman*. But Gamel's health seemed to require that we should winter abroad. I was anxious to improve my Por-tuguese, which I could read but not speak, so we decided to go to Portugal. In December therefore we sailed for Lisbon, taking our car with us, and after a brief tour of the country settled at Praia de Rocha in the Algarve. On the way there I caught flu and, owing to my stupidity in driving with the hood open, developed bronchial pneumonia and ran a high temperature. The local doctor came in. I was half delirious and Gamel in despair. Speaking in a mixture of Portuguese and Spanish, he said, 'I can inject you with gold, or I can inject you with silver. If I inject you with gold, your temperature will fall immediately to below normal, but the shock will probably kill you. So I will inject you with silver, which is not so severe.' He then gave me an injection of what he said was silver and my temperature fell at once. Within a few weeks I was well again – a recovery which has given me a high opinion of Portuguese doctors. We now, after a visit to Cape St Vincent, set out for Yegen, where we had agreed to spend a few weeks with the Culme-Seymours.

We arrived and were warmly greeted. Mark was a very good looking young man of twenty-three with a beautiful voice and a rather flashy smile. He had taken our house with the intention of writing a life of his hero Alfred de Musset and for this purpose had brought out a large suitcase of books that dealt with him. However literature did not seem to be his *métier* for he never, I think, got so far as the first page. His sister Angela was two years younger than he was and just as good looking. She was clever in a rather facile way – had learned Spanish quickly, painted recognizable portraits, played a little on a guitar and had written a novel in a couple of months in the manner of Gerhardie – but there was no great depth behind these attainments. Both she and her brother had thrown themselves into the life of the village and made themselves liked, but though Mark was much sought after by the local girls – one even came thirty miles to see him – he did not manage to have the kind of success he wanted because Spanish girls want a husband and not a lover.

Angela, whose slim figure contained a good deal of wiriness, was an athletic girl and so we took to going for long walks together. We would race down the hill slopes in a reckless way and then climb till we were completely out of breath. But although I could not help being attracted to pretty girls or, when the opportunity offered, flirting with them, I was determined never to injure my marriage by having an affair. I had chosen monogamy because I was sick of promiscuity and besides Gamel was a person so sensitive and defenceless that I could not bear the thought of hurting her. I therefore drew away from Angela, realizing how dangerous she could be to me because I found her so attractive.

In April we drove to Seville to see the Easter processions and then set about looking for a house. After much search along the coast we found what we wanted in the pueblo of Churriana, which lies a mile inland off the coast road from Malaga to Torremolinos. The house was not being offered for sale, but as we drove past it the street door was open and we got a view into the garden beyond. This greatly attracted us and the agent said that he would enquire whether the owner, whose name was Don Carlos Crooke Larios, would consider selling it. It turned out that he would, and we went to call on him.

We found a tall, well-built man in his early fifties living with his wife and six children. He belonged to an old Malaga family which like most old Malaga families had English blood in it, but things had gone badly for him and he found it a struggle to keep going by running a small poultry farm. The house was far too big for us since it contained five downstairs rooms as well as a kitchen, pantry, bathroom and coachhouse. Upstairs there were ten bedrooms with a *mirador* or tower, which had once been used as a billiard-room, rising above them. Behind the house there was a spacious patio with orange trees and a fountain, closed at the further end by a raised *alberca* or tank which was big enough to swim in. Beyond this was a walled garden planted with fine trees and covering three-quarters of an acre. But everything was very run down. The garden had been turned into a chicken run and the plaster was peeling off the walls in many of the rooms. The place would need a good deal doing to it before we could live in it. But, much too palatial though it was, we both fell in love with it and I was all the more eager to buy it because I thought that it would remind Gamel of her childhood in South Carolina and that she would be happy living there.

The bargaining started. The chaotic state of Spain, the continual strikes and the severe unemployment had caused a fall in the value of landed property. Everyone wanted to sell and get their money out of the country and Don Carlos more than anyone else. I saw of course that there was a risk in putting our money into such a large house in those uncertain times, but I thought it worth taking. So I spent three days beating down Don Carlos's terms and in the end got the house for £1,200. After the cost of doing it up had been paid and the furniture bought we had spent rather more than £2,000, of which Gamel contributed £600.

We signed the deed of purchase on the last day of May and left for Yegen. Then, as we could not obtain possession of our house before the end of the year, we set off for England, taking my daughter Miranda with us. She was a strange little creature, very backward on account of her up-bringing and still too shy to speak to us, but she sensed that a better future lay in store for her and was glad to leave her mother, who had neglected her, to come with us. Juliana was pleased to lose her too as she was on the point of getting married.

We were back at Lulworth by June, and settled down to spend the summer in our cottage. Llewelyn was still confined to bed in the cabbage garden. John Cowper Powys and his companion Phyllis Playter had arrived from America – he a tall, cadaverous man with a heavy stoop who looked as if he carried the sins of the world on his shoulders. He was by far the most intellectual and the best educated of the Powys brothers, but, though he had been a great friend of Gamel's, I never got to know him well.

At this time we had a visit from Louis Wilkinson. He was a friend of the Powyses, who had written books about them and generally contributed to their reputation, but he could not find a good word to say for John Cowper on account of what he regarded as his dishonesty. He had a good story to tell about him. One of the Powys family had recently married a very bouncing businessman whom none of the Powyses could endure. When Mr Perks, as they always called him, produced a copy of *A Glastonbury Romance* and asked John to inscribe it for him, he wrote: 'To Ernest Perks, in commemoration of the psychic spark of instantaneous sympathy that was struck between us on our first meeting.'

Such a gesture was typical. J.C.P. was a cynic about certain things and, unless he particularly liked a person, would say anything he thought would please him in order not to be bothered with him. Gamel had learned her indifference to the truth from him, except that she never flattered but merely signified her agreement with other people's opinions.

A few days after this visit a very sad thing happened. Roger Fry's servant had a mania for polishing floors till they were as slippery as ice and one evening the mat slid from under Roger's feet and he fell and broke his pelvis. A man in better health would easily have recovered, but the head surgeon of the hospital was away on holiday and he died after a badly performed operation. He was sixty-eight and as an art critic at the height of his powers. To Gamel and myself his death was an immense deprivation, which I still feel today. Virginia Woolf put aside the novel she was engaged on to write his biography – an act of devotion that few creative writers would be capable of. Then a few months later we learned of the death of my old friend Frankie Birrell from an abcess on the brain. He was one of the most delightful and lovable of men and a great many people besides myself felt his loss.

Meanwhile we had returned by ship to Spain. Our first act was to drive to Yegen to pack our books and furniture. Then on Christmas Eve we set off in two lorries. With us went Maria, who had been with me since 1929 and her sister Rosario, an able, energetic woman who had for some years served as cook at the *posada* at Cádiar. Her husband Antonio came as our gardener. I shall never forget our first night in our new house. The window panes were broken, an icy wind blew through the empty frames and rats scuttled about. Maria and Rosario were almost in tears for they could not believe that the place would ever be made habitable.

But now an army of masons moved in on top of us. They tore down the partition walls to make larger rooms, cut great gashes in the other walls and filled the house with noise and dust. Then they began to repair the damage they had done – like socialists rebuilding their country after a revolution, only a good deal more efficiently. This agony went on for five months. At one moment there were more than twenty masons at work in the house or remaking the irrigation system in the garden and after them came the whitewashers, carpenters and painters. It was a great satisfaction to have such able, hard-working men on the job, very different in their pace to the leisurely drones I had watched in England, but we looked on in terror as the bills mounted up. However at last everything was finished and we found ourselves in possession of one of the most beautiful houses and gardens on the coast. Then in June we sailed for Plymouth to fetch our furniture.

20

Bertrand Russell

Lulworth once more. We visited and were visited by our friends and one of these visits was to Bertrand Russell and Patricia or Peter Spence at Telegraph House in Sussex. But since this chapter is to be devoted to him and will contain extracts from his conversation which I took down at the time, I will begin by describing a visit that he and Peter had paid to us at Lulworth the previous summer.

Bertie had just finished his book *Freedom and Organization* and was in good spirits, though his divorce case with Dora was about to come on and he was very bitter about it. The subject obsessed him, but when he got tired of telling us about it his conversation became very entertaining. It was studded with anecdotes, many of which were directed against either the clergy or philosophers whom he disliked. I will give a few examples. After speaking of Hegel, whom he detested, he told us the story of an Oxford don, a Hegelian and a clergyman, who every term preached the same sermon to the bedmakers. Its subject was the philosophical evidence for the existence of a deity and it ran in this way: 'The force of the onto-logical argument has, I grant you, during the course of the last few years, owing chiefly to the criticism of Teutonic philosophy, sensibly diminished – but, at the same time ... '

Another of his stories was on the Behaviourists. 'I once,' he said, 'asked Dr Watson how it was that, if his views were true, when one said "Pepper" no one felt inclined to sneeze. He could not answer me.'

One afternoon we had a discussion about the arts and as to whether value judgements in them were meaningful or otherwise. He was inclined to be doubtful. That night I had a dream which I repeated to him next morning at breakfast. I had dreamed that I was standing with him in an aquarium looking at some fish. To my surprise I saw that they were musical fish and that they were producing the most delightful music. What is more, they were dancing in time to it so that it was clear that they appreciated it. But on my drawing his attention to it he had said severely, 'They can't possibly *hear* it. Sound is vibration in the air and there can be no sounds in water.' However on second thoughts he had agreed that they might feel it in some other way.

'Which only goes to prove,' he had gone on, still speaking in my dream, 'that, as I have always believed, the arts of music, painting and literature are a purely emotional exercise well suited to the lower organisms. But I should be very surprised if those fish could solve a problem in Euclid.'

Bertie was amused by the malice of this dream and in return he told me of one he had had when he was very ill with pneumonia in Peking. He had gone round the circle of the Universe, but instead of returning to the same place had through some lapse of a dimension come out, as it were, just below it. Here it was very dark and the air hot and full of dust and the inhabitants were negroes who sang very sweetly. He was much tempted to listen to their singing, but he knew that if he did so he would die.

The notion of death coming through listening to a song is often met with in folk tales and I suggested that perhaps Freud was right in asserting that there was a language of symbols in the unconscious that was common to everyone. But he was sceptical of most of Freud's theories: he would believe nothing without proof unless ordinary experience confirmed it and did not see how any of Freud's hypotheses about the unconscious could be verified. He would only admit that they were interesting.

I now come to our return visit to Bertie in August 1935 – that is, a year after the conversations I have just described. Telegraph House, where he was living at this time, was a modern but not ugly building built by Bertie's brother on the summit of the South Downs above Harting. Its only supply of water came from rainfall, for which catchments had been built. Behind the house there was a garden which was not kept up and beyond this there stretched forty acres of down and woodland, composed of ancient oaks and yews – a primitive forest where the trees had grown uncut and uncared for since Roman times. Bertie's study was at the end of a passage and the only other sitting room was the tower room, which was glassed in on four sides and provided a magnificent view over the summits of the trees as far as the Solent on one side and the North Downs on the other. This was the room in which he had worked when the house was a school, for nowhere else could he escape from the noise of the children. Another room, which might have been put to some use, was kept un-repaired and unfurnished apparently in the same state in which Dora had left it. All the furniture in the house was ugly. Bertie was aware of this and explained that it had once belonged to Wittgenstein and was on that account sacred to him. But I think that he was really indifferent to his indoor surroundings, though he loved Nature and was proud of his magnificent estate.

He was a very good host, considerate, hospitable and by turns serious and amusing. In the mornings he worked, but during the rest of the day we were together, going for walks through the beech woods after lunch and in the evenings talking and reading aloud to one another. I had feared that my incapacity for discussing philosophy, much less science or mathematics, would lead to my boring him, but he kept pressing us to stay on and in the end we stayed a fortnight.

He and Peter made an odd contrast. She tall, very young and willowy, with red hair and a creamy complexion, smooth pussycat face and a pleasant smile. Under the smile a rather determined chin. He with his flowing white hair, prominent nose and bright, eagle eyes overhung by dark, bushy eyebrows. It was the most alert face I have ever seen and one that became more striking with every year that marked it. His photographs show this, but not that he was rather short with that shortness that is straining to reach higher. Thus he always held himself very upright, never slouching even in an armchair and one felt a readiness for action in his whole body. This and his way of pulling out his large silver watch when meal time grew near – one cannot imagine him being ever late for anything – called up the picture of some very correct and methodical person, say a Victorian banker or statesman. Then his tight, clipped tone in talking, which brought out the flavour of every word, and incidentally reminded me of Asquith's voice on the radio, made me wonder whether it had not come down from the Whig speech once heard at Holland House. There was at all events something very old-fashioned about it.

I will again report some of the notes I took on our conversations. After talking of Virginia Woolf, whom he scarcely knew, we got onto the subject of Clive Bell.

'I like him,' he said, 'as one likes people who flatter one, but I despise him.' (He often said that he despised people.) 'I believe one might learn a great deal about one's own weaknesses by listening to his flattery. He is a master in that art and knows just where to apply it.'

I said that I did not think that was quite fair to Clive Bell, who only flattered people whom he genuinely admired, in which case it was not really flattery. It was true that he also flattered women when he wanted to go to bed with them, but all men did that. And even there his flattery took the form not so much of paying them compliments as of bringing them out and making them shine in conversation. That was his special art: he could make a shallow or silly woman appear brilliant and even witty and in that way he gave a lot of innocent pleasure.

Bertie went on to say that he had never known Bloomsbury well and had only the slightest acquaintance with the Stephen sisters. Was it true, he asked, that Virginia had been to bed with her half brother? I had never heard the story and doubted it. But her mother, he said, must have been a remarkable woman. She called her first child Stella and her second Vanessa. Fancy wanting to combine Stella and Vanessa in one family.

I said the reason must have been that she had married Leslie Stephen, the Victorian Swift.

'He was a dry old stick of a man. But what a subject for a novel! A person who had a day-dream about some figure in the past and then tried to carry it into actual life by marrying him.'

'Yet,' I said, 'without being in love with him.'

Bertie had an amusing story about the Archbishop of York:

'I knew Temple as an undergraduate. One day he came to my rooms and told me he was thinking of joining the Church. "Oh," I said, "and do you believe the dogmas of the Church?" – "I believe the Apostles' Creed." – "Do you then believe in the Resurrection of the Body?" – "In a sense I do." – "In what sense?" – "I believe it in the sense of the renewal of the spirit." – "If I told you that I had met a black man walking in the lane and when you questioned me I said that I meant black in the sense of white, what would you say?" He did not answer and I never saw him again.'

In the evenings Bertie read the Bible aloud and when he wished to smoke his pipe he asked me to read from it. He had a remarkable knowledge of its absurd and scandalous passages and could quote chapter and verse for them. He would start one of these readings by asking me, 'Do you know that edifying passage where God tries to kill Moses in a hotel?' I did not know it and he read out the verses in Exodus 4 that give it. Then he said, 'Do you remember that passage that begins, "Remember now thy Creator in the days of thy Youth"? Creator is a mistranslation for penis. Quaint, isn't it?'

I once spoke to Leonard Woolf of this strange familiarity of Bertie's with the less-known parts of the Bible and he said, 'All the atheists of his time had it. It was part of their equipment and in their search for damaging texts they probably read it as often as believers.' But it was not only the absurd passages that he knew: he had a genuine liking for its stories of human life and for its poetry. Thus when I read him the account of the death of Absolom, which he had forgotten, he was greatly moved. After that Gamel read him the beautiful passage on the Egyptian magicians from Chapter 17 of the Wisdom of Solomon. He did not know it and was much impressed by it. For in fact he was not without religious feeling, and did not call himself an atheist. No one as convinced as he was of the fundamental unintelligibility of the Universe – he used to say that we had not yet discovered a single certain fact about it – could fail to have some sympathy with the mystical attitude.

On Gamel's visiting him in Wales in 1967 she repeated to him a quotation from Spinoza which I had told her – 'God is to the Universe as the laws of stress are to a bridge.' He had not come across it before and was impressed by it. Since he admired Spinoza very much I felt tempted to remind him of that philosopher's maxim, *Non ridere, nec lugere, nec detestari, sed intellegere,* because in his ordinary practice he reversed it. Yet it was that of course that made his conversation so lively and entertaining.

When I asked him why he had given up writing on philosophy, he replied that he had shot his bolt and had nothing more to say. Every philosopher and mathematician, he said, had just one idea to express and when he had done that he had finished. If he continued to write it was merely to expand and develop his first idea. In fact, however, Bertie was soon to start doing original work again.

I told him that outside his philosophy, of which I was no judge, his great quality was his unfairness and that this was a literary quality when it led to conciseness and wit. Since he had read widely on history, politics and sociology and held strong views on them, why did he not apply his talent to writing a moral tale in the manner of *Candide*? There was a place for such a book in every century and he had more to draw on than Voltaire had had because, unlike him, he was an original thinker. But he replied that he could not write a story of any sort as he had no imagination or powers of invention. I said that these came by trying since one always had resources that one was not aware of, but he refused to be persuaded. I still think that had he set himself to do as I suggested he might have written a masterpiece even greater than *Animal Farm,* but he had no literary ambitions. Outside his philosophical works he could only turn out propaganda because he wished to influence the world *at once* – that is, as a teacher rather than as a literary satirist.

I found that he had an extensive acquaintance with even the obscure English novels of the last two centuries. His favourite novelist was Jane Austen, but he knew Dickens equally well and could quote abundantly from him. Gamel asked him if he knew *The Fairchild Family,* and he at once made a dozen quotations from it. His memory was certainly astonishing. Poetry however he knew less well. His favourite poet was Shelley, who alone, he said, understood the scientific attitude to Nature and expressed it in poetic language. He also liked Milton and Blake and, to my surprise, *The Waste Land.*

He was very well read in both English and American history of the last two centuries. He knew the United States as few Americans knew it since he had visited almost every part of it during his lecture tours. He did not like most Americans and especially objected to their intrusiveness, but he admired the United States as a political organisation and had great hopes of its future. He was far less prejudiced than most Englishmen are about it –

indeed I did not think that he had any prejudices on this subject at all. Of American learned men and scientists he said that they were all specialists and had too little general culture, but he excepted from this William James, whose work he greatly admired, and George Santayana whom he liked less. And he found the young Americans at the universities more open to new ideas than European ones were.

He was amused by the American ignorance of geography. When crossing the Mississippi in a train he found that there was no one in his carriage who could tell him what the river was called. When staying in St Louis at the house of a cultured lady he was asked what he would like to be shown there. 'Don't show me any more sewage works or electric light plants,' he said. 'I collect rivers. Take me to see the Missouri.' But the lady did not know where it was. 'I believe there *is* such a river about,' she said, 'only I have never seen it.' So she sent for her chauffeur, who took him there.

At Winnipeg he was sitting talking to a group of professors. 'Does your river here,' he asked, 'flow into the Arctic, the Mississippi or the St Lawrence?' Not one of them had any idea. It was typical of Bertie that before asking these questions he knew the answers. He merely wanted to find out if they knew them.

He was tolerant of ordinary people, but intolerant of many philosophers. To my surprise he had some good things to say of the Schoolmen, but he regarded Aristotle as a dull pedant and Plato, presumably on account of his political ideas, as 'very wicked'. Hegel, Schopenhauer and Nietzsche were beyond the pale. He was very free with the word scoundrel, which he pronounced with great vehemence, and one day he called Bergson that.

I protested, saying: 'Whether one agrees with Bergson or not one should surely give him some credit for providing the greatest novelist of our day with a theme. How many English philosophers have done anything to stimulate the imagination? Then isn't there something to be said for a philosophy that is inspired by evolution rather than by a mechanical science such as physics?'

But he wouldn't hear of it, saying again that he was a scoundrel because his arguments were demonstrably false, though later, I believe, he changed his mind about his. Another person whom he called a scoundrel was Dr Johnson. When I said that I thought him the most human and lovable of all English writers as well as one of the most intelligent, I could see that he thought the worse of me. For my part I found his violent vituperation of those whose views he disliked to be painful – all the more as he so often changed his mind about them.

In talking to people of the left wing one often doubts the sincerity of their idealism. They appear to love an idea rather than the increase of happiness and diminution of suffering which that idea is supposed to bring.

Thus for years the *New Statesman,* which was so sensitive to the least injustice in capitalist countries, had been glossing over or excusing Lenin's brutal starving of the bourgeoisie by refusing to give them ration cards, and Stalin's insane and ferocious purges. Credulity and hypocrisy would seem to be the occupational diseases of left-wing intellectuals. But in the case of Bertrand Russell no one could doubt for a moment the horror that any organized repression or policy of savagery caused him to feel, even if it were done in the name of socialism. He was a man of the most intense sincerity and depth of feeling and was not taken in for a moment by the tyranny that had been established in Russia because cruelty and inhumanity were the matters on which he felt more strongly than on any others and he was a socialist precisely because he believed that socialism would put an end to these. Next to that came intellectual dishonesty where, as I have said, I found his attitude less admirable because he saw everything in black and white. Besides, the strength of his feelings when aroused would often prevent him from taking in his adversaries' case, so that, shutting his eyes to all inconvenient facts, sweeping to one side the finer considerations, he would deliberately misinterpret and blacken them. Thus in intellectual matters he was often very unjust indeed.

On the other hand he was candid in speaking of many of his own failings. He told me that his vanity suffered deeply because he was not as well known as Wells or Einstein and that he often regretted that he had not taken up physics, in which so many great discoveries were being made, rather than Symbolic Logic, which led nowhere. Yet the men he would most have wished to resemble were not, he said, the men of intellect, but those who had exposed some great barbarity or injustice such as the conditions of slavery on the Congo or Upper Amazon rubber plantations. There was what one might call a Prometheus complex in him and he would gladly have gone to the stake in a good cause, especially if he could have done so publicly. Had the Germans invaded England he would have been the first to get himself sent to an extermination camp. Yet, though he was so ready to admit and, I think, exaggerate his longing to be universally admired, I never heard him blame himself for denouncing those people who disagreed with him on intellectual grounds as evil and perverted. A difference of outlook could be for him a difference between honesty and dishonesty. He showed this tendency to give a moral cast to his judgements even in his private affairs. Speaking of his first marriage, he told me that he had for a long time believed that his wife was a good woman, but one day he went for a bicycle ride and in the course of it he decided that she was not good at all, but a hypocrite. However he continued to live in the same house with her for some years after this, though he despised her. It would never have occurred to him that this change of opinion about her character might have been due to his loss of sexual interest in her, because he believed that in his judgements on people he was guided solely by reason. However in his *Autobiography* he has since then given a very frank and full explanation of this, without attempting to avoid blame for what he calls his priggishness.

The time had now come for Gamel and myself to leave Telegraph House, but before doing so it was agreed that Bertie and Peter should pay us a visit at Churriana in the early spring. We returned to Lulworth and sold our car, which we should no longer be able to afford, took the boat for Gibraltar and by October 1st, 1935 were installed in our absurdly palatial mansion. After five years of unsettled life I looked forward to a period of peace and tranquillity and started at once on a new novel. But the political situation in Spain soon began to look threatening and the little Eden we had built for ourselves seemed far from assured. Then early in February Bertie and Peter, who had just got married, arrived on a six weeks' visit.

Bertie was as delightful a guest as he had been a host. He seemed never to suffer from moods, but was invariably cheerful and full of conversation. He was also very active. Although he was now a man of sixty-four, we used once or twice a week to climb the mountain above the village, carrying a thermos of tea with us, and drink it on the summit. He took the steep ascent of 2,000 feet in his stride and came down the rough shale slope, wearing his English leather-soled shoes, without stumbling or feeling stiff afterwards. He was working at this time on his biography of his parents and in the evening would read out extracts from the typescript Peter had made. I found them rather dull, but his mind was running on the past and he talked freely of his early memories. Among other things he told us some amusing anecdotes. As I believe that they are not in his book, I will quote a few of them.

Here are two about his grandfather, Lord John Russell:

'The Queen said, "Is it true, Lord John, that you hold that under certain circumstances a subject may justifiably rebel against his sovereign?" "Speaking as I am to a sovereign of the House of Hanover," he replied, "I think I may say yes." '

The other is about his famous lack of tact:

'Lord John was sitting at a party beside the Duchess of A. at one end of the room, then he suddenly got up and sat down at the opposite end beside the Duchess of B. After the party was over his wife asked him why he had done this. "Oh, I was too hot." "Did you tell the Duchess of A. this?" "No, I forgot to. But I told the Duchess of B." '

Speaking of his childhood he said

'My only pleasure in Church used to be calculating the date of Easter. You divide by 19, excluding fractions. It was such a relief to be able to do that. One was never allowed to exclude fractions in arithmetic at other times.'

On another occasion he said to me:

'That reminds me of what someone once called Russell's Law – that the piety of mariners is inversely proportional to the tonnage of their vessels.'

One of the more attractive sides of his character was his love of children. He charmed my daughter Miranda, who was a very shy little girl of five, by all kinds of tricks, pretending to swallow things and then bringing them up again, tweaking his nose and making a comic noise as he did it. When there was a baby he would pull out his large silver watch and hold it to its ear. He told me that he had always longed to have children and had married Dora because she was the first woman he had been attracted to who was ready to have them.

As I have said, he talked very frankly about himself. Among other things he told me that when he had been young he had been a prig. (Both Molly MacCarthy and Roger Fry had told me this too.) He had felt that a gulf divided him from ordinary people because he had a much better mind than they had, so as this made him feel very isolated, he set out to bridge this gulf by making all sorts of silly jokes which he hoped would amuse them. I will give two examples:

'A certain boy in his school essay wrote, "Pins have been very valuable to human life." His master asked him why. "Because they have saved the lives of many people." "How's that?" "Because of not being swallowed." '

'If you look up Bounder in the *New English Dictionary* you will find that God is defined as the Universal Bounder.'

He often came out with little jokes of this sort as well as with puns, but his usual conversation ran on history, people, Nature, life, and he talked well on these because he possessed a large store both of experience and of reading. His curiosity about the world was limitless and he especially prized odd bits of what he called useless information. But sometimes he started to talk on mathematics or logic and then I was out of my depth at once and could not understand a word of what he said. He seemed to find this incomprehensible – why couldn't anyone follow a mathematical or logical argument seeing that each separate step was so easy to take in? But even then, little though I could grasp of what he said, the force and drive of his intellect used to amaze me. It was precisely that drive, always in a straight line, taking no account of the complexity of things, blind to incommensurables, that, when he left logic for life, caused him to make so many miscalculations. Yet, when not excited by passion, he did what he could to allow for the irrational element in human nature and was sometimes successful in this. He was not really lacking in what Pascal called *esprit de finesse,* only he often preferred to make use of his powerful logical mind to override it. This led him to adopting an oversimplified attitude on social questions such as sex, marriage and education, as well as on politics. For example he seemed to be convinced that all the world's troubles would be solved by socialist organization and by the provision of a high standard of living for everyone. He had in his head a blueprint of human happiness, whereas I believed that the solution of one problem led at once to the emergence of others.

Once I asked him if he would write a paper on aesthetics, or at least on the possibility of there being such a thing as aesthetics, and he replied that if he did he would have to start experimenting with babies and playing on trumpets to them. I thought this answer stupid, or rather as exhibiting the shallowness of the rationalist mind, for there is plenty of evidence of the existence among adults of aesthetic feelings, but now I see that my request was stupid too. That, no doubt, was why he answered me as he did.

I repeated to him an observation that Bismarck had made, that the measure of a man is his intelligence after his vanity has been deducted from it and added that since reading that I had decided that I must get rid of such vanity and conceit as I possessed because my intelligence was not sufficient to permit of any deduction from it. He was deeply impressed by this aphorism of Bismarck's because, as I have already said, he regarded himself as being a very vain man. Gamel agreed with him on this, but I thought that ambition was a better word. What he really wanted was that his great superiority of mind should be generally recognized so that he should be in a position to exert a useful influence on human affairs. He was always modest about his work, tending rather to depreciate it than to stress its value, and when he spoke badly of other philosophers it was because he disapproved of their tendencies and never out of envy.

One of his more agreeable qualities was his readiness to associate on equal terms with people who were far less intelligent than himself. I hardly ever heard him speak of anyone as being boring. He found human beings interesting, whoever they were, listened attentively to what they said and studied their characters. He had no prejudices about races or degrees of education and was prepared to enter into conversation with anyone who would talk honestly and frankly. I think that one reason for this openness of mind was that he hated cliques and felt imprisoned as soon as he found that he was seeing the same group of people too often. Yet he complained that he had lost most of his old friends because they had not got on with Dora. It is doubtful if this is true, and I imagine that it was really his dismissal from Trinity on account of his pacifism in the First World War that had thrown him out of the academic world into the wilderness of ordinary people. When I first knew him he was certainly very isolated.

One marked feature of Bertie's character at this time was his lustfulness.

As often happens with elderly men who have led quiet married lives, girls excited him sensually. His theories of sexual permissiveness encouraged him in this and his approaches to them were direct. Bertie had never, I believe, been a man to have much erotic appeal for women because he had no feminine element in his character and so could not talk their language. Though very pleasant, he was quite devoid of charm. Thus though he was always patient and considerate with them, I was conscious of there sometimes being a strain in his relationships with women. But it was perhaps not surprising that he should feel drawn to Gamel. She listened to what he said and appeared to agree with him and then her gentle Southern manners charmed him. She reminded him, he said, of those aristocratic ladies he used to know in his youth, so different in every way from the ultra-modern, left-wing women he had for so long been consorting with because they shared his opinions. She had poise, maturity and tolerance as well as a certain mysterious quality of her own that usually attracted older men. His gradually increasing inclination to her seems to have made him fear that I, as a young man, might be finding Peter's lovely body too alluring, for on one of our walks he suggested to me that we should neither of us complicate the situation by making up to one another's wives. In saying this he obviously thought it would be completely natural and *en règle* to do so. Those were his principles, but they were not mine and I was taken aback by the crudity of his suggestion.

Gamel, though she enjoyed Bertie's conversation, told me that she found him unattractive as a man. And like myself she treated marriage as a serious relationship. But I will let her speak for herself by quoting from a letter she wrote to Llewelyn Powys just after he left:

> I am so tired of seeing people – it sounds strange to say so, but so many people seem to come and the Russells stayed such a long time. And I only half like him. My heart never warms towards him at all. His guiding forces are vanity and love of power and to gratify them he wasted his amazing talent for mathematics and took to writing his books on happiness and marriage and all the subjects about which he evidently knows nothing worth saying. But in many things he shows great integrity of thought and character ... I get so tired of always talking. I wish human beings were more silent creatures. It would be lovely never to speak, but only to think and feel ...
>
> Today I heard the cuckoo. It was a cloudy, windy, restless day and suddenly out of the grey sky over the green fields I heard it. It was lovely to me. I might have been in England. And how beautiful the charm of the birds was when the sky was beginning to be light! I was sitting in the garden doing nothing at all, only looking at the stocks

and tulips and calla lilies in blossom. Do you suppose I shall be doing that all the year?

This letter tells one more about Gamel than it does about Bertie. She was not unsociable, but she liked to spend a good part of the day alone. Having visitors to stay in the house exhausted her unless she felt attuned to them and she could only feel attuned to people who had sensibility. But Bertie was not aware of this, for he did not take in women's feelings easily, and so his interest in her continued to grow. After his return from America during the last months of the war, she would meet him occasionally for tea when she went up to London. Then she ceased to see him or to answer his letters. Although she never told me her reason for this, I imagine that he made some sort of a pass at her or even asked her to leave me and marry him. One of his letters to her, which I have since read, contains a love declaration. At the time I knew nothing of this until one day I got a letter from him in which he asked me to persuade her to go and see him. An odd request from a would-be lover to a husband, but on my telling her of it she said that when she went to London she preferred to spend her afternoons at films or picture galleries. Then he married Edith Finch, so her objection to meeting him vanished. We had by this time returned to live in Spain, but every summer she would pay a short visit to England and spend a week or two in North Wales with John Cowper Powys and Phyllis Playter. Bertie lived close by and so she would drive over to see him for a meal or to spend a night. Now that she could see him on different terms she enjoyed these occasions greatly, all the more as she liked his wife. I never went to Wales because I did not fit in with John Cowper Powys.

To return to 1936 and Churriana, Bertie and I talked a good deal of the war with Nazi Germany which we both saw was coming. He had no illusions about either Hitler or Stalin, and yet he believed that England ought at all costs to keep out of the struggle, even if that meant submitting to a German occupation, because he thought that if we did not our cities would be totally destroyed by air bombardment. Millions, he declared, would die of either gas or explosive bombs and even more would perish by starvation. In support of this view he handed me a book by a so-called authority on modern warfare which, with many figures and statistics, foretold that this would happen. I read it and did not believe a word of it. I was particularly sceptical of the loss of life which it claimed would be caused by the dropping of gas bombs because my experience in the last war had taught me that they were of little effect in cities. The book was plainly a piece of alarmist propaganda full of exaggerations and hysterical forecasts and if Bertie had not seen this it was because there was something in his nature that made him wish to believe it.

Later he sent me a copy of his pacifist treatise, *Which way to peace?* I replied that it reminded me of a book written by an Archbishop of Canterbury on the question of whether the doctrine of the Trinity ought or ought not to be believed, for although it began in the most open and impartial way with a consideration of all the arguments there were against believing it, one knew that it was going to end with an emphatic affirmation. The sweep and clarity of his book were, I said, just what one would expect from an eminent theologian who knew from the first page where he was going although he pretended that he didn't. However, Bertie, who two or three years later was to reverse his opinion, was not offended by my letter and when he returned from America in 1944 we met several times in the most cordial way. I was amused to see the immense admiration he now had for Winston Churchill, whom till recently he had regarded as a dangerous warmonger. It never seemed to worry him that he changed his mind so often. Each new pronouncement of his on politics was as authoritative as his previous ones had been.

After this scrappy account of Bertrand Russell's character and conversation I will try to summarize my impressions of him. Both his mind and his work can be seen as split into two separate compartments. In one he is the logician and philosopher, the man of pure intellect who is completely cut off from all feelings. In the other he is the political writer, educationalist, teacher, prophet, moved by generous indignation at the follies and cruelties of the world, but also by a hankering for public esteem and applause. There is nothing unusual in such a division of interest in a scientist or mathematician, many of whom in the last three decades have been communists, but what was peculiar in Bertie's case was the amount of time and thought that he gave to these activities and the passion that he put into them.

But when engaged in this way he was severely handicapped. Pure reason is not a good instrument for plotting a course in politics, where so many imponderables have to be taken into account and so many popular feelings and prejudices allowed for, and though he was not lacking in the faculty of intuition he rarely gave it full play but drove his logical judgement through the maze of inter-related circumstances, simplifying everything that lay in its path till his conclusions no longer corresponded to reality. Then he was a man who, whenever his moral indignation was aroused, became blinded by passion. As is so often the case with pacifists, there was a strong streak of aggressiveness in his nature. The result was that, although in the course of his political and propagandist writings he has said many wise and just things, in the end he has generally lost his head and come out with foolish and desperate ones. A sceptic in everything else, in political matters he has always felt convinced that he was right and that those who disagreed with him were not merely mistaken but corrupt and evil. His incapacity for compromise, which went strangely in a man who believed in democracy, made him feel that most politicians were dishonest.

Yet when one talked with him one could never forget that he was a great man. Not only was his intellect a very powerful one, but his capacity for feeling was on the same scale. If much of this feeling was destructive, even more of it was channelled into a passionate concern for human happiness. Perhaps one might say that in the strength and depth of his nature he resembled Milton, though he lacked that poet's egoism and had less bitterness and rancour. For the same greatness of mind was there, an attribute of his character that could not be invalidated by his failings, and I believe that future generations will recognize it.

21

The approach of the Civil War

The Russells were not the only visitors we had that spring. Before their arrival Angela Culme-Seymour, who had rented a house at Yegen the previous year, came to stay with her newly-wedded husband Johnny Churchill. Johnny was a painter who devoted ten hours every day to decorating any surface he could lay his hands on with Renaissance frescoes. Before he left he had covered the walls and ceiling of several of our rooms with Amphitrites, nereids, tritons and fish-tailed monsters desporting themselves in a very jolly manner. He was a very pleasant guest, good-natured and tubby, and during the brief periods when he was not painting gave amusing imitations of his uncle Winston by whom he had been brought up. Then he and Angela moved to Torremolinos where they rented a house next to the Moorish tower. Her mother, Jan Woolley and her half-sister Janetta, then a girl of fourteen, settled next door. But Angela soon became bored by her husband's absorption in his painting and ran off with a French marquis. Johnny then stayed on alone.

Another person who was living at Torremolinos was an American called Jay Allen. He was a star correspondent of the *Chicago Tribune,* a warm, generous-minded man with a taste for adventure. As a socialist who spoke fluent Spanish he had become a friend and confidant of Largo Caballero and Alvarez del Vayo and was thus able to tell me a good deal about them and their revolutionary plans. Then at Churriana two artists, Clare and Sidney Sheppard, had rented a small house. Clare was a niece of my old friend Molly MacCarthy and a devout Catholic.

The victory of the Popular Front on February 16th of that year had been followed by a state of chronic upheaval and disorder. But before describing this and the outbreak of the Civil War six months later I must say something of my own political orientation because it conditioned my attitude to what was happening in Spain. From the time of the Armistice in 1918 I had thought that the main thing was the prevention of other wars and so I had supported the League of Nations until it became evident that it was only a paper league. I was also strongly opposed to colonialism. Not only did it seem to me tyrannical to rule people against their will as we were doing in India, but I thought that the practice of doing so had a bad effect upon the rulers and that many of the things that I disliked about the British upper classes of that time were due to the false sense of racial superiority which they had acquired by bossing Orientals. That is to say, colonialism hurt the colonizers as much as it did the colonized. But although my views on such questions were radical, I was not a socialist. If socialism meant, as it then did, the ownership by the state of all the means of production, I believed that it would inevitably lead to the establishment of a tyranny as it had done in Russia. Capitalism with its appeal to greed was not on the face of it an attractive system, but it provided a counterweight to the power of the state, besides quickening the life of society by providing competition. Socialism, or rule by bureaucracy, meant, I thought, the dead hand on everything, the life-destroying tyranny of the anonymous.

In London I had seen something of the poverty and unemployment that had been caused by the Depression. I could not understand why something should not be done to alleviate these by a programme of public works and I despised the Baldwin government for its lethargy and lack of imagination. But I felt no sympathy for the view then held by many left-wing people such as Harold Laski that a revolution was the only way out. That word had no charms for me, in the first place because I hated violence and secondly because I believed that both the French and the Russian revolutions had done more harm than good. Such play-acting in a solid parliamentary democracy such as England seemed to me silly because by waiting a little a new government would come in, other policies be adopted and the standard of living begin to rise once more. But now Hitler had come to power in Germany. From that moment the most pressing problem had ceased to be the social or economic one and become that of how to resist him. If we wished to avoid war, we must at once rearm and adopt a firm attitude. Or if war came in spite of this, we must win it.

Where Spanish affairs were concerned I was less clear. I saw that the Republican regime, which I had at first welcomed, had failed because it had no social programme and that by its attacks on the Church it had given the landowners a powerful ally and enormously increased the bitterness of feeling in the country. I felt that the best hope for the future now lay in the Socialists because in a stagnant, uncompetitive economy such as that of Spain, their solution was the more practical one. Only I thought that it should be introduced gradually and after an adequate preparation because a sudden nationalization of the big, dry farming estates would lead to chaos. For this reason I had not sympathized with the Asturian rising of October 1934. I believed in moderation and patience. But now, after the Popular

Front victory, I could see no solution. The Centre, which should have been the point of concentration, had melted away: the poles repelled one another. Through the operation of its peculiar electoral system the country had been split into two halves which felt a passionate hatred for one another. The working classes were also more or less equally divided between the Socialists and the Anarcho-Syndicalists, who had nothing in common but their small wage packets. The whole of the south, centre and east was simmering in a pre-revolutionary state and yet it was clear that no successful revolution could take place so long as the Liberal Azaña remained in power because the Asturian rising had proved that the army, when backed by the government, would always be able to suppress one. It never for a moment occurred to me that the generals would rebel with the support of the right because that would throw the government into the hands of the workers and spark off a revolution that would have every chance of being successful. The only hope seemed to be that the revolutionary fervour would in time die down without coming to a head and that some measure of agrarian reform would help to effect this. What I forgot was the generals might be able to get help from Nazi Germany and Italy. Only if they succeeded in that would they dare to rise.

The working classes of the province of Malaga, and indeed of almost the whole of Andalusia except Granada, were Anarcho-Syndicalists and belonged to the union known as the *Confederación Nacional de Trabajo* or C.N.T. They were controlled by a small organization of pure Anarchists known as the *Federación Anarquiste Ibérica,* or F.A.I. It was rare to meet a Socialist worker of the rival *Unión General de Trabajadores,* or U.G.T. Our deputy to the *Cortes,* a doctor called Cayetano Bolivar, was however, a Communist, although there were very few party members in the province. The reason for this was that, since the Anarcho-Syndicalists did not put up candidates because they disapproved of bourgeois politics, they voted in times of tension for one of the other parties. As a rule these were the Left Republicans, a lower-middle-class party led by schoolmasters, but in Malaga they chose to vote for a Communist because he was personally popular, in spite of the fact that the Communists were almost as much their ideological enemies as the Clericals.

The whole of that spring and summer was given over to an orgy of lightning strikes. The men would come out without any warning, demanding either a huge rise in their wages or impossibly short working hours, as well as heavy compensation for the days they had spent in prison. Then when their wives insisted that they must earn some money, they would return to work with equal suddenness. The purpose of these strikes was of course purely political – to create fear and despondency in the middle classes and encourage the workers with the hope of their approaching victory. All businesses began to lose money. An economic collapse seemed imminent. As one went about the streets every face, according to the social class and opinions of its owner, displayed either deep gloom or a confident expectation.

The look of triumph on the faces of the workmen was sometimes very striking. The men who drove the two-wheeled carts in the port stood sternly erect, holding onto their reins in the stance of Greek charioteers. Their proud, self-confident bearing showed that they already felt themselves the rulers of Malaga. Yet no one, however closely associated with the Right, was molested. Although certain sinister and ragged figures, the dregs of the unemployed, could be seen lurking in the shadows, the workers, when their day of victory came, did not intend to injure their class enemies. Such at least was the prevailing ideology: all men were to be equal and those who had previously lived in wealth and comfort would be taught how much happier they would be when they earned their bread like other people. Only those who plotted or resisted would be killed.

I had made a number of friends among the leading Anarchists. One was a man called Samper who kept a store of antiques near the British Cemetery. He was a member of the F.A.I. and like all the other Anarchists I knew a man of the strictest honesty who asked low prices for his goods and refused to bargain. He lived in a single room in a large bug-ridden wooden tenement, packed like one of the worst London slums with very poor families. In one corner was his bed, never made, while the rest of the room was a jumble of decaying furniture and pictures, piled on top of one another and never dusted. An old woman cooked his meals on a portable charcoal stove and he ate them sitting on the only available chair. In the evenings he would put on a black, well-brushed coat and sally out to a café, from which he would not return till after midnight.

I liked Samper and got on with him well. He had a genuine feeling for the sort of antiques that I used to collect – tiles, pottery and glass pictures – and would keep some of his best finds for himself and refuse to sell them. One Sunday afternoon he came out with a friend to Churriana and we sat drinking beer in the garden for an hour or two. But he was reserved and did not care to talk on politics. However, on running into him in a café one day, I told him of the pleasure it had given me to hear that some Andalusian *pueblos* had begun to manage their own affairs.

'By bringing back life into the small units,' I said, 'you are doing something that is very much needed. Probably it is only feasible in Spain, for everywhere else in Europe the seeds of social life have been destroyed. But I hope that if ever there is a revolution in this country you will be strong enough to prevent it from going the way either of the French or of the Russian Revolution.'

'We think,' he said, 'that there is no use in expecting liberty or justice in the world unless we can get it first of all in small bodies of men who work together and know one another. We believe in starting like that, putting our principles into practice in small groups. Our full ideal, libertarian communism, must come gradually. We no longer expect it to drop out of the sky all at once. But it is a great ideal and so worth working for and waiting for.'

'And meanwhile?' I asked.

'Meanwhile we shall try as far as is possible to establish these local conditions in pueblos and factories, and we shall fight all tyranny, whether it comes from the left as Marxism or from the right as military dictatorship. We are equally opposed to both.'

'Does that mean then,' I asked, 'that you would be ready to come to terms with a bourgeois regime that was willing to give you the local conditions you ask for?'

'When such a regime appears,' he answered, 'we will talk with them, but after the experience we have had we will not easily be convinced of their sincerity.'

This was the first time that I had heard an Anarchist speak of the possibility of compromise, but later I gathered that it was the opinion of most of their leading men in Malaga.

The atmosphere at Churriana was not as easy and pleasant as it had been before the election, though to us as foreigners everyone was friendly. The class struggle was very much in evidence. The people felt that they were on top and they meant to take every possible advantage of it. Even quiet workmen, indifferent to all ideologies, put on boastful airs, while not only had wages gone up by a third but farmers and landlords were compelled to take on extra hands whom they did not need. Everyone who could brought claims against the chief industry of the district, the sugar factory, which was a state monopoly, and because its manager did not dare to resist, their claims were automatically admitted. To give an example, a young painter who had been employed there at a good wage – ten pesetas a day – claimed and got fifteen hundred pesetas as arrears when the rate was raised. He came in great jubilation to tell me this, wearing a stiff straw hat and a pink shirt and riding a new bicycle. 'I'm very glad,' I said, 'to hear of your luck, but aren't you killing the goose that lays the golden eggs?' He was not politically minded so he merely laughed, but a committed worker would have answered, 'No, for we shall take the factory over and pay whatever wages we can. They may be less or they may be more, but anyhow we shall know that we are not being exploited.' Anarchists are the only revolutionaries who do not promise a rise in the standard of living. They offer a moral gain – self-respect and freedom.

But if there was class war, there were few signs of class hatred. Whenever the landowners or the factory owners submitted, as they nearly always did, the workers were satisfied. Only the priests remained objects of suspicion. Ours could not walk through the village without it being said that he was trying to overhear the conversation of the people around him. One day we were told that he and the verger had been caught attempting to set fire to the church so as to put the blame for this on the village. This story was started by a lorry owner and haulier, a militant Anarchist with the glum unsmiling face of a seventeenth-century Covenanter. The poor priest's position soon became so precarious that he judged it best to leave the village after distributing the sacred vessels and images among pious families, and to conceal himself in Malaga. He was lucky enough to survive the war.

The postman provided another example of this anti-religious mania. He was a nasty little man, a Left Republican in politics, and a great retailer of gossip - one of those people whose oath in court no jury would trust. His favourite theme was the licentiousness of the clergy. He had a number of highly coloured stories about priests, friars and nuns which he would pour out in the kitchen when he delivered the letters. They were all of them, I am sure, pure inventions, for though the priests were not invariably chaste, the nuns were above suspicion. Yet his own daughters were not sent to the state school, but were educated in a convent. His wife had insisted upon this, not, as one might suppose, because she was religious, but because she was a snob. Convent education was thought to give greater refinement. In fact the education given in both state and convent schools was of the most elementary sort, but the convent schools did turn out girls who could read and write, while the state schools, where the classes were very large, often did not. Also the nuns taught sewing and embroidery as well as good manners.

Another symptom of the times was the increasing eroticism of the book trade. One could not buy a book on elementary geology or physics that did not have an illustration of a naked woman on the cover. Then the kiosks took to stacking hundreds of little badly-printed paperbacks of a purely pornographic content and containing the crudest illustrations. They cost a couple of pesetas each and no word or act or situation was spared, not even women's unions with dogs. I do not think however that this flood of erotica corresponded to any increase of sexual permissiveness in the population: the small publishers were merely taking advantage of the recent abolition of the censorship to provide books that sold well. At the same time the bookstalls were flooded with cheap, hurriedly prepared translations of the works of Marx, Engels, Lenin and Stalin. It was of course the Communists who were responsible for these. From being a small and quite insignificant party they were gaining ground rapidly, especially among the middle classes, as the party that understood the techniques of revolution.

One afternoon in Malaga I ran into a Catalan engineer who many years before had stayed with me at Yegen while he was making an ordnance survey of the Sierra Nevada. I remembered him as an intelligent and very energetic man who was devoted to his work. He came of a well-to-do family and could have gone into business or led a life of idleness, but he had preferred to enter a profession in which he could feel that he was useful. Since he was too busy to come out with me to Churriana, we went into a café for a talk.

He told me that he was now attached to the Commission of Agrarian Reform and was going next day to Cordoba where some large estates were being broken up.

'So you've had to take sides in the end,' I said. 'Do you remember that you used to tell me that you were a Catalan and nothing more, and would never have anything to do with politics?'

'That is still true,' he replied. 'I merely support the Republic like a good Catalan because they gave us our autonomy. Apart from that I have no political opinions of any sort. But I like my work – and why not? I am doing for these wretched Andalusians what we Catalans did six hundred years ago for ourselves. Feudalism is today an anachronism.'

'It's worse than feudalism,' I said. 'What you have on these large estates is a free labour market where the supply is twice as great as the demand and all the work is seasonal.'

'All right. Call it what you please. The great thing is to cure it.'

'And are you curing it?'

'No,' he replied. 'In the province of Cordoba we are not. Most of the peasants to whom we are giving land will fail, while the rest will remain as poor as ever. But I think there will be less unemployment.'

'Are you setting up any collectives?'

'No indeed, there is to be no question of that. Anything which exists in a country called Russia is barred to us here. And collectives, it seems, are a Russian invention.'

'And also a Spanish one,' I said. 'In Leon there are large districts where the land, though separately owned, is worked in common too. This is not a new invention, but has come down from the Middle Ages.'

'Yes, I know villages in the Pyrenees where everything is managed in that way. But the people who live there wear eighteenth-century costumes and call themselves Carlists.'

'I see. The label's what matters,' I said. 'But I'd like to ask whether you have changed your opinions. You used to maintain that the only tolerable governments in Spain were the corrupt ones and that when the municipal councillors or the deputies to the *Cortes* were no longer allowed to make their millions, the deluge would come. Now I imagine you don't think that any longer.'

'The deluge *is* coming,' he said.

'What, a revolution?'

'Revolution! Surely you don't take all these speeches and strikes and newspaper articles seriously. These people have not the discipline nor even the sense to make a revolution. Read Spanish history. Read Galdós. This is just the old Spanish anarchy, simmering like a pot on the fire and leading nowhere. As soon as the water has all boiled away, it will quieten down. Then, if we are allowed to get to that point, everyone will go to sleep for ten years and we shall have a nice corrupt government once more. But we may not get to that point.'

'What do you mean?' I asked.

'There is an organization,' he said, 'in Spain called the army. I don't know whether you have noticed it. At the head of it there are five hundred generals. There has not been a turnover on army contracts since Primo de Rivera came in, and they are beginning to think that there may never be one again. But I must be going. I have an appointment at the Town Hall at five and as I am a Catalan I shall be so rude as to arrive there punctually to the minute.'

'I hope all these troubles will soon blow over,' I said. 'Spain is a country where the sun ought to shine.'

'Yes,' he said. 'The sun of bribery. Remember my words. It is not the bread hunger of those poor devils in the pueblos that matters, but the far more important hunger of the politicians, generals, *caciques* and hangers-on. This country can only be called healthy and in normal working order when all these people are adequately fed. *Vaya* – when we next draw up a new constitution I shall propose that as the first article. And now I must really go. If you are ever anywhere near Lucena, come and see me.'

My friend left. I watched his handsome bronzed face and athletic body moving quickly down the street. A puzzling man. I did not in the least believe in his boasted indifference to politics. There is a frontier where, strangely enough, the purest fascism and the purest communism meet. He might have belonged to either of these. However on thinking it over I decided that he was just what he said he was – a Catalan disgusted by the confusion and inefficiency of Spanish affairs and believing that what the country needed was less politics and better administration. No doubt his ideal was the mild but efficient dictatorship of General Primo de Rivera.

In May Clare Sheppard's mother, Mrs Balfour, came out to visit her. She was the sister of Admiral Fisher, who was then in command of the Mediterranean Fleet, and an ardent Catholic. After staying for a few days at a hotel she took a room in a convent which belonged to an order of nuns who trained girls for domestic service. It stood in a popular quarter close to the Plaza de la Victoria and, since there was so much feeling in the air against the religious orders, Clare became anxious for her mother's safety. But Mrs Balfour categorically refused to leave the convent. She was convinced that a revolution was imminent and that when it came all the sisters would be massacred. If so, she wanted to be massacred too. The martyr's crown was becoming very difficult to earn in these lenient days, and this seemed a providential opportunity for acquiring one. However it appeared that the nuns were not thinking along those lines. At the back of their convent there was a large garden which communicated by a door with the house of Dr Bolivar, the Communist deputy, and he had promised that if any attempt were made to molest them or to set fire to their convent they could take refuge with him and he would protect them. When Mrs Balfour learned of this plan her interest in these nuns declined and she returned to England.

Dr Bolivar was no doubt a humane man, but in offering his protection to the nuns he was following the party line. The Communists of Malaga, lost in the great sea of Andalusian anarchism, were mostly of bourgeois origin and as such had little sympathy with the rabid anti-Catholicism of their rivals. But they also happened to control the poorest and most wretched of all the syndicates, that of the fishermen, which had recently seceded to them from the C.N.T. These men were now demanding a higher price for their fish. But the fish vendors' syndicate, which was relatively prosperous, objected to paying more because that would reduce their earnings. Since they belonged to the C.N.T., the old antagonism between the Communists and the Anarchists, embittered by memories of how Lenin had repressed and liquidated the latter, flared up again. At this moment a young and energetic party member, who had a seat in the Municipality, discovered that the fish vendors' syndicate was dumping its rotten fish, left over from the market, on the hospital and lunatic asylum and demanding the same price for it as for fresh fish. The usual graft, in fact, and he ordered that in future only fresh fish should be provided. There was a great outcry when this appeared in the papers and that night a party of the fish vendors went to the young Communist's house, called him out and shot him. On the following day two of the fish vendors were shot in revenge and that night two more Communists. Then the leading men on both sides intervened and the vendetta was brought to an end. But the C.N.T. had lost face by it. Graft and dishonesty in an anarchist, like immoral acts in a clergyman, are more damaging than in anyone else. If a Republican or a Catholic should take bribes – *nada*. That was to be expected of them, but in an unwordly congregation such as that of the Anarchists it was deeply shaming. Altogether the incident did not augur well for the future of working-class relations after the revolution had been won.

In the countryside a reaction had begun to set in against the orgy of strikes, new labour regulations and so forth. It affected mainly the small farmers, better class workmen and artisans. A farmer whom I knew, an enthusiastic Republican, complained that when he asked the Syndicate for a man to hoe his vines, they sent him *cualquier tío*, any old buffer, whether he knew how to hoe or not. For the Syndicate's rule was to send in rotation the men who were on their list, irrespective of whether they could do the work or not. Antonio too, the master mason who had directed the repairs on our house, was disgusted because the team of men he had trained had been broken up and he had to take on new hands every week. Then our house painter, Alonso, told me that he intended to refuse the new wage of twelve pesetas and take only his usual eight. 'My work', he said, 'is not worth more than that and if I take more people will not employ me.' He was an elderly man who had voted left out of a feeling of solidarity with his class, but when one got him alone he would confess that the regime that had pleased him best had been the dictatorship of Primo de Rivera.

'We Spaniards', he said, 'are not like you English – wise and prudent. We are a bad, violent race and we need a strong hand over us. You have visited many countries of the world – don't you agree with me?'

'No, I don't,' I said.

'*Puñeta,* then you don't know us properly. You haven't understood that we are all *bribones* and scoundrels. There isn't one among us who wouldn't rob his father of his last penny. No good or true plant ever grew on Spanish soil. And then what justice is there? The law is always on the side of the rich.'

In those days one often heard people talk like that. As the proverb says, *Si habla mal de España, es español.*

Almost the last strike of that summer was the servants' strike. All servants were told to stop working and as a protest against their work to walk in a procession. Our servants joined in the procession because I said they must, but they continued working as usual. Since they were villagers from a remote *pueblo* they were strongly opposed to the Popular Front, but after the fall of Malaga to the Nationalists they changed their minds and moved to the left. The spate of executions had made them feel solid with their class and the fall in the standard of living confirmed this.

From the middle of June onwards everyone except the government seemed to know that the military were planning a rising. One day as I was walking down the Calle Larios, which is the main street of Malaga, an elderly man, Don Antonio Villa, who lived in the house next to ours, hailed me in loud tones.

'Good news, Don Geraldo,' he called out so that half the street could hear, 'Good news! Within ten days Calvo Sotelo will be King of Spain.'

Calvo Sotelo was the leader of the extreme right in the *Cortes* and the political organizer of the rising, but a week later he was assassinated by some Socialist policemen. It was clear that from this moment the military rebellion would not be long delayed.

22

The Civil War at Malaga

On the afternoon of Saturday July 18th I took the bus to Malaga to do some shopping. I had got so accustomed to seeing strained faces and frozen, apprehensive glances that I did not at first pay much attention to the atmosphere. Then I noticed that the police in the Plaza de le Constitución were looking unusually jittery. They were craning their necks up and down the street and fingering their belts and one of them had a positively haggard expression. I put it down to the fact that they had been on extra duty for many months and were not getting enough sleep.

After making the purchases I needed I went into a bookshop in the Calle Larios which was kept by two serious and immaculately dressed young men. They did not have the book I wanted, which was a new publication on agrarian reform, so I picked up a copy of the local paper *El Popular* and began to read it. The headlines said, 'Military Rebellion in Morocco. Ceuta and Melilla seized by the factious,' but there was a reassuring follow-up in a statement by the Prime Minister, Casares Quiroga – 'The Government is fully master of the situation. Nobody, absolutely nobody in Spain has taken part in this absurd plot.'

I decided to have a quick coffee, fetch my trousers from the cleaners and take the little train back to Churriana before anything happened. But before I could get to the café I heard the music of a band and saw at the end of the street a crowd of people, mostly men, who were walking along the Alameda. Behind them came a company of soldiers. An officer marched at their head looking straight in front of him and the men followed with their arms at the slope while a band took up the rear. Behind this the street was packed with workmen, while others walked alongside the soldiers and kept up a running conversation with them.

'Where are you off to?' they asked.

'To the Aduana to proclaim military law by order of the Government.'

'No, the Government has not ordered it.'

'Well, those are *our* orders.'

Everyone was shouting or talking in excited voices, so as I had no wish to become involved in whatever was going to happen, I decided to give up my coffee and return home at once. It appeared that other people had had the same idea as myself for the shops were putting up their shutters, the women and the better dressed people hurrying off and the side streets emptying themselves. Then suddenly from the top of the Calle Larios there appeared a stream of men running to join the crowd that was following the soldiers. But my trousers! I needed them badly, so I turned into the cleaners, which was close by, only to learn that they had been delayed by a strike and would not be ready till the following day.

Just as I was leaving I heard a few shots fired from the direction of the Aduana and then the rattle of submachine guns.

'*Ay, Dios mio,*' exclaimed the woman in the shop. 'What's that?'

'The military rising,' I answered.

'*Por Dios,* don't tell me that,' she said. '*Qué criminales!*'

Although no bullets were coming down our street everyone had begun to run, a few towards the shots but most of them in the opposite direction. I gave up the idea of reaching the station, which would have meant crossing the line of fire, and decided to catch the bus. It left from near the market, only a few minutes away.

The firing went on increasing. Behind the methodical tap tapping of the machine guns, I could hear the sharp bark of rifle and revolver shots. The volume of noise was surprising – one would have said that an infantry battle was going on. As I saw no reason for panic I did not run as everyone else was doing, but I walked fast. Then on rounding the corner beyond the market place, I saw the bus disappearing into the distance. An elderly man, one of our two village plumbers, came up at the same moment. Pulling out an enormous nickel watch, he looked at it.

'The bus has left seven minutes before time,' he said. 'All because a few shots are going off. *Vaya, qué cobardes!*'

'Then we must walk,' I said. And we set off.

But on reaching the bridge at the end of the Alameda we found that bullets were zizzing through the branches of the trees and ricocheting off the stone parapet. The bus had taken a chance in getting through. We did not feel inclined to take this chance so we turned back to cross the river by another bridge. Here we had to pass through a popular quarter. The streets were crowded with men and women who were milling about like ants when a stick is poked into their nest. A few of them were running with revolvers in their hands to join in the fighting, while the rest were talking excitedly. We made our way back to the main road and got a lift home in a lorry.

When I woke up next morning the first thing I did was to listen. Not a sound. I saw our maid Maria picking some roses in the garden and went out to ask her the news.

'They say that the Fascists have been defeated,' she answered, 'and that they are now going to make the revolution.'

She spoke in an angry tone and would hardly look at me, for she had a strong dislike of *Comunismo Libertario* and indeed of anything new.

'You can see it from the *mirador*,' she said. 'Half Malaga is burning.'

I went up to look. Tall columns of smoke were rising from several parts of the city. Two fires had been visible the previous night before we went to bed – now there seemed to be at least twenty.

We had breakfast as usual in the garden under a nispero tree. Antonio was hoeing his potatoes as though nothing had happened. The scarlet cannas and the dahlias and roses gleamed in the early morning sunshine and red admirals and brimstone butterflies fluttered lazily round them. It seemed impossible to believe that an anarchist revolution had just begun.

Maria came out in her grave way to clear the breakfast things.

'There's a fine sight to be seen in the street,' she said.

'What's that?'

She stood there with her arms folded and an ironic curve on her mouth.

'Go and see for yourself,' she said. 'Then perhaps you'll like to join them.'

We went into the house and looked out of one of the upper windows. Lorries and cars were tearing past crowded with workmen who were armed with guns, revolvers, knives and even swords. They sat on the roof, they stood on the running boards, they hung round the drivers' necks and leaned out of the windows and every one of them pointed his weapon towards the street so that the lorries literally bristled with them. They saluted everyone they passed with their left arm bent and the fist clenched and a greeting of *Salud,* and kept their weapons trained on them till the greeting was returned in the same way. All the cars and lorries fluttered with red flags and had letters painted on them – C.N.T., F.A.I., U.G.T., U.H.P., but never P.C. Some of them were driven at a furious speed amid muffled cheering, while others crawled along.

'What are they doing?' I asked.

'They are armed patrols,' said Rosario, 'and are looking for Fascists.'

'They shoot all the rich,' said Maria. 'Take care they don't shoot you.'

'*Calla, mujer,*' said her sister. 'Don Geraldo is not a Fascist. *You're* the only real Fascist here.'

'Yes,' I said. 'We'll denounce you.'

Alonso the house painter had followed us upstairs.

'I'll bet,' he said, 'that, if it comes to that, Don Geraldo is as good a Communist as any of us here.'

287

'Of course I am,' I said. 'I want everyone to be as rich as I am.'

'Now that's true Communism,' said Alonso. 'Most of the Communists here only want everyone to be as poor as themselves.'

'Well,' I exclaimed, 'so the great Revolution has come at last!'

'*Qué revolución!*' he said scornfully. 'What do you imagine is going to happen? Nothing. *Nada.*'

A couple of young men from the *comité* or village committee, carrying ancient matchlocks, came to search for arms. They were very polite. I said that I had none, but that they were welcome to search the house. Although they obviously did not believe me, since everyone in Spain who could afford to buy a revolver had one, they pretended to take my word for it.

'These are Don Geraldo's weapons,' said Rosario, coming in with a club of Irish blackthorn which I had carried on patrols during the First World War.

'It's at your service,' I said.

They handled it admiringly.

'*Caramba,* with that one could kill Fascists,' they said, 'But we will not deprive you of it.'

'Of course not,' said Rosario, who had something of the gipsy in her character. 'We need it ourselves. Although you don't know it, Don Geraldo is a greater libertarian Communist than you are.'

A great cloud of smoke now hung over Malaga. With my field glasses I could pick out some thirty or forty houses that were burning. They were setting fire, I was told, to all the houses of the Fascists. After dark it was a splendid sight and we walked down to the church to get a better view of it. A small crowd had collected there to watch, but no one seemed to know any more than we did what was happening. Because the military rising had been suppressed in Malaga, it was assumed that it had failed everywhere. Few of the working classes looked beyond their own province.

That afternoon I decided to walk over to Torremolinos to see if our friends there were safe. A continual stream of cars and lorries filled with armed workmen was tearing along the main road – all in a holiday mood, it is true, but given to pointing their weapons playfully at everyone they passed. As I guessed that few of them had handled a gun before, I preferred to take the track over the hill. I went first to call on our oldest friends there, Mr and Mrs Bush, since they lived on the near edge of the town. She was a voluble and energetic Spanish woman who had once kept a pension in Madrid and he was a silent and dried up New Englander. Neither of them had any sympathy with the Left, so I expected them to be in a state of gloom or alarm, but Mrs Bush was on the contrary in the highest spirits because she had a good story to tell. It seemed that two men from the local *comité* had come to requisition her small car, saying:

'It's for your sake as much as for ours. We need it to defeat the Fascists.'

'How will you use it?' she had asked gravely. 'As a tank?'

'That will be for the *comité* to decide,' they had answered with equal gravity.

'But we are American citizens,' she said. 'It would not do for us to compromise our neutrality.'

So they had gone away. But she had privately decided to hand it over after all because, sick of both military risings and popular fronts, she and her husband intended to leave Spain for good. As a preparation for this she had covered it with a large red sheet and stuck a red stuffed toy monkey on the radiator in place of the St Christopher. She was so pleased with this joke that she took me out to the garage to see it.

As I was leaving we saw a short elderly man standing just outside the gate, staring fixedly at the smoke that was rising over Malaga.

'He's a neighbour of ours,' she said, 'and the reddest Anarchist in the whole of the province. I'm going to speak to him. Listen well – he's sure to say something *gracioso*.'

'Good day, Manolo. How are you?'

'Very well, thank you.'

'And how is the garden?'

'Well also.'

'I thought your maize was looking a little dried up yesterday. I hope you've not forgotten to irrigate it.'

'No, no, it's very well.'

'I'm glad to hear it. And your potatoes? I was thinking of planting mine next week. Is that what you advise?'

'I advise nothing. I am looking at the smoke over there.'

'Oh yes. There seem to be some houses on fire.'

'They are burning down Malaga.'

'Really! How interesting!'

'They are going to burn it till not one stone stands upon another. Where Malaga is today, cabbages and potatoes will grow tomorrow.'

'Well, I've never liked the place very much. But why, can you tell me, are they doing this?'

The man stretched out his hand towards it with a solemn gesture.

'*Te van a destruir, Malaga. Tus vicios te han condenado.* Your last hour has come.'

'I'm delighted to hear it. I daresay we shall all be much better without it.'

'Another Isaiah,' I said when we had walked on. 'His language was quite biblical.'

But Mr Bush did not agree with me.

'Isaiah,' he said, the American capitalist coming out in him, 'never said a word against property.'

It was not the moment to start an argument on Bible texts so I said good-bye to them. But before I had gone more than a hundred yards I heard a shout and a bullet whistled close to my ear. Two men with rifles came up with their barrels covering me and I explained that I was English.

'Then walk more carefully,' they said. 'We thought you were a Fascist.'

'You might have spoken before you fired,' I said, and they agreed and offered to escort me past the next sentry.

I now went to call on Johnny Churchill. I found him walking up and down in front of his house, got up in a West End suit and velours hat and carrying a silver-topped cane.

'What's all this going on here?' he asked in his best Bertie Wooster manner. 'I've just been up to the main road and I find it crowded with armed workmen. What on earth do they think they're doing?'

He had been painting in his studio and had no idea that anything out of the ordinary had happened. I explained, and pointed to the smoke rising from Malaga, which he had not noticed.

'But how very peculiar!' he said. 'They've set fire to their own city, have they? Really I call that an extraordinary thing to do. Carrying eccentricity a bit far, don't you think?'

I said I thought he should go in and change into his ordinary working clothes.

'I think too,' I added, 'that it would be better if you didn't wear a tie, especially not a bow tie. They are regarded as being a sign of having fascist sympathies.'

'Well, of course you know this country better than I do. But I put on these clothes deliberately because I thought they would impress them. After all they are much better clothes than theirs. I can see though that you think they are a little out of place. All right then, I'll change. And meanwhile, I suppose, there can be no objection to our having a drink.'

'That would be very nice.'

'Do you know,' he went on, as he filled our glasses, 'this sort of thing makes me feel terribly English. As a rule when I am in a foreign country I try to forget that and be as the natives are. Eat snails and spaghetti and that sort of thing. But burning one's own city – I find that a bit hard to take. Not what we do at Bognor Regis is it? You've lived here a long time – what's your opinion?'

I left him ruminating over the differences between foreigners and Old Harrovians and went up the street to call on Jay Allen. But on reaching his house I found that he had left in a car for Gibraltar immediately on hearing the news of the rising in Morocco. He had been stopped near La Linea, narrowly escaped being shot as a Fascist and stuck into gaol. His chauffeur had been wounded in the arm, but had somehow managed to get back to Torremolinos with the story. Then I was told that Jan Woolley and her daughter Janetta, aged fourteen, had been caught in Malaga by the rising and had only got back that morning after terrible experiences. I hurried off to see them.

I found them both nervously and physically shattered and with a long story to tell. They had gone to Malaga, as I had done, to do some shopping. Then they had been struck by the state of tension in the city and had decided to return home. As they were on their way to catch their bus they had heard firing and were half way down the Calle Larios – it can only have been a few minutes after I was there – when they saw people starting to run in front of them and then a machine gun opened fire up the street. There was a doorway on the right opposite a café and they bolted in. They went up a staircase and knocked at the first door. There was no answer. Continuing their ascent they found the door on the second floor open, but the people inside slammed it in their faces, so they went on to the third floor, where a kind woman let them in.

The firing continued to be very heavy from the direction of the Aduana. A machine gun occasionally played up the street, though it was quite empty. Then towards nightfall a man appeared dressed in a red shirt with one arm tied up in a blood-stained sling. In his other he carried a tin of petrol. He threw some of it against the door of a shop that stood just across the street and set a match to it. It caught. As the flames mounted he performed a sort of dance of joy in front of it. Then, lurching and capering, he crossed the street towards them and threw the rest of his petrol against a bookshop – it was the same one I had visited a few hours before – which was next door to the house in which Jan Woolley and her daughter were sheltering, but separated from it by a narrow alley. After that he disappeared.

Both these houses blazed up quickly. The heat from the bookshop soon became very great and set fire to the tarpaulin of the café below. But now the soldiers, driven back from the Aduana building, had taken possession of the street. Pickets were posted in the side turnings and the officers walked up and down between the fires as though nothing was happening. The people in the flat with Mrs Woolley knew some of them and leaned out of the windows to talk to them. By this time the rifle and machine gun fire had ceased. Soon the soldiers began to dribble away and the officers vanished too.

Meanwhile the flames from the bookshop were making the heat almost unbearable and then the café below them caught as well and they saw that if they did not leave they would be burned alive. So they broke down the partition into the next house with a coal hammer and went on breaking down partitions till they had moved some way down the street. Hardly any of these expensive flats were occupied for their owners had been warned in time and had left for Gibraltar. But in some of the houses people had been shooting from the roof and Jan Woolley had the impression that that was why the family below had refused to receive them.

The rest of that night passed quietly except for the roaring of the flames which was so loud that one had to shout to make oneself heard, while the air was so suffocating that it made sleep out of the question. Then at dawn there was a terrifying moment. From the small streets that gave on to the Plaza de la Constitución on their left, a dense mass of workmen began to emerge, all armed and carrying red flags and marching steadily forward. As they marched they shouted and sang, yet the sound that rose from this angry pack was not like a human sound, but had the rhythmical whirring of a dynamo.

Straight forward they came, completely filling the broad street and then paused at a house. The door was broken in, the rooms were quickly searched and after that petrol was thrown on the furniture and it was set on fire. What struck Jan Woolley most was the methodical way in which they went to work. The houses were deliberately selected and the people in them warned before they were set on fire. Later the fire-engine arrived and stood by to prevent the flames from spreading to the adjoining houses. The principle of selection was not clear. No doubt it was usually the houses belonging to prominent right-wingers that were chosen, but sometimes it seemed that houses were burned because people had been seen firing from them. Jan could clearly see men running along the roofs and firing into the packed crowd in the street below.

By eight o'clock the mob had moved on to another part of the town and left the street to burn by itself. Jan and her daughter decided to get out and make a run for it, while their hosts, who had throughout treated them with great kindness, preferred to remain where they were. So they helped them drop through a window onto a lane at the back. Their immediate problem was to find a hotel where they could get some coffee and rest, but Jan did not know her way about the town and spoke little Spanish. They ran into an Englishman, apparently one of the local businessmen, but he was in a hurry and did not offer to escort them to a place of safety. Then a Spanish workman took them under his protection and led them to a hotel close to the cathedral. Here they felt safe. Coffee was being prepared and they had been given a room when one of the incendiary parties arrived and ordered the hotel to be evacuated because they were going to set fire to the Conservative press next door and there was a danger that the hotel might catch.

They then decided to get back, if they could, to Torremolinos. Again a workman came forward as a protector and tried to find them a taxi, and, when that failed, to procure them a lift on one of the armed patrol lorries, but none of them had any room. So there was nothing for it but to walk. Since the main road seemed too public, they decided to make their way along the beach. But their adventures were not over yet. As they passed the fishermen's shanty town on the shore they were mobbed by women demanding money and did not get away till they had parted with all they had. Then they had to wade the river, but on arriving at the sand spit on the other side found it occupied by a herd of black bulls. This meant a detour inland to the railway bridge, after which they followed the line till they came to Torremolinos. Altogether a distance of ten miles on rough ground.

The afternoon was drawing on and if I wanted to get home before dark I should have to start at once. My way lay over low hills of red earth planted with olive trees. On my left the mountain was hung with deep shadows like folds on thick cloth, while on my right I could see the sea, flat and smooth like a slab of marble and of so deep and rich a cobalt that is suggested less an element in Nature than a rare and precious *objet de luxe*. A patrol of two men armed with shotguns stopped me, but let me pass. Then I saw a column of smoke rising in front of me. On reaching the brow of the hill I perceived that it came from a large country house whose owner, Don Eugenio Gross, a genial but hasty-tempered man, was unpopular with his workmen.

When I got home my wife told me that a patrol had been round searching for arms. They had been very polite, explaining that they were acting under orders, and she had told them to search where they wished. They had begun with our bedroom where the first drawer they opened contained women's underclothes. Turning rather red, they closed it at once and went into my daughter's room where they pulled out a drawer containing headless dolls. Embarrassed again by this intrusion into family privacy, they expressed themselves satisfied.

'Don't give up so soon,' said Maria in her usual ironical tone. 'In the end you'll come on a heap of revolvers and bombs.'

But they felt they had done enough and left with many apologies to my wife for disturbing her.

A rumour had been going round that morning that they were going to burn some houses in our village and in particular that of Don Antonio Villa which stood next to ours. I had scarcely got back from Torremolinos when a lorry full of armed workmen drew up at the door with the apparent intention of carrying this out. I went out to protest, saying that unless they brought the fire-engine from Malaga our house would catch too. Why didn't they burn the furniture as a gesture and use the building for housing poor families? Possibly my words had some effect, for after arguing a bit among themselves they went off and I later gathered that a decision had been reached to burn no more houses. Indeed the only house to be fired outside the city was that of Don Eugenio Gross.

On the following morning Gamel and I decided to go into Malaga and find out for ourselves what had happened. The buses were not running yet, but we got a lift on a lorry. The city presented a strange and melancholy aspect. Half the houses in the Calle Larios were charred and smoking ruins, among these being the house over the café where Jan Woolley and her daughter had passed such a terrible night. Almost every house that was still intact had its balcony hung with red cloth. There were very few people in the streets and some of those I saw were not reassuring. An elderly workman with a withered hand, dressed in a red shirt and carrying a rusty iron bar, followed us up the street, shaking his bar and shouting, 'Look, look.' He was drunk and perhaps mad as well for it seemed that in the confusion some of the lunatics had escaped from the asylum as well as all the prisoners from the gaol. A few shops were open but no cafés or taverns as these had been closed by order of the Civil Governor. The churches had a notice chalked on them, 'Respect the property of the people' and signed C.N.T. and F.A.I. None of them had been burned, for Malaga had already had its orgy of church burning in May 1931, when some thirty churches and convents had been set on fire by Anarchists, and this was no doubt thought to be enough. In the era of *Comunismo Libertario* that was now coming in the churches would be found useful as meeting halls and cinemas where the marvels of Nature would be displayed to working-class audiences.

Outside the British consulate I ran into an English businessman whom I knew slightly. The expression on his face reminded me of those I had seen during the war on officers coming out of trenches after a nasty bombardment. He looked, to coin a needed word, revolution-shocked. He told me that most of the large villas in the rich suburb of the Limonar had been set on fire and that his wife had been in hysterics. A British destroyer, he said, had just arrived from Gibraltar to take off the first batch of English people and the Foreign Office had issued orders that everyone was to leave. 'Why?' I asked. 'Oh well,' he answered, 'you can't have British subjects left to the mercy of these Reds.'

I went into the Consulate. The Vice-Consul, Mr Clissold, was working calmly at his table as he would continue to do during all the alarms and bombardments of the following months. Outside his door there was a queue of Britishers who wished to leave in the destroyer. I went into the British Club upstairs and took out a membership to it. The battle between the troops and the *Guardias de Asalto,* aided by the workers, had taken place in the Parque just outside and the walls were riddled with bullet holes and most of the panes broken. I could not understand how such a large number of shots had risen to the third floor, but later I was told that unless one was well trained in firing a submachine gun, the barrel worked up.

The club was packed with people waiting to get passes for the boat. Some of them, especially the women, were in a very overwrought state. They imagined that people were being taken out and murdered all the time. The Reds, in their view, were burning, killing and looting to their hearts' content, which at this time was not true. No one had yet been killed in cold blood. That did not begin till July 26th, eight days after the rising, and then mainly as a reprisal for the air raids and for what was happening in Seville. Nor had there been any looting. As an example of the kind of thing that happened, the principal grocer in the city was a Catalan who was greatly disliked because he drove away with insults the poor who came round to his shop begging. I had seen him behaving in this way and it is something that is not done in Spain. As a punishment his house was cere-monially burned with all its stores of tins and hams and delicacies while a hungry crowd stood round and watched without appropriating anything. When I asked why the food had not been distributed I was told in a severe tone that that would have been stealing. But it would have been useless to tell these panic-stricken Britishers this, for they only believed what their fears suggested to them. Thus I had to listen to a long, excited story from a woman who said she could hear the executions going on all night, when what she was hearing was the exchange of fire between the police and the soldiers. At last I said, 'Well, after all, it was the military who started it.' But she had not taken that in. All she knew was that there was a Red Revolution. It was this crowd of terrified, hysterical people who, arriving that evening at Gibraltar, in a medium that was already strongly sympathetic to the insurgents, was responsible for the first batch of atrocity stories that reached the British Press.

I left this distasteful scene to see whether I could find someone who would give me a clearer picture of what had happened on the evening of the rising. I learned that the strength of the troops who had marched into the city had been under two hundred. The men, who were young con-scripts, had been told by their officers that in consequence of the rising in Morocco on the previous day the Government had ordered military law to be proclaimed from the Civil Governor's office in the Aduana building. The plan had broken down because the troops had taken so long to reach it that both the authorities and the workers' syndicates had been fore-warned. Thus on reaching the Aduana they found it defended by the Assault Guards and a furious exchange of fire ensued that went on for hours. Messages passed under white flags and in the end the men melted away and the officers surrendered on the promise of their lives being spared – a promise which incidentally was not kept. I learned later that the casualty list from these hundreds and thousands of shots was one soldier killed and a few from both sides wounded. Such are the battles of the Andalusians!

We got back to Churriana that evening without difficulty to find that nothing had happened in our absence. Then on the following morning we set out again for Torremolinos as Gamel wished to see Jan Woolley. We found that Jay Allen had got back from La Linea but was leaving again at once for Estepona, where he had arranged for a fisherman to take him to Gibraltar. As a parting present he gave us his small radio. We carried this back and almost my most vivid recollections of the Civil War are of listening to it. Every evening round nine we tuned in.

'Radio Barcelona speaking. Radio Barcelona speaking. Order has been restored here. Order has been completely restored here. The aeroplanes of the people of Democratic Spain have just left to bomb Saragossa. Order has been restored. Anyone firing from roof tops, anyone keeping his shutters closed, anyone not giving up his arms or sheltering Fascists will be dealt with summarily ... '

The shrill, high-pitched voice of the Barcelona announcer and his short phrases repeated like an incantation gave a terrifying picture of war and calamity. The Madrid station was calmer. The announcer spoke in correct, unhurried tones, almost as soothing and complacent as those of the B.B.C. But the frequent interruptions in the programme, the instructions for catching people who were firing from roofs and the immediate contradiction of everything said by Lisbon or Burgos were less reassuring. One evening at midnight the President of the Republic, Don Manuel Azaña, spoke. He made a moving speech, calling for firmness and resolution to meet an unprovoked rebellion by the armed forces of the state and offering the hope of liberty and justice for everyone, whatever his sympathies or opinions.

The only rebel station we could hear was Seville. Here the star performer was that amazing radio personality, General Queipo de Llano, who by his dash and energy had won the key city of Seville for the insurgents with only a handful of troops. His broadcasts, which were given late at night, were preceded by an introduction designed, like the rattle of castanets in the wings before the *bailarina* appears on the stage, to raise expectations.

'In five minutes the Most Excellent General Queipo de Llano, commanding the forces of the Army of Salvation in Southern Spain, will begin to speak ... In three minutes the Most Excellent General ... In one minute ... '

Then there would be the sound of someone coming in quickly, a question to his staff – 'They are waiting, are they?' and he would begin.

He was a magnificent broadcaster. His whole personality, cruel, buffoonish, satirical but wonderfully alive and actual came through on the microphone. And this was because he did not attempt any oratorical effects, but simply said what came into his head. His whisky voice, though we were later told that he did not drink, added to the effect. He sat there in full dress uniform, with all his medals on his chest and his staff, similarly attired and drawn up behind him, but he was completely natural and at ease. Sometimes, for example, he could not read his notes. Then he would turn to his staff and say, 'I can't read this. Is it five hundred or five thousand Reds we have killed?'

'Five hundred, *mi general.*'

'Well, never mind. Never mind if this time it's only five hundred. For we are going to kill five thousand, no five hundred thousand. Five hundred thousand just to begin with, and then we'll see. Listen to that, Señor Prieto. I think I can hear Señor Prieto listening in spite of, what shall I say? his hm, hm, *girth,* due to those hm hm, millions of pesetas of Government money he ate the other day and hm, hm, the terrible fear he is in that we shall catch him. Yes, Señor Prieto, listen hard, five hundred thousand to begin with and when we catch you, before we finish with you, we are going to peel you like a potato.'

His broadcasts were stuffed with scurrilous anecdotes, jokes, insults, absurdities, all wonderfully alive and vivid but horrifying when we realized the mass executions that were going on all round him in that city where every workman was either an Anarchist or a Communist and of which fugitives were bringing us reports. Certain figures appeared in his broadcasts every night – Prieto, the most moderate of Socialists, in the guise of fat *cacique* or racketeer and La Pasionaria as a prostitute escaped from a brothel. All the Right believed this, though actually she was the wife of a miner and a woman of an austere life. Her name had been given her for her passionate oratory.

But Queipo de Llano could not endure the Falange, though he had occasionally to allow them to broadcast. On one occasion he made a slip and said, in place of *canalla Marxista, canalla Fascista.* A pained voice corrected him.

'No, no, *mi general, Marxista.*'

'What difference does it make?' the General said. 'They're both *canaille.*' And then, sweeping on, 'Yes, you Red *Canaille* of Malaga, just you wait till I reach you in ten days time! Just you wait! I'll be sitting in a café in the Calle Larios sipping my beer and for every sip I take ten of you shall fall. I shall shoot ten of you,' shouting at the top of his voice, 'for every one you shoot of ours, if I have to drag you out of your graves to do it.'

Most of his broadcasts ended on this note. '*Canalla Marxista!* I say, *Canalla Marxista,* when we catch you we shall know how to treat you. We shall skin you alive. *Canalla, Canalla!*'

These broadcasts were all the more nauseating when one remembered Queipo de Llano's history. He had no reason to feel any grudge against the Republicans, who had favoured him and promoted him. Till a week or two before he had been on the best personal terms with Prieto, whom he now addressed so brutally. He had been a Republican since the fall of the Monarchy, had sworn allegiance to the Government, which had trusted him – and then broken his oath and betrayed them. Such are the people who come to the front in civil wars and revolutions, where ambition conquers every other feeling. Yet it must be said in defence of his broadcasts, which by the fear and anger they caused did so much to provoke reprisals on the other side, that he was holding down a city where all the working classes were hostile with (till a contingent of the Foreign Legion arrived) a handful of troops of doubtful loyalty, and so felt compelled to rule by terror. Not that he can have disliked doing so for he was a natural sadist and the executions went on without pause for months after his position was safe.

Just six days after the military rising my wife and I took our small daughter on a donkey to Torremolinos. The British tourists there were to be evacuated by a destroyer and Jan Woolley had offered to take her back and look after her till we returned. On our arrival we found them assembled with their luggage in front of the one and only hotel, the Santa Clara, which the place provided. The destroyer was lying off the shore but, being a warship, it could not land a boat without a special authority from Malaga, and that authority had not arrived. This created a storm of indignation among the tourists. 'Disgraceful! British subjects! How dare they treat us like this? What's the Consul doing?' The middle-aged, middle-class women were the loudest in their complaints and once again I was made to feel ashamed of being English. Their utter selfishness, their inability to feel the least sympathy for the plight of this unhappy country, their concern for themselves and their possessions alone was nauseating. They provided a vivid illustration that this, the Munich era, was one of the lowest and most deplorable epochs of British history. Then word came that the embarkation was to take place, not that evening at Torremolinos, but on the following morning at Malaga. The destroyer began to move off while one lonely figure, Johnny Churchill, standing by himself on the beach, held up his hand and uttered the word 'Stop'. After this two polite young workmen from the local *comité* arrived to say that everything had been arranged, that buses would arrive within the hour and that everyone would be lodged free of charge in a hotel in Malaga, where the British Consul would personally watch over them. How well, I thought, Spanish calmness and politeness contrasted with the fuss and bad manners of my compatriots!

The war was now beginning for us in earnest. One afternoon, as we were having tea in the garden, a plane passed overhead and dropped some bombs about fifty yards away. But they were only the size of hand grenades and, falling in the soft earth, did no harm. On the following day some larger bombs were dropped, damaging a few houses in the village but injuring no one. However they caused great panic among the female population. From now on, whenever the sound of a plane was heard, there would be a rush of black skirts for our house because it offered fair protection. There they would squat on the floor, groaning and wailing, and giving out the disgusting stench that great fear produces.

Meanwhile the men had been enlisting in a volunteer force which the Civil Governor had supplied with rifles, and a few infantry sergeants were endeavouring to train them. But time was short and after an hour or two of arms drill they were sent up in lorries to the front. Soon, according to the local paper and to the radio, they were advancing gloriously towards Cordoba and Granada, which were held by the insurgents. Then however, their progress was checked by small posts of Civil Guards. To judge by the press accounts, the fighting had taken on a medieval character. We read of Moorish castles and watch towers being besieged and when, in a sudden advance, Puente Genil in the province of Cordoba was captured, it was proudly announced that after the war it would be annexed to Malaga. It was a local war that we were fighting, as in the days of the Arab *taifa* kingdoms, and our enemies were Cordoba and Granada. What happened in the rest of Spain did not concern us.

The militia did not impress me as a fighting body. In the first place they were totally untrained and many of them did not know even how to fire their rifles. Then the Andalusians have never had much reputation as soldiers. There was little enthusiasm to be seen among the men, who wanted to fight the war in their own streets and town rather than outside it, besides which the Anarchist principle of freedom of choice was a handicap. A man volunteered to join, but he could also volunteer to quit and I spoke to one militiaman who, on hearing a bullet whizz by him, had got up and gone home without any objection being raised. Then morale was always bad at Malaga because it was surrounded by the enemy on every side except the east, where a single long corniche road following the sea coast connected it with the rest of Republican Spain. It could thus be cut off at any moment, and this led to frequent panics. When one evening it was rumoured that Moorish troops were approaching from Algeciras almost the entire population of Churriana decamped to the mountains and spent the night there. The Moors had a not unjustified reputation for killing and raping.

I had now, on Bertrand Russell's recommendation, been appointed a Special Correspondent for the *Manchester Guardian*. I procured a bicycle and rode into Malaga every day to get news. The bombing had by this time become a daily ritual and the bombs were larger. One hot afternoon – the thermometer stood regularly at over 90° in the shade – I decided to bathe from the wooden pier which then projected into the sea next to the restaurant of Antonio Martín. The battleship *Jaime I* was lying a few hundred yards off the shore when suddenly a couple of planes came over very low and bombs began to fall round it. For some reason it is much more unpleasant to be bombed in the water than on land and I got out quickly. On another afternoon a single plane flew over the city. The broad street where I was walking at once filled with workmen who began firing at it with rifles, shotguns and revolvers. On these occasions there were always accidents. Probably more people were killed by shooting themselves or their friends than by the bombs of the enemy. Indeed one young man, the *novio* of our servant Maria, shot himself dead on our doorstep with his rifle because he had not learned to use the safety-catch.

These air raids, though they did no military damage, provoked a deep anger and a longing for revenge. In reply the Malaga air force of four small passenger planes set out to bomb the Alhambra, close to which a battery of guns was said to have been mounted, and claimed to have hit it, though in fact they had missed. But the people in the streets demanded blood. During the first eight days after the rising, as I have since been able to check, no one had been killed, although the prison had been filled with suspects. Now it began to be mooted about that every time there was an air raid that inflicted casualties some of these prisoners ought to be taken out and shot. At the same time terrorist groups drawn from the F.A.I. began to make their appearance and to drive about the city and the countryside looking for Fascists. Suddenly, within a few days, this word Fascist, scarcely heard before, had come to signify a sort of mythical being, an enemy to the human race, much what the witches had been in the seventeenth century. General Queipo de Llano's nightly broadcasts had naturally played their part by evoking an image of sadistic fury and savagery. Such people must be exterminated.

The first glimpse I got of this sinister side to the revolution came at the very end of July. An armed lorry of the *Joventudes de la F.A.I.*, or Anarchist Youth, drew up in our village, declaring that they had come to take the local Fascists to the gaol in Malaga. One very unpopular man, a retired *carabinero* or coast guard, had been confined in the village lock-up and, as I was told that they also intended to carry off a friend of mine called Juan Navaja, I hurried up the street to see if I could intervene on his behalf. On arriving I found a lorry crammed with young men, all except one in their teens, got up in red shirts and armed with rifles and submachine guns. Juan had not been found but after a great uproar and many protests from the crowd that had assembled they carried off the *carabinero*. As a guarantee that he would not be shot on the way his wife and daughter were permitted to accompany him. But hardly had the lorry left than the two secretaries of the village *comité* arrived. Enraged at this high-handed way of behaving, they jumped into a car, caught up with the armed lorry and forced the young men to surrender their prisoner. For the principles of *Comunismo Libertario* required that each *pueblo* should be the judge of its own people.

That afternoon the two secretaries of the *comité* came to see me to ask for a subscription to their funds. One of them was a pleasant, well-spoken young man of under thirty, while the other was some dozen years older. Chosen for his eloquence, he might in another age have been a Franciscan friar, with his large moist eyes and soft, pleading way of speaking. They sat down to have a glass of beer with me and I congratulated them on having rescued the *carabinero*.

'I am in favour of killing the really bad,' said the first. 'Death is nothing. It is over in a moment, so why should one fear it? But this *carabinero* was only moderately bad and now that he has had a lesson he may repent and become good.'

His older companion supported him.

'It would have been terrible if they had shot him. He is an *hijo del pueblo,* a son of the village. His family live among us. How could we face them again if we let him be killed?'

And then he began to expatiate in lachrymose tones on the terror through which the poor man must have passed. But perhaps, as I wrote in my diary, there was not so much difference as one might suppose between a sentimental pity of this sort and a sadistic gloating. In revolutionary times, I reflected, one does well to suspect anyone who gets emotional stimulus out of the violent death or suffering of others. In a war between nations that does not happen.

But the *carabinero* had not after all been let off. A few days later the *Joventudes de la F.A.I.* returned in their blood-red shirts and their lorry that bristled with guns and took him away. The two secretaries of the *comité* had been warned that it might be dangerous for them to resist the will of the people and had left the village so as not to be present. No one else dared to oppose the terrorist gang. As I rode into Malaga on the following day I saw the poor man's body lying crumpled up on the side of the road – no longer a human being but a broken doll.

The people marked out to be killed were not however those whom one would have expected to be chosen. The committees of the *Sindicatos* had not prepared lists of their enemies before the rising. Indeed there was an almost touching naiveté about their ignorance of those whom, on ideological grounds, they ought to make away with. They simply killed the people they disliked, who were usually men of quite humble position who had exercised some tyranny over them. It was as though, in an army mutiny, the sergeant majors had all been shot, but few of the officers. One exception to this was that all priests and monks were killed and also all members of the Larios family, who were the owners of the large cotton mill. In every revolution of the previous century these had been the first to go. But not a landowner was touched. They lived on their estates, which were not large, and were well known to the men who worked for them. There was for example, my neighbour Colonel Ruiz, who was known as the 'Colonel of the million pesetas'. The story told of him was that, when he was serving in the pay department in Morocco, he had been tempted by the sight of a bundle containing a million pesetas worth of notes, had got into his car and driven off with it. Finding himself pursued, he had pulled up at a newspaper kiosk in Larache, wrapped the notes in a waterproof sheet and thrown them on top of it. He was stopped and searched, but as no evidence of guilt could be found against him he was released, only obliged to retire from the army. Two years later he had returned to Larache, found the bundle of notes still on the roof of the kiosk and taken them home. He spent the money on buying a fine estate at Churriana. A few years after this General Primo de Rivera came into power in Spain and he felt it advisable to retire for a time to Paris. But again no evidence against him could be found so he returned to his house where, having meanwhile been widowed, he married his housekeeper. But his marriage, even more then the financial scandal, estranged him from the other members of his class as they would not accept his wife. To pay them out for this he refused to subscribe to the Conservative paper *El Debate* and took in the Liberal *El Sol* instead, although he had no political opinions. This put him in good odour with the Left and when he died at about this time his son, a pleasant, amusing homosexual, inherited his popularity.

A more unusual case, however, was that of the Marqués de las Nieves. He was the eldest son of the Duque de Aveiro who owned a large country seat called El Retiro which had been built by an illegitimate son of Philip IV who became Bishop of Malaga. This house with its famous ornamental garden lay half way between Churriana and Alhaurín de la Torre. The family lived in Madrid and rarely came down to Malaga, while their land, except for their walled in park and garden, was let out to farmers. This meant that they were little known in the district. However a few days before the rising the Marqués de las Nieves arrived at his home.

Now Alhaurín de la Torre was a very Anarchist village where the land was well divided. A certain baker, who was a fanatical member of the F.A.I., was a member of the *comité*. Either from some personal grudge or because he disapproved of marquises, he thought that this young man should be 'taken for a ride'. But the people of Churriana had a traditional antipathy for the people of Alhaurín. This was the normal pattern – every *pueblo* hated its neighbour but had friendly feelings for the next *pueblo* but one. There was therefore a good deal of indignation when it became known that the people of Alhaurín were preparing to take the Marqués's case into their own hands. The question was debated in the *Casa del Pueblo*, the little parliament where village affairs were decided, and as it happened I was present that evening, standing near the door. The older lachrymose secretary addressed the assembly. This so-called *marqués,* he said, did not deserve to be hurt. He had shown his goodwill by contributing 200 pesetas to the expenses of the *comité.* When one considered the fact that he had been brought up in vice and idleness, this was a proof that he had a noble nature and was in sympathy with the new era of freedom and brotherhood that was beginning. No one dissented, and it was decided that the village should provide the young man with a permanent guard, which he would of course feed and pay for. So the Marqués de las Nieves survived till, in the general exodus from Malaga as the Italian troops moved in, he was shot by a *camarilla* from Alhaurín.

The baker of Alhaurín, who went by the name of *el Guacho,* the 'messed about person,' had for some time been quite a friend of mine. He made an excellent brown bread which he brought round every day on his donkey and, as he was the first Anarchist I had ever known, I used to draw him into conversation. He was well up in their literature and became very friendly when I told him that I had read one of Kropotkin's books and had even known a friend of his. He was fanatical about everything and especially about food. Wine, coffee and tea were in his opinion pernicious drugs which ought to be forbidden, while meat and fish poisoned not only the physical constitution but the moral one. Indeed he did not even believe that we should eat bread: if we wished, as we ought to, to follow Nature we must live solely on the unfired fruits of the earth.

One morning around this time I caught up with him returning to his village with his donkey and walked alongside him a short way. Somehow the question of the bumpings off by the young men of the F.A.I. came up.

'It's the only thing to be done,' he said, 'with certain incurables. For the sake of everyone we must begin by putting down a few or else we shall never succeed in getting the world into a better state. And why should men mind dying? They do not really mind it, they merely think they do. Life is only good for those who have good natures. Those who are corrupt and bad cannot get any real satisfaction from it.'

'You now say,' I replied, 'that only a few are bad. But when these few have been killed, you will find others. And when they are gone, more again. Once one starts killing the bad, where is one to stop since, as you must agree, all men have a great deal that is bad in them.'

'No, no,' he protested. 'We shall only kill the irreclaimables.'

'Then I daresay,' I answered, 'that you will end by killing me. For although I shall never oppose any regime of freedom and equality, I shall probably find it difficult to acclimatize myself to the life of, say, a field labourer. It is hard suddenly to change one's habits. The rich may be exploiters, yet to throw them suddenly into the street is only to introduce a new tyranny.'

'Ah, but you've got it all wrong,' he said. 'You are thinking of Russian communism, which to us is slavery. You will not be expected to change any of your habits, except perhaps a few which impinge upon the freedom of others.'

'Well,' I replied, 'I'll tell you this. I am an English Liberal and I hate all bloodshed and revolution. I believe that we should aim at changing social conditions gradually with as little use of force as possible. Given a few more years, scientific invention will enable us to abolish poverty and perhaps wealth as well. But now that it has come to revolution, and by the fault of the people on the other side, I hope that you will succeed in your plans and establish libertarian communism. Only I am certain that you will never do it if you kill too many people, because blood calls for blood. You must re-educate your enemies, not destroy them.'

'We shall win,' he said, giving his donkey a kick. 'Justice is in the air. It cannot be denied any longer.'

When six months later the Nationalists entered Malaga *el Guacho* refused to flee but set fire to his house and died in the flames.

One morning at 4 a.m., just ten days after the military rising had broken out, we were awakened by the crash of a large bomb coming from the direction of the military airfield. Hurrying on to the mirador we were just in time to see another bomb burst so far as we could judge on top of the villa which Don Carlos Crooke Larios, the former proprietor of our house, had built for himself adjoining the repair sheds. We threw on a few clothes and started out with bandages and disinfectant to see if anybody had been hurt. But when we arrived we found them all safe, for the bomb had fallen a little short. However their house was too close to the airfield to be pleasant, so we invited them to come and stay with us.

The family consisted of Don Carlos and his wife, with their two daughters and three sons, of whom the youngest was still a child. We soon found that we were lucky in our guests. Don Carlos was a tall, rather heavily built man with a fine Roman nose, a completely bald head and a vivacious almost boyish manner. His wife, Doña Maria Luisa, was one of the nicest women I have ever known. A devoted wife and mother, a good manager and cook, kind and well spoken to everyone and still handsome in spite of her forty odd years. They were a very close and united family, but they had no money. In their efforts to make some they had spent six or seven years sheep farming in Tierra del Fuego, but had returned from those icy regions as poor as they had gone out. After that they had taken up chicken farming. Ostensibly they had come to us to seek a refuge from bombs, but I was gradually to discover that they were even more in need of protection from other things because Don Carlos had been deeply implicated in the rising.

He was a sort of Micawber of a man, overflowing with optimism and high spirits and full of lively and amusing stories about his experiences. One of these concerned the evening of the military rising. He had gone into Malaga, he told us, to visit a friend who kept a hotel and had been stranded there when the firing broke out. While the contest in front of the Aduana was going on, snipers were firing sporadically from the roofs and windows of his street. After a little a body of armed workmen came up and told the proprietor that since someone was shooting from one of his windows they were going to burn down the building. He begged them to search all the rooms before doing so and they did this and found nothing. However, as they were still suspicious, they ordered everyone in the hotel to sit in the doorway so that they could be seen from the street. This was a disagreeable ordeal for people who were known to belong to the Right, but they had no option but to do as they were told.

Don Carlos was an observant man and earlier in the evening he had noticed that someone was firing at regular intervals from one of the bed-room windows. He now kept his eyes open to discover who it was. Of the twenty or so people sitting in front of the hotel one was a woman of about thirty, unmarried, spectacled, who worked as a clerk in the Telegraph Office. He noticed that every now and then she slipped away for a few minutes. Following her up the stairs, he saw her go to a window on the second storey and fire from it with a Browning revolver into the street. He spoke to the proprietor of the hotel and they stopped her as she came down.

'It's not a weapon,' she said, handing it over. 'I use it for shooting dogs with.'

The proprietor unloaded it, cleaned the barrel and handed it to the first patrol that came along.

'She must have been a little mad,' said my wife.

'Mad!' exclaimed Don Carlos. 'Oh no, she was just a typical Spaniard.'

As I have said, I used to ride into Malaga every day on my bicycle and return with the news. Almost every act of vandalism that I reported pleased Don Carlos. When I told him that both the right-wing bookshop and the Conservative Press had been burned to the ground he was enchanted.

'Good,' he exclaimed. 'Good. That will save us the trouble of burning them ourselves.'

I realized from this that he was a Falangist and that he had gone into town on the day of the rising with a revolver in his pocket and the intention of using it if things had gone well. Now every evening he sat glued to the radio listening to Seville. General Queipo de Llano's sadistic broadcasts delighted him, though his wife would not listen to them, exclaiming, *'Qué indecente! Vaya qué chulo!'*

Up to this time I had not felt impelled to take sides in the struggle. On the one hand I had no liking for social revolutions and no faith in the practicability of libertarian communism, and on the other I felt a strong antipathy for the insurgent generals. It was they after all who had started this fratricidal war – quite, as it seemed to me, without necessity. Yet why should I, simply on that account, become a partisan in the domestic affairs of a foreign country? But now the broadcasts from Seville were beginning to make me change my mind and incline me more strongly to the Left. The Republicans had no Queipo de Llano. I could not fail to see that the mass shootings that were taking place in Seville were on an incomparably larger scale than anything that was taking place in Malaga and moreover that they had begun from the first moment. While Seville, Cordoba and Granada were being drenched in blood, Malaga was only being sprinkled. I decided therefore that I would be for the side which killed least. The degree of ferocity shown was an inverse pointer to the degree of decency and civilization. Then, though I did not at the time attach so much importance to this, the rebel propaganda was bitterly hostile to the democratic countries. Liberalism, it proclaimed, was the first step to communism: Roosevelt and even Chamberlain were Reds or near Reds. They were shooting, as I knew, everyone who held their opinions. The leaders of the New Europe were Hitler and Mussolini. It seemed clear from this that Nationalist Spain would be on the side of Germany and Italy in the war that I saw was coming and would thus be in a position to close the Mediterranean to our fleet. Yet it was not really considerations of this sort that decided me. My natural sympathies have always lain with the underdog rather than with the oppressors. My feelings, if not always my judgement, were well to the Left. This meant that I should have to take sides with the working classes who were being so cruelly handled even though I had no faith in their blueprints for the future.

Inevitably this decision set up a painful tension in my relations with Don Carlos. He was my guest, he was in danger of his life, he was a very brave man, but he also had a cruel and destructive streak in his nature so that I often found it hard to control myself when listening to his sallies. Yet this was not because he was a Falangist. I knew that José Antonio, the founder of the Falange, was a humane man who had a real concern for the conditions of the working classes and I had read one of his books with interest. Had Don Carlos been a man of that sort I would have sympathized with his ideas even though I would have disagreed with them, as I did with those of the Anarchists. But this man had nothing of the idealist in his nature.

There was in Churriana a man whom I knew well and greatly liked called Juan Navaja. He was the village baker, but he also acted as house agent and in various other capacities. For example it was he who organized the yearly *romería,* turning out for it himself in full Andalusian costume with one of his nieces similarly clad riding pillion behind him. There was something old-fashioned and traditional in his whole bearing: one could imagine him in a play by the brothers Quintero or even in one by Lope de Vega. Discreet, measured, disinterested in the advice he gave, he embodied all the virtues of an Andalusian small-town worthy. It was characteristic of him that he had never married because, his *novia* having died when he was a young man, he had chosen to remain faithful to her memory. In normal times he would have been the most respected and best liked man in the pueblo, but these were not normal times. He stood out against the prevailing views and as a practising Catholic and moderate Conservative had acted as an agent for Gil Robles' party, *Acción Católica,* though, as a prudent man, he had refused to do so or even to vote when feelings ran high at the last election. This support for the Right had been marked down against him. Yet it was not so much this as the fact that he had lent money at a low rate of interest to various people that put him in danger.

It was some time in early August that we learned that he was wanted. Then one evening I got a message asking me to call at his house. I went and found him in a pitiable state. A brave man at ordinary times, his terror had reduced him to a state of utter inertia and indecision, like that of a rabbit mesmerized by a snake. His only companion apart from his niece was an idiot he had befriended, for other people were afraid of being compromised by visiting him. What he wanted of me was that I should take him in and hide him. But I knew that Don Carlos was in equal though less immediate danger, so before giving him an answer I went back to consult the Crooke Larios family about it. We all agreed that if I took in Juan the men of the F.A.I. would immediately hear of it and come for him, and that they would then almost certainly carry off Don Carlos and his grown up sons at the same time. I had therefore to tell Juan that I could not shelter him, but that I would leave the garden door unbolted so that if they came for him in the night he could slip round to my house by the back and conceal himself in the undergrowth. But I strongly advised him to get out of the village at once and either hide in Malaga or try to make his way along the sierra to the insurgent lines beyond Marbella. He was a sportsman and knew the country well.

A few days later we heard that he had been caught and shot. It seems that he had hidden in a cave not far from the village, where his family had brought him food, but that one of the men to whom he had lent money had followed them and betrayed him. When I returned to Spain thirteen years later his brother blamed me for his death, because he imagined quite wrongly that the Union Jack that we had hung from our balcony would prevent our house from being searched.

Meanwhile a number of small signs was showing me that the danger to Don Carlos was growing more pressing. He appeared to be well liked in the village, where he had never taken any open part in politics, and the *comité* had told me that they had nothing against him. During the first days that he had spent with us he had several times walked down the street and people had smiled at him. But then suddenly they began to look the other way. One evening a carpenter I knew who lived in Malaga dropped in to tell me that my protégé had better move somewhere else because he was wanted. One of his surnames was the fatal one of Larios and, though the Falange was a secret organization, it might well have leaked out that he belonged to it. To meet this situation we thought of a ruse. On the following morning I went in with him by the little train to Malaga carrying a suitcase and left him at a cousin's. That night he came back secretly in a taxi, driven by a man he trusted. Meanwhile we had given it out that he had left us.

Yet we could not be sure that this story would be believed. In case our house was searched we arranged a hiding place for him. This was a small alcove in the bathroom, above the false ceiling. The dangerous time was between two and three in the morning. Every night at this hour the patrol lorry of the *Joventudes de la F.A.I.* came up our street and turned round in a drive way that was opposite our house. As soon as Don Carlos heard it he jumped out of bed and clambered into his hiding place.

One morning at dawn there was an air raid over Malaga. My wife and I stood watching it from our bedroom window when a tremendous explosion from the direction of the port shook the air and a heavy column of smoke poured up into the sky. A bomb had hit the petrol and oil dump that supplied the city. To get a better view we went up on to the mirador and there we found Don Carlos and his sons jumping about in glee in a way that was plainly visible from the street below. He was even calling out the Nationalist slogan, *Viva España*. I was outraged by this act of madness and a painful scene ensued. I had to point out to him that if they came for him they might well take me too for those who sheltered Fascists incurred the same penalty as those who were Fascists themselves. If I was to continue to take this risk, he must show more discretion. That evening we listened to the B.B.C. telling us that Malaga had 'probably been completely destroyed'.

Soon after breakfast I rode in on my cycle to see the damage. Not all the petrol containers had caught fire. Some were still intact because they were buried underground and hundreds of workmen were engaged, at great risk to themselves, in covering them with wet sand. The heat was terrific and they had taken off their clothes and were working in their underpants. What with the roaring of the flames and the dense clouds of smoke it looked like a scene in Hell. But if some of the petrol had been saved all the heavy oil was lost and continued to burn with a prodigious column of smoke for two or three days. Then on my way back I came on a pitiful sight. A part of *Úngaros* or Hungarian gipsies had been encamped close to the main road with their mules and caravans. Only a few days before I had stopped to talk to them. Now a bomb had exploded plumb in the middle of their encampment just as they were eating their morning meal. Their mangled, blood-stained bodies with the carcasses of their mules were lying around among the black cooking pots. Out of more than forty gipsies only one, a little girl, had survived.

I came back in a nervous, tensed up state. As I reached my house I heard from the street the faint, raucous sound of Seville broadcasting. It was strictly forbidden to listen to any Nationalist station and very dangerous to do so, especially for people in our position. I had explained this to Don Carlos and impressed on him that he must only use the radio, and then turned on low, in one of the back rooms. And here he was for the second time that day acting with a childish irresponsibility. I flew into a rage and said more than I ought to have done. Yet something had to be said for that night three men were taken out of their houses in Churriana and shot. I saw their bodies lying by the roadside the next day.

In all revolutions there occurs a moment of delirium and intoxication when the chains of the past drop away and a golden future stands revealed. Everyone, even the enemies of the new order, are comrades, everyone loves one another. This moment had been exemplified at Malaga by the wild career of the motor patrols on the day following the rising, but the city itself had shown no signs of jubilation. Instead empty streets, charred and smoking houses and glum faces expressed the people's exasperation with the attack that had been made upon them. Only the red flags and draperies hanging from the houses and vehicles told one that a revolution was in progress. A sad sort of revolution in which no one seemed to know what to do or where to go.

But suddenly there was an at least outward change. Almost in a night the red flags vanished and were replaced by Republican ones. This was by order of the Government and was designed to impress the democratic powers upon whose attitude, it was thought, the outcome of the war would depend. Some attempt too was made to repress the unauthorized shootings that, as the military rebellion continued to progress, had begun to increase. Guards were stationed at the doors of the hotels and the centre of the city made safe, even at night time. Yet the killings went on. After every air raid a certain number of men were taken from the prison and shot as a reprisal. This was demanded by public opinion and had to be accepted. But the murders committed by the small terrorist groups were another matter. Although they were now kept out of the centre of the city, these Uncontrollables, as they were beginning to be called, had the run of the suburbs and of the outlying pueblos. The Civil Governor, who had been obliged to send his small police force to the front, could do nothing but appeal to the committees of the Syndicates or trade unions, who were the real rulers of the city. They responded, for they too were opposed to these unauthorized killings, so that Malaga became plastered with notices appealing in the name of the C.N.T. and F.A.I. as well as in that of the Socialists and Communists, for an end to these crimes that 'stained the fair name of the Revolution'. The reason why they went on lay in the nature of the F.A.I. It was not an organized body, but consisted of a number of separate groups with no real cohesion between them and no central authority over them. Probably the majority of its members genuinely disapproved of these killings, but they had no means of controlling the groups which instigated them except by employing force against them. This they were loathe to do. The first casualty in every revolution is moral courage.

The most terrible of the crimes of the murder gangs took place at this time. Three heavily armed lorries of the *Joventudes de la F.A.I.* drove up to Ronda and insisted that the *comité* of that town should hand over to them their prisoners. Others, whose names had been given to them by secret delegates, were included with them, apparently without any further enquiries. They were then taken out and thrown alive over the high cliff that bounds the public gardens. Five hundred and twelve people died in this way, among them some women. Since the fundamental principle of Spanish anarchism was that every pueblo should decide its own life and destiny, these forcible interventions by armed bands from the capital of the province made nonsense of all the Anarchists' claims to establish justice and freedom. Most, though not all, of the murders committed in the pueblos of the province occurred in this way – that is, by intervention from outside.

Another dreadful event of this time was the arrival of the refugees from the large pueblos of the Guadalquivir basin. Driven out by General Varela's 'Army of Salvation', which had advanced eastwards from Seville to open up communications with Cordoba and Granada, they had before abandoning their homes murdered their right-wing prisoners, often in the most terrible manner. In one place they had shut them up in the church and set fire to it. The Nationalist Government later brought out a book on the Red atrocities in Andalusia which I reviewed for the *New Statesman*. I had to admit that its reports were true because I had talked to people who had been present. There was a recurring pattern in these massacres. The Nationalists shot all men who had trade union cards because, being in such a small minority, they felt obliged to rule by terror. The workers imprisoned those of their class enemies whom they knew were hostile to them but, if they were on the point of being overwhelmed, they killed them in the way that came quickest to hand because they knew that if they themselves were caught they would be shot. A little foresight on the part of the military – a radio broadcast offering terms – might have prevented many of these massacres, but they were too full of blood-lust to care about saving members of their own side. They were in the grip of what the Flemings in the reign of Philip II had called the 'Spanish Fury'. So humane on ordinary occasions, Spaniards are prone in times of excitement to a hysterical passion for killing and destruction. And then a long service in the savage conditions of Moroccan warfare had warped the feelings of many of the officers of the African Army.

One day early in August I ran into Sir Peter Chalmers-Mitchell getting off a tram. He was dressed in an immaculate white alpaca suit, complete with a bow tie – the only man in Malaga except the foreign consuls who dared to wear such a bourgeois symbol. When I had last met him we had not talked politics so that I was surprised to hear that he not only sympathized strongly with the Workers' Revolution, but that he had several friends among the Anarchists, including some of the terrorists. At the same time he was sheltering in his house one of the most right-wing families in the city. The Bolíns were *nouveau riche* people whose wealth came from iron mines in the North. One of them, Luís Bolín, was the press chief of the Nationalists. (He was recently brought out a book, translated into English, in which he shows that during the course of the past thirty years he has continued to believe his own propaganda.) Another brother was now in the Malaga gaol and Sir Peter would visit him every day, carrying soap, chocolate and clean socks. On his invitation I went to tea with him at his small villa, which stood on the hill above the fashionable suburb of El Limonar. To reach it I had to pass up the Camino Nuevo where I saw the corpses of around a dozen priests laid out in a row, like the trophies of dead hawks and weasels which gamekeepers hang on branches. The rich and pious were supposed to look and take warning.

The Bolíns struck me as being typical of their kind and class – usually the worst in any country – but I was sorry for them on account of the strain that they were under. Señora de Bolín was expecting every day to hear that her husband had been shot, yet they had to listen to Sir Peter lecturing them on the evils of wealth and of how much happier they would be when they lost it. They had no idea, he assured them, how satisfying it was to cook one's own food and scrub one's own floor. Yet it was Señora de Bolín who was now doing the cooking, not the immaculate Sir Peter, whom one could not imagine dirtying his hands by any sort of rough work.

I cannot say that I liked him, although in the past I had enjoyed his conversation about zoos and animals. The moving spring in his character was his hatred of his father. Because he had gone to kirk, his son had become a passionate atheist. He seemed to be puritanical about sex but held extreme views in politics, wishing to see a thoroughgoing social revolution in England, though not taking any active part in bringing one about. He told me a story that illustrates both his Scottish closeness about money and his fanaticism. Walking down Oxford Street one day he had been waylaid by a group of ex-soldiers wearing their medals and playing on brass instruments.

'What will you do,' he had said, 'if I give you money? Will you spend it on bombs and revolvers? No, you will not, so I shan't give you anything.'

Yet his principal task when he had been secretary of the Zoological Society had been raising money to pay for the setting up of a zoo at Whipsnade. In pursuance of this he had frequented the houses of the rich, lunching and dining with them but concealing his revolutionary opinions. His manner showed that he was very much at home in that world. Tall and thin, with a red face, small mouth and white hair, he had a soft, persuasive way of speaking. No one meeting him socially could have imagined the fanaticism this gentle manner concealed.

Later I met him several times at the Spanish Embassy in London, where I gathered that he had drawn close to the Communist Party. The last occasion was after the publication of my book, *The Spanish Labyrinth*. In his sweet tone of voice he told me that he had found several parts of it interesting, but that I had made one capital error. There were no differences whatever, he said, between the Anarchists, the Socialists and the Communists. There were only the exploiters and the exploited.

All this time I had been trying to find a way of getting Don Carlos and his family out of the country. It was not easy. One could buy false passports, but they would be of no use because he was well known by sight. Could I though procure him a genuine foreign passport? His elder sons were both Chilean subjects because they had been born in Tierra del Fuego while he himself had once acted as Chilean Consul in the Argentine. I applied therefore to the Argentine Consul, who also represented Chile, and he cabled to Santiago to ask if he might issue him with one. But the reply was that he could not. I now approached the Civil Governor of Malaga and got from him a paper allowing Don Carlos to leave the country, but this was of no value unless it had been stamped by the Committee of Public Safety, which had recently been set up. Would it be wise to approach a committee that had such an ominous name? As it happened, Don Carlos had once worked on the Municipality with a Republican who, he thought, might have some influence. I went to see him and found that he was only too willing to help. Like all Spanish liberals he was appalled by the situation while his daughter, who kept house for him, was in a state of abject terror, equally afraid of the Anarchists and of the Nationalists. Don Francisco, hoping no doubt to find a protector for the day when the military took over, promised to do what he could.

Meanwhile the Chilean government had begun to interest itself in the expatriation of those Spanish families which contained a person of Chilean birth, provided they were not of military age. This allowed the Consul for the Argentine to make out for us a document which, though without legal authority – for it was only a recommendation – might serve our purpose. I got it stamped at the Civil Governor's office and through Don Francisco by the *Comité de Enlace*. This seemed sufficient, so, as an American destroyer was leaving for Gibraltar on the following day, we decided to take Don Carlos in with his family and put them on it. But how should we get to Malaga? Taxis were now being stopped and searched, so we decided to leave openly by the early morning train. As we walked down the village street we came in for some sinister glances, but no one stopped us and we reached Malaga in safety. Here I took Don Carlos at once to the British Club and left him there. Later I learned that we had left Churriana only just in time for within an hour of our doing so three heavily armed men of the F.A.I. had knocked at our door and asked for him.

After a quick snack we all set off for the docks, accompanied by both the American and the Argentine Consuls. The former, after a glance at Don Carlos's document, said he saw little hope of getting him past the barrier, so the long wait in the shed where the emigrants' papers were being examined, while the thermometer stood at near 100°, was pretty nerve-racking. Then, when Don Carlos's turn came, they refused to let him pass. Some other permit was needed.

But the Argentine Consul was indomitable. Jumping into a taxi we drove together to Don Francisco's house. We woke him from his siesta and bore him off to the office of the Committee of Public Safety, which luckily was open. Here the Consul, who was an indefatigable talker, launched into a stream of eloquence about the need of the Spanish government for creating a good impression abroad and especially in Chile. The tired men sitting round the table gave way and made out the pass. We drove back to the docks, where the destroyer was waiting for us, and Don Carlos and his family embarked. The date was August 26th. They had been with us just a month.

On the following morning we were awakened by some heavy bombs falling in front of our house. One of them broke the window and cracked the tall looking glass that stood by our bed. What could they be aiming at? I went down the street to see if any damage had been done. A boy had been killed and his body lay by the roadside surrounded by a group of people. His mother was kneeling with his head on her lap and the tears were streaming down her face.

'Cursed be the war,' she said, 'and cursed the Fascists who made it. What need had they to come and kill my son?'

That afternoon Gamel and I again went in by train to Malaga. We were sitting in a café when we saw at the table next to ours a fair-haired young man with a chubby innocent face which told us at once that he was English. We spoke to him and learned that he was a correspondent of an English newspaper. He had just arrived by car from Valencia and found it difficult to understand what was going on because he spoke hardly any Spanish. Was it true that the people here were all Anarchists? He seemed so lost in this unfamiliar environment that when he asked us to have dinner with him at his hotel and explain the situation to him we accepted.

We had finished eating and were sipping our coffee in the glass-covered patio when the lights went out. Then we heard the drone of a plane overhead, followed by the crash of a large bomb. At once the atmosphere in the hotel changed. The previously friendly waiters began to glower at us with suspicion as though we were in some way responsible. Angry, excited voices came from the street and armed patrols rushed by in their cars. Our young journalist jumped up with the intention of following them on foot, but it was not a night for a foreigner to be wandering about alone so I entrusted him to one of the motor patrols who promised to take him to where the bomb had fallen.

Since we now had no means of getting home, we asked for a room. In a harsh, angry voice the manager replied that he had only one, which he usually reserved for honeymoon couples, and that we would have to pay a good price for it. He then showed us into an apartment decorated with a pattern of gold and rose and containing a double bed hung with muslin curtains. Two large windows gave on to the Alameda. But it was not exactly a room in which to spend a night of air raids, for the ceiling was a shallow dome of glass through which I could see the full moon shining down on us. There we lay all night, listening to the drone of mosquitoes humming round us and to the more sinister drone of the Junkers circling overhead. Every time a bomb fell there were cries of 'Bring out the Fascists' and rightly or wrongly I got the impression that an armed gang was dragging people out of their houses. Next morning as we were having breakfast the young journalist reappeared. He had seen the mangled bodies of a few bomb victims and then those of forty men who had been taken out of the prison at dawn and shot as a reprisal. They had been lying in an open trench in the cemetery.

A couple of days later we were in Malaga again when we ran into another English journalist. He was a tall, extremely good looking young man with fair hair and blue eyes whom I vaguely remembered to have seen at a London party some years before. He introduced himself as Hugh Slater and said that he was acting as a correspondent for the *Daily Worker*. We had a drink together and he came out to our house for the night. He told us that a couple of years before he had become convinced of the frivolity of his way of life and had joined the Communist Party. They had sent him to live in the East End, which had completed his conversion because he had found the dockers to be more friendly and decent people than the raffish, arty set he had mixed with before. They had changed his views in many ways: for example, since his public school days he had hated and despised football – now he never missed the opportunity of watching a match. I found his gaiety and high spirits a great relief from the gloomy faces around us and yet there was an underlying sanctimoniousness about him which suggested the young curate who had just found God.

But it was a strange sort of sanctimoniousness. On his way down the coast from Valencia he had witnessed an execution and seen the bodies of those who had been 'taken for a ride' laid out along the edge of the road.

'I find one doesn't mind the bumpings off as much as one expected to,' he remarked in a cheerful tone. 'One learns to see them in their context.'

I said nothing, but I found that I minded them more with each day that passed.

One thing about him puzzled me. When I had met him before he had been called Humphrey. I asked him about this and he said that on joining the Party he had changed his name to Hugh because it sounded less feudal. When after the Nazi-Soviet pact he left the Party with John Strachey he changed it back to Humphrey again.

His account of the policy of the Communist Party was interesting, for it was not what at that time anyone had been led to expect.

'We are trying,' he said, 'as far as we can to protect the middle classes and rally them round us and incidentally to protect the Church as well. Also of course to put a stop to the illicit executions. This is not the moment to push on with a Socialist revolution. Victory in the war must come first.'

He was travelling in an old Rolls-Royce with a Spanish interpreter and wanted to have a look at the Antequera front. Since I was acting as a correspondent for the *Manchester Guardian,* he invited me to come along with him. We drove to the summit of the pass next to the Torcal, which was the front line. Three or four militia men were sitting there with a machine gun and a dozen others were in a hollow several hundred yards behind. The enemy lines were on the plain several miles away, but no patrols were being sent out. No trenches had been dug and, worst of all, not a single bridge on the narrow mountain road had been blown up. It was obvious that a few tanks and a battalion of infantry could reach the suburbs of Malaga whenever they pleased. The men looked bored and showed no sign of enthusiasm or of fighting spirit.

The time had now come for us to leave Malaga. My account in the bank was almost exhausted and I had no way of getting money in from England. I therefore gave our servants all I could spare and on September 7th we left for Gibraltar in an American destroyer.

We found the Rock packed with rich Spanish refugees, waiting till they could return to their homes. Among them was Don Carlos, who told me that he was working for the Nationalist Intelligence. I asked him when he returned to Malaga to protect Don Francisco, to whom he owed his life and who was in any case not a Red but a harmless liberal, trapped in a situation which he hated.

'He'll be shot all right,' Don Carlos answered breezily. 'We are going to shoot everyone who worked for the Reds.'

In ordinary time he was not an inhumane man, but in this war the words humanity and gratitude had ceased to have any meaning.

The English people we met were all strongly on the side of the insurgents. Perhaps this was natural, for in colonial life class-feeling is very strong and, as the spirit of Munich was already in the air, the Nationalists' admiration for Nazi Germany and their openly proclaimed contempt for the democratic nations passed unregarded. But their appetite for atrocity stories, where all the horrors were attributed to the Reds, was less agreeable. We had already noticed something of this in Malaga, but here, where it was less excusable, it was rampant. It was what my wife aptly described in her book *Death's Other Kingdom* as the pornography of violence.

It emanated too from the highest places. When that winter I got back to England my father hired a horse for me and I had a couple of days hunting. At a meet near Painswick I met an intelligent colonel of the Royal Engineers who was curious to have my impressions on the events in Spain.

'I had a letter the other day,' he said, 'from General Sir Charles Harrington, the Governor of Gibraltar. He told me among other things that the Reds had laid naked nuns down in the main street of the town and run a steam roller over them. Can that be true?'

'I hardly think so,' I replied, 'because Malaga did not possess a steam roller.'

In fact no nuns were killed at Malaga, either while I was there or later.

We had not been long in Gibraltar before we ran into Jay Allen. It was a pleasure to hear his kindly, tolerant, Western voice again. Since I had last seen him he had been to Morocco, where Franco had given him an interview, and after that to Portugal, from which he had secretly crossed into Spain to investigate the truth about the Badajoz 'massacre' by Colonel Yagüe's legionnaires. The number of those killed in the bullring had been put very high in the British and Portuguese Press but Jay reduced it to around two thousand. When I repeated this to an Englishman who got his views from the *New Statesman* his face fell. He would have preferred the larger figure because it made better propaganda.

Don Carlos had told me that Jay was followed about in both Gibraltar and Tangier by three *requetés* who had the Sacred Heart of Jesus embroidered on their breasts with orders to bump him off if he went into a lonely street. He seemed to think such procedure right and normal since he had written against them. I repeated this to Jay who told me that he had suspected it and taken precautions. He now asked me if I would go to Tangier and take his place there as a correspondent for the *News Chronicle*, since he was leaving at once for Toledo and Madrid. It was thought that there might at any moment be a rising of the Moors in the Spanish Zone, in which case the French would probably occupy it in the name of the Sultan. But he wanted me first to fly to Lisbon to investigate the mutiny in the Portuguese fleet which had just broken out and been suppressed. We therefore took the next boat to Tangier and went on next morning by a small Portuguese plane to Lisbon. Gamel, who seemed to be enjoying this life of adventures, insisted on coming with me.

After landing at the airport we took a taxi to the house of the representative of Vickers Maxim, who Jay had told me was a Communist. Every hundred yards the driver stopped to whisper our destination to a police agent in plain clothes. The government was evidently solving its unemployment problem by enrolling a sizeable proportion of the male population in that service. On our arrival we found the house heavily guarded and the man we wished to see in hiding, so we made our way on foot to the second address we had been given. It was that of a family of Jewish descent who owned large properties in the Azores. We were welcomed by a cultivated old gentleman of liberal views and by his son and daughter-in-law, who appeared to be Communists. The house was luxurious, the meal they offered delicious and I came away with all the information I required.

A certain English newspaper had a woman correspondent at Lisbon who ran an entrepot of Red atrocity stories. She got them from the Nationalist press agent and passed them on to London. Had she talked to the Portuguese journalists, who were the only foreign correspondents who were allowed to accompany Colonel Yagüe's column, she would have got atrocity stories of a different brand, but it was not in her plan to report any of those committed by the Nationalists nor, no doubt, did her employers wish her to do so. An atrocity, to have the right sadistic flavour, had to be a Red one.

I had intended out of curiosity to pay a visit to this lady, but she was out when we called and we had to catch the next plane back to Tangier.

The café on the Petit Socco was packed with the glum, despondent faces of Spanish Republicans and Socialists. The town was also overrun by Nationalist agents and gunmen so that any person connected with the Left who strayed into the suburbs ran the risk of being kidnapped and taken across the frontier. The Italians had filled their big new legation with Blackshirts and the warships of half a dozen nations lay in the harbour in case trouble should break out. Spies of all sorts abounded and the brothel and blue cinema run by the Hon. Mrs X. for the benefit of visiting liners was doing a brisk trade. But I had not come to Tangier for pleasure. My job was to get information about what was going on in the Spanish zone and since the frontier was closed to all traffic the problem of how to do so seemed at first insurmountable. In the end however I found a one-eyed Moor whose business took him across it twice a week. I met him regularly at a shop in the Petit Socco and he provided me with a stream of news about the unrest of the tribes which I daily passed on to my newspaper. However, since I could find no way of checking what he said, I gradually became suspicious. There seemed more than a whiff of the One-Eyed Calendar of the *Arabian Nights* about him. I went therefore to the French Legation and had a talk with their Intelligence attaché.

'But how have you found out all this?' he asked in surprise. 'Your picture coincides with ours.'

I told him about my one-eyed Moor and he exclaimed, 'Why, he's our agent. He has no business to sell his information to you. However, since he has done so, I will say that you can trust his reports implicitly. He has ways of finding out what is going on among the natives.'

From that time on I believed everything the Moor told me.

Then one day early in October I got the news that I had been waiting for. The Beni Uriaguel were up in arms, the Gomara had joined them and were besieging Tarquist. All the tribes of the Spanish zone had risen against the Spaniards. After checking this news at the French Legation I sent off a report which got headlines on the front page of the *News Chronicle,* and waited. And then nothing happened. The one-eyed Moor had vanished and it gradually became clear that I had been the victim of a hoax. I sent in my resignation as correspondent to the paper and left with Gamel on a sightseeing trip for Fez, Marrakesh and Taroudant. By the end of the month we were back in Gibraltar where, since it was impossible to get a passage to Malaga, we took the boat for Plymouth. As we had no winter clothes with us and were short of money, we landed in England wearing long, flowing *djellabas*.

23

Aldbourne

On arriving in England we bought a second-hand Morris car and went on a round of visits to our friends. Llewelyn Powys was preparing to leave for a sanatorium in Switzerland, from which he would obviously never return, so we took lodgings for some weeks at East Chaldon to be near him. I had come to like him much more than I had done at first and to admire the courage and gaiety he showed in his illness. Then after a couple of months at Farnham, where Jan Woolley had put our daughter Miranda to school, we set off for Cornwall and rented a house at Welcombe near Bude on one of the most beautiful and unspoiled stretches of the coast.

Meanwhile I had been caught up in the current of violent feelings about the Civil War that was sweeping through England and could think of nothing else. I began to do propaganda for the cause of the Spanish government. At first I merely wrote letters to the papers, as a rule in answer to others sent in by supporters of the Nationalists. These tended to be from Catholics and although it seemed to me perfectly natural that they should hate a regime which had closed their churches and was killing their priests, I did not see why they should have to lie so much about the savage actions of their own side. They must have known that in Seville and elsewhere large numbers of people were being shot in batches without trial, but on their return from touring Spain they denied that anything of the sort was happening. This attitude of theirs contrasted with that of the supporters of the Spanish government who freely admitted that unauthorized killings were taking place every night in their territory, though they excused them by saying, what was true, that the military rising had obliged them to send all their police to the front. In the course of this correspondence I scored an amusing hit. Sir Arnold Lunn, who was one of the leading supporters of the Nationalists in England, wrote a letter to the *Daily Telegraph* in which he lamented the fact that any decent Englishman should support a side which had been guilty of that atrocious massacre at Badajoz. Evidently, like so many of his fellow Catholics, he thought that atrocities and massacres could only occur on the Red side, and I got a lot of pleasure from correcting him.

My feelings about the Civil War were however of an altogether different sort to those of most of the other supporters of the Spanish government. They saw it as a contest between Fascism and Democratic Socialism, a preliminary jousting which would determine which of the two opposed ideologies would win in the European struggle that loomed ahead. I did not view it in this heroic light. To my mind this was a purely Spanish affair, to be seen in terms of Peninsular rather than European history, but intensified and distorted by the existence of two great power dynamos, Nazi Germany and Communist Russia, which operated from outside. What shocked and horrified me was the hatred and fanaticism that was tearing to pieces a country that I loved, so, though I gave my full support to the Government cause, I should have been only too pleased had it been possible for the contesting sides to come to terms. For this reason I supported the Non-Intervention Committee until it became clear that the weak and timid British government was not prepared to enforce it.

The propaganda for the Spanish Republic was being largely directed by the Communists. I did not mean to have any dealings with them. The purges that were going on in Russia did not seem to me to give them any moral right to speak for the cause of liberty or equality, and besides they were people whom one could not trust, for the same reason that the Jesuits could not be trusted by the Dominicans and other monastic orders of the seventeenth century. They had invented a new Macchiavellian morality which allowed them to lie and to intrigue against their allies for the greater glory of Stalin and Marx. In any case it was a waste of time to preach to the converted about the evils of the military rebellion; one must address one's arguments to people who had not yet made up their minds. When therefore I was introduced to the Duchess of Atholl I found someone with whom I could make common cause. She was a right-wing Tory and held views about India and the Empire with which I disagreed, but she saw clearly the menace of Hitler and how greatly a Nationalist victory in Spain would add to his power, and so she threw herself whole-heartedly into the struggle on the side of the Spanish government. In doing this she was of course acting logically. The menace of Hitler was at the door, that of Communist Russia remote, as any British Tory, whose stock-in-trade has always been the national interest, might have been expected to see. But too many of these Tories had been undermined by the Nazi propaganda about the Treaty of Versailles, whose unjust clauses, though they had long ceased to be operative, had been of their own making, while they could scarcely be expected to have much sympathy with the workers' rule in Republican Spain. Labour too was the victim of its own propaganda about disarmament and of its perennial illusion that good intentions are enough. Simply by making himself the master of Germany Hitler had exposed the weakness of purpose on which the Anglo-French alliance rested and destroyed the power of decision of the British government.

The result of my association with the Duchess of Atholl was that I was asked to address a number of Conservative M.P.s in a committee room of the House of Commons. I had never spoken in public before so that I felt extremely nervous. Even in ordinary conversation I easily get confused, forget words and names and lose the thread of what I am saying. I therefore wrote out my speech with the intention of reading it, yet when I got up and saw all those faces fixed on me I let my paper fall and talked freely with, I think, reasonable clarity. At all events the Duchess was pleased because, though the room was packed, no one went out in the middle as she said that some members usually did. I put down this trifling incident because it shows that in emergencies one can call on powers of whose existence one had previously had no notion.

We had spent the summer and autumn at Welcombe in a grey modern villa called Ley Park. Park simply means paddock in Cornwall, but the address had helped me to get my letters accepted by *The Times*. Now in November we rented a furnished cottage at Aldbourne in Wiltshire, half way between Hungerford and Swindon. It was close to Ham Spray, so that we could see the Partridges easily, and not far from London. My propaganda work had taught me how little I really knew about recent Spanish history, so I began making trips to London to read in the British Museum.

Just before Christmas that year my mother developed an incurable cancer. Although she was not told what she had, she guessed it and was alarmed at the prospect of dying – a thing which struck me as strange because the most firmly held part of her creed was a belief in a future life. But who can tell what comfort their fair weather beliefs will afford them when they see the blank wall in front of them? Her sufferings were happily shortened by large doses of morphia and she died in a coma on January 7th, aged seventy-six. I cannot say that I felt her loss very deeply because as she had grown older we had drifted somewhat apart, but I have never forgotten what I owe her and during the past twenty years I have scarcely passed a day without thinking of her. There is something about those who love others more than they love themselves that makes an ineffaceable impression.

My mother's death led to a sordid family quarrel over money. During the past year she had repeatedly said to me that when she died I and my brother would be better off because she had left us everything she had. As we had sunk more than £2,000 in our Spanish house and I was about to buy a cottage in Wiltshire, my fixed income of £360 a year had been reduced to almost half and I did not know of any way of increasing it at short notice. My brother too had just had a second child and found life in London expensive. So when after the funeral we came together in the drawing room to hear the will read, we took it for granted that we should each receive a half share of what she had left. My father produced the will. After coughing once or twice in his dry way,

'I know already what is in it,' he said, 'because I dictated it to your mother myself.' Then as he read it aloud we learned that she had left everything in trust to him for life, to come to us only after his death.

'Those were your mother's wishes,' he said in a decisive tone. 'Like a dutiful wife she left everything she possessed in my hands. However I will consider how far I can let you two boys have some of the interest accruing to me, though that must depend upon how satisfied I am with your conduct.'

My father was at this time very well off indeed. He had in fact just bought a Regency house with several acres of lawn and shrubberies on the outskirts of Cheltenham, to which he had intended to move with my mother in the spring. My mother's total capital, reduced by heavy losses in the family business and by contributions to the purchase of their house, amounted to £12,000, whereas my father's was around seven times that amount. With his parsimonious habits he was living well within his income, but he could not bear parting with the power over his sons which such a relatively small sum would afford him because the wielding of power afforded him a deep satisfaction. My brother and I at once protested that this will did not represent my mother's expressed intentions and an estrangement ensued which was never entirely healed, even when on war breaking out he renounced the income in our favour in order to escape the greatly increased income tax. My brother, who had always been his favourite son, was even more indignant than I was and never, I think, entirely forgave him.

After another summer in Cornwall we moved into a cottage at Aldbourne which we had bought for £800 and done up. It was called Bell Court. We chose the furniture in London on the day of the Munich Agreement, expecting war to break out at any moment. On our way home we stopped for lunch at Ham Spray. Ralph and Frances were both ardent pacifists and a quarrel broke out between us in which Ralph accused me of longing for another war. As a matter of fact I had not been opposed to the Munich settlement, but only to the spirit in which it had been made and received. I felt certain that, since we had let everything drift for so long, war was bound to come soon, but there were factors of which I was ignorant, such as the state of our air defences, which might provide a reason for postponement. Besides nothing had been done to prepare the country psychologically. England still lived in its smug pacifist dream, hiding its head in the sand like an ostrich. Before we could challenge Hitler it seemed to me essential that everyone should realize that his territorial ambitions were unlimited and that therefore no alternative to a firm stand was possible. If there had to be war, the whole country must be united. However Ralph needed a scapegoat and, being when excited a very emotional and aggressive man, he rounded on me till Gamel and myself were more or less driven out of the house. Such quarrels were breaking out all over England at this time, between parents and children, between brothers and sisters, between old friends, but on the following day I wrote Ralph a conciliatory letter and our quarrel was made up.

A few weeks later the Duchess of Atholl resigned from her constituency of West Perthshire in order to recontest it as a protest against Chamberlain's refusal to appoint a Ministry of Supply or to speed up rearmament. She wrote to me asking if I would come up to help her. I wholeheartedly agreed with her stand, for Chamberlain's attitude of self-complacency gave me the feeling that we were being driven headlong in a car by a man who was either drunk or drugged, but I did not see what use I could be. I was not the sort of person she needed. However when I spoke to her on the telephone she begged me so earnestly to come to her help that much against my will I promised to do so, though on the understanding that I should not have to make any speeches.

I had never stayed at a ducal house before, but I imagined that evening dress would be worn at dinner. I had one of course at my parents' house, as they dressed every night, but it was old and frayed. I never wore it in London because I made a point of avoiding occasions where one would be necessary. So I went to Moss Bros. and bought a new evening suit with shirts and collars to go with it. However on my arrival in Perthshire I found that my hosts did not dress nor even have dinner. Every evening I went off with the Duchess in a car with a thermos of coffee and sandwiches.

This was the winter of the great frost. Rivers and streams were hard bound in ice: a white lace covered all the branches. Steam hissed around the wheels of the Flying Scotsman as I rode northwards. Then as I drove through the dour little town of Dunkeld, I caught sight of large posters with my name and army rank on them. Clearly I was going to have to make speeches after all.

The family seat, Blair Castle, was opened only during the summer months. The Atholls normally occupied a large modern house on the edge of the town. It was warm and comfortable, but furnished in the plainest and drabbest way. However the Duchess was kind and hospitable and the more I saw of her the better I liked her. She was a small woman in her sixties with aquiline features who dressed very simply in dark colours. Her father had been a Scottish historian and till her marriage she had helped him in his work, so that there was nothing she did not know about local history. She was also a pianist of note who had played at the Queen's Hall, but since she had taken up politics she had given her whole time to them. A childless woman, they had become her obsession and her husband, who was proud of her ability and intelligence, gave her his strong support. Her energy was inexhaustible. Every morning she woke at six and wrote for a couple of hours before getting up, and from then on till midnight or later she was never idle.

My mornings were spent in writing letters to the Press, after which there would be an excellent lunch served with very good Moselle. Sometimes there would be visits from Liberal M.P.s, for nearly all the Conservatives – 'the tame cats', as Churchill called them in a letter of support he wrote to the Duchess – were for Chamberlain. Then in the afternoons I would set off with her in a car to meetings in the glens. On the way she would point out places where famous events had taken place – usually combats or slayings – sometimes citing in support a ballad. The Duke's clan was the Murrays and I was struck by the fact that in Scotland all the legends attached to places were historical, whereas in Ireland they would most of them have been mythological. The meetings were held in the schools and presided over by the minister, who would usually open the proceedings with words such as these: 'As I was saying to you in my sermon last Sunday, when I put before you the terrible situation of the people of Czechoslovakia ... ' Then the Duchess would stand up, a long wand in her hand with which to point to the map of Europe, grave and high-minded as the headmistress of a large girls' school, and I would be hurried on in the car to the next schoolroom to hold the platform till she arrived. In front of me I would see three or four rows of red or white faces, as void of expression as turnips or tomatoes, fixed on me in a pudding stare. The ministers, who were all on the Duchess's side, struck me as well-educated men, but what the vegetable faces thought, if they thought anything at all, was another matter. Sometimes I would be accompanied by a young Englishman and his girl who had come up from London to help the Duchess and who each time made the same speech. 'Take a young man (or girl) like me,' they would begin, 'growing up with democratic ideas and a belief in liberty and progress. What does he see but a world that is being rapidly taken over by fascist tyrannies that threaten to destroy all his hopes of a better future. And when he looks to his own government to defend him, he finds ... ' This young couple kept very much to themselves and I judged that they were Communists. The Duchess had not chosen her helpers wisely.

The Duke had failed to put in an appearance because, to everyone's relief, he had broken his ankle and could not leave his bedroom. He was restless and impatient for news and on my second day I was sent upstairs to soothe him. I found him reclining on a lounge chair with his leg in plaster and a glass of whisky beside him. He motioned to me to sit down, but did not offer me a drink.

'Know Argyll?' he began in a gruff voice.

'No, I've never met the Duke of Argyll.'

'He's a dirty little shit. Didn't want to serve in the war so I got George [George V] to talk to him. He needed a good spanking.'

'Know Montrose?' he started off again.

'No, I've never met the Duke of Montrose. This is my first visit to Scotland.'

'Then you've missed nothing. He's a complete rotter.'

And so on through all the Scottish dukes. Gradually I realized that for him the election was not being fought on a matter of national importance, but was merely a phase of the age-long contest between the Murrays and the other clans.

I was wearing a pair of red Morocco slippers which I had bought in Burlington Arcade. I had worn shoes of this sort for many years and now they were the fashion. But the Duke took such a violent dislike to them that he could not keep his eyes off them. It was the usual military reaction and I had gone through it before with my father. Then a nephew and a niece of his appeared wearing them and his aversion for mine seemed to grow a trifle less. One evening I remembered that he had been the colonel of the 4th Hussars, which was my Uncle Charlie's regiment, so I asked if he remembered him.

'Charlie Graham your uncle, is he? A splendid fellow! A very fine soldier! – Help yourself to some whisky.'

After that his manner to me completely changed.

Some months later I met a woman who had been a guest at Blair Castle during the previous duke's time. Her bedroom had been next door to the ducal bathroom and every morning she could hear him singing loudly to himself as he sponged and splashed. The words he sang were always the same, repeated over and over: '*Blair* is mine and *Atholl* is mine and *I* am the Duke of Atholl. Ha!'

During my last days at Dunkeld I was turned onto canvassing. My first assignment was to win over the railwaymen who usually voted Labour. For them the Duchess was the arch-enemy and I had to talk to their leaders for six or seven hours before I succeeded. I had never met men so slow in mind before. I was less successful with the lairds, though they were just as canny. Most of them were baronets who had risen to be colonels and they lived in grey stone houses surrounded by lawns and shrubberies and wore heavy tweed suits with plus-fours and thick stockings and were accompanied by Scotch terriers. They listened to my arguments and made no reply and I saw that they were going to vote for the official candidate because one could not imagine their having any opinions that were not totally conventional. I also attended a meeting addressed by one of the Duchess's leading Conservative adversaries. He had just returned from Germany. Benes, he asserted, was a secret Communist and the British Empire had no better friend than Germany. He therefore saw no need for rearmament. The Duchess, as was to be expected, lost the election and I took the train home to spend Christmas with Gamel.

I must now describe the place and cottage where I was to pass the next fifteen years. Aldbourne is a large downland village lying in a hollow where seven roads or sheep tracks meet. It had thus the shape of a wheel and at its hub there stands a circular pond about which legends have gathered, one of them being that after the battle of Mount Badon King Arthur set up his round table here. In the eighteenth century it became a small industrial centre with a corduroy factory and a bell foundry and after a fire many of its cottages were rebuilt in brick on a larger scale. These now provided convenient homes for retired gentry, most of whom were either widows or spinsters.

Our cottage, Bell Court, owed its name to having been a messuage of the bell foundry that had been set up in Queen Elizabeth's reign. It was a long, low brick building set at right angles to the village street and looking onto a narrow court, which I sowed with grass. One entered this court by a door and saw in front of one a long strip of lawn, contained between the cottage and a flint and mortar wall, and expanding at the end into a small garden shaded by a pear tree. We put up a plaster bust of Venus, a stone urn and a marble table set round with heavy cast-iron seats and added a small pillared porch, taken from a church, to the front door. A Burmese rose with evergreen foliage and large, single petalled white flowers was trained up the wall with other roses of an old-fashioned sort such as Gloire de Dijon and General Jacqueminot. Lilac, moss roses, lilies, tulips and peonies were planted in the beds. An unpromising cottage had been turned into a pretty and unique one.

Inside, even more than outside, everything was on the smallest possible scale. The four rooms into which the ground floor was divided measured no more than eight feet by ten, while my head only just cleared the ceilings. There was also a minute two-roomed cottage on the opposite side of the street door, which we used as an annexe. Seen by night from the lawn, with all its windows lit up, our cottage looked like a ship, but from the inside it was more like a doll's house.

Not long after my return from Spain I had got to know an Austrian sociologist called Franz von Borkenau, who had just brought out a brilliant book, *The Spanish Cockpit,* on the early months of the Civil War. I had already begun reading what I could find on recent Spanish history because I wanted to get a better idea of how that war had come about and he encouraged me to put down the result of my discoveries in book form. This was the origin of *The Spanish Labyrinth.* During the next few years Borkenau paid us several visits and we became good friends. He was the son of an Austrian civil servant and did not learn that he was of Jewish origin till he was grown up. The discovery was a great shock to him and his reaction to it was to become a Communist and to take employment in the Comintern. After some years of this he became disgusted by the lack of political realism shown by the Party as well as by the total failure of the Russian Revolution to implement its ideals. So he left the Party, took a course of training as a sociologist and set off to do field work in Panama. Here he learned Spanish and when the Civil War in Spain broke out he saw his opportunity and went straight to Barcelona.

He was an uncouth, clumsy man with an absurd moustache and little aptitude for getting on with people. A Nietzschean romantic rather than a Marxist, he always thought, like a Prussian professor, in terms of force and power. In conversation his judgements were often wild and it was only when he sat down to write that his intelligence and his sense for reality came out. He completely failed to understand the English, whom he regarded as decadent and spineless, and was so convinced that we would yield to the Nazis that the outbreak of war found him in Italy. He was a courageous man, as his book shows, but so extraordinarily nervous that he could not sit or walk without continually turning his head to see if he was being watched or followed. We called him 'the spy' because he looked like a comic cartoon of one by Hervé.

Another person who helped me over *The Spanish Labyrinth* was a young Dutchman called Arthur Lehning who till the war had been a librarian at the International Institute for Social History in Amsterdam. He was an Anarchist who had represented the Anarchist International at Barcelona and knew all the leading militants there. He was a man in his thirties with the disposition of an intellectual rather than of a man of action, and he and his attractive wife became great friends of ours. With his help I was able to obtain books and periodicals from Amsterdam that were unprocurable in England and so to make my chapters on the Spanish Anarcho-Syndicalists the most reliable in my book. Another friend I made was the Spanish working-class writer Arturo Barea and his highly-educated Austrian wife, while I paid several visits to Oxford to stay with Don Alberto Jiménez, the director of the cultural branch of the Institución Libre de Enseñanza and his wife Doña Natalia de Cossío. I also got valuable information on Communist tactics from Luis Araquistáin, the only really indoctrinated

Spanish Marxist, who till recently had been the *éminence grise* of Largo Caballero, the Socialist prime minister. Then for three months that summer we took in a wounded Spanish refugee, who before the war had been a shop attendant, and his young Valencian wife.

As the outbreak of the war drew near I put down my name for the special reserve of officers with a recommendation by my sister-in-law's uncle, General Gwynn. I also got in touch with the Foreign Office who offered me a post as Press attaché at the British Legation in Nicaragua. While waiting for the appointment to be confirmed I decided to read up the Central American republics in the British Museum. So on the day on which war was declared Gamel and I drove up to London. A stream of cars and vans loaded with bedding and furniture was pouring out along the road to Reading, while we seemed to be the only people moving in the opposite direction. I had so little faith in Bertrand Russell's prediction that London would be destroyed within a few days that I was glad to put my disbelief to the test. That night my brother and I went to a delightful production of *The Importance of Being Earnest,* which put us in better spirits.

The British Museum Reading Room was shut but I managed to obtain an authority from the Foreign Office to use it. I was the only reader in the huge domed room. The librarian thought I must be engaged on top secret war work so they were surprised when I asked for books on the Central American republics. Their surprise increased when I asked for Nicaraguan and Guatemalan poetry, for I had discovered that my best entry to political circles in those countries, where every general had had to win his spurs as a poet, would be through the local Muse. Meanwhile I had rented our cottage at Aldbourne to the Carrington family, which comprised Noel (Dora Carrington's brother), his wife Catherine, their three small children and their cook-nurse. Hardly had I done this than the Foreign Office told me that they had decided not to appoint Press attachés in Central America for fear of offending the United States, so we were left without a house. Very kindly the Carringtons allowed us to squeeze in with them, so there we all spent the winter together. Luckily Noel went up to London every day, but I had to work in our tiny dining room while the cook, a great hulking girl aged eighteen, would burst in every few minutes with a clatter of plates and toasts and scuttles of coal for the iron range.

This was the coldest winter within living memory. The rain froze as it fell and turned each blade of grass to an icicle. Then a warm rain came down and melted the ice and snow, flooding the village to a depth of a couple of feet. In March I contracted stomatitis or trench mouth, which I had caught from drinking tea out of the chained mug in Paddington Station buffet. Cups and saucers had become so difficult to get that people stole them. It is a nasty complaint in which the throat and mouth swell up and there is a high fever, so in April I went to Brighton for a few days to recuperate. On my way home I listened in Hyde Park to speakers from the British Union of Fascists talking in a way that seemed highly detrimental to the war effort. The papers were full of stories of how fifth columnists in France and Belgium had helped the invading German troops so I wrote a letter to the *Daily Telegraph* in which I suggested that these people should be locked up for the duration of the war. This letter was to cost me dear.

I had at this time a painful quarrel with Ralph Partridge. The Battle of Britain was on and everyone's nerves were in a bad way. He and his wife Frances were, as I have said, ardent pacifists and when we met he could not resist pressing his views on me. After one such occasion, when he had been more than usually determined, I rang him up and suggested that when we saw one another again we should not discuss the war. 'But it's impossible,' he said, 'to talk of anything else.' I sat down at once in a state of emotion and wrote him an unforgivable letter. Usually when I write a letter to relieve my feelings I keep it overnight and then destroy it, but I posted this one at once, as I now see because I unconsciously wished for a breach with him since I could not endure any discussions on this subject. He did not answer and we ceased to see one another till the end of the war.

I had joined the Home Guard and been made a sergeant, but after the threat of invasion had passed I felt that I wanted some closer participation in the war so in November I went up to London and enrolled as an air-raid warden in Addison Road, where my brother and sister-in-law and their children shared a house with a doctor called John Dent. There was something very stimulating about London in those days. During the first war the women and older men whom one met when on leave had been in a thoroughly nasty mood, full of hatred of everything German, of tin trumpet patriotism and talk of imaginary atrocities. Now the bombs had put them in the front line and given them the cheerful, stoical spirit of soldiers. After any bad bomb incident a miasma of gloom and despondency would hang about the wrecked area, but except on these occasions morale was high and people talked to one another on buses and in shops as they had never done before. Londoners had lost their love of privacy. This had a sad effect upon Dr Dent. His patients had consisted almost entirely of elderly neurotics and hypochondriacs, principally women. When the bombing began a few of them went off to the country, but the majority stayed and, finding themselves faced with a real danger instead of an imaginary one, their fears and neuroses left them and they no longer had any need of his services. He lost all his patients and it was not till he took up a new treatment for curing alcoholics and drug addicts that he was able to earn money again.

When the sirens began to howl the air-raid warden had to leave his shelter and patrol the streets. This was far from pleasant, for pavements provide no shelter from flying fragments. The bomb explosions sometimes had surprising effects. One would see houses which had been completely destroyed except for the chimney stack, yet whose occupants had suffered only minor injuries. Or one would enter a bombed building that was so choked with dust that one needed one's torch to see across the room and find a man or woman with all his clothes ripped off by the suction of the air yet suffering merely from shock, or else a person streaming with blood as though dyed with paint. When taken to hospital these were found to have only superficial cuts caused by window glass.

One of the warden's duties was to make sure that no lights were showing from windows. If he saw a crack of light, he knocked at a door and made his complaint. But lonely or frightened women sometimes took advantage of this to draw a warden to their house. On one occasion I was admitted by a girl in her early twenties who asked me to adjust her curtain. I did so and she poured me out a whisky. She was decidedly attractive, but when she suggested I should stay and spend the night with her because she could not bear being alone, I had to decline because I was on duty. Then there was a woman of around forty, a fading belle, who lived on a fourth floor and showed a light every night to attract a warden. A human glow-worm. In the end she had to be threatened with arrest if she did it again.

Another strange feature of the times was the prestige which air-raid wardens enjoyed. In working-class districts they became more important than doctors. I was sent for by a woman who was suffering from acute asthma and felt herself to be dying. 'But she needs a doctor,' I said. 'I'll send her one.' 'No, no,' came the answer. 'She doesn't want a doctor – she wants an air raid warden.' On another occasion my services were requested for delivering a child.

My sister-in-law was a dyed-in-the-wool Londoner who felt that safety lay only in large cities. She could have stayed in the country, either with us or with her uncle Stephen Gwynn, but after trying this for a week she decided that there was more danger from the children's eating watercress, which might give them typhoid, than from German bombs, and returned to Addison Road. Here she strengthened the ceiling of a basement room with wooden posts and fitted bunks into it. Although the house next door was levelled to the ground the attitude she took up was that there was no danger at all. Everyone kept a stiff upper lip and the bombing was never alluded to. Londoners were in fact testing themselves and liking it, because it is invigorating to discover that one is braver than one had supposed oneself to be. Gamel, who several times came up to visit me, enjoyed the experience and I have often wondered whether women, though less aggressive than men, are not generally speaking more courageous. I certainly felt some nasty twinges myself, though I concealed them.

The spring and summer of 1940 saw an outbreak of spy fever pass through Wiltshire. This emanated from the Chief Constable, we were told, who seemed to think that the country was alive with fifth columnists. None of the country magnates, who, out of fear of Russia, had shown a readiness to come to terms with the Nazis, were suspected, but only new arrivals whose antecedents were unknown. For example, Anthony West, the son of Rebecca West and H. G. Wells, had recently bought a farm in a village close to us. Like his mother, he was a strong liberal who detested everything German, but the police suddenly descended on his house and searched it. He had a collection of French books, but the police did not know the difference between French and German so they carried some of them off to have the language verified. Then they came to a locked cupboard. With some reluctance Anthony produced the key and they found inside a collection of toy soldiers with cardboard banners inscribed with revolutionary slogans such as 'Up the Proletariat'. It seems that the Wells children had played with these and that Anthony sometimes took them out when his wife was away and set them out on the table. The police duly carried them off to Marlborough and all his farm papers and accounts with them. Here they kept them through the summer at great inconvenience to himself and were only persuaded to return them when his mother complained to the Home Secretary.

Another case was that of my friends the Bomfords. Jimmy Bomford was a successful stockbroker who, seeing the war coming, had decided to leave the City and invest in land. He learned the latest techniques in farming, bought a large tract of good grazing land and built himself a house on the top of the Downs some two miles out of Aldbourne. He made few efforts to mix with the local gentry while his modern methods of farming created a good deal of jealousy by their immediate success. The result was that, though he was totally unpolitical, he came under suspicion. Because he wore blue shirts he was said to be a Gauleiter; because his wife was beautiful and dressed in expensive and somewhat theatrical clothes she was said to be French – and that now meant almost the same as German – although she was actually the daughter of a civil servant called Smith; because they had a small flat roof for sunbathing it was thought that they had built it as a site for a radio station. Their house was therefore searched twice by half a dozen policemen, while other policemen hung about in the woods and hedges for several months on end.

The man in charge of these operations was a Dundee marmelade manufacturer called Keiller. He was a well-known archaeologist who had excavated at his own expense the great stone circle of Avebury, setting up again the stones that had fallen. He was one of those people who love mysteries. Thus he had made himself an authority on the Scottish witches of the seventeenth century and had written a book, which he presented to me, on certain covens. He also believed that the slightly different shapes of the Avebury megaliths were not accidental but contained a symbolism which, if it could be deciphered, would reveal their meaning, though I do not think that he ventured to publish his views on this. Now when the war broke out he joined the Special Police and was made a sergeant. At once he discovered that he had a talent for criminal investigation and in particular for spy hunting. He also found that he got a deep satisfaction from saluting. Whenever a police officer appeared he would spring to attention with an audible click of the heels and give a smart salute. Every time the officer came into the room he would repeat the action.

Jimmy Bomford had asked me to be present when the police searched his house for the second time in case they endeavoured to plant anything on him, so I went up and spent the day there. They combed through all his papers, dug holes in the garden and ransacked the whole house. When Jane Bomford wished to go to the lavatory, a policeman was stationed outside the door and the plug was detached, since it was supposed that she might be intending to destroy a secret paper. It was, I believe, an order by Winston Churchill that put an end to these preposterous scenes, which incidentally were not extended to the south-eastern counties but only to those where the authorities were panicky.

My own case, however, was quite different. I began to realize that I was under some sort of suspicion in June 1940. A visitor, who opened her bedroom window one night so that the curtain flapped, brought a policeman next day to the door accusing me of signalling to the enemy. This had become the usual term for accidentally showing a light and there was even a case reported in the papers when a magistrate convicted a man of that offence – and fined him two pounds. Then one day nearly a year later, while I was on night operations with the Home Guard, I flashed my torch into a ditch and two policemen sprang out with the same accusations. I realized that I was being watched and that the whole village knew it. Yet one of my fellow sergeants, an ex-Mosleyite, was under no suspicion at all.

Two years passed without my having any idea of the reason for this. Was I, I wondered, with my public record as a supporter of the Spanish Republican government, regarded as a 'premature anti-fascist'? Then one day a detective drove up to my cottage and asked me to come with him to the Marlborough police station. A police officer who was sitting at a desk invited me to sit down. Then he told the young detective who had brought me to conduct the interrogation, obviously because he was new to the job and needed practise.

'You seem to get about the country a good deal, Mr Brenan,' he began.

'I go to London every week to speak on the B.B.C. and in the summer I take a few weeks' holiday in Cornwall. Otherwise I never go anywhere.'

'When were you last in Southend?'

'About ten years ago I went down there for the day. Since then I have not been back.'

The police officer now intervened.

'I will put my cards on the table,' he said. 'How do you explain this?'

And he handed me a sheet of partly burned paper, on which were written the words: 'Gerald Brenan, German Embassy, Dublin', followed by a row of meaningless signs, representing a child's idea of a code.

'I will tell you how this came into our possession,' he said. 'In May 1940 the office of the British Union of Fascists at Southend were burning their papers because they expected to be arrested, and this piece of paper was blown over the wall into the garden next door.'

'I can explain that perfectly,' I said. 'The week before this I was in Hyde Park where I heard the Fascist speakers talking what I considered to be treason, so I wrote a letter to the *Daily Telegraph* suggesting that they should be locked up. In this piece of paper they were obviously trying to pay me out.'

'Precisely,' replied the police officer. 'I have the cutting from the *Telegraph* here.'

And he handed it to me.

'Then what the hell,' I said, 'do you mean by suspecting me? I have a public record of having been on the Republican side during the Spanish Civil War. I have well-known friends who can vouch for me. Is this the way to conduct a police investigation in war time?'

'I'm sorry, Mr Brenan,' he replied, 'but this is not our doing. Your case has been in the hands of MI5, who send us their instructions which we have to carry out. But I may tell you that you are now cleared from all suspicion.'

The little detective drove me home.

'All the same, Mr Brenan,' he said, 'I think that there is quite a lot to be said for the British Union of Fascists. Mosley is a very patriotic man.'

A few weeks later I was promoted from sergeant to lieutenant in the Home Guard. I had not been called up as a reservist though I might have been of some use in Africa, but a little later I was asked if I would care to command a landing craft in the Normandy landings. As I know nothing of boats I declined.

24

Aldbourne and Cornwall

The fifteen years I spent at Aldbourne were years of hard and steady work. The first book I wrote there was *The Spanish Labyrinth,* which took me just three years. It was written in considerable stress of mind. The Spanish Civil War had affected me far more deeply than the war with the Nazis because of the savagery with which it was conducted and I had to struggle continually with the strength of my feelings in order to avoid undue bias or prejudice. When I began to read for it I was almost totally ignorant both of working-class movements and of Marxist dialectics, so I had plenty of ground to cover. On finishing it I saw that what I had written was really an indictment of the follies and illusions of the left, with whose general aims I sympathized.

My next book was a novel on a Spanish theme which I called *Segismundo.* I had started it as a short story about a boy who had begun life in an orphanage, but it grew into a vast work with more than seventy characters, all of them Spaniards. These characters were first of all established and then the Civil War came and they were obliged to take sides, some in accordance with their political opinions and others with those of the territory, Nationalist or Republic, in which they found themselves. I had been drawn into writing this book by my desire to fill in the bones of *The Spanish Labyrinth* with the flesh and blood of real life and so continue the *Episodios Nacionales* of Pérez Galdós. But the attempt was absurd because I did not know nearly enough about Spain and Spaniards, so after spending nearly five years on it and writing more than 200,000 words and still finding myself far from the end, I gave it up and burnt it.

When in the summer of 1946 I abandoned *Segismundo* I had for some time been spending my evenings on reading French medieval literature and Provençal poetry. From there I moved on to Spanish medieval poetry, which I had hitherto known only imperfectly. I became so enthusiastic about this last that I decided to write a book on it and that is how *The Literature of the Spanish People* began. I finished the book in February 1949 after less than two and a half years work, and in which the reading took up far more time than the writing. While engaged on it I put it aside for a couple of months to write two articles for *Horizon* on the life and poetry of St. John of the Cross.

Immediately after finishing this book I went with Gamel on a trip to Spain which led to a travel book, *The Face of Spain,* which I wrote in ten months. I then worked for four months on my old novel of the 'twenties, *A Holiday by the Sea,* and on getting once more held up in it began my autobiography, *A Life of One's Own* and finished it within two years. I submitted it to Chatto and Windus who on Day Lewis's advice refused it.

During most of this time I was working regularly for the B.B.C. So long as the war lasted I gave regular broadcasts to Spain and when these ended I wrote plays on historical subjects for Children's Hour. I took on this work because we were finding it increasingly difficult to live. My wife's tiny income had suddenly and mysteriously dried up, my mother's bequest gave me less than £180 a year and I was obliged to sell out some of my rapidly diminishing capital. Such is the writer's life – precarious and harassed in every age. Everything conspires to prevent him from writing what he wants to write.

My father had meanwhile sold the large house he had bought in Cheltenham and purchased a Regency one on the Evesham Road. It was a handsome stuccoed building with a sitting-room that extended from the street to the garden and containing two fireplaces. Since however he preferred comfort to grandeur he divided it in half with a plywood partition and further impaired its elegance by fitting its tall windows with curtains that ended three feet above the ground. This was done out of economy. Another economy was to provide his occasional visitors – an Anglo-Indian judge who spent his days doing crossword puzzles, a retired colonel or two who played golf – with the cheapest South African sherry, which, as he would frankly tell them, cost only 3/6 a bottle. He was in very prickly moods these days and, if it had not been that he had conceived a great admiration for Gamel, I do not think that I should have been asked to his house at all. He detested my sister-in-law, because in spite of her gentle way of speaking she always stood up to him, but had her to stay once a year with my brother and his two children out of a sense of duty.

Now he suddenly wrote that he was getting married. The lucky girl, Mabel Constable Curtis, was the daughter of a very old man who lived in a large house opposite and had never had any profession. She was about three years younger than I was, plain and limited in mind, but at the same time good-tempered and sensible, especially when it came to keeping an eye on the pennies. This last was a quality that my father particularly appreciated. After his marriage, to which my brother and I were not invited, my father sold his Cheltenham house and bought a modern villa at Budleigh Salterton in Devon. Here he and his wife Mabel lived quietly, without any of those scenes that had punctuated his life with my mother. He seemed to have at last got what he wanted.

We had sold our car when the war broke out and taken to bicycles. This set a limit to the number of our friends. The principal ones were V. S. Pritchett and his wife Dorothy, who in 1939 rented a Georgian manor house called Maiden Court close to the village of East Shefford in the Lambourne valley. We used to bicycle over every week or so to have tea and supper with them and I have vivid memories of coasting down Baydon Hill on frosty nights when the stars shook and sparkled overhead and of warm summer afternoons when the carthorses stood lazily under the pollarded willows swishing their tails. V.S.P., as everyone called him because he disliked his first name of Victor, was the best company imaginable – alive to his finger tips, amusing, sagacious, always in good spirits and of course very intelligent. His wife Dorothy, a big, dark Welsh beauty who acted both as his cook and secretary, was completely devoted to him so that with their two children they made up a very united family.

In appearance V.S.P. is short but sturdily built, tough and wiry. He is both a very sensual man and a demon for work. He likes good food and plenty of it – meat, cheese and pudding with plenty of cream on it – and to watch him eat is like watching an engine being fuelled with coal, for what he takes in is at once converted into intellectual energy. Every morning he works from breakfast till lunch and then, after a short siesta, is at his desk again and writing hard till supper and often after that till midnight. He has powerful muscles to his mind, and the ability to get through a lot of work is the thing he most respects in other people.

Essentially he is a family man, wrapped up in his wife and children. The perfect husband and father. With them he has followed the narrow, uneventful course of the dedicated writer which he has described in his admirable autobiography, driven on by the pressing need to make money (for many years he supported his parents) and lacking the leisure for making and keeping friends. When I first knew him he had none. In this he differs from the Bloomsbury Group for whom friendship was sacred, but then they had a university background, as well as private means.

When I first met him in London during the Civil War he was reacting against his Spanish experiences, which he has described in *Marching Spain*. The beauty and drama of Spanish places and landscapes had hit him hard, but he now wanted to suppress the poetical side of himself and write according to the realistic canon that one should show no indulgence to the gentler feelings, but look for the weak spot, the tell-tale self-deception or hypocrisy under the public mask. Now that I have come to know him better I can see that he was haunted by the spectre of his Christian Scientist father, of whom he talked continually and about whom he has written in his brilliant novel, *Mr. Beluncle*. At all events he had conceived a great contempt for anything that could be called romantic or poetical, though later he learned to find more subtle applications for those words.

I greatly admired his short story, *The Sailor,* which he wrote in the early war years. I still think it is one of the best short stories in English, but I cared less for those that immediately followed it. A marvellous observer, the best eye I have ever known, he looked at people without malice, but with the aim of discovering their weak points. He once told me that he saw all his friends and acquaintances in the form of animals. This is no doubt the vision of the comic writer, but it excludes the sympathy one had felt in *The Sailor*. The greatest comic novelists, such as Gogol, are really satirists, but there is no satirical element in V.S.P.'s stories because, lacking an ideal inner world with which the actual world could be contrasted, he took people and things as they were. Later he developed his notion of gentle, Meredithian comedy and in *The Key to my Heart* he achieves the delicate balance he had been seeking.

To meet he is the most friendly and genial of men. Though highly strung, one cannot imagine him ever being angry or impatient. No one has ever been snubbed by him, no one brushed off in a review. He is completely without bad feelings or malice. Then his conversation is very stimulating – witty and full of fantasy yet also balanced and judicious. The hard struggle he had to survive in his early years caused him to mature early and it also rubbed off the rough corners so that he has no eccentricities, but is always sanity itself. One can sum him up as a man who keeps down to earth, a man without false hopes or illusions, an accepter and recorder of things as they are. Yet the imagery in his writings often betrays a half-buried sense for poetry.

I must end with a few words about his wife Dorothy. She is a tall, handsome, buxom woman with a vivacity and clearness of colouring that make her seem many years younger than her age, and the best wife any hardworking writer ever had. She types all her husband's business letters and manuscripts – no easy task since his handwriting is almost illegible – criticizes his work and reads books for him. She is also a splendid cook and housekeeper and a lively and amusing talker. But it is her warmth, generosity and exuberant hospitality that I would like to single out because I have so often been the recipient of them. They pass all bounds.

Other neighbours of ours of whom we saw a good deal were Jimmy and Jane Bomford. I have already said something of them. On leaving the Stock Exchange Jimmy had bought some thirty paintings by the masters of the École de Paris. Although he had acquired them solely as an investment, he came very soon to like them. This set him dabbling in the English art world, inviting young painters down for weekends and sometimes buying their work. He was in most things a simple, unsophisticated man, but he had an Onassis eye for money and an amazing rapidity in calculation, while competition was the breath of his nostrils. He had to win and would never do anything unless he could do it better than everyone else. In his own house he was a splendid host. The food, which he often cooked himself, was excellent and he gave parties which provided a welcome relief from the dullness of country life.

At Jimmy Bomford's house I met a number of amusing people. One was Diana Dors, whose real name was Dora Fluck, to which she wisely gave a better sounding form on going into films. At that time she was a big, strapping girl of eighteen, good natured and devoted to her mother who lived in a back street in Swindon. Other frequent visitors were Tambimuttu, a Singhalese who edited *Poetry London,* and Desmond Morris, later famous as the author of *The Naked Ape.* On another occasion Henry Moore came down, but finding Jimmy's conversation too much for him, spent the day with us. I found his directness and simplicity engaging. However the real friend I made among Jimmy's visitors was a Polish Jewish painter called Jankel Adler. He had been a pupil of Paul Klee and was an artist all through with a technical knowledge and skill which made most English painters seem amateurs. He had also that kind of maturity and wisdom about life which is possessed by Jews who have been exposed to pogroms, and the sight of his stolid, casually dressed figure and bright, twinkling eyes was always welcome. I found his conversation on art and literature stimulating, for, though he had read little, whenever he opened a book it was always one of the great classics, which gave him food for meditation. Jimmy Bomford had bought a number of his big canvases and regarded himself as his patron and now in 1948 he found him a cottage in Aldbourne and set him up there with a fine studio next door. Up to this time Adler's big paintings had been, in my opinion, over-dramatic or fussy. The liquidation of his co-religionists in Germany and Poland had deeply affected him, but now he had reached a calmer period in his life and wished in quiet country surroundings to open a new phase of his painting. He was fifty-two and his best work was before him, but at this moment a disaster occurred. His show in New York had been a total failure and his application for a British passport, on which he set great store, had been refused because, though he was totally unpolitical, he had described himself as an anarchist. I saw him shortly after his return to England and he was in great distress of mind and on the following day he had an attack of angina pectoris which killed him.

It was nearly a year before this – in February 1948 – that Dylan Thomas turned up one day in Aldbourne with his wife Caitlin accompanied by Mrs Taylor, the wife of the historian, who generously made him a monthly allowance. He came with the vague idea of settling in the village, thinking perhaps that, as he had liked my first novel, *Jack Robinson*, I might make a congenial companion. He struck me as being a basically simple man, a lost, frightened baby who could not bear to be alone but hankered for the warmth and friendly contentiousness of boon companions. He tended to become upset by people who talked literature, even sometimes by Mrs Taylor because she wanted him to be poetical. When once, as we went down the street, she exclaimed 'Look at the stars, Dylan', he replied with a bawdy joke. It was his craving to be surrounded by friendly faces that made him love pubs so much. The hour of their opening was always present in his mind and after ten-thirty in the morning he would keep looking at his watch, which I imagine he only wore for that purpose since he observed no other fixed times. Then with a glass of beer before him he felt at home, surrounded by the stolid faces of country people, drawn together by their love of company and ale.

It is a mistake to regard Dylan as an alcoholic. He drank to produce a flow of feeling between himself and the outside world. It is true that, like the Elizabethans, he never tasted any other liquid but alcohol and would make a face if he was offered tea or coffee for breakfast, but he was perfectly satisfied with beer. In the Aldbourne pubs, of which there were five, he did not drink anything else. He would drink slowly and quietly from eleven to one and more rapidly in the evenings, his best hour coming between seven and eight. Then he would warm up and, especially if he had a companion of the right sort to drink with, he would become increasingly vivacious in a slap-happy, often rather mischievous way. His conversation would also become bawdy. He had a large repertory of dirty stories which he told with great gusto, bringing out all their dramatic flavour. Then when the pubs closed he would if possible move on to a friend's house, going to bed comfortably lushed at twelve or one. Yet next morning he would come round to our cottage as fresh as a daisy, for so long as he stuck to beer he did not have hangovers.

After a week at Aldbourne Dylan and Caitlin decided to move on. On their last evening they came to our cottage after the pubs had closed and I got out some wine. Then the last bottle was emptied. I feared for a moment that he might break up the furniture as he had been known to do before when the drink had run out, but he left quietly. A full moon was shining outside. Close to the street door there stood four large metal dustbins that gleamed in the moonlight. Suddenly his hands shot up, as if in terror. 'Ali Baba!' he cried. 'Ali Baba!'

Dylan was a man whom one could not help being fond of. Although his conversation gave no bridge to his poetry, it conveyed a warmth and richness of nature as well as a complete freedom from that class awareness that the Englishmen of those days never seemed able to escape from. Thus he could be the spokesman for average human nature in a way that no other of our poets except Blake and Hardy have been. His gift for giving imaginative expression to emotion without passing it through an intellectual filter has led, in my opinion, to his writing some poetry of a high order, though often the method seemed rather a hit or miss one. Although he planned his poems carefully and corrected them afterwards, they draw or appear to draw almost too heavily on inspiration – that is on a free passage for language and images from the unconscious. Perhaps it is because it is the popular view that poets should be vaticinal and should pour out their verses in a frenzy of rich rhythmical language that the obscurity of his work has not been an obstacle to his popularity. What is certain is that in the poetical climate of today, among so much dry, flat, colourless verse, his poems with all their faults and weaknesses stand out and show one what poetry can be.

Early in the war a Jewish family called Lowinsky settled in a large house in our village. Thomas Lowinsky was a painter and aesthete, two of whose morgue-like pictures are in the Tate, and he had also very inappropriately been an officer in the Horse Guards. Soon after their arrival he died and his wife became a good friend of ours. Her mother had been an immensely wealthy woman who had settled at Littlecote Park, a large Elizabethan manor close to Hungerford that contained a wainscoted gallery lined with suits of armour and at least two ghosts. After her marriage she kept a literary and artistic salon in London, a more modest version of those of Lady Colefax and Lady Cunard, and then retired with her husband and children to Garsington Manor, which till that time had been the home of Lady Ottoline Morrell. Now she and her husband were less well off and had adjusted their life accordingly.

Ruth was a short, stout woman with great exuberance and zest for life. She woke up every morning feeling that the world had been newly created. She and her husband had been collectors of old furniture and prints, so that the house was as crammed with rare objects as a museum, while the food she offered was superb since she was a famous *gourmet* and had written several books on cookery. Her weekend visitors were mostly art lovers and collectors who were also bridge players. I do not play bridge, but in spite of the great difference in our incomes and ways of life we became real friends. I admired her tremendous gusto and love of the good things of life, among which she included Nature, and also her curious mixture of innocence and intelligence. As an example of the first, she told me that her brother, when at Eton, had pulled her leg by saying that the boys were obliged to use different brothels from the masters and that she had firmly believed this till she was nearly thirty. Her intelligence was chiefly shown in social matters, but she had a great respect for learning and brains in other people and could herself read Hebrew, though she had been brought up as an Anglican. We also had a special link: she had adored my old friend Franky Birrell, whose floods of conversation and warmth of heart had roused an echo in her. She herself had a lot of heart and her son's death in the war was something she never recovered from.

I had also kept in with most of my old friends, among them Helen Anrep. After Roger Fry's death she had taken a flat in Charlotte Street, where she became the mother-figure of a group of young painters who were known as the Euston Road Group. Among them were Victor Pasmore, Bill Coldstream and Lawrence Gowing. But she soon found that she could not afford even the simplest forms of entertainment and as they became famous they drifted away from her, though so long as her *engouement* with them lasted I saw less of her. My friendship with Arthur Waley, on the other hand, grew steadily closer. During the war he had worked at the Ministry of Information, where he had also enrolled as a stretcher-bearer. One night a bomb shattered the large Y.M.C.A. building in Tottenham Court Road. There were heavy casualties, among them many cases of people badly cut by window glass. Arthur told me that as he went upstairs with his stretcher he had to walk through a stream of blood that came trickling down. Since he had always been prone to faint at the sight of blood, he thought at first that he would not be able to go on, but then a line from the ballad of *Thomas the Rhymer* came into his head – 'They waded thro' red blude to the knee' – and he immediately felt all right again. He saw a literary parallel in everything.

Beryl de Zoete had withdrawn from London when the bombs began to fall, but on her return I found that both she and Arthur had fallen into the then fashionable vogue of sympathy – not for the Russian people, which I shared – but for Russian communism. Arthur's usual ideological sustenance consisted of books of mysticism, especially when they had an Oriental flavour, but now he was reading Marx and Engels with approbation, while Beryl had become a real fellow-traveller. Arthur soon tired of this craze whereas Beryl, to whose silliness there were few limits, contrived for some time to enthuse over Stalin. After the war she set off, though in her late sixties, for India, but I used to come up to London to see Arthur to consult him about popular poetry, in which he took a great interest.

In 1942 my friend Hope-Johnstone returned from China to England. A year or two before the Spanish Civil War broke out he had inherited a little money from his mother and set off for the Far East. After some months spent in Bali and a visit to Indo China and to the frontiers of Tibet, he had settled in Peking, where he earned a small living by teaching English to Chinese children. He got on badly with the foreign colony but liked the Chinese and indeed the years he spent there would seem to have been the happiest of his life. He made a collection of pictures, materials and other antiques, which he stored in crates, intending to bring them back to England and sell them at a high profit. But then the war with Japan broke out and, though he himself got away in a ship, his crates were all confiscated by the Japanese. It was his usual luck.

As soon as I heard of his arrival I asked him to come down and stay with us, but he did not seem eager to accept. He was busy seeing his rich friends in London. Six months or more passed and then he asked if we could put him up for a fortnight. He had had all his teeth pulled out and did not want to be seen till his gums had hardened enough for him to have new ones put in.

He arrived and surprised me by the intense interest he showed in the Spanish Civil War. My *Spanish Labyrinth* had just come out and I gave him a copy. He took it, but never referred to it again, though the reviews I was getting were very favourable. Instead he talked incessantly and pointedly on Madiaraga's book on Spain, which he praised warmly. I realized that he was jealous of me.

The years passed and he returned again. Obviously he had not come to see me out of friendship, but only because he thought I could be of use to him. He had little money and was living in one room of a house in the country with some people whom he did not like. I told him that if he wished he could have the small annexe to our cottage. He accepted at once and moved in. This annexe consisted of one very small room on the ground floor and of two tiny bedrooms above it and into these he had to fit his library of around three thousand books, all very carefully selected, and his art photographs and gramophone records. One of the two upstair rooms was entirely filled with them, stacked up round the walls or put away in boxes, while his bedroom was so choked that he had only a square yard of floor to stand on beside his bed. Downstairs there were more books on shelves and also the latest type of radio and record player, which had had to be fitted onto a concrete base by a technician who came down from London. There was only one chair, but it was the most expensive armchair that money could buy, and so large that visitors, when he had any, were obliged to perch on the single small table. There was a sort of cupboard with a sink in it at the foot of the stairs in which he washed and shaved, and he had baths in our house.

Here he settled down to a hermit's life of reading and listening to music. For breakfast he would have a pot of Lapsang Souchong tea with a special toast which he ordered from London. Lunch he took in the village where a

343

woman called Mrs Barnes provided a substantial and very cheap meal for a dozen or more people. For supper he ate nothing but one or two Bath Oliver biscuits with some Camembert cheese and a glass of orange juice. However he had a good many meals with us. When he felt hungry he would drop in just before breakfast or supper and we would keep him to share what we had. I must say that I dreaded his breakfast visits, for they were usually the occasion for his starting off on one of his furious diatribes against the ignorance of the B.B.C. speakers and the mistakes they made over Latin quantities. He had a few friends in the district who would fetch him to lunch or supper in their car, but his closest companions were the village children. His passion for little girls of ten or twelve had increased and in the evenings there was usually a group of them waiting outside his door. His manner with them was just right – friendly, natural and straight-forward without any sort of condescension. He would join in their games and I remember him refusing an invitation to tea because, he said, he had an appointment to play hopscotch with some little girls. He was then verging on seventy and with his straggling white hair and his corduroy coat and heavily rimmed spectacles looked very attractive.

But I was always aware of his ambivalent attitude towards me. He was so consumed with jealous feelings that he did not read my *Literature of the Spanish People* when it came out although he had dabbled in Spanish poetry and took a great theoretical interest in it. Then I gathered from other people that he considered that I ought to pay him half the money my great-aunt had left me because he had originally suggested to her that she should do that. I did not share that view at all because even without his interven-tion she would have ended by adopting me as her heir, but I did feel some responsibility for him as an old friend who had fallen on hard times and did what I could to help him. But age, continual disappointments and a life-long habit of calculating what he could get out of people were leading to a steady deterioration in his character.

Every summer we went to Cornwall for a few weeks' holiday. We took rooms at Home Farm, Welcombe, with two old ladies, Mrs Cottle and her sister Miss Box, and for fifty shillings a week each lived off the fat of the land. The Cornish people paid no attention to wartime rationing so that we got all the cream and butter we wanted, with legs of lamb and roast chicken for lunch and supper, followed by gooseberry or blackberry-and-apple tart and custards. I have never eaten better. And then the air was like a drug. One could walk all day without getting tired and sleep for eight or nine hours at a stretch without stirring. Everything spoke of sleep. The long, low hills looked like bolsters and pillows, the dogs yawned when they tried to bark and even the cockcrows, though they began well, ended in a snore. Only the flowers were awake. They gleamed and sparkled in the clear light like that which one sees rippling under the surface of chalk streams – the light of a subaqueous world, thick, watery yet infused with drowsiness.

Every lane led towards the sea. It was impossible to keep away from it just as it is impossible to keep away from a party that is being given by friends in the next street. Presently one came out through a hedge and saw it, blue and faintly ruffled like a velvet carpet that had been swept by a careless housemaid against the pile of the cloth. The shadows of one or two white clouds lay on it like the shadows thrown on to long grass by apple trees.

Down below the ceremonies on the beach were in full swing. Bright figures danced about in the waves, children dug their sand castles or collected shells, the old sat immersed in their daydreams. In the hollows between the rocks the lovers lay side by side. The sound of the sea in their ears had changed time to eternity. But eternity can also, when measured by the clock of time, be boring, so after sitting there for a little, looking stupidly at the countless white and black pebbles and grains of sand, I would start to climb over the rocks that lay prostrate in long ridges and dykes under the cliffs. Up and down I would go, crossing one rib of jagged rock after another, till I came to a deserted pebble beach. The sky was a silky blue, the sea barely moved and as I clambered over the slippery rocks and slithered between the blue, seaweedy pools, the reflection of the light in my eyes, the soft splash and wallop of the water would produce a sort of intoxication. The gulls circled and screamed but no one was in sight, nothing could be seen except the towering cliff above and around me the labyrinth of black rocks gleaming in the sunlight like herds of feeding elephants. I would throw off my clothes and plunge naked into the sea, then lie, drunk and dazzled by the sunlight, on the beach.

There was a jutting out point called Gull Rock, only to be reached at low tide and even then separated from the mainland by a gulf of a few yards in breadth through which the sea poured. A cave ran right through the rock, the breeding-place of a pair of seals, and one could bathe in the narrow inlet, protected from the strong current that ran round the point, without being seen from the beach. Here I used often to go to wallow in the swirling water or lie stretched out on a slab of black rock, and drink in the pungent savour of the sea. Or else, by choosing the exact moment of the tide, I could go on under the towering cliffs, across the rock-ribbed empty beaches until I came to the path that led up the cliff to Morwenstow. The coast was savage, littered with timber from wrecks and bunches of slimy sea-wrack, and I had to travel fast to get to the path before the sea cut me off. The solitude, the emptiness, the sense of being squeezed between sea and cliff weighed on me. One fall on those slippery rocks, a broken ankle and I would fail to make it and this knowledge sent a delicious thrill of fear down my spine. I would arrive soaked in sweat, have a drink at the pub and walk home.

But it was not only the beach at Welcombe that drew me. Since Gamel found the steepness of the hills too much for her, I used to go for long walks by myself along the cliff top as far as Hartland Point on one side and Combe on the other. The gorse, the heather, the foxgloves, the privet and the sea thrift growing on the broken cliffs rise in my mind when I think of them. I can call up their scent in my nostrils as I sit here. And then there were the dense, impenetrable woods, carpeted with hart's tongue and osmundia fern, where the trees, nipped by the salt sea gales, twisted and writhed like the trees in illustrations to books of fairy tales. Only I could not work in this intoxicating climate. I wrote a poem or two – the first I had written in more than twenty years – but for prose I needed the neutral air of Aldbourne.

Gamel and I made two life-long friends at Welcombe in Ronald and Rosemary Duncan. Ronnie had been brought up by his mother in a cottage a few miles along the coast and in 1937, soon after coming down from Cambridge, he rented a small dilapidated mill house that stood on the stream that divides Devon from Cornwall. He was a very undersized man, in body little more than a child though in face old and mature, with a mass of straight black hair and dark aquiline features that evoked Giotto's portrait of Dante. Rosemary, whom he later married, was a complete contrast, for she was a tall slim girl with long golden hair and bright blue eyes. She had great charm of manner and a bewitching smile which enabled her to get her way with everyone, but she could be difficult to live with as she had a capricious temperament. Since Ronnie has written his autobiography I need say little more about him except that both he and his sister were manifestly of Indian descent and, though there is some mystery about the connection and whether it was legitimate or otherwise, it seems certain that his paternal grandmother belonged to the family of the Rajahs of Cooch Behar, who owned vast estates near Calcutta. Ronnie's mother, on the other hand, was the daughter of an engine driver. But if her origins were humble, his father's family was rich, two of his uncles having houses in Park Lane, and he was eventually to come into enough money to buy up most of the land in the parish of Welcombe and so preserve it from vandalism. But there were no concrete signs of this when I first knew him for he and Rosemary lived in the most primitive style, collecting their timber and firewood on the beach and carrying their milk and groceries down the steep hill from the village.

Around the time of the Munich Agreement he bought the mill house he had been renting and a few acres of land from the miller and set out to combine the life of a poet with that of a farmer. Most of his land was either woodland or marsh and the few strips of run-down arable were half over-grown by bracken and capable of producing only the poorest crops. But he bought three cows and some poultry and a second-hand tractor and set to work. No Italian peasant ever lived on a simpler footing. Their cottage was furnished with a couple of wicker armchairs, a wooden bench and a table, while their bedroom upstairs contained only the plainest of beds and a wash-basin. There was a peculiar charm in seeing this strikingly handsome couple, with their cows and poultry and brood of newly hatched chickens combining farming with poetry in such Arcadian surroundings.

When the war came Ronnie declared himself a pacifist and was permitted by the authorities to continue with his task of what he optimistically called food production. A contingent of half a dozen other young pacifists arrived to assist him, for he had by now added another stretch of soggy or wooded acres to his estate. Such an amateurish team can rarely have been seen before in the annals of farming. One of the cows burst from having eaten too much grass, the tractor broke down every ten minutes and in any case the crop of wretched, rain-soaked oats was not worth reaping. Only the poultry, which Rosemary herself looked after, did well. At the same time Ronnie would launch out into the wildest ideas about the lack of enterprise in English agriculture. Why did we have to import bananas? If this valley were roofed over with glass we could grow thousands of tons of them. Why didn't we grow our own tobacco? Later he did so, planting a whole field on the hill top, and, though few plants came up, he had some dried leaves made up into cigarettes and sent a box of them to T. S. Eliot, who replied, 'I can recommend them strongly to anyone who wishes to give up smoking.' Yet by dint of reading he came in the end to acquire a good deal of theoretical knowledge of farming and his articles in the *Evening Standard,* which have since come out in book form, are first-rate journalism because he has the gift of writing terse, pungent prose.

This little group of pacifists were not opposed to war as such, but only to war with Nazi Germany. Ronnie had studied *Mein Kampf.* I should have found it hard not to have quarrelled with him if I had not reflected that at his age Shelley had also held opinions which he later changed. And what about myself? Ronnie was still under Ezra Pound's influence and needed to grow up and see the world as it was, and in time he did this with the help of more sophisticated friends such as Benjamin Britten and Lord Harewood. His success in the 'forties as a playwright and librettist also did a good deal to modify his opinions, for he has always been intensely anxious for the public recognition he well deserved.

I have always found Ronnie's charm irresistible. Although there is a bitter tinge to his mind, which has been increased by the neglect shown of late years for his poetry and plays, I know of no one whose company I

347

would prefer to have if I were in trouble. Confide in him and he shows an almost feminine sympathy and understanding. Then he is always calm and relaxed. One can sit by the fire in his company watching the flames without saying a word. At such times he gives the impression of being all of one piece, for there is a definiteness and completeness in his nature as though a line had been drawn round it. He is the only poet I have known who looked and talked like one. Another of his characteristics is his contempt for superficiality and cleverness. This has made him enemies, for as he has no small talk he passes over completely people who do not interest him. Arrogance and modesty, gentleness and bitterness, naivety and disillusion all show up by turns in his conversation. One curious anomaly is that, though he is a man of great natural dignity, he has a clowning streak which comes out of his relations with some of his friends. He can be either Dante or a little boy.

In May 1946 my father's sister died, leaving me £3,000. Then in the following June my stepmother wrote me that my father had developed an incurable cancer in the prostate. I went down to Budleigh Salterton and stayed with her till the end came. This happened early in the morning. I was keeping the night watch and he was lying back, apparently unconscious, in an armchair. A few years before he had lost one of his eyes and his new glass eye had been set in badly, so that it peered out to one side. But now it had suddenly taken another angle and looked upwards. Towards four o'clock a heavy laboured breathing began, the Cheyne Stokes respiration, which I had first witnessed as my mother lay dying. One of his eyes looked downward while the other, the glass one, stared steadily upwards, as if it already had a vision of heaven. How strange, I thought, that the mode of breathing by which during the past million years men have died should be given the name of an obscure Victorian doctor! Strange too that in order to die one must learn a new rhythm to that which one learned at the moment of birth!

The funeral banquet at the hotel had the rather ghoulish cheerfulness that such meals usually have. 'The old boy was seventy-seven, wasn't he?' my Uncle Bertie remarked. 'I wonder what he will cut up for.' And his widow and sons were wondering too. Then the lawyer, who had come down from London for the ceremony, read out the will. My father's estate, it appeared, totalled £62,000, which owing to the appreciation of capital would amount to £100,000 or more today. My stepmother was left the house and furniture, £1,000 in capital and the life interest on £12,000. I got £9,500 and my brother, as was just, a little more, our portions being assured to us by my father's marriage settlement. The rest was taken by death duties. My stepmother already had a certain income of her own, but hardly was my father dead than she came into a great deal more, and within a few years was better off than he had ever been. She moved to Surrey, where she lived with three servants in the lap of comfort, till her mind went and she was relegated to a private home where she still is today.

To sum up, I have at different times in my life inherited a total of around £23,000. I give these particulars because money is the controlling factor in a writer's life and without some private income I could never have written anything. Since the British free library system deprives an author of so much of his royalties and channels his work into commercial grooves I do not consider what I have got by inheritance to be exorbitant. In the case of only two of my books have I earned as much for the time I spent on writing them as the compositor who set them, and in some I have earned far less.

As soon as the funeral was over I went with Gamel to Cornwall. Although I had never loved or even liked my father, I felt so exhausted that for a few days I could scarcely walk. To be present at the death of someone one knows very well is a racking experience, because it is one's own death that one is witnessing. I was now at the top of the moving staircase and would probably be the next of my family to go over the edge.

My life with Gamel had all this time been a very happy and tranquil one. A woman came in every morning for an hour to get our breakfast and clean up, but Gamel did all the cooking while I washed up afterwards. Every afternoon we went for a walk over the Downs while, to keep us company and provide subjects for small talk, we kept a cat. It was a huge male tabby, by name Poffet, an animal of great beauty and character, and when after twelve years of life with us it died, we felt its loss. I have always been fond of cats while Gamel had that passion for them that is often felt by childless women. For we had not succeeded in having children. During our first years together her health had not allowed it and when, after settling into our house at Churriana, we tried to have one, we found it too late.

Marriage is a difficult thing to write about. The links that bind two people together can be of so many kinds. When Llewelyn Powys died in Switzerland in December 1939 Gamel seemed little affected because she had been expecting it for a long time. She buried him in the well of her mind, where like a true Southerner she buried all her past, to bring him up twenty years later as the one love of her life. For since she had strong ideals of what married love should be, she was more aware than I was that, though happy together, everything was not perfect between us. In a letter to Llewelyn dated perhaps in 1932 she wrote:

'Gerald has never got in touch with most of my mind at all, or even wanted to, or would be interested if he did. And I am sure that large tracts of his mind are equally sealed to me.'

I think that there is some truth in this. The barrier that separated us was due to something more than the existence of Llewelyn. I felt a lack of sympathy with the deeper parts of her mind. The happiest marriages are those in which two people are in accord with one another down to the roots of their being. But I could not share Gamel's deeply pessimistic and melancholic view of life, which sprang from some inherited weakness and lack of energy in her constitution and I felt even less sympathy for the romantic aura in which she invested her past. She liked to talk of her childhood, but I never believed what she told me about it because she saw it completely *couleur de rose* whereas I knew that it had in many ways been painful. So I stopped listening and it was this that made her feel that I was not interested in her mind, whereas it was only one tendency in it that I did not care about. Her favourite reading at this time was fairy tales: everything that took her back to the magic days of childhood delighted her. True lovers share their childhoods, but even if I had been completely in love with her I could not have shared an imaginary childhood because I require some portion of reality in everything.

One could call her, in some aspects of her nature, a narcissist. As she passed forty she began to be obsessed by her appearance; wherever she sat she had a large silver hand mirror tucked into the chair beside her and every ten minutes she would examine her face with care to see if any new lines had appeared. This preoccupation with their looks is often to be found in beautiful women who feel the years stealing over them, though she carried it to greater lengths than I have seen in anyone else. Yet, as I used to tell her, age would never destroy her beauty, which depended on fine bones and a clear skin as well as on the intelligence and sensitivity one read in her features.

But if in the depths of our natures we were not in contact, we were very close on the upper levels. We had the same tastes in everything, the same feelings for books and places and paintings. This gave us ample subjects for conversation though often I was too taken up with my work to be an enlivening companion. Writers' wives have to suffer from an overflow of their cogitations on the book they are working on. Yet, this apart, she had little time in which to feel bored. Not only did she do the cooking but she typed my manuscripts and besides we had many visitors. Although when she was left to herself she would sink into her melancholy musings, she enjoyed seeing people and was gay and lively when they came. Then she depended on me in everything, for she was one of those people who cannot initiate the smallest thing by themselves. As for myself, I was completely satisfied with my marriage. It gave me peace of mind, which I had not known since I had got entangled with Carrington, and therefore leisure for work, which was the only thing I wanted. And then I loved her. Her face was a perpetual pleasure to look at. With her calm bearing and gentle voice and ways and dreamy aspect she created an atmosphere of romance and poetry that other people were aware of as well as myself. I felt that I was extraordinarily lucky to have as my wife a woman who was of so much finer a mental and moral texture than I was.

And yet, if I am to be completely honest, Gamel's passivity of temperament sometimes weighed on me. Her conversation could be delightful, but it did not stimulate. It was precise and lucid, yet it did not engage her whole nature. It has usually been vitality, the quick give and take, the sense of entanglement with another mind, that has attracted me in women and called out a vein of spontaneity I could never show with her. One could not tease her, for, since she had no sense of humour about herself, she regarded all teasing, however mild, as a form of bullying. One could not flirt with her because she did not understand flirting. One could not quarrel with her or even, without a sharp tone coming into her voice, disagree with her. Our intercourse was therefore conducted on one level. We met only on neutral territory and that left something lacking.

But if these were my feelings about her, what did she think of me? Although one can never really know how one appears to other people, I would say that when we had first met at Chaldon and begun to fall in love with one another she had seen in me an active and self-assured man, not without literary imagination, who would give her the love and support she needed. She had even compared me to Jane Eyre's Rochester. But this flattering opinion of hers did not last. She soon came more accurately to see me as a very self-centred person, obsessed by the problems that the deficiencies of his own mind made for him. I used to say that I was like a man engaged in a motor race whose engine gave him such continual trouble that he was compelled to give more of his attention to it than to the course. Then I was a realist about life, which must have seemed a flat sort of thing to a woman of dreamy, romantic modes of feeling. If I was still, where practical things were concerned, a man of some self-assurance and energy, a hedgerow tree round which the honeysuckle could climb, in our quiet literary life there was little scope for such qualities. I can understand best what I lacked for her when I look at Llewelyn Powys or at one or two other men to whom at various times she was drawn. This was sweetness and simplicity. These qualities I did not have and in their place could only offer reliability, deriving from my sense of responsibility, which has always been strong. Gamel knew that whatever happened I would never leave her and that, with all my defects, I gave her the security and companionship she needed.

For these reasons our relationship came gradually to approximate to that of brother and sister. At length, when I was fifty-seven, I became so conscious of this that marital relations between us began to appear as a sort of incest. Soon I was unable to continue them. No doubt it seemed to her a sign that she had ceased to be attractive to me because she was growing old, but this was not the case. I continued to love and admire her as much as before. But it also affected her because, though past fifty at the time, she was of a sensual disposition.

During these years at Aldbourne my old attraction to girls would return from time to time and I would have a brief, surreptitious adventure. So long as no serious feelings were involved, I saw no harm in them. Girls had become freer in their habits since the 'twenties and young bodies have a special charm. One of these adventures however was different. I was drawn to a young actress who came to live with her parents next door. She was a shy but impulsive girl, too thin-skinned for the racket of stage life, with delicate features that reminded me of my old flame of the 'twenties, Vivien. She was in love with her husband, who was at the war, and was hardly a girl to have affairs, but somehow as we went for walks or read poetry together, a current of feeling sprang up between us and for a few weeks we imagined that we were in love. Then just as I was getting alarmed by the situation, her husband returned unexpectedly and her feelings for me collapsed. We promised eternal friendship and never met again. Although I was taken aback by the suddenness of the change, I was also relieved. A good marriage has a pull like the earth's gravity. A passing moon can raise a tide, but it quickly subsides again.

My daughter Miranda had meanwhile grown into a tall, strong and remarkably handsome girl, bad at her books but a good dancer and with a talent for practical things. To complete her education we sent her to Paris *en pair* with some French friends of ours and she became engaged to the young man of the family, who was finishing his studies to be a doctor. I went out to see her and spent a rapturous fortnight there in May 1950 and they were married that autumn from my brother's London house. It has turned out to be a very happy marriage. My son-in-law, who is a first-rate doctor and a very delightful person, has a practice in Paris, while she has become a real Parisienne, dressing with taste and elegance and managing her house and bringing up her children well.

In the April of the following year Gamel and I went to Italy on a two months' trip. Our object was to visit the sites of all the Greek cities south of Naples, whether they had important remains or not. We made the tour of Calabria and Sicily, travelling by bus and train, and the high-spots of our trip were, after the Sicilian temples, Locri and Sybaris. Later I wrote an article called *The City of the Sybarites,* which came out in *Encounter,* in October 1957.

Gamel's mother had died in Florida and in December 1951 we flew to New York so that she could claim her inheritance. We spent a few days in New York, meeting E. E. Cummings and Horace Gregory, but as soon as we had seen the picture galleries I was glad to leave. The scale of its architecture is inimical to human life. The South, however, pleased me. The little towns with their white frame houses were pretty, even though they were all alike, and then there was the size of the country. It never composed as the scenery of Europe does: its beauty lay not in any particular scene but in its vastness and monotony. Gamel's family were very hospitable and kind. Her half-brother, Bill Woolsey, drove us all over the state and then through Georgia to Jacksonville, where we spent a couple of weeks seeing lawyers. In the end it turned out that Gamel had inherited some six thousand dollars.

We returned to England sooner than we would have liked because Ruth Lowinsky had offered to drive us out to Malaga. Since our previous visit three years before we had heard that the state of Spain had greatly improved and this made us wish to go back and live there. In fact we found that the drought and famine were over and American aid pouring in, so we decided to do this. We returned for the last time to England to pack our books and dispose of our cottage, and took the boat back to Gibraltar in January 1953.

25

Churriana again

It was a great change to find myself occupying once more a large house whose rooms were airy and spacious instead of a diminutive cottage where I had to stoop every time I went through a door. It was also a change to leave the cold, grey English winter for the warmth and sunlight of southern Spain. I love large rooms and I love light. The garden too had come on surprisingly since we had laid it out twenty years before. The trees had grown taller and more spreading, roses and wysteria smothered walls and trellises and there was a look of semi-tropical exuberance breaking through the formality of the edged flower beds. This was the house that I had dreamed of so often during the war years, searching for it but never finding it, inquiring but always put off, and now that I at last had it I could say that it was even better than I had imagined it to be.

We had however to resign ourselves to one great drawback; almost half of the house was occupied by a tenant whom we could see no way of getting rid of. During the war years the British Treasury had not allowed me to send out money to pay the taxes or the wages, so that Rosario, the wife of our gardener Antonio, had been obliged to let off the rooms of the house to raise enough money. The families who took the first floor were Spaniards and, with the self-respect that is natural to their nation, assisted by a little key money, found other lodgings for themselves as soon as they learned that I and my wife were returning to live in our house. But the ground floor had been rented to an Englishman and his French mistress and they showed no intention of leaving. He paid a rent of 125 pesetas a month – that is 80p – for half this large house furnished with good furniture and with several hundred books thrown in. That was the situation we had to face.

My tenant was a strange sort of man. He had served as an officer in Kenya during the First World War and after that had come out to Torremolinos. Here he had settled down with a French girl in a small farmhouse. They had bought horses and before the Civil War I would see them riding about the country clad in riding habits made by the local tailor and imported bowler hats. Then when the war broke out the horses vanished, but for many years after that he continued, summer and winter, to wear the bowler hat, presumably for its symbolical value.

My housekeeper Rosario had taken pity on his poverty and let him have half the house at a very low rent, but no sooner were they installed in it than she quarrelled violently with his companion. All the other tenants quarrelled with her too and this led in 1949 to a lawsuit which Rosario lost.

We had then to accustom ourselves to sharing our house with another couple. We occupied the top floor and they the ground floor, except for a garden room off the patio which we retained. They had the front door and we the back, so that we never met, for since the lawsuit we had not been on speaking terms. Otherwise we had nothing to complain of except the inconvenience, for our tenant was a complete hermit. No one ever visited him, not a sound ever came out of his rooms. All we knew of him was that he would go for long walks carrying his shoes and socks in a basket and that he took in *The Times Literary Supplement*. So we lived in the same house for sixteen years without any communication between us.

When in March 1949 I had visited Torremolinos for the first time since the outbreak of the Civil War I had not seen a single Spaniard in the place. A few villas – that was all – had been put up by people from Madrid. But now in 1953 the foreign influx was begining and, once started, it continued to grow at a prodigious speed. Within a dozen years this little place had become a town with fifty or more hotels and innumerable apartment blocks, while the whole coast from the Pyrenees to Algeciras, which till then had been the most beautiful and deserted coastline in Europe, had become a chain of villas and hotels.

The building explosion was accompanied by a parallel explosion in the standard of living. Wages rose by several hundred per cent within a few years and the cost of food and services followed them. Every Spaniard who had a shop or a business or who worked in the building trade was making money, with the result that, whereas in 1953 there had been only one car in our village and no motor bikes, very soon there were several hundred. The street on which my workroom looked, which had formerly echoed only to the sound of horses trotting and of flocks of goats pattering, now shook with the screech of motor traffic. Then the nightingales, which had rested in our garden, took wing and left and the house martins and golden orioles followed. Only the blackbirds with a sprinkling of warblers and sparrows remained. Although certain material benefits such as refrigerators and washing machines became available, the *douceur de vivre* of Churriana had gone.

Almost at once we began to have visitors. Ralph and Frances Partridge would come out for a couple of months almost every year and rent a house that lay just outside the village. Then in the winter of 1954–5 Augustus and Dorelia John took rooms in a hotel in Torremolinos. Augustus had become very genial in his old age and had adopted an elaborately courtly style of address with women, while Dorelia was one of my best and oldest of friends and got on well with Gamel. We also had many friends to stay in our house – indeed we had never before been so social.

I must say something of the visit of my oldest friend, John Hope-Johnstone, though it was a painful one. He arrived in May 1953 and stayed for a couple of months and I can only say that he was detestable. He had been staying in Switzerland with a rich man who collected Chinese works of art to advise him about cataloguing them and he had eaten so well there that, though a very slim man, he had developed a paunch and could no longer fasten his top trouser buttons. He complained of everything, especially the food. Why was the bread so bad? Why was there no French cheese? There he sat in his city clothes, collarless and with his flies undone, boasting of his aristocratic descent and reviling middle-class mores. There was a perpetual sneer in his voice and I could only congratulate myself that, if this was how he liked staying with us, I need never invite him again.

There were several hundred books on our shelves that belonged to him and which I had brought down from Yegen where he had left them some thirty years before. He spent several days going over my library selecting those he wanted. I then had them crated and sent off to England, while those he did not want I bought from him at an agreed price. Then shortly before he left I noticed that a large empty canvas bag that he had brought with him was now full and bulging with what were obviously books. One day therefore when he had gone into Malaga I decided to investigate. The bag was locked but I found a key that opened it. As I had expected, it was full of my books, some of which I particularly needed. As I had no wish to humiliate him by confronting him with his crime I removed those I could not afford to part with and substituted for them mathematical tomes which belonged to him but which he had said he did not want. I had always known that Hope filched books from other peoples' libraries, but I felt indignant that he should do so from mine, all the more as he was living rent free in the annexe of my old cottage at Aldbourne, which at some sacrifice to myself I had stipulated that he should have for his life.

Six years later there was a sequel to this. He had been on a visit to a cousin who lived at Algeciras and on his way back to England he called on us. 'Just for an hour or two,' he said, but, remembering our old friendship, I persuaded him to stay for a fortnight. Since the only luggage he had brought with him was a very small valise and a string bag full of books 'to read on the train', I did not suppose that he could do any more pilfering.

But in this I was mistaken. After he had gone I found that several of my most treasured volumes were missing and that in their place he had left behind some trashy modern novels, which he had taken from his cousin. Yet he was pathetic, for his mind had began to go. When he set off by train it was with a rucksack so heavy that he could hardly lift it and a large suitcase which before coming to see us he had deposited at the station cloakroom. With these he intended to visit a number of places in Castile which were only accessible by motor bus. I bought him his ticket to Cordoba and settled him in his carriage – then, just as the train was starting, he asked, 'Where am I going to? I've forgotten the name.' 'Cordoba,' I shouted back to him, and the train drew out. I got a card from him from Madrid saying he was ill and returning to England, but since that day I have not seen him nor heard from him.

He died in January 1970 at the age of 87. He had come into a little money before then and bought a large cottage in the same village. I am told that in his last years he had talked badly of me, telling people that my autobiography, *A Life of One's Own,* was a pack of lies. Yet before I left Aldbourne I had showed him the typescript of this and offered to cut any passage he did not like, but he made no comments. So ended a friendship that had lasted for near on fifty years, though I think that it would have ended twenty years sooner if he had not seen some material advantages in continuing it. Prolonged poverty, that deformer of character, had brought out the calculating side of his nature, which, if he had had an adequate income, would have been early buried.

My life during these first five or six years back in Spain was a very quiet one. I worked in the mornings and usually again after tea and in the afternoons went for a walk with Gamel. To make these walks more interesting I took up botanizing. The first book I wrote was *South from Granada.* I began it on the suggestion of Merwyn Levy that I should write something on Spanish life for a paper he edited in Berlin under American auspices. It made me around £1,400. Then I took up *A Holiday by the Sea* and finished it four years later, though I did not work at it continuously. It made me less than £700. After this I took up my autobiography, *A Life of One's Own,* revised it and added a couple of chapters on what I could remember of my war experience.

It thus happened that, although these books all got good reviews, I made little money on them. If it had not been for the steady and increasing income brought in by *The Spanish Labyrinth* and *The Literature of the Spanish People* I do not know how we should have managed. Our house was unsaleable because no one would buy it so long as an irremoveable tenant occupied the ground floor. Yet to live in it we had to keep a gardener, a cook and a maid. I often felt trapped, but I have a gift for survival and

357

somehow we managed to surmount every crisis.

Gamel's mode of life began to change soon after our settling in Chur-riana and to revert to the old Southern pattern in which she had been brought up. Since we had servants she did not need to cook and since she could not bear to give orders or even enter the kitchen (she always talked to Rosario and Antonio as if she was not the mistress of the house but a visitor) she left the housekeeping to me. This took up little of my time, but her relegation of all responsibility for the house or garden meant that she had no stake in them and therefore nothing of a practical kind to occupy herself with. She would sit all day in her armchair in the *cierro* with the *New Yorker* on her lap or on the floor beside her, looking out over the garden in a dreamy state of mind. She had spells of reading poetry or novels and then to everyone's amazement she took up science fiction and developed a pas-sion for it, devouring not only all the books on it she could lay her hands on but the little magazines that appeared every fortnight in Spanish. She even wrote a science fiction story about the loneliness of living on one of the planets which was published in the *Saturday Evening Post*. She knew her failing – lack of energy. As I would tell her, energy can be generated by sitting down to a table at a fixed hour every day, but she would never write except when the mood was on her, seated upright in her armchair with an exercise book on her lap. And even then her pen would often drop and she would sink back into her dream. Yet if practical problems arose that re-quired immediate action, she would pull herself together and meet them. She was admirable in emergencies because they gave her the stimulus she needed.

Before we came out to Churriana she had translated a novel by Pérez Galdós called *La de Bringas* under the title of *The Spendthrifts*. She was a first-rate translator, rendering the text in pure and idiomatic English, and the book sold 70,000 copies. For this she received £100. I wanted her to continue translating, but she preferred to do original work. This turned out to be poetry. Soon after settling in Spain she wrote a long poem in *vers libre* entitled *The Search for Demeter* which was published in *Botteghe Oscure*. Its subject was the remorse she felt on hearing of her mother's death. A year or two later she began a series of sonnets. The form suited her better than *vers libre* and these verses show a fine ear and are delicately and pre-cisely phrased. Had they been published in the 1920s they would have been well received, but now in the post-Auden years they struck no new note. Although she had refined her technique, she was still the romantic poet she had been in her youth and so those sonnets are really distillations of all the poetry that had been written in England between Keats and Eliot. Then every one of them has the same theme: they speak of deep sadness, a vain regret for the past, a lack of hope for the future. That is, they express the melancholy side of her character and not the gay and happy one which she also possessed. It is for this reason that, taken together, they do not exhilarate, as Matthew Arnold said that all true poetry, however melancholy in tone, must do. One can read two or three of them with pleasure, but in the mass they are monotonous because they always strike the same note.

Our servants, who were strongly attached to Gamel, compared her to a nun. Much of her life at Churriana was indeed a long, dreamy meditation. I sometimes felt that a root in some form of Christianity would have helped her, but religious faith was something that she totally lacked. Her father had been a deist and her mother an agnostic and her first introduction to religion had come from Frazer's *Golden Bough,* which she read before she was ten. She used to say that when she first came across Christianity she took it to be just another mythological cult of the Attic-Adonis sort. Yet the religious mood was something that she felt spontaneously, for her favourite poets, who had once been Donne (for the love poems), Blake and Wordsworth, were now George Herbert and Eliot. Only the energy required for positive faith was lacking.

I can see her now sitting in her favourite chair watching the sunset. She preferred sunsets to sunrises, ruins to perfect buildings, old people to young, the past to the present. Indeed the last dozen years of her life were spent in brooding over the past and recreating it in her mind. The United States, her childhood, Llewelyn Powys were all worked over and built into something new – something hugged secretly to herself which she could never speak of to anyone except to those two women, Alyse Gregory and Phyllis Playter, who had shared her youth with her. Every summer she went back to England to visit them and renew her memories of the past.

There is a special charm about people who have renounced struggle and effort as a means of getting their way. Gamel was a quietist, totally devoid of both selfishness and egoism. She welcomed the stimulus provided by social life, especially when it offered intelligent conversation, but what she most liked was to be left alone to read and dream. Someone had to provide the outer framework of her life – that was all. She never asked anything for herself, but accepted the suggestions that were made to her, just as she agreed to other people's opinions because that saved her trouble. Yet her habitual air of calm was deceptive: under it she was racked by obscure feelings of guilt and above all by the belief that she had frittered away her literary talent. Why did she have so little energy? Such thoughts gave her a secret impatience with herself which she rarely revealed even to me. All through the war years she had longed for the life she now led – the large house, the beautiful garden, the mild climate, the leisure to read and write, the continually growing library, and now she found that she could do little to the point with them. Given the clear mind and the fine sensibility that she knew she possessed, her inability to make better use of them was tragic. Yet the effect that she produced on other people was different. By her mere presence, sitting in her chair, pacing slowly about the garden, entertaining her visitors, talking to her cats, she gave off a sort of poetry that everyone who got to know her felt. She was the spirit of the house, of the house in which she lived as if she were a guest because any sort of possessiveness or assertion of authority aroused guilt in her, and I still feel, almost two years after her death, that she inhabits it.

I now come to an event which brought a sudden though temporary change in my life. On April 2nd, 1957, a girl of twenty-five called Joanna Carrington came on a visit to us. She was the niece of Dora Carrington, and had been born in the year of her suicide. As a child of seven she had spent the first winter of the war with us in our Wiltshire cottage. Then she had grown up, developed a talent for painting and was sent to an art school. Here she had met a young designer and gone out with him to Nigeria, where he had been appointed to a post in the government publicity department. But although she was deeply in love with her good looking, communist husband, the marriage had gone badly from the start owing to temperamental incompatibility. She fell ill of relapsing fever and was invalided back to England, feeling that she could never live with him again. Under this distress of body and mind she became moody and neurotic, so her mother asked me if we could have her to stay since she needed rest and sunshine.

She arrived. I saw a singularly lovely girl with long golden hair and intense blue eyes – the same far-sighted eyes that Carrington had once had. Her features were regular except for her thick, almost negroid lips which gave a sensual look that contradicted the pure lines of the rest of her face. Her limbs and her body were slim and perfectly made. In repose she had a sulky expression, but when she talked she lit up and her smile was full of encouragement. Since she felt a strong admiration for her aunt I gave her the packets I had of her letters to read. They fascinated her and, as she told me later, made her feel that she wanted to draw me away from Carrington's memory and secure my attention for herself.

A flirtation began between us which soon carried me out of my depth. The culminating moment came when we climbed a mountain behind the house and picnicked on the top. For the first time in thirty-five years I found myself totally carried away. 'It seems', I wrote to Ralph Partridge, 'that I can only lose my head over members of the Carrington family.' I went at once to Gamel to tell her what had happened. She was naturally distressed, but I pointed out to her that nothing could possibly come of my *engouement* for a girl who was nearly forty years younger than myself. Within a few weeks it would be over, for Joanna would return to London, where she was already interested in a young man, and I would pass out of her life as a temporary aberration. Whatever I felt for her now, my feelings for her, Gamel, would never change. She, although clearly upset, took my explanation well and showed her usual tact by leaving us together frequently. She knew as well as I did that it would not last.

Flirtation, however fervent, might not have been enough to put me in the state I was now in had Joanna not suffered from such changeable moods, moving from ardour to coldness every few hours. She was full of theories about love and could discuss its tactics and strategy by the hour, yet under her theories there lay an ambivalent attitude towards me which was beyond her control. Thus, she told me, she could not help despising any man who was in love with her because he was in her power and this propensity, I supposed, must be turned with greater force upon me, who was so far removed from her in age. I had therefore to put up with her 'afternoon moods'. Affectionate in the mornings before she went off to paint, she would usually feel a strong reaction against me after lunch. If people came to tea she would make ironic remarks about me and, should a man be around, flirt with him in order – or so I thought – to make me jealous; it did not matter how unsuitable he was – to snub and hurt me, an elderly queen would do. But then in the evenings she would change completely: we would sit up till two or three drinking cognac and chain-smoking till the little sitting-room was thick with cigarette smoke. Only for once it was not I who did the talking. The breakdown of Joanna's marriage followed by her illness had left her in a very lonely and unbalanced state so that she felt an obsessive urge to communicate everything about herself and her life. I had to be content with little more than that because, with Gamel in the house, there could be no question of our relations being carried further, even had Joanna been ready for it.

We quarrelled of course. When she treated me too badly I would shut myself up in my work-room and refuse to see her and she would knock on the door full of repentance at having hurt me, but also with a renewed interest in me because I had rejected her. She liked to make the advances herself, so that only a man who was emotionally detached from her could hold her for long. In this she resembled Carrington, except that she sometimes enjoyed hurting me, which Carrington, who had hurt me more, had not done.

So the weeks passed. Evenings of intoxicating happiness were followed by afternoons of frustration. This is the treatment that drives the arrows of love deep into the system. I was falling more and more under her spell: outside her nothing existed. Yet I knew that this vertiginous course could not last. She would leave and find a young man in London and I would return to my quiet life with Gamel. I was in the position of a child at a fair, revelling in the thrills of speed on the scenic railway, yet not really wishing that they would continue indefinitely.

At length the end came. Joanna left for London, where she had to appear in court to get her divorce, but holding out a qualified promise that she would return for a longer visit in September. A correspondence followed – two or three letters from each of us every week. Some of hers were enormously long – one of them, I remember, covered thirty pages. They were what she called 'pour out' letters, describing her very intense and always changing feelings, her agony over her divorce and her complicated life in London. In this troubled period of her life she was a compulsive relater of everything she did and felt, and it became my function to receive her letters, just as I had once received and answered Carrington's. Only Joanna's were far fuller and franker because she kept nothing back, whereas Carrington had always been secretive.

Meanwhile a dreadful emptiness had descended on me. For some days I kept entirely to my room and could not bear to enter the little sitting-room with its yellow armchairs where I had sat up on so many nights talking to her. I ceased to be able to read or to work on my novel, but either lay on my couch going over the past weeks in my mind or else wrote letters. Then I suddenly began to write poetry and for two months continued to do this every day, turning out in that time a quantity of verse that was greater than all I had written since 1918. This calmed me. It was the best verse I had produced so far and only a small part of it was about Joanna.

September came at last and she arrived. It had been agreed that our relations should from now on be on an entirely different footing. Both my and her regard for Gamel demanded this even if, which is highly doubtful, she would have been ready to resume them as before. However, to compensate me for this change, she promised me that there would be no more 'afternoon moods'. We would be merely good friends and against a friend she could have no hostile reactions. But in this it turned out that she had promised more than she could perform. Aware of how I still felt about her, she continued to blow alternately hot and cold, so that, as I was no longer receiving what she had given me before, I began to feel more and more bitter about her. Whenever she wished she could charm me, but she could also make me hate her and when she left in January I was not sorry to see her go. The strain had become too much for me. In a few months I had lost some sixteen pounds in weight, which is a good deal for a man who is naturally thin.

Today I feel nothing but gratitude to her. She turned a flirtation into a stirring and deeply felt experience and drew out of me a store of feelings that had long been dormant and which I had never supposed could rise to the surface again. She is now happily married and whenever I go to London I see her.

The spring of that year brought another girl into my life. This was Hetty. She had been picked up by an American friend of ours, penniless and ill, and he asked us to take her in because he was leaving Spain. I went to Torremolinos to see her. I found a sturdily built girl with long straight black hair and enormous brown saucer eyes fringed by thick eyelashes. She had the face of a doll and the melancholy expression of Mary Magdelene in a baroque painting. Both in appearance and manner she was unlike any girl I had ever met and I did not feel drawn to her. But then as we sat on the verandah together and she told me her story I became more interested.

It seemed that she was the daughter of an Anglo-Dutch stockbroker called Scholten and his much younger wife, who had been a hospital nurse. When she was eighteen she had shown a marked talent for drawing and had been sent to an art school, after which she had worked with some success in London as a lithographer. But adventure was in her blood and she had suddenly developed a craze for jazz and jazz orchestras. Falling in love with a man who played in one, she had dropped her art for a life of wild and often sordid adventures which had ended in her marrying an American junky. After knocking about for a year in Greece and Turkey, they had come out to Spain with their baby, intending to settle there. Her husband's pension as a wounded soldier gave them enough to live on. Then suddenly he had vanished with all their money, leaving her in hospital recovering from a mild addiction and their baby with the Spanish woman with whom they lodged.

Rather unwillingly I invited Hetty to stay with us; her baby and her numerous possessions were fetched from Marbella, and then her husband turned up. He proved to be a completely broken-down man, filthy and bedraggled and dressed like a down-and-out. For many years, it seemed, he had led the life of a petty criminal, stealing, poncing and performing abortions with a pair of rusty iron forceps which he carried about with him, but now he was too far gone on junk for that. After collecting a little money from me for 'medicines', he staggered off and did not appear again for several months, after which he left for Mexico. The strange thing was that Hetty had an unshakeable trust and confidence in this unappetizing husband of hers, although she declared that she would never live with him again until he gave up heroin. Her recent experiences had cured her of any desire to go back to that, yet drugs of one sort or another were for her the great romantic experience of life – what travel in exotic countries is to other people – and it was not long before she was smoking marijuana.

As the days went on I began to feel more and more drawn to her. I liked her for her tremendous vitality as well as for her warmth and good humour, which contrasted so strongly with Joanna's prickly moods, and then I was fascinated by the adventurous career she had had. She appealed to that side of me which had once been attracted to aberrant or borderline girls of working-class extraction, for these were the circles in which she had spent the past five or six years so that her middle-class origins had been almost entirely rubbed off. I also felt physically attracted to her, but here I had no success for early in our acquaintance she announced that if I ever made a pass at her she would leave at once.

Hetty therefore stayed on and when in June Gamel left for England she remained alone in the house with me. We went to parties, got drunk together, talked and played records, but though Hetty, who was proud of her firm little body, would undress and walk about naked in front of me, we never in any way made love. Then she left for Torremolinos, where I supported her for a few months, hoping she would make money by her painting. She had real talent, her drawings especially being full of power and vigour, but her passion for sitting in cafés and bars or dancing till 3 a.m. as well as the total disorder of her daily life usually prevented her from getting down to work on a picture. That winter there was a large influx of beatniks into Torremolinos. They were most of them New York Jews and they sat around all day in cafés, not so much talking as staring at one another, beginning a sentence with 'Like, man … ' and then stopping from lack of anything to say. In their pads they smoked large quantities of pot. Hetty found these people very congenial and took pleasure in introducing me to them. I was fascinated. This was a new world to me and through her flattering introductions I entered it on almost equal terms and not as an elderly square. I felt as though I was an anthropologist who had been adopted by a tribe of Solomon Islanders. Or, to vary the simile, as though I was the old lady who got on so well with the elephants in the Babar books. I also derived a snobbish pleasure from mastering their vocabulary and learned to use phrases such as 'turn on, be way out, goof for, flip, be hung up, put someone down, dig something, be with it, make that scene' and so forth, at a time when they were not known outside jazz orchestras in England. Hetty was introducing me to 'life', those mysterious goings on that since I was a boy of sixteen I had craved to be admitted to, but which had always been outside my reach. She was also making me, what every man in his sixties longs for, feel young again. Her zest and enthusiasm and the affection and encouragement she gave me were powerful stimuli. I made notes on what I saw as I was intending to write a novel on my experiences.

The high point in our relation came in May 1959 when Gamel left for England and I decided on the spur of the moment to take Hetty on a trip round Morocco. We were to travel as beats, hitch-hiking whenever possible, sleeping in Arab *fondaks* and taking no luggage. In fact we carried nothing but a haversack between us, containing our washing things and

(for me) a clean nylon shirt and pair of drawers. Then when we got to
Tangier Hetty bought an Arab *foukiya* and left her European clothes behind.

We went first to Marrakesh, where she picked up a young Moroccan
who introduced her to the secrets of the preparation of pot and hash. She
was crazy on the subject of all drugs – a side of her nature which bored me
because, though I occasionally smoked to please her, I got nothing from it.
From here we crossed the Atlas to Taroudant and continued to bus to
Goulimin, where we slept on a straw mattress in a shop and saw the marvellous dances of the Blue Men, or rather of their girls. From this place we
got on to Ouarzazate and then descended the Valley of the Dra to Zagora.
I have not space to put down the many adventures we had for Hetty was a
person who made friends everywhere and we were travelling like poor
people. But unfortunately we had both caught heavy colds at Goulimin
from being too lightly dressed and now mine turned to flu and I developed
a high temperature. However the thermometer had risen to 100° Fahrenheit in the shade and the sun heat was stunning, so, as I was not afraid of
getting pneumonia, we went on as usual, returning by Ksar-el-Souk to Fez
and from there to Tangier and so home. During the last week I had seen
everything through a film of fever, but a few days in bed put me right.

After our return I began to see rather less of Hetty, who took to living
with a succession of boy friends, most of them American beats. She would
fall violently in love, expect her relation to last forever and then quarrel
and leave. The last of them was a crippled and mentally retarded Australian
with whom she settled in one of the wildest of the Canary Islands, where he
went berserk and beat her up. But nothing could get this girl down for
long: she came bobbing up to the surface like a rubber ball and, as soon as
she had got back to Spain, set off with her son for Mexico where she hoped
to renew her relations with her husband. She found him living alone in a
shack on a remote mountain side, but, sunk in heroin, he refused to have
anything to do with her. The obvious move after this was to Haight Street,
San Francisco, where she supported herself for some years by illustrating a
hippy magazine called *The Oracle*. Here she was in her element, taking
L.S.D. and having colour visions. But soon the cops began to turn nasty
and the great diaspora of the hippies began. After a short spell in gaol she
set off with her new English husband for a deserted island off British
Columbia, where they hoped to found a self-supporting colony. But before
their log hut had been finished the Canadian police moved them on, so,
tired of being hunted down, they sailed from New York to Pondicherry in
India. Here they joined an *ashram* that had collected round a French lady
aged ninety-seven who was known as 'Holy Mother'. Hetty became a
devout Buddhist and her letters would contain packets of dried flowers that
had been blessed by her, but then, the summer heat proving too great, she

went on to Nepal. At present she is living in a Tibetan monastery, dressed in scarlet nun's robes and being taught to speak and read Tibetan by a young monk with whom she hopes to bring out a Tibetan primer for English people. Her last letter was full of Tibetan words and Lamaist doctrinal terms and she assured me that this form of Buddhism with its Shamanistic roots was greatly preferable to the sort that 'Holy Mother' taught. She had always been the most gullible of girls.

Gamel had first looked askance at Hetty's intrusion into our life. But then with her usual kindness and tolerance she came to like her and to see that she was a harmless girl with no designs on me, but merely a need for moral and, in emergencies, financial support. Hetty's feelings for me became in time those of a daughter for her father while Gamel, whom she was equally devoted to, became her mother figure. So though often bored by her obtuseness, which could in her credulous moods be very great, Gamel became genuinely attached to her and would defend her to me when I was annoyed with her. What she disliked was the obsessive interest I took in her during the first year or so of our acquaintance and the fact that I talked so continually to everyone about her latest exploits. She was right about this and looking back over these years I feel that I often behaved stupidly and insensitively. The sixties are the classic age for silliness in men because they feel that their power to attract the other sex is rapidly failing.

My association with Hetty led to my making friends with a number of other young people who were by no means beats or hippies. In the summer months while Gamel was in England they would pack into my house and conduct their amorous musical chairs. I was tasting in my elderly way the sort of dissipation I had missed when I was young, only it was a vicarious one. I sat around in night clubs and flirted, but in none of these girls did I take any real interest. It was the atmosphere that I liked.

The excuse I made to myself for leading this sort of life was that I was writing a novel on the coast. I said to myself that I had never become a novelist because I had not had a fixed society to draw on. The people I had known in England had come from all over the place. But the Costa del Sol, where I now lived, was a mixing bowl. Beatniks and millionaires could meet and know one another and this provided something equivalent, though in a superficial and shoddy way, to the world from which the great Russian novelists had been drawn. I wanted to write an open novel, exhibiting a large range of characters and situations, and the theme was to be disintegration, for that was what all the non-Spaniards on the coast were doing. They were people who had cut themselves off from their roots and were destroying themselves. Then there would be a subsidiary theme on the plight of young writers and painters. There must be several hundred thousand of them in the world today and, though many of them have some small talent, hardly any of them come to anything, either because they lack character or a sense of direction or because they have no regular means of support. I thought of them as offering a parallel to the hermits and ascetics of the Middle Ages, set on drawing some illumination out of themselves, but almost invariably failing.

My novel, which I entitled *The Lighthouse always says Yes,* came out in 1965 and was a complete failure. I agree with the critics that it was a bad novel, partly because I had made my anti-hero so feeble and negative, but I would claim that some of the scenes in it, especially that of the flamenco show at Seville, were vivid and well written. Incidentally most of the characters in it were drawn from real people.

In the same year in which we settled in Churriana an American couple, Bill and Annie Davis, had bought a very large house just outside the village. They were people of a literary turn of mind and strong Anglophile tendencies, while Annie was the sister of Cyril Connolly's first wife. They often had congenial house guests and, as they were hospitable people, would invite us to dinner to meet them. Now in the spring of 1959 Ernest Hemingway came to visit them and remained all the summer. Although he was at this time exclusively taken up with bullfighting, which I do not like, he had read some of my books and wanted to meet me.

I find it difficult to describe him because he was totally unlike anyone else I have ever known. At first sight he suggested one of those famous sea captains of past ages who have spent their best years in the Arctic, fighting the ice floes in their struggle to make the North-West Passage. His eyes, which were blue and very bright, had something fierce and mischievous about them. They sparkled continually as if they were there to give warning signals rather than to see with. His jaw was aggressive but, contradicting this, there was a softness and almost an innocence in his features such as one sees in many Americans. His body was very powerful and made for action and I suspected that it was this rather than his fame as a writer that gave him his self-confidence.

There was nothing remarkable about his conversation. He was not easily drawn to talk on literature, though in answer to my question as to what contemporary writers he liked, he expressed a great admiration for Salinger, Carson McCullers and Truman Capote. Speaking of the Spanish Civil War, he said that he had never felt much enthusiasm for the ideologies of the Left, but had gone to Spain for the sole reason that he liked wars. But in general he avoided these topics and talked on whatever came up, telling anecdotes and making wisecracks, all in what a European would regard as a very American style. It was as though he wanted to emphasize that he was not a writer but a sportsman, a good mixer in bars, a man whose friends were either simple uneducated people or else very rich like himself.

And although he had a courteous manner with women, I suspected that he was not really at ease with them. He obviously preferred male company and spoke with contempt of homosexuals, beats and bohemians – that is, of all those people who in his eyes had failed to make the grade.

Although his manner to me was friendly, I did not find that I could make any real contact with him. His personality, backed by his physical strength, weighed on me. In his presence I felt myself to be a weak and ineffectual person, not manly enough to drink five whiskies running or to face a bull in the arena, and I remembered how, when I was a young man, Augustus John had produced the same effect on me. I spoke too in the effete southern English dialect, not in the slow, rasping, dominant American one. Did he, I wondered, set out to make this impression on people or was it, as in John's case, that he was bound and confined by a physical presence that was in excess of his brains? Or was it, as some people said, that he had built himself a mask and then with the passage of time grown into it? I could not say, but what was certain was that all the masculine elements in his nature had been drawn out into his body and manner of expression, leaving the sensitive feminine ones, which had made him such a fine artist, hidden within. He had, it was clear, evolved his peculiar style of composition by deliberately cutting out all those elements that did not seem strictly necessary to his purpose. A more ascetic, less sonorous Flaubert. My objection to his novels, admirable though they were, was that, moving in the opposite direction to Proust, he had reduced and simplified his characters to a point at which they displayed only two or three facets, such as fear, courage and lust. He himself must be a very sensitive and complex man, but on meeting him one realised that, in pursuit of his ideal of manliness, he had applied the same method to his own character.

However anything I write on Hemingway must be mere speculation. I did not see him often enough nor do I know the American scene well enough to be able to speak of him with any conviction. I will only add that, in spite of his damaged kidney, which prevented him from sitting down except to eat, he exuded vitality. One did not need to have read his books to feel his greatness as a man.

In the autumn of the following year my old friend Ralph Partridge died suddenly of an angina. He had been ill for some time, but his end was sudden. He was by a long way my best friend. We had quarrelled over Carrington and again over his pacifism, but each time we had made it up. Since I had come out to Spain we had written to one another every fortnight so that his death left a gap in my life that nothing could fill. The effect on Frances was shattering for they had had a very close marriage. She sold Ham Spray House and took a flat in London, but it was many years before she recovered from the agonizing void his death had left.

26

Finis

Gamel had been shaken by my infatuation for Joanna and irritated by the fuss I had made over Hetty, though with her natural tolerance she had shrugged this last off. But now something happened which distressed her far more. She had sent her sonnets to Fabers to see if they would publish them and T. S. Eliot replied, refusing to do so. Since he was her favourite poet, this was a severe blow. I offered to get them printed privately, but she would not hear of it. The ambitions of a lifetime had been shattered and from now on she abandoned all thought of literary work.

I had saved up a little money so, to give her a change of scene, I suggested that we might make a trip to Greece. We left in March 1961 and spent three months in travelling about the country by bus, train and taxi, visiting the principal islands from Thasos, Lesbos and Samothraki down to Crete. Our tour was an immense success. At the age of sixty-one Gamel was still an indefatigable traveller, ready to put up with the worst foods and beds and unfailing in her zest and enthusiasm.

Through these years we had been seeing a good deal of the novelist, Honor Tracy. I had first met her in London after the war when she was about to set off for Japan as a special correspondent for, I think, the *Manchester Guardian*. After this I did not see her again till 1955 when she turned up in Malaga and we invited her to stay with us. From then on she would come out every couple of years, sometimes spending as much as a month or a couple of months with us.

She was a delightful guest. I hardly know anyone whose conversation I have enjoyed more than hers, for she had a very good mind and was at the same time full of what she called fun and nonsense. We met few good talkers on this coast so that her visits were something to look forward to. Though not Irish, she was a Catholic, but so far from being narrow that most of her friends were either Anglicans or agnostics. In Ireland, where she had made her home, she was in closer sympathy with the old Protestant Ascendancy than with the native Irish, whom she ridiculed in her novels for their shiftiness and two-facedness.

At this time she was a stout, heavy woman with reddish yellow hair and a large head. When she was younger she had had the frame of a pugilist. To match her appearance she had a very strong personality, passionate both in her friendships and her hates, and when she did not like anyone she could be formidable. But she had a wonderful smile – one of those warm, expansive, generous smiles that seem to come straight from the heart. At such moments she was beautiful.

A strong friendship grew up in time between her and Gamel. Honor turned all her charm and sweetness onto her and Gamel melted. I was naturally pleased as she was often in low spirits, needing sympathy and intellectual stimulus to draw her out of herself. For her health had now began to fail and she worried a good deal about it. Just at this time our friend John Whitworth bought a Volkswagen and invited us to make a trip with him along the north African coast, perhaps as far as Egypt. This seemed an admirable idea, so in March 1966 we set off. We travelled through Algeria and Tunisia in a leisurely way as far as the ruins of Lepta Magna in Tripoli and then turned back to Tunis where we took the boat to Sicily. From there we continued up the leg of Italy, taking a devious route to see pictures and buildings, and on through France to Paris, where we stayed with our daughter. This journey through the length of Italy at the highest point of the spring was an experience I shall never forget, and yet I enjoyed our passage on to Paris in a different way, for I love the quiet, solemn French countryside more than almost any in the world. As Renoir said of Gaugin when he set off for Tahiti, *Pourtant on est si bien à Batignolles.*

After a visit to London, where I saw Arthur Waley on his death bed, we returned to Spain and for a time Gamel seemed to be in better health and spirits. But then in July 1967 her left arm began to swell. Though she insisted that it was only rheumatism, I took her to see a doctor, who found that she had cancer, emanating from her left breast and spreading down the lymphs through her body. There was no hope for her living for more than a few months. Since it was necessary to deceive her about the nature of her complaint, we flew at once to London as we had previously intended to do. Here I saw Honor and asked her if she would come out to Churriana and help me nurse her. She said yes, she would.

I hardly have the courage to write down my memories of the next few months, the saddest and most terrible of my life. I felt racked with pity for Gamel, who wished intensely to live, all the more as she had not fulfilled any of her literary ambitions. To the very end she refused to admit the truth to herself. The pain began to increase after Christmas. The opium suppositories she was taking to relieve it were ceasing to work and the village doctor categorically refused to give her morphia. Her heart was so weak, he said, that one injection would probably kill her and, though he admitted that she could not possibly live for more than a few days, his Catholic conscience refused to take on the responsibility of shortening her life. Mercifully the end came very quickly, on January 18. She was buried on the following day at the British cemetery. Later I put up a stone and had inscribed on it the first two lines of the song from *Cymbeline*.

> Fear no more the heat o' the sun
> Nor the Winter's furious rages.

They were lines that she had been particularly fond of.

27

Sequel

For a time everything seemed to have ended for me. Since the onset of Gamel's illness I had realized that I should not be able to continue living in our big, ramshackle house by myself. I decided that I would sell it for what it would fetch and start a new life either on a Greek island or in Central America. And then a miracle happened. An English girl of twenty-four who had a strong feeling for poetry and a very great desire to study literature and philosophy came to live with me. A new chapter in my life began.

I had met Lynda quite briefly a few months before Gamel fell ill. A friend had brought her to our house because she was interested in St John of the Cross's poetry and had read in an American edition of his works that I had written two essays on him. When she entered the room I saw a tall, slim girl with dark brown hair hanging to her shoulders, dressed in a shirt and jeans. I noticed vaguely that she was attractive and had a fine nose and lively eyes. I gave her my two essays to read and she came back on the following evening to supper. Gamel liked her, as she liked anyone who cared for poetry, and we invited her to pay us a long visit in the autumn. When she left I gave her a copy of my autobiography, *A Life of One's Own*, and a correspondence between us began. Through this I came to see that, though she had spent five years at Chelsea Art School, she was a girl of pronounced intellectual tastes, as much interested in ideas as in poetry and drama, but that she had never had much leisure in which to read and study. At that time she was trying to learn Spanish and, to support herself, worked in a shop in Toledo, selling swords and armour to American tourists. It was a job that kept her all day on her feet so that, as her health was far from robust and she suffered from severe migraines, she was usually too exhausted to read when the evening came. When therefore I asked her if she would like to share my quiet writer's life at Churriana, she agreed at once.

I had come to hate my big, run-down house with its sad associations.

Sequel

The squalid housing estates of the coast were creeping up to the village and I could no longer afford to keep a staff of two women and a gardener. Besides my cook Rosario, envious of the high wages offered in the Torremolinos hotels, had turned surly and this set up an unpleasant atmosphere. Luckily just at that moment I came across an American sculptor who was willing to pay me three million pesetas, or £18,000, for the house and walled garden. But what about the English tenant? After some lengthy negotiations he agreed to leave if he were given half a million pesetas out of the sale price and the permission to build a house in the garden. The new purchaser resigned himself to that and also agreed to keep on the gardener Antonio at a good wage and to leave him and his wife their little cottage rent free for life. I gave them a substantial present but, since it was only a fraction of what I was compelled to pay the tenant, Rosario was so far from satisfied that she wrote me a bitter letter. So ended our thirty-year-old relation.

Lynda and I had now to find a suitable spot on which to build our new house. After some search we found a piece of land some thirteen miles inland from Churriana and overlooking the large pueblo of Alhaurín el Grande. It consisted of a long strip of hillside planted with ancient olive trees and bounded on one side by a broad, dry stream-bed and on the other by a steep rocky escarpment. A mountain forested with pines rose steeply on one side while in front there was an enormous view of the whole range of the Ronda mountains, which in winter were often covered with snow. Below them lay the large white pueblo, gleaming in the sunlight. It seemed an ideal place on which to build a house, but the price was high because it contained an excellent well and both electricity and telephone wires.

We looked, we returned, we looked again. Every visit to the Cañada de las Palomas, as the dry water course was called, confirmed our first impression. This strip of red soil between the stony stream bed and the boulder-strewn hill slope lay secret and secluded among its bushy olive trees, yet open to a great view and to a wide tract of empty air in which we sometimes saw eagles and ravens. Three badgers had dug their sets in the sandy soil under the boulders and this seemed a further proof of its isolation and remoteness. We decided we must have it and I bought it in Lynda's name because I wished her to feel that the days of her insecurity were over.

We drew up between us the plans for the house, then we signed a contract with a German constructor for a little over a million pesetas and started building. On the ground floor one long room, 37 feet by 27, ran the length of the house and opened on to a broad covered terrace. Behind it there was a library and kitchen. Upstairs each of us had a bedroom-study that gave on to a balcony where we could sunbathe or sleep in summer. The only other rooms were a visitors' room and a bathroom. Our German proved to be an excellent and conscientious constructor, who prided himself on building houses that would last for five centuries, but he was less strong on economics for he ran out of money before the work was finished and finally went bankrupt, leaving debts behind which we had to pay. But our house suited us perfectly and we could now live much more simply and economically than before since we did all the cooking and housework between us, while I looked after the small garden. The only help we had was provided by a woman who came in once a week. I cannot say what a relief it was to get rid of servants and do the housework ourselves.

Meanwhile Lynda and I had decided to write between us a book on the life and poetry of St John of the Cross. It seemed fitting that we should collaborate in a work on this great poet who had been the cause of our first meeting one another. I wrote the life and followed it up with a discussion of the verse while Lynda translated the poetry. The book was accepted by the Cambridge University Press and came out in May 1973.

In the spring of 1969, before completing the sale of the Churriana house, we had made a short trip by motor bus through Morocco, crossing the Atlas from Marrakesh to Taroudant and Goulimin and continuing across the desert almost as far as the Spanish colony of Rio de Oro. Now we bought a car, a Seat 600, the smallest car on the road, and this offered us better opportunities for travel. It was thirty years since I had been able to afford a car and I found that the sense of freedom it gave me was exhilarating.

We decided that our first long trip must be to Greece. Lynda had a particular desire to see it because she had spent more than a year reading Greek literature and philosophy from Homer and Thales to Aristophanes and Aristotle. The mythology especially attracted her since it offers so much to the poetic imagination.

In the spring then of 1972 we put our car on a boat for the Piraeus and spent a month and more touring Greece and seeing some of the islands. After this we drove to Istanbul and from there southwards through Asiatic Turkey, visiting on the way all the ancient Greek sites as well as Troy. The places that stand out in my memory are Priene and Didyma and then the incredibly beautiful ruins of Heraclea, standing among enormous boulders that had rolled down the slopes of Mount Latmos to the edge of the Bafa Lake. I must also mention as one of the high points of our journey the huge mosque put up at Edirne (Adrianople) by a certain Sinan which I felt, so far as its interior goes, to be the greatest religious building in Europe.

We returned home through Yugoslavia, and, after spending a few days at Venice and visiting the splendid cities that lay near by, made our way back across France to Malaga. The journey had lasted two and a half months and we had seen almost more than we could digest.

Sequel

Lynda and I have now completed five years together, but since these years form part of my present and are still going on I cannot write about them as if they were over. I have therefore recorded them in a factual and impersonal way. But I must say this – that they have been very happy years for both of us. Different though we are in character, there would seem to be a natural sympathy and accord between our minds that gives us the same range of interests as well as agreement in practical matters. To meet, Lynda is a strikingly attractive and lively girl, easily drawn out in conversation and with a vein of gaiety and irony, yet under this there lies a contrasting substratum of calmness and serenity. This and her innate truthfulness are her most characteristic features and with her insight into other people's minds they make her a very easy person to live with. I on the other hand am fifty years older than she is and the question I see on everyone's face is – what can possibly hold this incongruous pair together? I would reply that the first link between us is a strong sense of companionship: we enjoy one another's society. The other is that we both have the same plan of how we wish to live, which is to give the best of our time to our work and to cut down on social life with its inevitable distractions. Thus Lynda writes her poems and plays in her room while I work in mine, and we meet chiefly for meals and in the evenings. But outside the house we go everywhere together, do everything together, even the shopping and the marketing. This habit has become so strongly established that I can say that I have never before felt so inseparable from another person. It is when I think of this that I feel how incredible was the chance that our paths crossed in such an apparently casual way just at the time when we had most need of one another. For me, in my situation, at my age, it was nothing less than a miracle. She declares that it was the same for her.

Index

Index

Ham Spray House, 68, 75, 105, 108
Heard, Gerald, 254
Hemingway, Ernest, 367–8
History of Poor Robinson, 178
Holder, Lily, *see* Connolly, Lily
Holiday by the Sea, A, 115–17, 199, 336, 357
Hope-Johnstone, John, 17–18, 28, 30, 43, 51, 69, 115–17, 121, 136, 146, 178; ceases to be editor of *The Burlington Magazine*, 29, 37; to Yegen, 35; at Yegen, 37–41; helps edit *The Gramophone*, 53; returns to London, 75–7; with Beryl de Zoete, 95; leaves for U.S.A., 158; in U.S.A., 189–90; 'A Theory of Hope', 190–93; return from China, 342–3; settles in Aldbourne, 343–4; his visits to Churriana and death 356–7
Huxley, Aldous, 20, 190, 254

Jack Robinson, 199–200
James, the Rev. Frank, 132–5
Japp, Darsie, 108
Jensen, Miss, 88
Jiménez, Don Alberto, 328
(Jiménez), Doña Natalia de Cossío, 328
Joad, Marjorie, 67, 78–9, 109
John, Augustus, 39–40, 43, 52, 80, 157, 239, 245–6, 248, 356, 368
John, Dorelia, 80, 157–8, 239, 245–6, 248, 356
John, Robin, 39–41, 53–4
Joyce, James, 157, 220, 229; *Ulysses*, 157, 220
Juliana, 210–17, 251, 257

Lawrence, D. H., 20, 93
Lehning, Arthur, 328
Life of One's Own, A, 336, 357
Lighthouse always says Yes, The, 367
Lisbon, revolution in, 317
Literature of the Spanish People, The, 335–6
Lorca, Federico García, 57
Lowes Dickinson, Goldsworthy (Goldie), 254
Lowinsky, Ruth, 93, 341–2, 353
Lucile, 197–8
Lulu, 168–9

MacCarthy, Sir Desmond, 81, 184–5, 188, 246

MacCarthy, Mary (Molly), 99, 184–6, 227, 268, 274; *A Nineteenth Century Childhood*, 185
Mackenzie, Sir Compton, 53, 75, 158, 185
Mansfield, Katherine, 57
Marguérite, 164–6
Maria, servant at Yegen (Black Mary), 15–16, 53, 207–9, 212, 214
Maria *see* Martín, Maria
Marie, servant at Toulon, 170–71
Marion, 183
Marshall, Frances, later Partridge, 68, 103, 109, 179, 368; with Ralph, 113–14
Martín, Maria ('White Mary'), 214, 258, 276, 287, 293, 300
Mitrinovitch, Serbian seer, 76–7
Moore, Ann, 194
Moore, Henry, 339
Morrell, Lady Ottoline, 20, 341
Mortimer, Raymond, 155
Murry, John Middleton, 20, 57

Navaja, Juan, 300, 307–8
Nicholson Price, Lynda, 372–5
Nieves, Marqués de las, 302–3

Paco, 214–16
Partridge, Ralph, 20, 54–5, 179, 250; in love with Carrington, 21–8; at Watendlath, 30–33; with the Bollards, 43–5; his affair with Clare, 47, 49; breach with author, 49–50; letter to author, 52; visits Yegen, 67–8; at Shalbourne, 105; relations with Frances, 113–14; his character, 114; at Toulon, 171; after Lytton's death, 243, 246–7; quarrels with author over pacifism, 323, 330; at Churriana, 355; death, 368
Penrose, Alec, 154, 162
Penrose, Bernard (Beakus), 154, 244–5
Penrose, Sir Roland, 154, 162–3
Pepita (of Seville), 61–3
Pound, Ezra, 95, 347

Powys, Gertrude, 223, 225–6, 228, 235, 239
Powys, John Cowper, 220, 222, 237, 239, 258, 271
Powys, Llewelyn, 98, 220, 222–6, 228–31, 234–9, 250, 255, 257, 270, 320, 349, 351, 359; *Love and Death*, 237

Index

A Note on the Type

The text of this book was set on the Monotype in a type face called Garamond. Jean Jannon has been identified as designer for this face, which is based on Garamond's original models but is much lighter and more open. The italic is taken from a font of Granjon, which appeared in the repertory of the Imprimerie Royale and was probably cut in the middle of the sixteenth century.

Display typography and binding design by
Earl Tidwell